THE FUR TRADE ON THE UPPER MISSOURI, 1840–1865

THE FUR TRADE ON THE
UPPER MISSOURI, 1840-1865
By John E. Sunder

UNIVERSITY OF OKLAHOMA PRESS : NORMAN

BY JOHN E. SUNDER

Bill Sublette: Mountain Man (Norman, 1959)
(editor) *Matt Field on the Santa Fe Trail*, collected by Clyde
and Mae Reed Porter (Norman, 1960)
The Fur Trade on the Upper Missouri, 1840–1865 (Norman, 1965)

Library of Congress Catalog Card Number: 65–10111

Copyright 1965 by the University of Oklahoma Press,
Publishing Division of the University.
Composed and printed at Norman, Oklahoma, U.S.A.,
by the University of Oklahoma Press.
First edition.

To Ralph Paul Bieber, Western Historian

Preface

BACK IN THE 1870's, William Wright (Dan De Quille), the Nevada journalist, prefaced his *Big Bonanza* with the remark that he had put all he had to say "into the body" of his book. So have I—with these additions.

I wish to express my appreciation to the University of Texas and to the American Philosophical Society for research grants in the summers of 1960 and 1962, and to the many librarians who made my research a pleasant task—particularly at the Missouri Historical Society in St. Louis, in the libraries of the University of Texas at Austin, in the National Archives and the Library of Congress in Washington, D.C., and in the Bancroft and Huntington libraries in California. Also, I wish to thank the following institutions (not cited otherwise in this volume) for their assistance: the American Historical Association in Washington, D.C.; the American Lutheran Church Library at Dubuque; the Baker Library at Harvard; the British Museum; the Boston College Library; the library of the Catholic University of America; the Concordia Historical Institute in St. Louis; the Glenbow Foundation in Calgary; the Gonzaga University Library at Spokane; the Historical and Philosophical Society of Ohio in Cincinnati; the Historical Society of Pennsylvania at Philadelphia; the Hudson's Bay Company in London; the Massachusetts Historical Society at Boston; the Mutual Insurance Company of New York; the Museum of the City of New York and the New York City Public Library; the Princeton University Library; the Public Archives of Canada at Ottawa; the Saskatchewan Archives Board at Regina; the Smithsonian Institution's River Basin Surveys Office at Lincoln; the South Carolina Historical Society at Charleston; the State Historical Society of Iowa and the State University of Iowa Library at Iowa City; the Steamship Historical Society of America in New York City; the United States Military Academy Library at West Point; and the libraries of the Universities of London, Manitoba, Notre Dame, San Francisco, and Wyoming.

AUSTIN, TEXAS   *John E. Sunder*
JANUARY 1, 1965

Contents

Preface   vii

List of Abbreviations   xiii

I. "A sort of bastard East India Company . . . on a small scale"   3

II. "In these degenerate days"   26

III. "The green cotton commenced to dry"   52

IV. "Notorious for their misconduct"   78

V. "Still the heroes of the day"   105

VI. "Rapacity, envy and sickly emulation"   131

VII. "Under the influence of Christian civilization"   159

VIII. "For Fort Benton or bust"   187

IX. "Political troubles involving everything"   215

X. "Tired and out of spirits"   242

Bibliography   266

Index   282

Illustrations

BETWEEN PAGES 66 AND 67

Pierre Chouteau, Jr.
Charles P. Chouteau
Ramsay Crooks
Andrew Drips
Andrew Dawson
Malcolm Clark
Honoré Picotte
Alexander Culbertson, his wife Na-ta-wis-ta-cha,
    and their son Joe

BETWEEN PAGES 146 AND 147

Fort Benton, from a sketch by Gustavus Sohon
Fort Berthold on the Upper Missouri, by William Cary
Fort George, from a drawing by Alexander H. Murray
Fort Mortimer, from a drawing by Alexander H. Murray
Fort Pierre, from a drawing by Alexander H. Murray
Fort Union, from a drawing by Alexander H. Murray
A mackinaw boat with cordelle
Buffalo Crossing the Missouri, by William Cary

BETWEEN PAGES 226 AND 227

Joseph A. Sire
Daniel M. Frost
James B. Hubbell
Joseph La Barge

David D. Mitchell
Father Pierre Jean De Smet
The Reverend Stephen R. Riggs
General Alfred Sully

MAPS

The Lower Missouri Valley and Adjacent Areas, 1840–1865   13
The Upper Missouri Valley from the Big Sioux to Fort
   Union, and Adjacent Areas, 1840–1865   39
The Upper Missouri Valley from Fort Union to Three Forks,
   and the Valley of the Yellowstone, 1840–1865   45

List of Abbreviations

To AVOID EXCESSIVE REPETITION, the following abbreviations have been used in the footnotes and in four sections of the bibliography.

ABCFM: American Board of Commissioners of Foreign Missions
BMHS: *Bulletin of the Missouri Historical Society*
CHSM: *Contributions to the Historical Society of Montana*
CHSND: *Collections of the State Historical Society of North Dakota*
CLUC: Clark Library, The University of California, Los Angeles
CSmH: Huntington Library, San Marino, California
CtY-WA: Yale University, Western Americana Collection, New Haven
CU-B: Bancroft Library, Berkeley, California
DMR: *Daily Missouri Republican* (St. Louis)
DSI: Smithsonian Institution (Archives), Washington, D.C.
DSI-M: Smithsonian Institution (Natural History Museum Library), Washington, D.C.
FCHQ: *The Filson Club History Quarterly*
FRC, KC: Federal Records Center, Kansas City, Missouri
HED: *House Executive Document*
HR: *House Report*
ICN: Newberry Library, Chicago
KHi: Kansas Historical Society, Topeka
MM: *Massachusetts Magazine*
MnHi: Minnesota Historical Society, St. Paul
MOSA: Academy of Science of St. Louis (Archives)
MOSB: Missouri Botanical Gardens (Archives), St. Louis
MoSHi: Missouri Historical Society, St. Louis
MtHi: Historical Society of Montana, Helena
MVHR: *Mississippi Valley Historical Review*

NA: National Archives, Washington, D.C.
NdHi: State Historical Society of North Dakota, Bismarck
NDHQ: North Dakota Historical Quarterly
NH: Nebraska History
NHi: New-York Historical Society, New York City
NLA: New York State Library, Albany
OIA: Office of Indian Affairs
PNQ: Pacific Northwest Quarterly
RG: Record Group
SD: Senate Document
SDHC: South Dakota Historical Collections
SdHi: South Dakota State Historical Society, Pierre
SDHR: South Dakota Historical Review
SED: Senate Executive Document
SMD: Senate Miscellaneous Document
SOT: Office of the Solicitor of the Treasury
SR: Senate Report

THE FUR TRADE ON THE UPPER MISSOURI, 1840–1865

CHAPTER ONE

"A sort of bastard East India Company . . . on a small scale"

PIERRE CHOUTEAU, JR., was proud of his new Laurel Street office and warehouse overlooking the St. Louis levee. Skilled carpenters, tinsmiths, painters, and masons had built the imposing business block in record time, and in mid-November, 1840, Pierre Chouteau, Jr., and Company moved into the functional and attractive structure. The new four-story office building and salesroom, together with the large three-story warehouse, constituted the "most extensive" and "no doubt the best" business quarters put up in St. Louis in many months. The buildings, joined by a heavy, airtight, double iron door to prevent the spread of fire, surmounted limestone vaults and storage cellars drained by large sewers. The business block was Chouteau's answer in stone to those who prophesied that the fur trade was dying. His company, the most powerful western fur business of the day, refused to be frightened out of the fur and robe market by the depression, now under way since 1837, and looked ahead optimistically.[1]

St. Louisans who dropped by Chouteau's office to see the new business buildings, spacious ones in comparison to the old Company quarters less than a block away, stayed to congratulate the owner. Pierre Chouteau, Jr., was a tall, straight, distinguished-looking man. He was not handsome, certainly, since his nose was too large for his round, clean-shaven face, his mouth narrow and his cheekbones pronounced, but his eyes flashed and his smile and friendly manner, suited to drawing room or counting room, hid

[1] *Daily Evening Gazette* (St. Louis), June 12, September 10, 1840; *Missouri Argus* (St. Louis), November 21, 1840; *Hunt's Merchants' Magazine*, Vol. XI (September, 1844), 291; Pierre Chouteau, Jr., and Company to Ramsay Crooks, November 16, 1840, American Fur Company Papers, NHi.

from visitors another more thoughtful, solemn look known best to his office staff. Visitors left Chouteau's office to tell their friends that the American Fur Company was still very much alive. Legally speaking, of course, the business was known as Pierre Chouteau, Jr., and Company, but the public called it the American Fur Company, since Chouteau had earlier acquired a portion of John Jacob Astor's old fur empire and the name of Astor's company had passed directly to the fur tycoon's successors.

Pierre's father, Jean Pierre Chouteau, earned a fortune in western trade and, until his death in 1849, ruled as patriarch of the large, powerful Chouteau family. When the weather permitted, octogenarian Jean Pierre looked into his son's downtown office and passed a few genial minutes with the staff. Time, however, had mellowed the old gentleman. His "excitable and sometimes tempestuous" younger days were over and his iron will no longer directed family business strategy.

Most St. Louisans knew old Jean Pierre and were familiar with his son's career. They remembered that Pierre, Jr., was educated at home, had clerked in his father's store, had engaged briefly in the lead trade, and during the War of 1812 had opened a general store with Bartholomew Berthold, his brother-in-law. Twenty years later, Chouteau was in partnership with another relative-by-marriage, Bernard Pratte, Sr., in Pratte, Chouteau and Company and was bound closely to American Fur Company operations west of the Mississippi. When Astor retired from the great firm in 1834 —a painful retirement because John Jacob hated to give up control —Pratte and Chouteau purchased the Western Department of the American Fur Company. The Upper Missouri Outfit, or trading region, of the Western Department became Pierre Chouteau's prize possession. For thirty years, he, his partners, and his son, Charles Pierre, stood behind it on the upper river.

Pierre Chouteau was a wealthy man who kept his financial affairs secret, but secrecy bred newspaper and magazine speculation on the size of his fortune. Was he the "wealthiest man" in Missouri? Was his annual trade in furs and buffalo robes worth

4

$300,000? None knew accurately, yet many believed both stories. Circumstantial evidence suggests the tales were true. He belonged to the most prominent family in St. Louis, was related by blood and marriage to the old Creole aristocracy of the city and profited financially from those connections, and associated with influential political friends in Missouri and the East. To his admirers, he epitomized the wise merchant and patron of the arts and sciences, and was, decidedly, a man of the world; to those who contested his might on the Upper Missouri, he was a monster, a dragon of evil intent.[2]

Chouteau's relative and business partner, Bernard Pratte, Jr. (son of Chouteau's old partner, Bernard Pratte, Sr., who died in 1836), was the politically ambitious scion of a brilliant and talented family. Unfortunately, the Pratte family also produced violent-tempered, mercurial men who were not ideal business associates for long-range planners such as Pierre Chouteau. Pratte eyed political power. In 1838, he won a seat in the Missouri Assembly, dropped from active participation in Pratte, Chouteau and Company, and later, in the mid-forties, was elected mayor of St. Louis. When Pratte left the Company, Chouteau immediately increased his share in the business, changed the Company name to reflect the new management—Pierre Chouteau, Jr., and Company—and carefully reviewed Company fur-trade policies.[3]

Pierre and his father controlled slightly more than 50 per cent of the $500,000 capitalization of the firm. Three close associates, John B. Sarpy, Joseph A. Sire, and John F. A. Sanford, each held $80,000 in stock during the first two years of the new venture.[4] Sarpy eventually accumulated a fortune as a merchant-financier

[2] Harriette J. Westbrook, "The Chouteaus and Their Commercial Enterprises —Part II," *Chronicles of Oklahoma*, Vol. XI (September, 1933), 962–63; Paul Beckwith, *Creoles of St. Louis*, Chouteau Family entries; William J. Ghent, "Jean Pierre Chouteau," and Stella M. Drumm, "Pierre Chouteau," in *Dictionary of American Biography*, IV, 93–94; *Missouri Argus* (St. Louis) December 29, 1840.

[3] "The Reminiscences of General Bernard Pratte, Jr.," *BMHS*, Vol. VI (October, 1949), 59n.

[4] Division of Capital and Dividends in Pierre Chouteau, Jr., and Company, 1839–1841, Chouteau Family Papers (Uncatalogued), MoSHi.

and, through his Whig sympathies, brought the firm useful political contacts. His sterling character and willingness to entertain lavishly won the Company many friends in St. Louis and furthered his personal interest in railroading. The Company expressed its thanks by naming two western posts in his honor: Fort John on Laramie Creek and Fort Sarpy on the Yellowstone.

Sire immigrated to the United States from France when he was in his teens, and after a short residence in the East, he learned to run a western sawmill and to pilot paddle-wheelers on the Mississippi. He was the ideal man to advance Chouteau's interest in water transportation on the Upper Missouri and, time and again, took the firm's annual steamer to the Dakotas. Sire knew as well as anyone that the Missouri was a river "with a personality, a sense of humor, and a woman's caprice; a river that goes traveling sidewise, that interferes in politics, rearranges geography, and dabbles in real estate; a river that plays hide and seek with you today and tomorrow follows you around like a pet dog with a dynamite cracker tied to his tail."[5]

The third Company associate, John Sanford of Virginia, was liaison man between St. Louis and the East—Washington, Philadelphia, and, particularly, New York City. During the early thirties he had served as federal Indian agent to the Mandans; he then took a job under Chouteau and moved up quickly in Company ranks. He dabbled in Illinois railroads, but preferred the whirl of New York business and society. The Company needed a man of Sanford's abilities, someone who could dash from West to East and back again, since Chouteau, although he too enjoyed New York City and maintained an office there (listed as Chouteau, Merle and Sanford), could not be everywhere at once. Eventually, Sanford left the Company and settled in New York City, but not in peace and quiet, for his sister and her second husband were wrangling with the courts over custody of the slave Dred Scott. After intricate legal maneuvering, the case was heard by the United States Supreme Court. Sanford was the defendant, the

[5] George Fitch quoted in Robert G. Athearn, *High Country Empire*, 89.

court declared Scott property, and eventual civil war moved a little nearer to every American.

Pierre Chouteau, Jr., and Company was an unincorporated association, or partnership, of friends and relatives. Corporation laws were lax—weak enough to permit a few men to form a half-million-dollar enterprise, operate it in various states and territories for nearly a generation, and realize from it substantial profit without interference of outside investigators.[6] Whenever a partner retired or died, whenever a new man bought into the Company, Chouteau's accountants reviewed the business and made the necessary adjustments in shares held per partner. The Company reorganized almost yearly during the forties. The bookkeepers, harassed and overworked, simply numbered each reorganization as if it were a new French Republic! "Company 3" followed "Company 2" and was, in turn, succeeded by "Company 4."

The bonds of matrimony tied Sarpy, Sire, and Sanford to the Chouteau family as strongly as dollars bound them to the Company. Interweaving family trees strengthened the partnership, as it existed in 1840 and for several years thereafter, and gave the greater part of St. Louis business a stake in the fur trade. Sarpy's grandmother was old Jean Pierre Chouteau's sister. Sire's first wife was Pierre Chouteau's cousin and his second wife was the widow of another of Pierre's cousins. Sanford married Pierre's eldest daughter, Émilie. Remarkably enough, although the wives of the partners were all related and the families enjoyed frequent social gatherings, the Company kept most of its business secret and safely removed from family gossip.

The new direction given to Company policy by Chouteau between 1838 and 1840 when Pratte left the organization was extremely important to the entire western fur trade. Pierre and his associates decided to maintain their investment on the North Platte River, to withdraw gradually from the rendezvous-anchored Rocky Mountain trade, and to strengthen their trade on

[6] E. Merrick Dodd, Jr., "American Business Association Law a Hundred Years Ago and Today," in *Law: A Century of Progress, 1835-1935,* III 257-62.

the Upper Missouri. The first significant step, taken in 1838, adjusted the Company claim on the Platte. Chouteau agreed with Bent, St. Vrain and Company, his Platte Valley competitors, to restrict American Fur Company trade to the region above the South Platte, and they agreed to avoid the North Platte. Old, timbered Fort William, near the junction of Laramie Creek and the North Platte, was reconstructed of adobe, renamed Fort John (although Fort Laramie was its popular name), and designated center for the American Fur Company's Platte Outfit.

Chouteau's agents at Fort Laramie struggled to keep the Platte trade alive. They gathered small amounts of fur and large quantities of buffalo robes—1,000 packs of robes in 1843 and 1,100 in 1846 represented average seasonal trades—and shipped them by mackinaw down the Platte to the Missouri. After each late-spring rise, the Platte's sandy, treacherous bottom lay dangerously close to its watery surface, and many shipments grounded, sank, or were transferred to wagons and pack animals to complete the journey to the Missouri. At times, the Fort Laramie agents, to avoid the Platte route, sent furs and robes overland by trail from the North Platte to Fort Pierre on the Upper Missouri, where mackinaws or steamboats picked them up and floated them downriver to St. Louis. Moreover, Company supplies bound from St. Louis to Fort Laramie reached the Upper Platte country with difficulty.

Barely a mile below Fort Laramie, Lancaster P. Lupton built Fort Platte in 1841. Lupton, an upstart in the fur trade on the South Platte in Colorado, told his friends he had been kicked out of the army for criticizing President Jackson and that any man who dared to take on the former President certainly had the nerve to compete with the American Fur Company. He depended upon liquor, smuggled into the Indian country from Missouri and New Mexico, to enliven his business, but he lasted only a year at Fort Platte. Sibille, Adams and Company bought the post and continued Lupton's liquor policy, to the chagrin of the American Fur

Company, and for years the Platte River fur trade soaked in illicit alcohol.

Both the American Fur Company and the Fort Platte opposition used liquor in the Indian trade, despite laws to the contrary, and bartered containers of watered-down alcohol for choice furs and robes. The American Fur Company realized, however, that unlimited trade in liquor demoralized the tribes, turned red-skinned hunters into idle sops, and threatened the career of any trader whom government agents caught with unauthorized liquor on hand. Sensible fur men traded reasonable amounts of liquor for furs; foolish fur men depended heavily upon alcohol as a trade item. Chouteau viewed the Fort Platte traders, as well as many other Platte Valley fur men, as improvident profit seekers who deserved to be apprehended by federal investigators. Encouraged by the American Fur Company, the Commissioner of Indian Affairs cracked down on the liquor trade. In June, 1842, he appointed Andrew Drips as Indian agent and liquor investigator on the Upper Missouri, and Drips's subagent, Joseph Varnum Hamilton, the Iowa-born son of a professional soldier, looked into the Platte Valley liquor trade. Late in the summer of 1843, Hamilton searched the posts on Laramie Creek and heard many rumors of liquor supplies in the area, but failed to find a single keg.

Before the end of the year, Sibille and Adams transferred their controversial post to Bernard Pratte and John C. Cabanné. Pratte was dabbling in the fur trade again, and Cabanné brimmed with hate for Pierre Chouteau, his cousin. Cabanné's father, who died in 1841, was one of Chouteau's old business partners, but the two men had quarreled repeatedly: the "old close family ties . . . were broken up," and the wound remained unhealed.[7] Pratte and Cabanné ran Fort Platte until 1845, when they moved out and built Fort Bernard, a tiny log trading post, just seven or eight miles

---

[7] Ramsay Crooks to Pierre Chouteau, Jr., and Company, July 11, 1841, Chouteau Family Papers, MoSHi. On Sibille and Adams, see the Adams (David) Family Papers, MoSHi.

east of Fort Laramie. Pratte soon gave up his share in the new post, and Cabanné relied upon John Richard, a professional liquor smuggler and former Sibille and Adams employee, to manage Fort Bernard. Cabanné, however, pulled out of the trade before his manager could do him irreparable harm, leaving Richard to reign as firewater king of the Upper Platte.

The overland trail along the Platte passed the gates of Forts Bernard and Laramie. Increasing emigrant traffic over it forced the buffalo herds back into the hills, turned Fort Laramie into a roadside supermarket dispensing food and utensils to Oregon-bound parties, and gave the hundreds of Indians congregated in the area plenty to stare at and wonder about. Chouteau and his partners, thoroughly irritated by Platte Valley troubles, sold Fort Laramie to the United States Army in 1849. Since the Indians claimed the land, the Company received only $4,000 for the buildings. The military—two companies of mounted riflemen and one of infantry—moved into the post between June and August. Although the American Fur Company profited little, financially, from the sale, it welcomed the transaction.[8]

Actually, the old center of the mountain fur trade was located west and southwest of Fort Laramie and the Platte Valley. Between 1810 and 1835, hundreds of trappers and traders worked the mountain streams of Wyoming, Idaho, Montana, Utah, Colorado, New Mexico, and Arizona. The Rocky Mountain Fur Company built an enviable reputation in the twenties and thirties for successfully harvesting the fur crop of the mountains, and the annual rendezvous, where trapper, Indian, and eastern supplier met to exchange furs and goods, became the hallmark of the mountain trade. To the American Fur Company, however, the rendezvous was frequently a costly, nerve-shattering, and, at times, even humiliating event. Opposition fur companies beat American Fur Company supply caravans to the meetings, usually held along the

[8] LeRoy R. Hafen and Francis M. Young, *Fort Laramie and the Pageant of the West, 1834–1890*, 67–156.

Green River or in near-by well-watered valleys, or undersold American Fur Company agents at the annual frolic. But neither Astor nor Chouteau risked capital on reckless trading, and both refused to plunge their full resources into the mountain trade. They remembered that the Upper Missouri was the cornerstone of their western fur empire—the Rocky Mountain region was not —and there were many pitfalls in the mountains. The American Fur Company preferred to allow opposition traders to explore and open new mountain trade areas, then follow along, trade in the safer new locations, keep power in reserve on the Upper Missouri, and commit only limited supplies and business energy to the rendezvous. The American Fur Company and its Canadian counterpart, the Hudson's Bay Company, believed in the same business tactics: avoid the cost of exploration, forego immediate profit for distant gain, and plan for the long haul. The Rocky Mountain Fur Company, principal opponent of the American Fur Company in the mountain trade, and the North West Company of Canada, onetime outstanding adversary of the Hudson's Bay men, exhausted their resources in costly exploration and short-range planning. In Canada and the United States, the giant fur companies survived the longest; the small groups of adventurers did not.

By the mid-1830's the mountain trade had passed its prime. Men preferred silk hats to beaver hats, and the supply of furs, to fill the dwindling demand, was small and unpredictable. American Fur Company trapping parties met only halfhearted opposition in the mountains. Experienced trappers sensed that the boom days of the mountain trade were over. Entire river valleys had been trapped out and needed years of rest while nature restocked the animals. In other areas, four or five poor trapping years followed as many good ones. Few Mountain Men fully understood fur cycles or realized how disease, weather, and forage worked together to reduce animal population. Style, heavy trapping, the ever present fur cycle, and the movement of settlers across the

Rockies to Oregon disrupted the mountain fur trade. The beaver pelt, grand prize in the fur hunt, was in short supply on the St. Louis market in the late thirties.[9]

Dwindling fur supplies forced many trappers to leave the mountains or to expand their hunting territory, and it became difficult, even impossible, for some of them to attend the yearly rendezvous. Consequently, outfitters such as the American Fur Company gradually abandoned the annual gathering and pulled in vulnerable supply lines. In 1839, Chouteau sent only a small supply caravan—four two-wheeled carts piled high with goods—to Green River under a handful of men led by Moses (Black) Harris, "a mountaineer without special education, but with five sound senses."[10] Asahel Munger and his wife, Congregational missionaries bound for Oregon, attended the meeting, complained that the American Fur Company traded liquor to the Indians, and jotted down that Chouteau's forty-man party "made a poor collection of furs [that] year."[11] The following season, Indians and trappers in "great numbers" met at the Green River site,[12] but when John Bidwell's overland party encamped on the same stream a year later, in July, 1841, they exchanged goods with only a few trappers in a quiet gathering very much unlike an old-fashioned rendezvous.[13]

The British in Oregon, pleased to see the rendezvous system

[9] Hiram M. Chittenden, *A History of the American Fur Trade of the Far West*, I, chap. XXII; Paul C. Phillips, *The Fur Trade*, II, chap. XLIX; Ian M. Cowan, "The Fur Trade and the Fur Cycle: 1825–1857," *The British Columbia Historical Quarterly*, Vol. II (January, 1938), 19–30.

[10] F. A. Wislizenus, *A Journey to the Rocky Mountains in the Year 1839*, 28–29.

[11] "Diary of Asahel Munger and Wife," *The Quarterly of the Oregon Historical Society*, Vol. VIII (December, 1907), 395. See also Joel P. Walker, "Narrative of Adventures," MS, CU-B.

[12] Hiram M. Chittenden and A. T. Richardson (eds.), *Life, Letters and Travels of Father Pierre-Jean de Smet, S.J.*, I, 262.

[13] John Bidwell, *A Journey to California . . . by John Bidwell* (ed. by Herbert I. Priestley), 11.

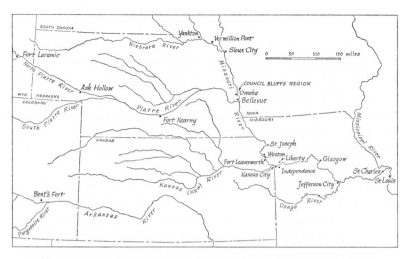

The Lower Missouri Valley and Adjacent Areas, 1840–1865

end, renewed trapping in the Idaho-Montana Rockies, but only temporarily and on a limited scale, and scores of American free trappers shifted allegiance from the rendezvous suppliers to the outfitters in Taos and Santa Fe. The New Mexican merchants and Bent, St. Vrain and Company seized the new windfall and sent their whiskey, flour, and other commodities to the trappers ranging the mountains north of Taos. A north-south line of exchange grew during the forties, penetrated the Platte Valley, and replaced much of the older east-west supply line between St. Louis and the Green River country.

Encouraged by supplies and new blood from New Mexico (a few Spaniards and Mestizos learned to set traps and maneuver robe-laden mackinaws), the mountain trade limped along through the forties. The Robidoux brothers traded at Fort Uintah in northeastern Utah and at Fort Uncompahgre near Delta, Colorado, but they poured too much alcohol into the Indian country. Between 1844 and 1847, the Utes rose and burned both posts. Jim Bridger, who built a fort on Black's Fork of the Green in 1843, traded with roving Indians and trappers and, following the example of Fort Laramie, supplied passing emigrant parties. East of the Continental Divide, Bent, St. Vrain and Company continued profitable trading at their large Arkansas River post, Bent's Fort, near the Purgatoire and, for a few years, at Fort St. Vrain on the South Platte. By the 1850's, however, even Bent's Fort was abandoned. The robe and fur trade on the Arkansas declined as overland emigrant traffic multiplied, crisscrossed the Bent family kingdom, and wrote *finis* to the fort.

By the mid-1850's, Minnesota and the Upper Missouri Valley led in furs and robes produced in the Trans-Mississippi West. American Fur Company trade in the Iowa country had collapsed ten years earlier when the Sac and Fox Indians ceded their lands to federal negotiators. Far to the west, the Hudson's Bay Company, once powerful along the Columbia, in the Rockies from Utah to Montana, and in California's interior valleys, lost its political position south of the forty-ninth parallel in 1846 when the Buchanan-Pakenham Treaty settled the old Oregon dispute. The company retained considerable prestige in Canada, but posed no great threat to American fur traders in the Northwest. Fort Hall, the old Hudson's Bay Company post in Idaho, supplied trappers and emigrants as late as the fifties, but competed little with the American Fur Company for the Upper Missouri trade. The years of vicious Anglo-American competition for northwestern furs and Indian loyalties had ended without war.

Pierre Chouteau, housed comfortably in his Laurel Street office early in the forties, had correctly visualized Minnesota and the Upper Missouri Valley as the two strongest bastions for his company's future robe and fur trade. Having withdrawn from the mountain rendezvous and reorganized his business on the Platte, he looked for opportunities to extend further his trade in the North and Northwest. In 1834, Astor's fur empire in the Great Lakes country (the Northern Department of the old American Fur Company) had been sold to an investors' group led by Ramsay Crooks, a Scot immigrant. Crooks was an experienced hand in the fur trade, Bernard Pratte's son-in-law, and one of Astor's closest business confidants. The depression beginning in 1837 struck a heavy blow at Crooks's Minnesota trade; then independent traders, many unlicensed, infiltrated the Upper Mississippi Valley, struck a second sharp blow at Crooks, and brought him to his knees nearly bankrupt.

Anxious to pull out of Minnesota, he offered Chouteau the Upper Mississippi trade. Chouteau accepted the proposal, since he believed the Minnesota fur supply was far from exhausted and could be exploited profitably by steamboats carrying trade goods upriver to Minnesota from St. Louis and fur cargoes downriver in return. After considerable difficulty with creditors, Crooks relinquished the Minnesota trade in 1843 and Chouteau picked up the Upper Mississippi. Henry Hastings Sibley of Mendota, who was previously associated with Crooks, acted as Chouteau's spokesman in the Minnesota trade, but the fur business remained small, profits were limited, and Sibley's political inclinations brought Chouteau's firm under regular fire in Minnesota for its "shameless, grinding monopoly." Actually, the monopoly was weak, since several of Chouteau's competitors tapped the Red River trade in furs and robes, carried annually after 1843 by cart from Pembina southward. The monopoly charge was based as much upon Minnesota's growth—expanding population, investment in lumbering and agriculture, and political evolution (territorial status in 1849 and statehood in 1853)—as it was upon Chouteau's power.[14]

Crooks retired from Minnesota and reinvigorated his New York City commission house. The establishment, incorporated by the state of New York shortly after Astor retired from the fur trade, legally carried the American Fur Company name. In addition to Astor's old Northern Department (in Chouteau's hands after

[14] William W. Folwell, *A History of Minnesota*, I, 162–65, 371; J. Ward Ruckman, "Ramsay Crooks and the Fur Trade of the Northwest," *Minnesota History*, Vol. VII (March, 1926), 27–30; John P. Pritchett, *The Red River Valley, 1811–1849*, 248–49, 255.

1843), much of the fur trade east of the Mississippi was still in Crooks's control.[15] His use of the American Fur Company name, related, as it was, to the popular use of the name for Chouteau's company, brought semantic confusion and charges—in 1842, when Crooks failed in Minnesota—that Chouteau held a block of stock in the Northern Department. Chouteau denied the insinuation and stated that Pierre Chouteau, Jr., and Company was "separate and distinct from the New York Company" and was "interested only to the extent of a few shares of stock in that concern."[16]

Undeniably, however, Chouteau and Crooks corresponded periodically and worked together closely to market furs and robes from all parts of the western country. Crooks, advantageously situated in New York City close to merchants who shipped pelts to the London market, regularly sent dependable news to Chouteau from the British furriers. "You must exert yourself to keep *every thing* out of rival hands," wrote Curtis M. Lampson, the leading London auctioneer and agent of American fur dealers, to Crooks in April, 1839. Crooks passed Lampson's warning to Chouteau and added, the following month, that "there has been a 'great fall' in London prices of your raccoons and in almost all other articles in which you have interests."[17] Since fluctuations in the international fur market followed closely the whims of European clothiers and fashionable Americans dressed as the Continent dictated, fur dealers in the Mississippi Valley resented Chouteau's ready access to dependable European auction reports and to detailed catalogs sent from Lampson to Crooks.

In the winter of 1841–42, a few months before the Northern Department failed, Crooks sent a few buffalo robes (by then robes had replaced beaver pelts as the biggest item in the American fur

[15] Grace Lee Nute, "The Papers of the American Fur Company: A Brief Estimate of Their Significance," *The American Historical Review*, Vol. XXXII (April, 1927), 519–38.

[16] *St. Louis New Era*, September 23, 1842.

[17] Ramsay Crooks to Pierre Chouteau, Jr., April 12, May 3, 1839, Chouteau Family Papers, MoSHi. See also the letters of Ramsay Crooks to Pierre Chouteau, Jr., and Company, March 14, April 16, August 20, 1842, American Fur Company Papers, NHi.

trade) to furriers in Hamburg and Leipzig. The dealers admitted that robes made excellent military coats and covers, but sheep-skin cost less in Europe. Crooks junked the robe project, except for the London market, where buffalo products found buyers, and advised Chouteau to build an American market big enough to consume most of the western robes.[18]

Chouteau's American Fur Company took the challenge and made Americans buffalo-robe conscious. Now that beaver skins, priced in St. Louis at an average four dollars per pound in the 1820's and early 1830's, brought only an average two to four dollars per pound by the late thirties—extraordinarily good skins sometimes sold at four to five dollars—the beaver market seemed dull to fur dealers. The day had passed when prime beaver com-manded six dollars a plew; when beaver pelts, packed sixty to eighty to the bale, filled the levee warehouses. A few beaver ship-ments continued to reach St. Louis in each annual trade, but deer, muskrat, and, especially, buffalo robes led on the St. Louis mar-ket. Robes, pressed ten to the bundle, were worth three to six dollars each, depending upon the supply. Twenty years earlier, they seldom brought more than three dollars each, but robes were the new staple of western fur dealers. According to the Jesuit missionary Father Pierre Jean De Smet, Chouteau brought 45,000 robes to St. Louis in 1839 and approximately 67,000 the following year. The rapidly expanding St. Louis market averaged 90,000 per year during the 1840's and 100,000 during the fifties and sixties. Dried buffalo meat, buffalo tongues, and pemmican also found growing markets in St. Louis and points east.[19]

Clearly, the mid-nineteenth-century fur trade was still valuable to St. Louis, yet its relative importance, when compared to the

[18] E. Douglas Branch, *The Hunting of the Buffalo*, 101–102.

[19] Walter B. Stevens, *St. Louis, the Fourth City, 1764–1909*, I. 164; *DMR*, September 14, 1838, March 15, 1839; *Missouri Argus*, July 18, 25, 1839; Chittenden, *Fur Trade*, I, 7; Chittenden and Richardson, *Father de Smet*, I, 179, 207; Bernard De Voto, *Across the Wide Missouri*, 103; Isaac Lippincott, "A Century and a Half of Fur Trade at St. Louis," *Washington University Studies* (Humanistic Series), Vol. III, Pt. 2 (April, 1916), 222, 225, 238 (n. 115), 241.

city's total business, was considerably less in 1840, 1850, or 1860 than it had been in 1820. St. Louis's annual commerce expanded from $2,000,000 to $200,000,000 between the time of the Missouri Compromise and the Civil War, but the value of the annual fur trade fell from $500,000 or $600,000 to between $250,000 and $500,000. Statisticians frequently quoted $300,000 as an average yearly trade through St. Louis after 1840. The total value of furs and robes did not equal the entire value of the trade, however, since "men familiar with the trade" judged that the fur dealers purchased annually more than $225,000 in trade goods to be shipped west from St. Louis. According to the Chamber of Commerce, the fur trade, far from dead, suffered more from federal failure to protect traders in the Indian country and to improve the waterways than it did from changes in the fur market.[20] If the government allocated enough money to deepen the St. Louis harbor and clear the rivers of navigation hazards, the fur trade would grow, or so "a number of citizens of St. Louis" assured their congressmen.[21]

Pierre Chouteau agreed with the Chamber of Commerce that the fur trade was alive, and he had moved into his new business quarters convinced that it would prosper. He had survived a long contest with the Hudson's Bay men, had abandoned the rendezvous and reorganized Company trade on the Platte, and had always overcome opposition traders—American Fur Company men called them "rats"—on the Upper Missouri. Chouteau's business house was in order. Bales of robes filled the new warehouse, overshadowed smaller piles of beaver, muskrat, and otter skins, and competed with deer hides from Arkansas and Texas for storage space. The robes, most of which came from the Upper Missouri, gave Chouteau clear, visual proof that he was right, correct in his decision to expand American Fur Company power on the giant

20 *Proceedings of the St. Louis Chamber of Commerce, in Relation to the Improvement of the Navigation of the Mississippi,* 15–16.

21 "Memorial of a Number of Citizens of St. Louis . . . for the Improvement of the Harbor of That City," 28 Cong., 1 sess., *SD No. 185,* p. 10.

waterway that meandered through thousands of square miles of buffalo and beaver range.

According to the American Fur Company definition, the Upper Missouri country started above the mouth of the Big Sioux River and reached out in a great semicircle. On a map, it resembled a sickle lying across the Dakotas and Montana, its handle at the Big Sioux, its point touching gingerly the front ranges of the Montana Rockies. The Missouri River, uncertain as "the state of a woman's mind," was the main highway crossing the region.[22] Fur traders traveled by water whenever possible in the Dakota-Montana country or followed Indian trails to reach distant tribal campgrounds and scattered interior trading posts. Even by 1865 no major overland trail carried large parties of emigrants into or across the country. It was a region reserved, set aside by nature above the high tide of travel until the seventies and eighties. Reservation (or was it isolation?) gave the Upper Missouri fur trade life and profit beyond 1840.

French and Spanish traders exchanged goods with the Dakota tribes years before Lewis and Clark took American sovereignty to the Upper Missouri. Numerous trading posts sprang up, many lasting but a few months or years, in the river valley between Council Bluffs and the Marias. Chouteau's American Fur Company owned several posts, pursuant to the transaction with Astor in 1834, but ownership was an empty claim unless they were adequately provisioned, defended, and supervised. Men, supplies, and trade goods were needed regularly, and the furs and robes accumulated by the posts were needed in St. Louis. Dependable steamboat transportation from St. Louis to the Upper Missouri and back again answered the American Fur Company's problem. Steam unsealed the upper river: unsealed its isolation, kept the seal broken, and strengthened, through improved communications, the Company's hand in the upper valley.

In 1831, when Astor and Chouteau decided to experiment with

[22] A Sioux City editor quoted in Athearn, *High Country Empire*, 89.

steam above the Platte, they realized that the life of the American Fur Company was at stake. Except for the tiny *Western Engineer*, a steam vessel navigated, under government auspices, to Council Bluffs in 1819, and a handful of regular steam packets operating on the Lower Missouri, steam craft were unknown on the waterway. Kenneth McKenzie, the outstanding American Fur Company agent on the Upper Missouri, pressured Chouteau and Astor to make the unprecedented decision to send a steamboat to Fort Union, then the principal Company post, far upriver. Pratte and Cabanné, both Company stockholders, opposed the plan, but Mc-Kenzie was an energetic, hard-driving, ambitious Scot who wrote convincing, well-phrased letters to his superiors. When the new side-wheeler *Yellowstone* tied up at the St. Louis levee in April, 1831, it was clear that McKenzie had won his point.[23]

Chouteau boarded the *Yellowstone* and witnessed the trip up-river to Fort Tecumseh (near modern Pierre, South Dakota). At the trading post, the crew loaded on furs, robes, and buffalo tongues, and the little 130-foot craft headed back to St. Louis. It was midsummer and the river was low—too low to allow the boat to continue upstream to Fort Union. The following year, how-ever, the *Yellowstone* churned up the Missouri on the spring rise, reached Fort Union in mid-June, and proved the Missouri navigable at least to the mouth of the Yellowstone. In 1833, the Company added the stern-wheeler *Assiniboine* as companion vessel to the *Yellowstone* in upriver trade, but within two years the newer vessel burned near Heart River. The fire, supposedly set by a deck hand, consumed thousands of robes along with the boat.[24]

Throughout the thirties, American Fur Company steamers paid annual visits to Fort Union. The *St. Peter's*, under the young Bernard Pratte, who entered the Company after his father's death, carried supplies upstream to Fort Union and a cargo of robes and furs downstream from the fort to St. Louis in 1837. The *Antelope*

23 William E. Lass, *A History of Steamboating on the Upper Missouri River*, chap. II.
24 *DMR*, June 29, 1858.

made the round trip in 1838, but the next year, she fell short of Fort Union, her goal, by four hundred miles. Since her hull was improperly designed for the Missouri and she drew too much water for the shallow upper river, she was sent to the boatyard before the end of the summer.[25] Boatbuilders were just beginning to learn how to design and construct light-draft mountain boats for the shallow Missouri. Nevertheless, experience soon taught them to build with lightweight materials; to broaden steamer beams; to install smaller, lighter, high-pressure engines; and to favor stern-wheel design—side wheels invited damage—which allowed them to launch easily loaded narrow boats with greater cargo space.

The new mountain boats sent into the Missouri fur trade faced the toughest stretch of inland water in the country. River silt easily clogged boiler valves and pipe connections and buried many boats in early graves on the muddy bottom. Careful engineers kept their boilers clean; careful pilots sailed, or steamed, only by day and tied up at night to avoid the snags, sawyers, and bars of the river; and careful masters kept close watch for thickets along the banks where crewmen could cut the many cords of cottonwood needed for each day's journey. Wooding was dangerous, particularly in the Dakotas, where Indian war parties harassed river traffic. The hazardous Missouri River taught Chouteau a lesson: it would be cheaper and safer for the American Fur Company to charter boats for the upper-river trade than to build and operate its own steamers. Thus, as soon as enough mountain boats were built or old boats rebuilt by the boatyards, the Company adopted a charter policy.

The weaving, wandering river menaced light-draft boats less than larger, heavier ones, yet menace them it did, nevertheless. Three thousand miles of water flowed between St. Louis and western Montana. Much of the muddy waterway was navigable, especially the section below the Platte, where rainfall was ade-

[25] *Ibid.*, July 17, 1837, July 17, 1838; John F. A. Sanford to Pierre Chouteau, Jr., June 12, 1839, Chouteau Family Papers, MoSHi.

quate. From there to the Yellowstone, the design of the new mountain boats paid dividends in trade to pilots who took advantage of the snow- and rain-fed April and June rises. Halfway across Montana, however, the sandy character of the river—sluggish, silt laden, debris filled, moving over dangerous sand bars and beneath undercut banks—gave way to the so-called "rocky river," reaching approximately two hundred miles from Cow Island to Fort Benton. The rocky portion of the Upper Missouri roared down from the west clear and relatively straight, yet still shallow, tumbling over a boulder-strewn bed.[26]

For the time being, however, in the thirties and forties the American Fur Company was content to send steamboats to Fort Union and the mouth of the Yellowstone, but not beyond. Furs and robes from the headwaters of the Missouri and Yellowstone were packed aboard mackinaws and floated downriver to Fort Union, or perhaps to some other point, where they were loaded on steamers. Until the Blackfoot-Crow trade expanded and pilots learned more of the sandy river, of the violent storms and devastating winds that whipped the high plains adjoining the Upper Missouri, and of the navigation season, usually late March to late November (or from ice to ice), American Fur Company boats dared not risk the channel above Fort Union.

Mackinaws not only linked the headwaters of the Missouri to the steamboat trade, but frequently supplemented the steamers engaged in the carrying trade below Fort Union. The mackinaw, or mackinaw batteaux, lineal descendants of earlier but smaller craft used in the Canadian fur trade, were cheaply built at upriver posts. The average mackinaw was a forty-foot-long, ten-foot-wide scow-shaped cargo carrier well suited to float down the Missouri under the command of a steersman, or patron, and his four oarsmen, or *voyageurs*. The oarsmen usually sat in the bow or in groups fore and aft; the cargo, covered tightly with drawn "lodge skins" fastened over a wooden frame, filled the center of the boat; and the steersman perched atop an elevated stern seat. Mackinaws

[26] Lass, *Steamboating*, chap. I.

were fairly comfortable, fast-moving boats that drew only fifteen to twenty inches of water, even when loaded with ten to fifteen tons of robes, furs, and supplies. At St. Louis or other downriver ports, they could be broken up, sold cheaply, or simply abandoned.[27]

After 1839, when the American Fur Company mackinaw fleet landed in St. Louis with $100,000 in robes and furs, many mackinaw cargoes were transferred to steamboats west of St. Louis because the insurance companies refused to cover mackinaw cargoes on the busy river below St. Joseph.[28] The boats were poor insurance risks. Mackinaws were lost regularly on snags, and the *voyageurs* drank heavily on the way downriver and thereby endangered the cargo they carried. Many mackinaws, however, continued to float downriver to St. Louis after 1839. In time, upriver boatbuilders increased the over-all size, cargo-carrying capacity, and passenger space of mackinaws to meet the demands of changing river commerce, and served miners and settlers, in the sixties and seventies, with the same ease earlier accorded fur traders.

Pierre Chouteau's steamboats and mackinaws carried most of the Upper Missouri River traffic by 1840 and supplied the American Fur Company a sturdy, although floating, foundation for greater Upper Missouri trade in the forties and fifties. But before the Company expanded upriver trade, it needed to create—to borrow a convenient term from American advertising—a better "public image." Granted, business conduct seldom follows the Sermon on the Mount and the American Fur Company was a shrewd business organization guilty of doing in any opposition by fair means or foul, yet poor conduct might be masked effectively by

[27] *Daily Evening Gazette*, July 3, 1839; Hiram M. Chittenden, *Early Steamboat Navigation on the Missouri River: Life and Adventures of Joseph La Barge*, I, 94–99; George M. Kingsbury, *History of Dakota Territory*, I, 48; Anne McDonnell (ed.), "The Fort Benton Journal, 1854–56, and the Fort Sarpy Journal, 1855–56," *CHSM*, Vol. X (1940), 264 (n. 38); John Palliser, *The Solitary Hunter; or, Sporting Adventures in the Prairies*, 203.

[28] *DMR*, July 4, 1839; Charles Larpenteur, *Forty Years a Fur Trader on the Upper Missouri* (ed. by Elliott Coues), I, 160.

better public relations. The Company needed an improved public image and set out to manufacture one. Chouteau knew full well that opposition companies would always regard the American Fur Company as "a sort of bastard East India Company . . . on a small scale," but the public was encouraged to take a more favorable view.[29]

Joseph (Jean) Nicolas Nicollet of the French Academy of Sciences was a perfect example of a renowned geologist and mathematician won over by the American Fur Company. In 1835, when Nicollet ascended the Mississippi, Pierre Chouteau, Jr., and Company "contributed liberally towards [his] . . . outfit and expenses, looking for no other remuneration than the general information which would be the result."[30] Four years later, in 1839, Nicollet, accompanied by a German botanist and young John Charles Frémont, reached St. Louis on his way to the Upper Missouri. The "old French residents" of the city received Nicollet's party with "profuse hospitality," and the Chouteaus provisioned them and gave them space on the steamer *Antelope*, bound for the upriver fur posts.[31] Several important American Fur Company agents, including John Sanford, "whose remarkable presence of mind and ingenuity in surmounting difficulties" excited Nicollet's "admiration," accompanied the scientific party aboard the steamboat.[32] At Fort Pierre, the Company transferred six men to Nicollet's service and sent him off pleasantly to his map making and specimen collecting. He was pleased with the Company's interest in science—correctly so, since Chouteau and several other American Fur Company leaders were ardent amateur scientists—and later told Congress, the newspapers, and his many influential friends of his pleasure.

[29] *Iowa Territorial Gazette and Burlington Advertiser*, July 6, 1839.

[30] Henry H. Sibley, "Memoir of Jean N. Nicollet," *Collections of the Minnesota Historical Society*, Vol. I (1872), 187–88.

[31] John Charles Frémont, *Memoirs of My Life*, 31–32.

[32] "Report Intended to Illustrate a Map of the Hydrographical Basin of the Upper Mississippi River Made . . . Under . . . the Corps of Topographical Engineers," 28 Cong., 2 sess., *HED No. 52*, pp. 41–42.

If eminent travelers (artists, missionaries, and, particularly, scientists, such as Nicollet) were welcomed warmheartedly by the American Fur Company to the Upper Missouri and given Company assistance to make their upriver visits memorable, they were likely to tell the world of the American Fur Company's virtues rather than its vices. And besides, the Chouteaus and other Company leaders enjoyed entertaining renowned visitors who passed through St. Louis to or from the upper river. Was it not a Creole aristocrat's Christian duty to assist missionaries, especially Roman Catholic ones, headed for the upper valley, and for westerners of substance to patronize the arts and sciences? Should the Upper Missouri robe and fur trade succumb within fifteen or twenty years to settlers tramping across the Dakotas and Montana, the American Fur Company might then point with pride to the assistance it had given to the scientific, artistic, and religious harbingers of civilization on the high plains. Who could tell what the future held for the American people? Was the American Fur Company to stand in the way of the nation's destiny? Not if Chouteau could avoid it. The American Fur Company would strive to build a better public image in the forties, continue for as long as possible to make a profit from the upper river, and then, later on, step aside with all possible grace and dignity (or so Chouteau hoped) before the surge of land-hungry emigrants to the Upper Missouri.

CHAPTER TWO

"In these degenerate days"

The election of 1840 dealt a hard body blow to Jacksonian Democracy. Military hero William Henry Harrison and John Tyler, his enigmatic running mate, carried the Whigs (or, as the political pundits said, were carried by Clay and his commandos) to victory. The Whigs, in a mudslinging contest, branded Van Buren a spendthrift responsible for the Panic of 1837 and the hard times afterwards. They bamboozled the Democrats and, before the opposition caught on, grabbed the banner of the common man, waved it high above Harrison, their old log-cabin, hard-cider hero, and dashed across the finish line with a popular majority of 150,000 and many, many electoral votes to spare. The Whigs won the presidency with Democratic political tactics, and the Democrats were aghast.

Throughout the winter before Harrison took his oath of office, Chouteau and his junior partners and clerks scurried to patch the American Fur Company's broken political fences. For twelve years the Company had spoken with a loud voice in the Federal City. The Office of Indian Affairs was staffed with many good Company friends, many now likely to be turned out, and Chouteau knew his Upper Missouri trade would suffer if the Whigs patronized men opposed to the American Fur Company. Thomas Hart Benton of Missouri, still in the Senate, was an old Company supporter, but he was a Democrat and his power less under the new administration. Chouteau saw clearly the new political problem: before the Company was harmed by the Harrison Administration, he must act to smooth over ruffled political feelings, to win friends in the new Whig regime, and to convince key Whigs that the American Fur Company was not anti-Harrison—but that was difficult since many Whigs knew otherwise.

The Superintendent of Indian Affairs in St. Louis and Indian agents west of the Mississippi River exercised enough power, as federal officeholders, to make business life grim or enjoyable for any fur company operating in the Indian country. Joshua Pilcher of Virginia, Upper Missouri agent in 1837–38, had been appointed Superintendent at St. Louis in March, 1839. Pilcher was a Democrat and a well-known professional fur trader, first in Manuel Lisa's employ, then in the ranks of the American Fur Company during the thirties. He ran his St. Louis office in co-ordination with American Fur Company interests, purchased most of his supplies from the Company, and was an outstanding example of an Indian Superintendent favorable to Pierre Chouteau.[1] When politics demanded, Pilcher rose to defend the Company. Shortly before Christmas, 1840, he wrote to Lieutenant-Governor elect Marmaduke of Missouri to oppose the recurrent agitation in favor of moving the superintendency from St. Louis to some site in western Missouri. Pilcher said the plan was preposterous, threatened to harm St. Louis business, and, by inference, was certain to weaken American Fur Company control of the superintendency.[2]

Indian agents stationed on the Missouri, whether friendly or unfriendly to the American Fur Company, understood that they held their jobs by sufferance of Chouteau and his men. The agents were alone in a hostile land, usually lacked adequate quarters, and depended upon the Company for most of their supplies. "The Company traders adroitly worked on their fears until they were fain to place themselves under the shelter of the trading posts."[3] Once that was done, the Company blended its business with the agents' duties, and the result was Company control of Indian

[1] Accounts of the Superintendent of Indian Affairs at St. Louis, 1839–1842, Clark (William) Papers, KHi.

[2] Joshua Pilcher to [Lieutenant-Governor elect] Meredith M. Marmaduke, December 16, 1840, Marmaduke (Meredith M.) Papers, State Historical Society of Missouri, Columbia.

[3] Chittenden, *Early Steamboat Navigation*, I, 177.

agents. Gifts from the agents to the Indians became gifts from the Company to the Indians, or so the Indians thought, and only a few exceptional agents possessed the strength of character to stand up against the Company.

The Upper Missouri Indian Agency was an old office originally established in 1819 at Council Bluffs. After twenty years of tribulation, it was discontinued, and the Indians above the Platte were left entirely to the mercy of the fur traders. It was not a tender mercy, and humanitarians demanded that the government reestablish the agency, but nothing was accomplished until 1842. In the meantime, the American Fur Company flexed its political muscles and strengthened its hand in the Indian trade. Indian annuity goods, paid out yearly by the federal authorities to specified tribes according to treaty agreements, flowed into the Yankton Sioux country by the late 1830's. Chouteau held the delivery contract, issued on a so-called "competitive-bid basis," and meant to keep it against all comers. T. Hartley Crawford, the new Indian Commissioner after 1838, balked at the American Fur Company hand in annuities, but John Sanford talked to the Secretary of War, Crawford's superior, and the Company prevailed. A few competing suppliers, appalled by the brazen use of influence, threatened to take the squabble to Congress, where congressmen favorable to the Chouteau-Sanford group prepared to challenge Crawford. Actually, the government had little choice but to give the American Fur Company each annual annuity contract, since the Company ran the only dependable steamboats on the Upper Missouri River and willingly underbid all competitors to keep the river trade monopolized. The Company could afford to lose money on carrying annuities if it kept control of the river.[4]

Despite Harrison's triumph in November, 1840, and the political skirmish with Commissioner Crawford, the Company fared well under the new Whig administration. Company agents and

[4] John F. A. Sanford to Pierre Chouteau, Jr., January 3, 7, 19, 1839, Chouteau Family Papers, MoSHi; E. A. Hitchcock to T. H. Crawford, February 8, 1839, Letters Received, 1839–1865, OIA, RG 75, NA.

partners lobbied vigorously in Washington during the winter after the election, convinced some of the less discerning Whigs that American Fur Company men were Harrison supporters, and fought to keep Joshua Pilcher, known to his enemies as a "Bentonian wire worker," in office as Superintendent of Indian Affairs in St. Louis. Although Pilcher had campaigned against Harrison and deserved to feel immediately the ax wielded by Whig spoilsmen, he survived in office until the summer of 1841. Harrison's sudden death in early April tossed the new administration into the lap of Vice-President Tyler, who was a Whig in name only and disliked frenzied firing and hiring. The battle to find Pilcher's successor dragged on into the summer.[5]

John Dougherty, a Whig member of the Missouri Legislature and respected expert on Missouri Valley Indian and fur trade affairs, was the leading contender for Pilcher's position. Dougherty understood as well as any fur trader, and better than most, the importance of furs, robes, and Indian goods to the Upper Missouri. He hated the American Fur Company, its agents, and its friends and expressed his hate frequently and vehemently: "I never wo'd ... play into their hands, and they know me too well to entertain a hope that I wo'd do so were I Superintendent."[6] Senator Benton, Dougherty remarked, "willed" Pilcher into office in 1839, but now the Whigs were in power and Dougherty was again in pursuit of the superintendency. This time he refused to rely upon verbal and written promises of support—they were insufficient; he knew that from 1839—this time he fought doggedly and tore the Company at every opportunity.

He won the first match a month before Harrison's inauguration. During the winter, Chouteau's friends in the Missouri Assembly presented a bill to incorporate the American Fur Company in the state of Missouri. Chouteau believed incorporation would strengthen the Company on the upper river and would im-

[5] John Dougherty to Samuel Churchill, February 27, 1841, Dougherty (John) Papers, MoSHi.
[6] John Dougherty to James H. Birch, March 15, 1841, *ibid.*

press the Whigs in Washington. But Dougherty opposed the "bill to incorporate the Missouri Fur Company." He threw his fur-trade knowledge and experience into the debate and asked why so many leading Democratic legislators, who regularly opposed acts of incorporation, supported Chouteau's proposal? Were they hirelings? Tools of the Company? On February 6, 1841, the bill lost in the House by a tie vote of forty-four to forty-four, with eleven members absent. Dougherty's opposition weakened the bill, and it died of overexposure.[7]

The Company, smarting from the stunning defeat suffered in the Missouri Legislature, threw its entire political force into the battle to retain Pilcher as Superintendent. He had committed a grievous political error, however, by telling the press before the election that if the Whigs won, he would "at once resign and apply his energies to the support of Col. Benton."[8] By the first week in June, rumors circulated that Pilcher had lost his job to Charles Keemle, a prominent St. Louis newspaperman and Beau Brummell. Keemle declined the office, however, and "an association of wealthy persons, having trading posts amongst all the important tribes of Indians of the West"—obviously the American Fur Company—advocated Pilcher's retention.[9] Unimpressed by American Fur Company pleas, the Administration narrowed the list of candidates to six, three of whom (Dougherty; George C. Sibley, a Whig humanitarian and philanthropist; and David Dawson Mitchell) were Missourians. Pilcher was ruled out; he was simply too controversial. Mitchell was an experienced fur trader who had worked under the American Fur Company for many years, but he was not a member of the inner circle of Company leaders and was said to have a mind of his own. The Company, with Benton's approval, supported Mitchell's candidacy: "with all his sins," he was the least of several evils and would do for a while. He was

<hr/>

[7] Ibid.; *Journal of the House of Representatives of the State of Missouri . . . One Thousand Eight Hundred and Forty*, 373.

[8] *DMR*, April 12, 1841.   [9] *St. Louis New Era*, June 18, 1841.

appointed Superintendent on September 13, and for the first time in months, political tension relaxed within the Company.[10]

Once the political crisis had passed, Chouteau gave greater attention to the upriver trade. The record of annual trading licenses taken out through the office of the Superintendent of Indian Affairs in St. Louis reveals that between 1839 and 1842 the Company increased its Upper Missouri capital investment from $36,000 to $60,000, it trading force from 90 to approximately 130 men, and its trading locations from fourteen to eighteen.[11] The Company expanded trade amongst the Crows in the Yellowstone Valley and with the Blackfeet along the far Upper Missouri. By the early fall of 1840, Chouteau had cleared away the remains of his old partnership with Bernard Pratte and had closed a troublesome chapter of business relations with the renowned fur trader Kenneth McKenzie. McKenzie re-entered the American Fur Company in 1842—only as a minority stockholder, however—and never exercised the power he had held at Fort Union a decade earlier.

Fortunately for Chouteau, the American Fur Company had met little strong competition in the Upper Missouri trade in the critical years between Astor's retirement and the political battles of 1841. The last major upriver opposition, from William L. Sublette and Robert Campbell, had ended in the mid-thirties. In the half-dozen quiet years that followed 1835, only small, weak, short-lived opposition groups contested the Company on the upper river. In 1840, Pratte and Cabanné, after one of their predictable, periodic disagreements with the Company, threatened to take a large outfit up the Missouri but changed their minds at the last minute. One small opposition outfit, however, led by C. A. Beauchamp, invested approximately $5,000 in a trading license on Christmas Eve, 1840, and took a wagon and five two-wheeled

[10] Ramsay Crooks to Pierre Chouteau, Jr., June 27, 1841, Chouteau Family Papers, MoSHi.

[11] Trading Licenses Granted Pierre Chouteau, Jr., and Company, 1839–1842, Letters Received, OIA, RG 75, NA.

carts, piled high with supplies and Indian trading goods, from Council Bluffs to the Sioux country around Fort Pierre. There the men split into three parties, traded over the remainder of the winter along the White, Bad, and Cheyenne rivers, and returned to civilization in the spring. They made a profitable trade, yet bothered the American Fur Company about as much as a gnat would an elephant.[12]

Chouteau's most aggravating competition, during 1840–41, came not from an organized fur company but from Joseph La Barge of St. Louis. La Barge was a young, energetic steamboat pilot who had worked for Chouteau in the fur trade during the thirties and refused to be intimidated by Company power. In 1840, he quarreled with his superiors over his duties as a riverboatman and scraped together enough money to buy a cargo of Indian trade goods. At Council Bluffs, he loaded the goods on wagons and set out for the Dakotas, but winter caught him and forced him to resort to sleds to move his outfit. Below the White River, he met a band of friendly Indians and an American Fur Company trader who admitted, once in his cups (La Barge provided the liquor), that the Company was determined to destroy all opposition. La Barge took the challenge, moved upriver to a trading site near Fort Pierre, and waited. Soon, an Indian messenger invited La Barge to accompany him to the fort. In his memoirs, La Barge charged that the Indian was under orders to shoot him on the trail, but, he said, he found the red man's gun, prevented the murder, and reached the fort, to the surprise of the American Fur Company garrison.[13]

On the second day of La Barge's visit to the post, the Company agent proposed that "the company should take [his] entire outfit at an advance of ten per cent upon the cost . . . while [he] was to engage [himself] to the company [as a pilot] for a period of three years."[14] At first La Barge refused the offer, but then agreed when he learned that one of his men had taken one-third of his

12 Kingsbury, *Dakota Territory*, I, 46–47.
13 Chittenden, *Early Steamboat Navigation*, I, 59–63.   14 *Ibid.*, 66.

goods, without his orders, to the Yankton Sioux. Still afraid for his life—at first he had refused even to eat or drink with the Company agent—La Barge left Fort Pierre and dashed through the bitter cold to the Cheyenne River country, where he settled his business, then returned to Fort Pierre and his own post. By April, 1841, he was on his way downriver to St. Louis, bringing a fair profit to his two merchant backers, J. B. Roy and Henry Shaw. La Barge was convinced that the American Fur Company was a completely unscrupulous monopoly guilty of hiring renegades and Indians to commit murder and "vile deeds" and was never to be trusted by any opposition concern.

La Barge's fear of death at the hands of Company assassins was only one of many fears prevalent amongst fur traders on the Upper Missouri. Honoré Picotte, a Company man with twenty years' experience in the upriver trade, complained of isolation at his tiny post on the Cheyenne. He was afraid of boredom and suffered from loneliness when his employees were away. "A few old Squaws" hung about his post "like as many rats—Knawing and Scratching and Stealing" whenever they got the chance, thoroughly irritating Picotte, who promised to harm any Indian or Company trader who made a poor hunt.[15] The Company, he said, did not send him adequate goods or personal supplies (candles, books, and writing paper) and he could not compete with opposition traders. To his fear of boredom he added fear that Chouteau disregarded his advice and planned to promote others to better Company positions. But Picotte was not the only man to feel lonely. Scores of traders, both Company men and opposition men, sensed the same isolation and frustration and complained of neglect on the upper river. Many, including some leading agents of the American Fur Company, turned to the bottle for consolation. Charles Larpenteur, an abstainer, called the Company leaders at Fort Union during the winter of 1840–41 a drunken "Trinity" who lost money to Indians who stole robes they had sold previous-

---

[15] Honoré Picotte to Jacob Halsey, February 24, 1839, Chouteau Family Papers, MoSHi.

ly to one inebriated trader in order to resell them to another equally as drunk.

Low upriver morale amongst isolated traders northwest of St. Louis was matched by complaints from fur dealers east and south of Missouri. Many dealers simply did not trust the American Fur Company to supply them regularly with quality robes and furs. At any moment a shipment of poor pelts might follow a shipment of good ones from Chouteau's warehouse, and any bale of robes might contain a variety of grades, perhaps even a few well-rotted hides. The Company explained that all big businesses made mistakes and errors were unavoidable in preserving, grading, storing, and shipping perishable furs and robes, but dealers thought some of the numerous errors were deliberate Company attempts to rid its warehouses of inferior stock. Dealers everywhere complained that the robes brought into St. Louis in 1839 were poor, and demanded allowances for shoddy packing. One small eastern furrier's protest summed up the over-all feeling: "The upper Missouri robes are not what they ought to be for the price. . . . We opened 3 packs to find a good handsome skin the other day without success and had to open a Bale of No. 1 before we could find a skin to suit."[16] Chouteau admitted to Crooks that packaging was slipshod at times and the American Fur Company sorters in St. Louis had held back "twice the amount as usual" of robes from the 1838 hunt, but he ignored most of the protests and waited for a better season to improve his business reputation. The hunt of 1839 was good, and a better market came quickly in 1840. Choice buffalo tongues sold well at the Company store, market quotations on St. Louis furs and robes advanced, and by November the Company had sold 90 per cent of all robes on hand.[17]

Although Chouteau was guilty of sharp market practices, he was victimized also by his own Upper Missouri traders, who passed along the skin-grading job to St. Louis and paid more at-

[16] Byron Greenough to the American Fur Company, January 4, 1840, *ibid*.
[17] Pierre Chouteau, Jr., and Company to Ramsay Crooks, November 24, 1840, American Fur Company Papers, NHi; *St. Louis New Era*, September 25, 1840.

tention to quantity than quality in the robe and fur trade. Each year, Indians killed thousands of buffalo on the northern plains, laid in the meat and robes needed for the winter, and prepared the remaining hides—perhaps one-fourth of the total kill—for market. The raw (or "green") hides, stretched on pole frames, were scraped and piled away until the end of the hunting season, when the squaws dressed them. Dressing hides was hard work, even by Indian standards. First the skin was scratched clean of the last pieces of flesh; then "brained," or smeared with buffalo brains and grease, after being sprinkled with water; and, finally, after further drying, rubbed soft and pliable with a sinew cord. Buffalo skins taken in the summer were usually thin, poor, and brought little from the traders. Skins from buffalo bulls over three years old were also unwanted, since the hide was thick and the hair uneven in length: short over the hindquarters, long in front. The properly prepared skin of a buffalo cow, however, when carried by an Indian to a distant upriver trading post or to a near-by temporary (seasonal) trading house (outfit), brought, in barter, since money was valueless to Indians, approximately three or four pounds of sugar, or two pounds of coffee, or two gallons of shelled corn. The robe cost the trader less than one dollar on the upper river, but transportation charges to St. Louis were high and the average robe sold finally for little more than its total cost to the trading company. As a result, robes had to be procured and sold in volume to be profitable items of trade.[18]

To the average trader, bartering goods for robes was a complex, drawn-out procedure. Whenever the skins were ready for trade —and that was usually during the winter months—the Indian braves loaded them on their women, or on convenient pack animals, and moved them to a trading post, where the agent in charge

[18] Thaddeus A. Culbertson, *Journal of an Expedition to the Mauvaises Terres and the Upper Missouri in 1850* (ed. by John F. McDermott), 91; "Report of Brevet Colonel W. F. Raynolds ... 1859–60," 40 Cong., 2 sess., *SED No.* 77, p. 11; Rudolph F. Kurz, *Journal of Rudolph Friedrich Kurz* (trans. by Myrtis Jarrell; ed. by J. N. B. Hewitt), 236; Henry A. Boller, *Among the Indians* (ed. by Milo M. Quaife), 304–305.

or his representative welcomed the party with small presents, and a gunpowder salute if an important chief accompanied the caravan. After the robes and furs were unpacked, the traders feasted the Indians upon coffee, bread, and whatever else was at hand. Then the red and white men passed the pipe and exchanged long-winded remarks. If the Indians were suspected of treachery, they were denied access to the post, and in unsettled times, only a few Indians were allowed in the trading room. The red men preferred to trade slowly and would accept a larger quantity of goods in preference to better goods in smaller quantity. A striped blanket or a blanket of a striking color brought more furs or robes than a dull-colored blanket of the same size and quality, and alcohol, of course, was always worth far more than its weight in blankets. Only the most inexperienced trader or a trader in fear of his life or the loss of his post to the Indians extended credit to the tribesmen, since they were notoriously poor risks.[19]

Upper Missouri traders marked up substantially prices on goods bartered with the Indians or sold to post employees. The markup, estimated at from 80 to 2,000 per cent, depended upon the item, the post, the trader, and the trading season, yet exorbitant prices were necessary to cover the costs of trade and to return the investors a dividend. The upriver markup and the sale of inferior summer robes, old bull skins, and water-damaged or vermin-infested robes shipped from St. Louis were regular business practices of the fur companies. Buyers who visited the fur warehouses in St. Louis were less likely to lose money, however, on furs and robes. They could personally examine the goods, select bales of well-seasoned pelts and robes, buy a few excellent buffalo-calf skins or used robes that were durable and evidenced little wear, and, on occasion, pay well for a rare light-skinned (white) robe for display purposes.[20]

[19] Kurz, *Journal*, 171; Edwin T. Denig, *Indian Tribes of the Upper Missouri* (ed. by J. N. B. Hewitt), 458–60; Harold E. Briggs, *Frontiers of the Norwest: A History of the Upper Missouri Valley*, 150–53.
[20] Kurz, *Journal*, 251; *St. Louis New Era*, June 29, 1841.

The cutthroat character of the trade, from markup to marketing, frightened other businessmen. A few fortunate amateur traders might profit for a season or two on the river, but most shrewd investors refused to back competition with the American Fur Company on the Upper Missouri. Nevertheless, a few St. Louis capitalists who disliked the American Fur Company for personal or business reasons quietly supported Company competitors. In June, 1840, Wayman Crow, a prominent merchant and civic leader, and Robert W. Taylor, whose father-in-law was a St. Louis alderman, stood bond for John A. N. Ebbetts in a new Upper Missouri fur-trade venture. Ebbetts employed twenty-nine traders to man trading locations on the west side of the Missouri between the White and Heart rivers. He sent one small outfit to the Black Hills, but the total cost of all his outfits was only $5,776.60—a small investment, yet enough to challenge the American Fur Company in the heart of the Sioux country.[21]

The nomadic, warlike Dakota Sioux claimed the Missouri Valley from the Big Sioux River to the Heart River (in present North Dakota), the adjoining country east of the Missouri as far as Lac qui Parle and the Turtle Mountain–Pembina River region, and the area west of the Missouri to the Powder River and the North Platte. The Yankton (southernmost) division of the Dakotas congregated close to the Missouri between the mouths of the Big Sioux and the James, and, by the fifties, were relatively peaceful. North of the Yanktons, the fierce, treacherous Yanktonai Sioux roamed from the Upper James and Big Sioux valleys to the Red River on the north and to the Missouri on the west. The large Teton Sioux division of the Dakotas, as hostile as the Yanktonais and more numerous, hunted from the Missouri west through the Black Hills to the Powder, north into enemy Mandan territory around the Little Missouri and Knife rivers, and south to the Pawnee lands on the Loup Fork of the Platte in Nebraska. Dakota

[21] Trading License of John A. N. Ebbetts, June 7, 1840, Letters Received, OIA, RG 75, NA.

Sioux warriors were ideal American Indians, tall and sinewy, be-feathered, painted—the perfect "Indian of the nickel"—and spoke a language pleasant to white men's ears. And since they were good hunters, wherever they gathered, traders would go, or try to go, with a temporary outfit, or would urge the Indian hunters to carry their robes and furs from their camps to the valley trading posts, some permanent, some only makeshift wintering houses strung out along the edge of the Missouri from the Big Sioux to the Heart.[22]

Before the end of the summer, 1840, Ebbetts had taken his trade goods into the Sioux country to feel out the power of the American Fur Company. Few St. Louisans seemed to know, or wished to say, much about Ebbetts' background. Evidence suggests he was a New York City importer backed by eastern capital but probably inexperienced in the Upper Missouri fur trade. He centered his 1840 fur operations in the White River–Old Fort Lookout country below the Great Bend of the Missouri, yet did not build a permanent river post until 1842. He lacked sufficient funds to charter steamboats in St. Louis to carry his supplies, men, and trade goods to the upper river or to transport his furs and robes downriver. He relied, instead, upon equipment purchased upriver from established traders (he bought a complete blacksmith's shop from a trader at the mouth of the Vermillion) and upon goods carried up annually in small river craft laboriously moved by cordelle, oar, pole, and sail, and sent his robes and furs downstream in mackinaws to St. Louis.

Ebbetts traded heavily in illicit alcohol, disregarded thousands of dollars that he owed his employees, and hammered away at the American Fur Company. By the spring of 1842, Chouteau was thoroughly irked by Ebbetts' business tactics and successful up-river trade. Honoré Picotte wrote Chouteau from Fort Pierre that

---

[22] Clark Wissler, *Indians of the United States*, 157; Edwin T. Denig, *Five Indian Tribes of the Upper Missouri* (ed. by John C. Ewers), references to the Sioux.

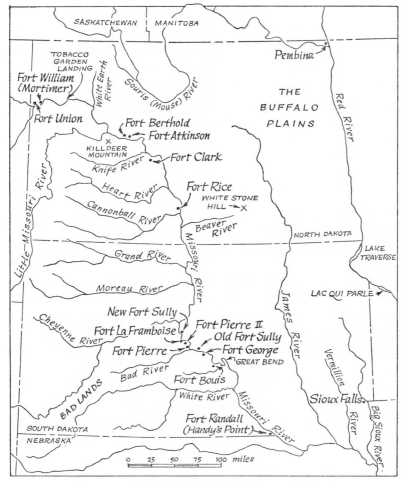

The Upper Missouri Valley from the Big Sioux
to Fort Union, and Adjacent Areas, 1840–1865

Ebbetts took 350 packs of robes in the winter trade, and advised
Chouteau to buy out Ebbetts "without making too great a sacrifice."[23] Chouteau refused to buy, however, and Ebbetts, rather

[23] Honoré Picotte to Pierre Chouteau, Jr., and Company, May 6, 1842, Chouteau Family Papers, MoSHi.

than sell, reorganized and expanded his business. On July 16, when he renewed his trading license, he increased the number of his employees, raised his capital to $32,000, and extended his trading area into the Yellowstone and Big Horn valleys. Taylor and Crow dropped out as sureties on the bond—Taylor was nearly bankrupt, fled St. Louis, and hired on with Ebbetts to trade on the upper river—and two New York City investors, Fulton Cutting and Charles Kelsey, stepped in.[24]

By August, 1842, the firm of Ebbetts, Cutting and Kelsey had opened business at Fort George on the right bank of the Missouri twenty miles below Fort Pierre.[25] The post stockade, approximately 155 by 165 feet, was guarded by "projecting blockhouses at two opposing corners." Recent excavations indicate that the enclosed post buildings, "several . . . equipped with adobe brick fireplaces," stood free of the walls (most fur-post buildings joined the walls), separated from them "by a wide alley or yard."[26] Fort George was built to last, built to withstand the American Fur Company and to give it strong competition. Since Ebbetts, Cutting and Kelsey (Kelsey was placed in charge of the new post) intended to remain on the upper river come hell, high water, or Pierre Chouteau himself, the American Fur Company sharpened its battle-ax for a lengthy campaign. As long as Ebbets bartered liquor for robes and pelts, he would make a profitable trade and the great Company would suffer "an indifferent business." Until Ebbetts' poisoned cup was drained, the American Fur Company could do little but wait, maintain strong upriver posts, and plead for help from the Indian Office.

The Sioux trading country from the James River to the Black

[24] Trading License of Ebbetts and Cutting, July 16, 1842, Letters Received, OIA, RG 75, NA; Benjamin Clapp to Pierre Chouteau, Jr., December 13, 1842, Chouteau Family Papers, MoSHi.

[25] Two Articles of Agreement made at Ft. George, August 22, 1842, Fur Trade Papers Envelope, MoSHi.

[26] Smithsonian Institution River Basin Surveys, "Archeological Progress Report No. 7" (October, 1962), 8–9.

Hills, from the White to above the Cheyenne, was the fief of Fort Pierre. Built in the winter of 1831–32, the post consisted of two acres enclosed by a cottonwood-log stockade protected by two blockhouses and stood one-half mile back from the west bank of the Missouri approximately three miles north of the mouth of Bad River. Although placed on a dreary, desolate, sun-baked river plain surrounded by treeless hills (firewood was cut upriver and floated down), it defied its environment and stood as a monument to American Fur Company power. The walls surrounded shops for carpenters, tinners, saddlers, and blacksmiths; a trading house and two large buildings containing living quarters; kitchens and storage buildings; stables; and a powder magazine. Corn, potatoes, and hay grew on fertile bottom land between the fort and the river. At Chantier Creek, approximately fifteen miles above Fort Pierre, artisans handsawed lumber and built and repaired river boats in the Company navy yard.[27] In the spring and summer of 1843, masons and carpenters put up a "new Row of Buildings . . . with 7 Doby chimneys in them," rebuilt the carpenter shop, and effected "numerous minor improvements" to embellish the appearance of the fort and to strengthen its competitive position with Fort George.[28]

Meanwhile, in St. Louis, the Company received the overland winter express with news and letters from the upriver posts and with last-minute estimates of supplies needed for 1843. Once the express was in, Chouteau completed arrangements for the spring shipment of men and material by mountain boat to the Upper Missouri. The steamer *Antelope* had made her last run to Fort Union in 1840. The following year, the *Trapper,* under Sire as master, completed the St. Louis–Fort Union round trip in 101 days. The *Trapper* left St. Louis on April 7, waved away by the

[27] Chittenden, *Early Steamboat Navigation,* I, 96; Frederick T. Wilson, "Old Fort Pierre and Its Neighbors" (ed. by Charles E. DeLand), *SDHC,* Vol. I (1902), 273–74.

[28] William Laidlaw to Pierre Chouteau, Jr., and Company, September 8, 1843, Chouteau Family Papers, MoSHi.

handkerchiefs of "a number of the fair sex . . . standing on the levee, with the heartfelt tear in their eyes."[29] Loaded with fur hunters and tons of paraphernalia, the mountain boat struggled upriver through low water and survived the abuse of an "indifferent" pilot who slept when he was tired, hunted ashore when he wished, and played cards whenever he pleased.[30]

The *Trapper* was lightened occasionally because of low water on the 1841 trip. Lightening, however, was one of the easiest, although time-consuming, methods to free a steamboat from a river bar or to move it ahead in shallow water. Enough of the cargo was sent ashore—sometimes even the passengers—to enable the boat to float free of the river obstacle and to move into deeper water, where she was reloaded. When the river bottom was soft and permitted logs to be sunk in the sand or mud, a steamer might "warp" itself ahead over a bar or shallow. In warping, a line was sent ahead from the boat and tied to a sturdy tree, a fixed log, or an anchor and slowly reeled in with a winch or a line pulled by the crew as the wheels churned. The boat, if lucky, moved ahead bit by bit, but the line might break, snap back, and injure passengers, crewmen, or cargo. If the pilot preferred, he could "grasshopper" his boat over the bar by setting a spar, connected to a winch, on each side of the boat. When the lines were drawn in by the winch, the boat rose, spun its paddles, moved forward (unless the grasshopper poles broke and splintered), and gradually, after the spars were reset several times, the steamer pulled free. Many bars were avoided by careful pilots who regularly sounded the channel, increased speed at just the right moment to send the vessel skimming over a shallow spot, or quickly reversed the wheel to back off a bar before the entire steamboat grounded.[31]

Landing at an Upper Missouri post posed other problems, since

[29] *Hawkeye and Iowa Partiot* (Burlington), April 15, 1841.

[30] Joseph A. Sire's Log Books (1841–1846) of the Annual Voyages of the Supply Boat of the American Fur Company from St. Louis to the Upper Missouri, Typescript, MoSHi.

[31] Louis C. Hunter, *Steamboats on the Western Rivers*, 252–55; Lass, *Steamboating*, chap. II.

the shifting river channel might in one season turn a deep landing spot near a post into a bar, sand spit, or shallow pool. In such an event the steamer landed across from the post and the master sent the cargo over in small barges or scows; put into shore above or below the post and dispatched the cargo by land; or simply waited for a rise in the river. Until the mid-1860's, many boats bound upriver resorted to cordelling to move against contrary currents and over the rapids below Fort Benton. One end of the cordelle (stout cord) was attached to the vessel and the other placed on the bank, where crewmen, aided by passengers if necessary, grabbed it and tugged. The method was crude, the work dirty and a great strain on passenger muscles unaccustomed to labor, but usually sufficient to edge the boat over a cantankerous current.

In 1842, Sire took the *Trapper* from St. Louis on April 11, bound for Fort Union with 150 traders and trappers and supplies for the upriver posts. The vessel's engineer was remarkable for his "know-how [and] . . . knowledge of making repairs," but the river was low and the boat did not unload at Union until late June.[32] The fort, "the principal and handsomest Trading post on the Missouri," had been constructed over a period of several months, beginning, probably, in the fall of 1829.[33] It commanded a "high gravelly bank" of the Missouri approximately six miles by water above the mouth of the Yellowstone, ideally situated near the confluence of the two rivers. Behind the post, prairies stretched back to McKenzie's Butte and a line of hills. Within the rectangular (240 by 220 feet) cottonwood palisade of the fort stood a comfortable two-story agent's house, living quarters for the employees, a powder magazine, artisans' shops, storehouses, and stables. Two double-storied stone bastions guarded the southwest and northeast corners of the twenty-foot wall, a strong double gate blocked the entrance, and a cannon flanked the base of the tall flagpole in the center of the post yard. In 1842, Fort Union

[32] Sire's Log Books, MoSHi; *St. Louis New Era*, April 12, 1842; *DMR*, April 13, 1842.

[33] Edwin T. Denig's Description of Ft. Union, July 30, 1843, Montana Manuscripts Collection, CLUC.

was the American Fur Company's largest, most heavily manned, and most elaborately furnished and supplied post on the Upper Missouri.[34]

From Union, the Company's tentacles of trade reached the Crows, Blackfeet, and Assiniboins. Although the Crows concentrated in the Yellowstone–Big Horn country, Crow hunting parties ranged into the valleys of the Musselshell, Powder, North Platte, and Sweetwater. The average Crow warrior was an excellent horseman (and horse thief), nomadic, generally friendly to white traders, an exceptionally good buffalo and beaver hunter, and a bitter enemy of the Blackfeet and the Missouri River Sioux. The Blackfeet, particularly the Piegan band, held the land around the junction of the Missouri and the Marias. They and the Gros Ventres (Atsina band of Arapahos) in the Judith Basin were greatly feared and distrusted by traders. Nevertheless, since large buffalo herds roamed the Judith and the mountain streams sheltered excellent beaver, white traders risked their lives and outfits to reach Piegan–Gros Ventre country. In comparison to the Blackfeet and the Crows, the Assiniboins, hard hit by smallpox between 1837 and 1840, lived closer to the walls of Fort Union. They roamed the land, in pursuit of the buffalo, from the Souris west to the Milk and from the Lower Yellowstone northward into Canada. Although "generally friendly to the whites" and willing to trade with the American Fur Company, they and the Blackfeet were wanderers who moved back and forth across the international boundary line, seeking at both American and Canadian posts the best barter they could find and the best bric-a-brac they could steal.[35]

Chouteau protested repeatedly to the Indian Office that the border-crossing tribesmen hurt American Fur Company trade and

[34] Chittenden, *Fur Trade*, II, 958–60. See also Frank B. Harper, *Fort Union and Its Neighbors*.

[35] Chittenden, *Fur Trade*, II, 857. Many fur men, in their reports on Indian trade, confused the Gros Ventres of the Judith Basin with the Blackfeet, since only a few Piegan Blackfeet traded regularly with the whites.

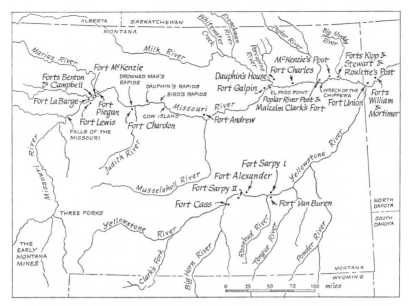

The Upper Missouri Valley from Fort Union to Three Forks,
and the Valley of the Yellowstone, 1840–1865

gave the British an economic toe hold on the Upper Missouri. Superintendent Mitchell supported the Company charges and noted, early in 1842, that at least one American trader, William P. May, had crossed to Red River and returned with British goods to trade with the Missouri River tribes. Such a "palpable violation" of the law, Mitchell added, would create British influence in new portions of the Indian country.[36] The Indian Office recognized the validity of the Company's charges, but could do little until the greater political issue of joint Anglo-American occupation of the Oregon country was settled in 1846. The American Fur Company was forced to tolerate the competition of the Hudson's Bay Company north and west of the Missouri and to hope that in time Con-

[36] Unfortunately, the manuscripts of the Hudson's Bay Company contain only brief, indirect references to the Upper Missouri fur trade after 1840, and are not particularly significant to this study. But see David D. Mitchell to T. H. Crawford, February 16, 1842, Letters Received, OIA, RG 75, NA.

45

gress might lower the tariff on Indian goods imported into the United States and so give the American traders a better competitive position in the Upper Missouri Indian trade.

In the meantime, the Assiniboin, Crow, and Blackfoot robes and furs accumulated at Fort Union in 1842 were loaded hurriedly aboard the *Trapper*; Captain Sire swung the vessel about and headed downriver, running with a falling channel. At Fort Clark, atop a high hill overhanging the Missouri eight miles below the mouth of Knife River, Sire landed and took on additional robes and furs. The small post, "a poor miniature representation of Ft. Pierre," was built in 1831 by James Kipp and named in honor of William Clark.[37] At first, the post was the nucleus of trade with the near-by maize-growing Mandans, but the Upper Missouri smallpox epidemic of 1837 had decimated the Indians surrounding the post. Those who survived continued to live a village life, although their civilization lay broken before the plague. They no longer resisted successfully the attacks of Sioux and Assiniboins, nor had they hunters sufficient to bring in many packs of robes for the Fort Clark trade.

Again the *Trapper* turned into the current, leaving behind the little leaky-roofed post encircled by its kitchen gardens. Near Fort Pierre, the Missouri seemed to run out of water entirely. The *Trapper* grounded and held firm, and Captain Sire and his crew transferred the cargo to several small boats, arranged to store the steamboat for the winter at the navy yard, and floated downstream in the smaller craft. When Sire reached St. Louis in mid-August— via river packet from the Vermillion—he learned that Chouteau had sent a second Company boat, the *Huntsville*, with goods to the upper river. The season was late and the risk great, but Chouteau had to expand upriver inventories to meet the threat from Ebbetts, Cutting and Kelsey in 1843. Although the *Huntsville* was "little more than a wreck," she carried her cargo to the up-

[37] Marie R. Audubon and Elliott Coues (eds.), *Audubon and His Journals*, II, 13–14.

river posts and returned to St. Louis on October 30 "with a few furs and skins."[38]

Most Upper Missouri robes and furs arrived in St. Louis on mackinaws rather than on steamers during the summer of 1842, despite both insurance-company unwillingness to cover mackinaw cargoes and the regular loss of mackinaws on river snags and sawyers. Thirteen to fifteen of them landed at St. Louis between mid-May and mid-August, carrying cargoes for the American Fur Company, and one to three others put in with cargoes belonging to Ebbetts, Cutting and Kelsey. Two additional mackinaws, however, both Company boats, sank. The first went down early in May between Forts Clark and Pierre, probably because the steersman failed in his duties. Fortunately, only 30 per cent of the robes aboard were lost. The second sank near the mouth of the Kansas, taking with it to the muddy bottom of the Missouri a cargo of approximately 2,600 robes, 4,000 buffalo tongues, and miscellaneous skins and castors. Nevertheless, enough Upper Missouri robes and furs were unloaded in St. Louis in 1842 to make the year a profitable one for the American Fur Company. Ebbetts, Cutting and Kelsey had wounded the Company, yet not mortally.[39]

In the summer of 1842, Chouteau acquired a new weapon of politically tempered steel sufficiently strong, he believed, to kill the opposition on the Upper Missouri. For years complaints had poured into the Indian Office that fur traders were demoralizing

[38] *DMR*, November 1, 1842; *Daily People's Organ* (St. Louis), August 23, 1842; *Native American Bulletin* (St. Louis), August 17, 1842, Transcript in Dale Morgan Collection, CSmH; Chittenden and Richardson, *Father de Smet*, I, 401–402; Pierre Chouteau, Jr., and Company to Ramsay Crooks, August 20, 1842, American Fur Company Papers, NHi.

[39] *St. Louis New Era*, May 16, July 22, 1842; Honoré Picotte to Pierre Chouteau, Jr., and Company, May 6, 1842, and John B. Sarpy to Pierre Chouteau, Jr., September 29, 1842, Chouteau Family Papers, MoSHi.; Pierre Chouteau, Jr., and Company to Ramsay Crooks, August 9, 16, 1842, American Fur Company Papers, NHi. In 1840, approximately thirteen mackinaws reached St. Louis with Upper Missouri cargoes, and at least one was lost on the way downriver; in 1841, ten mackinaws landed in St. Louis.

the Indians with liquor and flagrantly violating federal law forbidding alcohol trade in the Indian country. In 1840–41, when Ebbetts opened the firewater floodgates on the Upper Missouri, the American Fur Company realized at once that its old, carefully limited, carefully concealed upriver liquor business might be swept away by Ebbetts' tide. Chouteau wrote Superintendent Mitchell in October, 1841, requesting that Mitchell pressure the Indian Office to appoint a special, roving Upper Missouri Indian agent to curb the liquor trade.[40] Chouteau suggested that Colin Campbell, a halfblood Sioux who lived on the upper river and exercised great influence amongst the tribes, be appointed. Campbell wanted the job; the Company wanted him. Mitchell told the Commissioner that although Campbell was a "bold and energetic" man, he would need dragoon support to conduct a thorough investigation on the Upper Missouri. According to Mitchell, within the previous year more than one hundred Indians had fallen in drunken brawls in the Sioux country. Local civil wars threatened, hunting would fall off if war came, and villages would starve in the midst of plenty if the liquor trade continued.[41]

The Commissioner delayed action, however, and the delay provoked new pleas from Mitchell: "I would earnestly recommend the appointment of an agent for the upper Missouri. The whites, trading and residing in that country, as well as the numerous tribes of Indians inhabiting that vast region will soon cease to respect, or perhaps acknowledge the U.S. Government without some manifestation of its authority."[42] Finally, in March, 1842, the War Department instructed the army to clamp down on the liquor trade. Troops were sent to oversee the "half-dozen widely separated

[40] David D. Mitchell to T. H. Crawford, October 25, 1841, Letters Received, OIA, RG 75, NA.

[41] Pierre Chouteau, Jr., and Company to Colin Campbell, August 23, 1841, and to David D. Mitchell, October 7 (?), 1841, and David D. Mitchell to T. H. Crawford, October 25, 1841, *ibid.* Edwin T. Denig denied, in 1854, that liquor ever had killed many Upper Missouri Indians. He said that disease, rather than alcohol, had taken the heavier toll of Indians and that not more than one hundred Indians had died from drinking liquor in the previous twenty years.

[42] David D. Mitchell to T. H. Crawford, December 18, 1841, *ibid.*

trading posts" near the mouth of the Platte and to help the Indian subagent at Council Bluffs enforce the liquor laws.[43] The subagent and soldiers examined the cargoes of boats bound upriver, but Chouteau said he was dissatisfied with the investigation, since his cargoes were rigidly examined but some of his competitors' were not. He charged that the Indian Office had failed "to fulfill its promises or pledges" to appoint a special Upper Missouri agent.[44] Mitchell bristled at Chouteau's censure, yet dared not antagonize the Company openly, and continued to press Washington for an agent. Meanwhile, in late June, the Commissioner decided to still the tempest and appointed an "agent to reside in the Indian Country for the purpose of suppressing the whiskey."[45] His choice— the choice of Chouteau, Sanford, and Mitchell—was Andrew Drips, widely known as a Company man temperamentally better suited to the agent's job than the unpredictable Colin Campbell.

Although Drips was born in Pennsylvania, he had traded on the Upper Missouri before the age of thirty and counted Pilcher, Chouteau, and most American Fur Company men as his friends, patrons, and employers. Both Sanford and Chouteau encouraged him to examine the Indian trade of friend and foe alike, however, and to favor none, since the Company intended to stash its liquor while Drips made the investigation. If his examination halted, even temporarily, Ebbetts' alcohol business on the Upper Missouri and Richard's on the Platte, the halt might be long enough to kill all American Fur Company opposition. After some delay in the Senate, which Chouteau labeled "a piece with all public business at Washington in these degenerate days," Drips was confirmed and his nomination sent to St. Louis in mid-September.[46] Mitchell in-

[43] Charles Preuss, *Exploring with Frémont* (trans. and ed. by Erwin G. and Elisabeth K. Gudde), 76.

[44] David D. Mitchell to T. H. Crawford, August 23, 25, 1842, Letters Received, OIA, RG 75, NA.

[45] T. H. Crawford to John F. A. Sanford, July 2, 1842, Drips (Andrew) Papers, MoSHi.

[46] Pierre Chouteau, Jr., and Company to Andrew Drips, September 12, 1842, *ibid.*

structed him to examine Fort Pierre, then move overland to the Platte, and from there return to Fort Clark on the Missouri before winter set in. When spring came in 1843, he was ordered to investigate Fort Union and the Blackfoot country and, after that, descend the Missouri to intercept boats bound upriver and look into their cargoes. Mitchell believed that Drips should conduct the "experiment" from camps pitched amongst the Indians rather than at trading posts. Drips, however, thought otherwise. The American Fur Company had promised him shelter and sustenance, co-operation and companionship from old friends, and he was not about to sacrifice Company hospitality.[47]

He reached Fort Pierre in November, enjoyed a friendly reception, and left quickly on circuit into the Cheyenne River country, but notified Company traders in advance of the Company posts he planned to visit and instructed them to destroy or remove any liquor they had on hand. He did not visit the Platte, however, as Mitchell advised. Instead, he spent the winter on the Missouri and complained to the Indian Office that he needed money and dragoon protection. Mitchell admitted to Washington that the experiment so far had brought little reform in the liquor trade, yet steadfastly supported Drips and the re-establishment of the Upper Missouri Agency.[48]

Chouteau had forged his weapon, Andrew Drips, and the weapon was poised to strike on the Upper Missouri, but would it cut clean, destroy the opposition without touching the American Fur Company? Or would it leave a ragged edge and harm the Company as well as Ebbetts, Cutting and Kelsey? Only time would tell. For the moment, the winter of 1842–43 closed in upon St. Louis and upon "the regal buffalo across the plains" and "the Beaver's lurking place."[49] Chouteau heard midwinter rumors that

[47] David D. Mitchell to Andrew Drips, October 6, 1842, *ibid*.

[48] Andrew Drips to Colin Campbell, November 28, 1842, and to A. Raynald (?), December 15, 1842, *ibid*.; David D. Mitchell to T. H. Crawford, February 27, 1843, Letters Received, OIA, RG 75, NA.

[49] E. Peabody, "The Backwoodsman," *The Western Messenger; Devoted to Religion and Literature*, Vols. II–III (1836–37), 661.

Pratte and Cabanné had associated with Ebbetts, that a strong eastern transatlantic shipping firm was backing Ebbetts, and that Ebbetts was building at least two new upriver posts.[50] But was any rumor true, was any false? Chouteau did not know, could not guess accurately until the early-spring express came from the upper posts, until the ice broke and opened the river to trade. But whether all rumors were true or none was true, 1843 promised to be a busy year in the upper valley.

[50] Benjamin Clapp to Pierre Chouteau, Jr., December 1, 1842, Chouteau Family Papers, MoSHi.

CHAPTER THREE

"The green cotton commenced to dry"

THE NATION'S BUSINESS PULSE beat a little faster in the spring of 1843, faster than it had throbbed in six years—since the Panic of 1837 sent the country into an economic tail spin. The American Fur Company girded itself for impending warmweather competition with Ebbetts, Cutting and Kelsey and examined its corporate armor for dents and breaks. Since Drips's upriver probe had not uncovered proof, at least so far, of Ebbetts' liquor trade, and might not for some time to come, the Company, anticipating even greater opposition from Ebbetts in 1843, attacked his backers in New York City. Chouteau, supported by Sire and a majority of stockholders in the American Fur Company, opened a campaign in February and March to obstruct the Boston and New York City robe and fur markets by underselling the eastern agents who handled Ebbetts' Upper Missouri returns. Once again, the Company sacrificed short-range earnings for long-range gain, and, although some of Chouteau's associates disliked the temporary cut in profits, instituted the new policy nevertheless.[1]

Ebbetts' New York City supporters fought back, successfully blunted the point of Chouteau's eastern attack, and proved anew to the American Fur Company that the upriver opposition possessed sturdy financial support. The year before, Ebbetts, on a visit to the East, had won the financial backing necessary to hold up his sagging bank account. Fulton Cutting and the elderly Charles Kelsey contributed capital to Ebbetts' business, or so the

[1] Benjamin Clapp to Pierre Chouteau, Jr., March 18, 1843, and Joseph A. Sire to Pierre Chouteau, Jr., March 20, 1843, Chouteau Family Papers, MoSHi.

evidence suggests, and ascended the Missouri with him later in the summer of 1842 to take charge of portions of his trading empire. Cutting, the sixth son of a distinguished eastern lawyer, had briefly attended Columbia University. After leaving college he became a merchant and in 1839 senior partner in a Pearl Street importing firm. Kelsey, a well-established exchange broker in Brooklyn, gradually trickled an estimated $20,000 into Ebbetts' Upper Missouri venture and probably lost a fair share of the sum.[2] Cutting, who was a black sheep of the Cutting-Livingston family (his mother was a Livingston), gave Ebbetts less money, it seems, but more of his time and energy.

In midsummer, 1842, when Ebbetts and his partners Cutting and Kelsey reached the Sioux country, they carried with them a new trading license taken out in St. Louis and the confidence and financial support of Curtis Bolton, Samuel M. Fox, and Mortimer Livingston, who operated a flourishing line of transatlantic packets out of New York City. Curtis Bolton had built an excellent business reputation in the East, following earlier mercantile service in Savannah and a childhood spent as an orphan in boarding school. He had bought a large interest in a shipping line in the 1830's and had taken into the business two close associates, 37-year-old Samuel M. Fox and a Columbia University graduate, Mortimer Livingston, both of whom had married daughters of Francis Depau, the original owner of the line. Bolton retired from the firm after a few years, with a personal fortune estimated at $250,000, and devoted his time to philanthropy. Fox stayed with the business until his death late in 1849 and left his heirs an estate of $100,000 to $200,000, most of it accumulated in the shipping business. Livingston remained with the company for many years, served for a time as vice-consul for Granada in New York City, and eventually suffered heavy financial reverses in competition with the Cunard Line, a British firm.[3]

[2] Larpenteur, *Forty Years*, I, 179.
[3] Robert G. Albion, *Square-Riggers on Schedule*, 127, 138, 270, and *The Rise of New York Port*, 253, 325; J. A. Scoville, *The Old Merchants of New York*

In the firm of Bolton, Fox and Livingston, Ebbets found a New York City distributor for his robes and furs, a reservoir of capital strength, and a ready source of European trade goods derived directly from men in the shipping business. With Cutting and Kelsey by his side on the upper river, his power increased in the Indian country, and he was encouraged to expand his upriver domain to reach out to the Yellowstone, as his new license indicated; to finish building a permanent post (Fort George) near Fort Pierre; and to open trade at various new locations, particularly near Fort Union, along the river. St. Louis businessmen recognized at once the heavy hand of Bolton, Fox and Livingston in Ebbetts' company and gave the name of the New York City shippers, sometimes shortened to Fox and Livingston, to Ebbetts' enterprise or simply called the entire organization the "Union Fur Company."

Cutting moved up the Missouri from Fort George in the fall of 1842 with trade goods and liquor for the Mandan-Assiniboin country. Approximately three miles by land east of Fort Union, almost opposite the mouth of the Yellowstone, he opened trade near the ruins of old Fort William, named for William L. Sublette of the firm of Sublette and Campbell, archfoes of the American Fur Company on the Upper Missouri during the mid-1830's. Cutting christened his post Fort Mortimer in honor of his relative and business associate, Mortimer Livingston.[4] According to Charles Larpenteur, an American Fur Company man whose roving eye caught much of the drama in the Upper Missouri trade over a period of forty years, Cutting was "still green cotton." He bar-

---

City, I, 211; Moses Y. Beach, *The Wealth and Biography of the Wealthy Citizens of the City of New York*, 12, 32; Henry C. and Reginald P. Bolton, *The Family of Bolton in England and America, 1100–1894: A Study in Genealogy*, 418–42; *New York Evening Post* (New York City), December 11, 1849. See also the New York City business directories for the years 1839–53 in the Minnesota Historical Society, St. Paul, and in the Library of Congress, Washington, D.C.

4 W. A. Shoup to C. N. Kessler, January 15, 1917, Montana Manuscripts Collection, CLUC; Ray H. Mattison, "Report on Historic Sites in the Garrison Reservoir Area, Missouri River," *North Dakota History*, Vol. 22 (January, 1955), 64; Merrill G. Burlingame, *The Military-Indian Frontier in Montana, 1860–1890*, 77.

tered liberally—too liberally—for robes and furs and on one occasion presented the Assiniboin Chief Crazy Bear with a full military outfit, "fine fur hat and feathers," and a "beautiful sword." The Chief took his gaudy new costume to the agent at Fort Union and turned it over to him as a sign of Assiniboin loyalty to the American Fur Company. Cutting was astonished by the Indian's lack of good faith, and Larpenteur remarked: "The green cotton commenced to dry."[5]

By the spring of 1843, the Union Fur Company had opened trade at two new locations: tiny Fort Cotton, on the right bank of the Missouri in Blackfoot country just above the site of later Fort Benton, and at a trading house near the mouth of the Little Big Horn. Union Fur Company men manned both of them for approximately one to two years, then passed them to the American Fur Company when the opposition failed. Although the posts tapped briefly the trade of the Missouri, Marias, and Big Horn valleys and antagonized American Fur Company traders in each area, they were never a major threat to Company power above the mouth of the Yellowstone.[6]

Cutting was not the only green member of the Union Fur Company resident on the upper river during the winter of 1842–43. Charles Kelsey learned quickly that conditions in the trade were not entirely as Ebbetts had pictured them to him in New York City. The Indians and small traders were not anxious, as Ebbetts said they were, to desert the American Fur Company and take their robes and furs to the representatives of Fox and Livingston. By the time Kelsey reached Fort Union, he better understood the position of the American Fur Company on the river and remarked candidly to Alexander Culbertson, Chouteau's agent: "Had I known how the American Fur Company was situated, I would have kept clear of investing in this opposition."[7] As an experienced broker and money gambler, Kelsey knew that his chance to turn

[5] Larpenteur, *Forty Years*, I, 181–84.

[6] Burlingame, *Montana Frontier*, 76–77; McDonnell, "Forts Benton and Sarpy," *CHSM*, X, 238 (n. 1); Charles Mercier, "Reminiscences," MS, MtHi.

[7] Larpenteur, *Forty Years*, I, 179.

a profit on his investment was slim, that he would be fortunate to recover even his capital. In the meantime, he settled down at Fort George, as resident trader, and made the best of a poor situation while his temper grew short and his disgust for Ebbetts the dreamer increased. He imagined vividly what Fox and Livingston would say when they learned the full story.

Ebbetts believed, however, that as long as he controlled most of the liquor on the Upper Missouri—the "damnd agent [Drips] of the Co's notwithstanding"—he would make a successful trade. By January, 1843, he was ready to take liquor into the Sioux camps near Fort Pierre. His alcohol, mixed with river water and a few condiments (usually chewing tobacco, Jamaica ginger, molasses, and peppers) looked like whiskey, at least to an Indian, and tasted spirited. He dared Drips to stop his trade and threatened to harm Frank Beeman, the American Fur Company trader sent from Fort Pierre in November, 1842, to compete with Kelsey at Fort George. Ebbetts first warned Beeman to move away from Fort George or else, then cut Beeman's lodge "in several places and materially damaged" it, and, finally, offered to hire him and buy part of his outfit. Beeman, in fear for his life, hid the remains of his goods and fled to Fort Pierre, but was ordered back to Fort George in the company of Joseph V. Hamilton and James Illingsworth. Ebbetts threatened Beeman again, and on February 1, the American Fur Company man petitioned Fort Pierre for help.[8]

On the same day, Hamilton and Illingsworth sent similar letters to Honoré Picotte, the American Fur Company agent at Fort Pierre, and to Drips, asking them to do something about the Fort George liquor trade. Hamilton and Illingsworth said that they had talked to Kelsey, then in charge of Fort George, and had requested that he control the ruffians in his employ. Kelsey replied that he could not control them and would not interfere with them or be responsible for their violent acts against the American Fur Company. He was afraid to cross his employees because they were

---

[8] Honoré Picotte to A. Drips, January 20, 1843, and Frank Beeman (Frederic Behman?) to A. Drips, February 1, 1843, Drips (Andrew) Papers, MoSHi.

drawn from the dregs of upriver traders. The Indians who hung around Fort George received liquor from Kelsey's men, and "in one instance two Indians . . . drunk and with a bottle of liquor" left Fort George and forced their way into the near-by lodge of the three American Fur Company men, who expected an attack at any moment from the red men and opposition traders in one of their "drunken frolics."[9]

Perhaps Ebbetts could have controlled the drunken brawlers at Fort George; Kelsey could not. On February 16 or 17, Kelsey appealed to Drips for help, claiming that a group of rebellious traders led by John Bull (Jean Carriveau) were billeted in a log cabin on Simoneau's Island, where cattle grazed, opposite Fort George. Kelsey stated that the insubordinates had treated him outrageously and that he had dismissed Carriveau. According to William White, another of Kelsey's employees, Carriveau, together with Michoux Marley and Jack Boyle, had sworn to kill Kelsey if he set foot on the island and intended to ship him downriver if he "did not do as they wanted him to do." When Kelsey warned the troublemakers to leave the island, they refused and again threatened him. This time he returned to the fort, gathered friends and arms, and insisted that the rebels evacuate the island. The hostiles defied his authority, and, in answer, he and his followers assaulted the cabin. Marley and Carriveau fell. Carriveau, shot by Kelsey, died with a "leaden bullet" in his right breast. The other insurgents fled posthaste.[10]

Kelsey, sick and tired of life on the Upper Missouri, left Fort George shortly after the battle and with considerable difficulty made his way downriver. He returned to New York City, to the bitterness of defeat by the Upper Missouri trade, and to the disgrace of an indictment for murder brought in the United States Circuit Court for the District of Missouri. Although the indictment rested in the court from 1844 until 1847, it was finally

[9] Joseph V. Hamilton to Honoré Picotte, February 1, 1843, and to A. Drips, February 1, 1843, and James Illingsworth to A. Drips, February 1, 1843, *ibid.*

[10] Statement of A. Drips, February 22, 1843, and Statement of William White, March 25, 1843, *ibid.; St. Louis New Era*, April 27, 28, 1843.

57

dropped by the federal district attorney and Kelsey was freed.[11] Robert Taylor, Ebbetts' original partner, had fled Fort George with several companions either shortly before or immediately after the attack on the log hut. They traveled overland through deep snow until they stumbled onto an ice-free stretch of the river where they built a canoe and drifted down to Council Bluffs. The "peculiar circumstances" under which Taylor departed Fort George suggest that he was party to the battle, yet he was not indicted by the Circuit Court.[12]

Within two months after the clash on Simoneau's Island, a second unexpected outburst struck the upper river, this time at Little Bend, near the mouth of the Cheyenne, where the American Fur Company and Ebbetts each maintained a trading post. William P. May, an unlicensed independent trader (the one Superintendent Mitchell branded for trading British goods on American soil in 1842) reached the Cheyenne, accompanied by an American and a Red River halfblood. The three men encamped overnight with the local American Fur Company agent, and while breaking camp the following morning, the halfblood announced that he intended to remain behind to join Ebbetts' company. May refused to release him until they reached Fort Pierre. The halfblood, however, was adamant, and May had no choice but to accept the loan of a man from the American Fur Company and to set out downriver without the Red River métis. May was scarcely afloat when eight or ten of Ebbetts' men, most of them drunk, fired upon him from the bank where the channel was narrow, forced him ashore, and, before they permitted him to escape downstream, seized from his cargo several choice beaver skins and a quantity of salted tongues. Ebbetts made no effort to stop the attack. Anthony R. Bouis, the American Fur Company agent at Little Bend, reported to his superiors that May had been attacked, confirmed that Ebbetts' men drank heavily and brawled frequently, and added that they

[11] File of *U.S. v. Charles Kelsey*, Case No. 392, Records of the United States Circuit Court, District of Missouri FRC, KC; Law Record, United States Circuit Court, District of Missouri, Vol. A, 1838–1848, p. 349, FRC, KC.

[12] *St. Louis New Era*, April 28, 1843; *DMR*, May 11, 1843.

threatened to destroy his lodge at the Cheyenne as Kelsey's men had destroyed the lodge of the American Fur Company agent at Fort George.[13]

The Upper Missouri spawned many outbursts between traders, however, and May's loss was not unusual. In 1840, an American Fur Company employee robbed the store at Fort Union and when apprehended two years later was shipped downriver to be released from the Company in St. Louis. Individual traders or those traveling in small parties were at times robbed on the trail by competing traders. Other fur men, disgusted with life on the river, deserted posts and steamers, taking with them supplies, firearms, and packages of robes and furs. The trading companies expected desertions and periodic robberies, yet beginning in the spring of 1843, major acts of violence on the upper river increased. A barbed plant of hate grew in the heat generated by the rivalry between the American Fur Company and its competition and sent forth blossoms of destruction.

In St. Louis, the leaders of the Company—Chouteau, Sarpy, Sanford, Sire, McKenzie, and Benjamin Clapp—reflected upon the late news brought down from the Upper Missouri in the spring of 1843 and prepared to resist the Union Fur Company more stoutly.[14] On April 18, Chouteau received licensed permission from Superintendent Mitchell to expand Company trade on the Upper Missouri and Yellowstone in order to counteract the trade of the opposition. The Yellowstone Valley had assumed greater importance to the Company now that Ebbetts and Cutting were trading beyond Fort Union. The old Company post, Fort Cass, built in 1832 on the right bank of the Yellowstone two miles below the mouth of the Big Horn, was abandoned seven years later. Fort Van Buren (1835), east along the Yellowstone at the mouth of the Rosebud, replaced Fort Cass (the names of the two posts expressed clearly the political preference of the American

13 Anthony R. Bouis to A. Drips, April 18, 1843, Drips (Andrew) Papers, MoSHi.

14 Shareholders in Pierre Chouteau, Jr., and Company, 1842–1846, Chouteau Family Papers, *ibid.*

Fur Company) and controlled the Company's Crow trade until 1842, when Fort Alexander (Culbertson) was placed on the north bank of the Yellowstone, approximately twenty miles above Van Buren, nearer the center of the opposition trade developing at the mouth of the Big Horn. Charles Larpenteur, in charge of constructing Fort Alexander, burned palisaded Fort Van Buren, under Company instructions, before setting twenty men to work on the new post.[15]

The Yellowstone Valley was the crossroads for Sioux, Blackfoot, and Crow war parties and, consequently, was a dangerous land for all traders and trading posts. The Yellowstone River equaled in ferocity the epic intertribal struggles enacted along its edges. When the river was high, the sandy banks gave way and the swift current carried a heavy load of debris; when the stream was low, mackinaws struck sand bars, snags, and rocky ledges. Annual supplies for the Yellowstone posts were cordelled laboriously upriver from the Missouri, and each season's trade in robes and furs was sent down through the rapids, where boats and cargoes were lost frequently unless voyageurs portaged around the difficult sections of the river. Any mackinaw that landed, however, was in danger of attack from Indians concealed in ravines leading to the river or lurking in the matted, timbered bottom lands.[16] The valley of the Yellowstone was a 300-mile gauntlet from the mouth of the Big Horn to Fort Union, and only very powerful or very desperate fur companies dared trade along the river.

In 1843, the American Fur Company also reinvigorated its trade along the Missouri west of Fort Union. Twelve years earlier, the Company had built Fort Piegan, the first of a series of posts in the Blackfoot country, near the junction of the Marias and the Missouri. Fort Piegan was first garrisoned during the winter of 1831–32, but the severity of the weather, the post's remote location, and the danger of Blackfoot attack caused James Kipp, post bourgeois,

[15] Larpenteur, *Forty Years*, I, 170–71; Trading Licenses Granted Pierre Chouteau, Jr., and Company, 1839–1843, Letters Received, OIA, RG 75, NA.

[16] Denig, *Five Indian Tribes* (Ewers), 201.

to abandon the location in the spring. David D. Mitchell, then employed by the Company, replaced Fort Piegan with a new post, Fort (Kenneth) McKenzie, raised in 1832 approximately six miles above the mouth of the Marias. Fort McKenzie was protected by two corner bastions projecting above a log palisade and was secured by a double gate facing across a river plain bounded below by the Missouri, a few tiny islands, and bluffs beyond.[17]

By 1841, the Blackfeet were annually trading 21,000 robes at Fort McKenzie, and the post held the key to American Fur Company success above the Yellowstone. The commercial life of the fort was cut short, however, when Francis A. Chardon took command. Although he was an experienced Company agent from Fort Clark, he was also a hotheaded Frenchman who bartered liquor freely, befriended the wrong people, and left a trail of tension from post to post. While at Fort Clark, he was accused of murder, but the Company valued Chardon's trading ability, overlooked the charge, and transferred him to Fort McKenzie. Unfortunately, he misunderstood the Blackfeet and when one of his men was killed by them in January, 1844, he conspired with Alexander Harvey, another Company employee, to massacre the next Blackfoot party visiting the post. In February, when a Piegan band arrived at the gates of the fort, Chardon and Harvey opened fire upon them with small arms and cannon. At least six Indians were killed and others wounded before the survivors turned and fled pell-mell, leaving behind many horses, robes, and arms. The whites, so the storytellers said, scalped some of the fallen red men and that night danced around the bloody trophies in the safety of the fort compound.[18]

Chardon's irresponsible attack on the Blackfeet seriously damaged the American Fur Company's policy to maintain a vigorous

[17] James H. Bradley, "Affairs at Fort Benton from 1831 to 1869. From Lieut. Bradley's Journal," *CHSM*, Vol. III (1900), 203–205.

[18] Joshua Pilcher to Pierre Chouteau, Jr., January 7, 1840, and Pierre Chouteau, Jr., to William Laidlaw, January 10, 1840, Chouteau Family Papers, MoSHi; John C. Ewers, *The Blackfeet: Raiders on the Northwestern Plains*, 66–67; Annie H. Abel (ed.), *Chardon's Journal at Fort Clark, 1834–1839*, 246 (n. 186).

trade along the Missouri west of Fort Union. After the attack, the Blackfeet shunned Fort McKenzie, and Chardon secretly selected a site for a new post at the mouth of the Judith. There he built a rush stockade and when spring came, burned Fort McKenzie and moved its inventory to the Judith post, christened Fort Chardon in his questionable honor. The Indians, however, remembered the massacre at Fort McKenzie (afterwards known as Fort Brûlé, or "the burned fort"), and instead of trading at Fort Chardon, they harassed all white traders unfortunate enough to enter the region.[19]

The Company, anxious to restore the Blackfoot trade and to prevent Ebbetts' men from strengthening the Union Fur Company toe hold above Fort Union, chose Alexander Culbertson to replace Chardon. Culbertson, a native Pennsylvanian who had served in the First Seminole War in Florida, clerked briefly in the Minnesota fur trade after the Florida campaign and entered the American Fur Company trade on the Upper Missouri in 1833. After several months' duty at Fort McKenzie, he was given greater responsibilities in the Company and shortly was appointed bourgeois at Fort Union and ex officio trouble shooter on the Upper Missouri. His honesty, acute business sense, native intelligence, and mastery of Indian languages endeared him to the Company and won Chouteau's respect. Culbertson's second wife, Na-ta-wis-ta-cha (Medicine Snake Woman), was the attractive daughter of a Blackfoot chief. She advised her husband in the Indian trade and, although she did not speak English, adopted the manners and dress of white society. Her love for fast horses and jewelry was matched by Culbertson's love of alcohol and hunting. Few fur men, however, knew more of the Indian trade than Culbertson or

[19] Father Nicholas Point, "A Journey in a Barge on the Missouri from the Fort of the Blackfeet [Lewis] to That of the Assiniboines [Union]," *Mid-America*, Vol. XIII (January, 1931), 245; Hiram M. Chittenden, "The Ancient Town of Fort Benton in Montana," *Magazine of American History*, Vol. XXIV (December, 1890), 412; *DMR*, May 10, 1844; McDonnell, "Forts Benton and Sarpy," *CHSM*, X, 269 (n. 71), 292 (n. 205); Bradley, "Affairs," *CHSM*, III, 238. The *St. Louis New Era*, June 24, 1844, reported that 1,102 packs of robes and furs from Fort McKenzie had just landed in St. Louis.

worked as hard to accommodate missionaries, artists, surveyors, and other visitors to Company posts on the Upper Missouri.[20]

Chouteau sent Culbertson to the Marias in the summer of 1845 to right Chardon's wrongs. Within a few months, Culbertson sent Chardon into exile downriver; built a new post, the Fort of the Blackfeet (also known as Fort Henry, Fort Honoré Picotte, and Fort Meriwether Lewis), probably on the site of old Fort Cotton on the south bank of the Missouri above old Fort McKenzie; and revived the Blackfoot trade. By the spring of 1846, Culbertson was settled behind the log palisade of Fort Lewis and Fort Chardon was a smoldering heap, burned deliberately under his orders to remove the last vestige of Chardonism from the upper valley. Unfortunately, Fort Lewis was located several miles from a good stand of timber, and the Indians north of the Missouri complained that they could not cross the river easily at or near the post. Culbertson hunted a new location and found one three miles downriver on the opposite bank. His men dismantled Fort Lewis in the spring of 1847, floated the materials downriver, and rebuilt the old fort on the new site. Although the new post was at first variously called Fort Lewis and Fort Clay, within a year the Company settled on Fort Benton, after Missouri's stanch champion of the fur trade, and at Christmastide, 1850, formally christened it with the Senator's name.[21]

Fort Benton was in part the product of Chardon's temper and in part the result of the struggle, after 1843, between the American Fur Company and the opposition. A new phase of the conflict had opened in April of that year when the Company, determined to

[20] Charles E. Hanson, Jr., "Marking the Grave of Alexander Culbertson," *NH*, Vol. XXXII (June, 1951), 120–21, 126; Leslie A. White (ed.), *Lewis Henry Morgan: The Indian Journals, 1859–62,* 167; McDonnell, "Forts Benton and Sarpy," *CHSM,* X, 240–42 (n. 2), 243–45 (n. 3); Bradley, "Affairs," *CHSM,* III, 206–52; Culbertson, *Journal,* 2 (n. 6).

[21] Father Point, "Journey," *Mid-America,* XIII, 238–40; Gilbert J. Garraghan, "Nicholas Point, Jesuit Missionary in Montana in the Forties," in J. F. Willard and C. B. Goodykoontz (eds.), *The Trans-Mississippi West,* 51 (n. 8); McDonnell, "Forts Benton and Sarpy," *CHSM,* X, 239–40 (n. 1).

build up the Crow and Blackfoot trade, renewed its trading licenses. Within a week after the renewal, the Company steamer *Omega* backed away from the St. Louis water front, waved channelward by a late-morning crowd of loafers gathered on the congested levee, and nosed upstream toward the high Missouri. The boat's passenger register, truly a cosmopolitan document, listed at least one hundred trappers (all boisterous, many drunk), a party of Indians, and a small band of gentleman scientists, including the eminent, rather elderly ornithologist John James Audubon; his young, wealthy New Jersey farmer friend, Edward Harris; Isaac Sprague, a New England landscape artist and botanical illustrator; a "strong, active . . . and well to do" young traveler, Lewis M. Squires; and John G. Bell, a New York taxidermist. Captain Sire was master of the *Omega*, Joseph La Barge pilot.

The trappers, whom Harris labeled as "the very offscouring of the earth," saluted the vessel's departure with an hour-long barrage, later repeated, at least for a few minutes, at each bankside village passed, while the crew put the boat in order for a long voyage against a strong current.[22] The *Omega* progressed upriver slowly, fighting high water, piles of debris carried into the river from flooded farmland, and a steady headwind. Audubon received every courtesy of the boat (some crew members, however, thought him reserved and overbearing) and was charmed by Chouteau's floating hospitality, an extension of the kind reception given him on land. Before departing, he had not only visited the Company offices in St. Louis, where he purchased supplies at wholesale prices, but on two occasions had called upon Jean Pierre Chouteau "and . . . found the worthy old gentleman . . . kind and . . . full of information about the countries of the Indians."[23] The Audubon-Chouteau love feast started with a first course served in St. Louis and moved up the Missouri to the Yellowstone country. As long as the noted ornithologist and his friends wandered about

[22] Edward Harris, *Up the Missouri with Audubon: The Journal of Edward Harris* (ed. by John F. McDermott); Sire's Log Books, MoSHi; Chittenden, *Early Steamboat Navigation*, I, 141–53; Audubon and Coues, *Audubon*, I, 455ff.

[23] Audubon and Coues, *Audubon*, I, 454–55.

the Upper Missouri, the fur agents kept the proverbial red carpet unrolled, and Audubon's party reveled in the welcome.

Near the site of Omaha on the west bank of the Missouri a few miles above the mouth of the Platte, army Lieutenant Patrick Noble examined the cargo of the *Omega* for illegal alcohol but discovered none, although there was probably a quantity of it hidden aboard. A week later, on May 16, the *Omega* reached the first American Fur Company trading post on the Upper Missouri, the "Vermillion houses," ten miles by water below the mouth of the Vermillion River, and Audubon saw several buffalo carcasses, the remains of a drowned herd, floating down the Missouri. The small yet "strongly picketed" trading house was in charge of Pascal Cerré, "a handsome French gentleman, of good manners."[24] In 1843, however, the post had passed its trading heyday, was no longer very important to the Company, and was slowly becoming "a very miserable little place."[25] The *Omega* remained two days at Vermillion Post while the engineer repaired a damaged boiler, then pushed upriver.

A Santee Sioux war party—La Barge estimated eight or ten warriors—fired upon the steamer at Handy's Point (later the site of Fort Randall) on the morning of May 22 when the boat ignored an Indian signal to land. Several shots hit the steamboat. One tore a hole in a cabin wall, passed "through the pantaloons" of a sleeping trapper, and lodged in a trunk, another hit the water just in front of where Audubon stood by a chimney, and a third crashed through the pilothouse window and drove the relief pilot to shelter, yet, surprisingly, none of the passengers crowded on the deck was struck.[26] The following day, after the *Omega* had outrun the war party, it grounded on a sand bar. For thirty hours the crew battled sand, shattered spars, and a broken rudder before the boat slid free and continued upriver.

Between the Vermillion and the Bad rivers, the *Omega* passed two small fleets of mackinaws carrying robes and furs down-

[24] *Ibid.*, 493–94   [25] Palliser, *Solitary Hunter*, 69.
[26] Chittenden, *Early Steamboat Navigation*, I, 149.

stream to St. Louis. The first fleet, four boats under command of a hard Scot taskmaster, William Laidlaw of the American Fur Company, and Agent Drips, tarried briefly with the *Omega* at Vermillion Post. A few days later, a second fleet of three mackinaws laden with Union Fur Company returns met the steamboat near Great Cedar Island.[27] Sixty miles by land below Fort Pierre, three messengers left the *Omega* to carry dispatches to the posts ahead. Such express messenger service was quite commonly employed by captains bound upriver to notify fur posts that a boat was near and to forward important business messages to post agents.[28]

At Fort George, Audubon and Squires met Fulton Cutting. Squires had traveled in Europe with Cutting's brother Robert, and Audubon's son Victor had toured Cuba with Fulton himself. Cutting, just in from the Yellowstone, was laid up with a foot injury, earned in a buffalo hunt, and planned to return soon to St. Louis. Having paid their respects to Cutting, Audubon and Squires rejoined the passengers on the *Omega* and three days later, on May 31, reached Fort Pierre. Across the river from the post, the steamer *Trapper* waited at the bank, ready to complete its downriver voyage to St. Louis, which had begun the previous year. Negro pilot Jacques Désiré and chief mate John Durack had gone upriver on the *Omega* under Company orders to return the *Trapper* to St. Louis. On June 12, when the river rose eighteen inches, they took the *Trapper* and a cargo of twelve hundred packs of robes downstream on the rise and docked at St. Louis on the twenty-first, nine days from Fort Pierre—"a pretty serious undertaking," since pilot Désiré had no assistance on the down-

---

[27] *DMR*, May 29, July 31, 1843; *St. Louis New Era*, May 29, June 15, 1843. The American Fur Company Mackinaws—increased from four to five by the addition of one, presumably from the Platte—reached St. Louis on May 27 with 1,400 packs of robes and a small amount of furs. The three Union Fur Company boats landed in St. Louis on June 15. Two other mackinaws, probably American Fur Company craft, reached the city late in July.

[28] Sire's Log Books, MoSHi, contain examples of messenger service.

PIERRE CHOUTEAU, JR.

Courtesy Historical Society of Montana

CHARLES P. CHOUTEAU

Courtesy Missouri Historical Society

RAMSAY CROOKS

Courtesy Minnesota Historical Society

Andrew Drips

Courtesy Missouri Historical Society

ANDREW DAWSON

Courtesy Historical Society of Montana

MALCOLM CLARK

Courtesy Historical Society of Montana

HONORÉ PICOTTE

Courtesy Missouri Historical Society

ALEXANDER CULBERTSON, HIS WIFE NA-TA-WIS-TA-CHA,
AND THEIR SON JOE

Courtesy Historical Society of Montana

river trip and had stuck "at the wheel" each day "from daylight to dark."[29]

After landing half her men and cargo at Fort Pierre and taking on a few trappers bound upriver, the *Omega* resumed her journey in the afternoon of June 1. At Square Buttes, the boat passed James Kipp, who commanded four barges, manned by a rough-looking crew, headed for St. Louis, and the following day, June 7, pulled up to Fort Clark in a heavy wind- and rainstorm. Scores of Indians crowded aboard the boat for free coffee, biscuits, and speeches, and the passengers locked their belongings in their state-rooms and kept "a sharp lookout besides to prevent thieving." Peter Garrioche, one of the Company traders who boarded the *Omega* at Fort Pierre, said that every Indian woman at Fort Clark was anxious to "co habit" with the whites. Parents led their daughters aboard, warriors their wives: every female was sold into prostitution (at least Garrioche said so), and bargaining was heavy all day. In his words, the traders paid "Fifty percent premium for the hind-quarters of old women of the Mo!!—Better than any Bank in the United States. Go it Yankees!"[30]

Captain Sire pulled his boat away from Fort Clark as soon as possible and on the twelfth, saluted by a booming cannon, tied up at sunset below the gates of Fort Union. Culbertson, in a style more appropriate to the Hudson's Bay Company than to the American Fur Company, led a cavalcade down to the landing to welcome the vessel and assigned Audubon's party quarters within the fort. Two days later, the *Omega*, unloaded, repaired, and partially reloaded, headed away from the post. Downriver, past Fort Clark, Fort Pierre, and Vermillion Post, she skimmed along, reaching St. Louis on June 29, two weeks from the Yellowstone. Audubon sampled two months in the upper Missouri country, collecting specimens, hunting, and passing pleasant hours amidst the

[29] Quotation from Harris, *Up the Missouri*, 83–84. See also Chittenden, *Early Steamboat Navigation*, I, 149; Chittenden, *Fur Trade*, II, 995; *DMR*, June 22, 1843; *St. Louis New Era*, June 21, 1843.

[30] Diary of Peter Garrioche, 1843–1847, Typescript, NdHi.

plain yet sufficient comfort of Fort Union. On August 16, he and his friends left the Upper Missouri aboard a newly launched mackinaw and eight weeks later, on October 19, stepped ashore in St. Louis "in good health and spirits."[31]

The *Omega* landed in St. Louis two months before the Union Fur Company steamboat *New Haven* left for the Upper Missouri. Financial difficulties may have delayed the sailing of the *New Haven*, yet it is more likely that Cutting's injury, his late arrival in St. Louis from the upper river, and slow business negotiations with his eastern backers occasioned the boat's belated departure. It was August 10 before Cutting renewed the opposition trading license. George Collier and his young brother-in-law William Morrison, two St. Louis wholesale commission merchants, stood bond with Cutting for the new Union Fur Company license—and so, incidentally, stood up to be counted in opposition to Pierre Chouteau. Seventeen days later, on August 27, the *New Haven* whistled good-by to St. Louis and turned upriver, carrying Cutting and sixty tons of freight for Forts George and Mortimer. The Sioux, possibly Santees, fired on the steamer as it splashed upriver in the Dakota country, and "a good many balls" hit the cabin. The men aboard returned the fire, but no one was injured on either side. Later, when the *New Haven* descended the Missouri, fighting cold, snow, and drift ice much of the way, the Sioux opened fire again. This time the chiefs were warned that if the shooting did not cease, the crew would attack the Indian camps, destroy them, and leave the red men homeless for the winter. The firing stopped. The *New Haven* tied up safely in St. Louis on or shortly after November 30 and unloaded "about 160 bales of Buffalo robes and a small lot of furs."[32]

Cutting found conditions poor at Fort George, where violence remained the order of the day, and poorer at Fort Mortimer. At George, two independent traders had opened a tiny trade on

[31] *DMR*, June 30, 1843; Harris, *Up the Missouri*, 184 (n. 10).

[32] Trading License of Fulton Cutting, August 10, 1843, Letters Received, OIA, RG 75, NA; *St. Louis New Era*, August 30, December 4, 1843; *Niles' National Register* (Baltimore), December 16, 1843.

Simoneau's Island. Honoré Picotte, American Fur Company agent at Fort Pierre, anxious to restore a Company post to the Fort George area, had offered to buy them out. The offer was rumored about, and in early November, "one or more Indians," according to Picotte, under the influence of the Fort George opposition, burned down the independent post.[33] At Fort Mortimer, Cutting looked over the remains of the post (the river had undercut it and carried off the front portion) and gave food to the starving garrison. John Collins of Kentucky, the agent in charge, and his men had barely survived the spring and summer, living on stolen food, wild game, and small gifts of food and medicines from Fort Union, where they were not particularly welcome. To add to their misery, they had suffered an Indian attack during the summer, had quarreled with Fort Union over an Indian woman and a stolen mackinaw, and had taken only a few robes in trade.[34]

The Union Fur Company was discouraged by the 1843 robe and fur return. The American Fur Company, however, had turned a higher yearly profit, but was upset, nonetheless, by Drips's failure to find evidence (alcohol) in the hands of the opposition. Drips had spent the year investigating the Indian country up and down the river from his base at Fort Pierre, and his reports to Mitchell in St. Louis were filled with general conclusions and recommendations but no liquid evidence: he was overworked and needed an assistant agent; the Sioux favored an end to the liquor trade and were surprised that the Great White Father had not sent soldiers to control it; Ebbetts should be removed immediately from the Indian country. Drips's own interpreter, Théophile Bruguier, was said to be trading in robes illegally. Mitchell regretted his agent's failure and told him so, but after Drips returned to St. Louis and conferred with Mitchell, early in the summer, they parted as friends and Drips went upriver to continue his liquor hunt. In April, he had suggested that Joseph Varnum Ham-

[33] Honoré Picotte to A. Drips, November 16, 1843, Drips (Andrew) Papers, MoSHi.

[34] Harris, *Up the Missouri*, 113, 117–18, 123, 127, 131, 168; Audubon and Coues, *Audubon*, II, 36–37.

ilton, the American Fur Company trader who had recently withstood the dangers at Fort George, be appointed his assistant investigator. Mitchell agreed and in May certified Hamilton as special subagent, but then, in July, dismissed him when Drips returned to duty.[35]

Hamilton, at Fort Pierre when dismissed, "took it upon" himself to journey overland to the Upper Platte to examine Forts John (Laramie) and Platte for smuggled liquor. Drips, who remained on the Missouri to check the cargo of the *New Haven*, approved of Hamilton's ex officio war on the "swindling whiskey peddlers" in the Platte country. After nine months of investigation, however, from September, 1843, to May, 1844, Hamilton found nary a drop of alcohol. The Platte traders had carefully cached their kegs, and although Hamilton wrote Mitchell a detailed account of the Platte Valley liquor trade, his mission failed for lack of proof. Nevertheless, his investigation dampened the enthusiasm of the Platte Valley liquor kings, for the time being at least, and may have even saved a few Indian lives.[36]

Hamilton was certain that Pratte and Cabanné were guilty of breaking the liquor laws on the Platte. "They do not deny having liquor but defy me to find it," he reported to Drips in September, and strongly advised his friend to confiscate the Pratte and Cabanné keelboat on the Upper Missouri and to watch the Cheyenne Valley for illicit alcohol. After several months of indecision, Pratte and Cabanné had decided to open an Upper Missouri outfit and had received a license from Superintendent Mitchell to trade with the Sioux in various new locations between Forts Pierre and Clark. Until 1843, the Indian Superintendents at St. Louis had always granted annual upriver licenses "in conformity with" American Fur Company licenses: where the Company traded, the oppo-

[35] Andrew Drips to David D. Mitchell, January 2, April 4, 7, 1843, and to Joseph V. Hamilton, May 12, 1843, David D. Mitchell to A. Drips, April 20, July 25, 1843, William Laidlaw to A. Drips, March 26, 1843, and Honoré Picotte to A. Drips, April 30, 1843, Drips (Andrew) Papers, MoSHi.

[36] Joseph V. Hamilton to David D. Mitchell, March 7, 1844, and to Thomas H. Harvey, July 5, 1844, Letters Received, OIA, RG 75, NA.

sition might trade, but in no additional locations. Mitchell, however, under pressure of a licensing technicality brought to his attention by Pratte and Cabanné, had allowed them to place trading houses wherever "the Indians and traders [thought] it to their mutual advantage."[37] Accordingly, Pratte and Cabanné applied to Drips for permission to build wintering houses on at least four new sites, near the mouths of the Cheyenne, Moreau, Grand, and Beaver rivers, all within the country covered by their license, and Drips, still lacking proof that Pratte and Cabanné had violated the liquor law and having no power to defy Mitchell's license, consented. The American Fur Company said Mitchell had "made a fool of himself" and of them by granting opposition traders rights in new areas, but the Company was enmeshed in the web temporarily and had no choice but to request permission from Drips to build competing trading houses at the same points granted to Pratte and Cabanné. Drips agreed. The Union Fur Company, of course, heard of the American Fur Company's plight and opened trading houses at the new locations after receiving special permission. Throughout the winter of 1843–44, the three companies skirmished for trading sites on the upper river while Mitchell, booted out of office in October (he was replaced by Thomas H. Harvey), savored the bitter flavor of Company power.[38]

Drips continued his unproductive liquor hunt during the winter and into the spring of 1844. His presence on the upper river, however, jeopardized Company trade, since as long as he was there the Company held down its liquor traffic. Honoré Picotte wrote

[37] Quotations from William Laidlaw to Pierre Chouteau, Jr., and Company, December (?), 1843, Chouteau Family Papers, MoSHi. See also Honoré Picotte to Pierre Chouteau, Jr., and Company, January 4, 1844, *ibid*.

[38] Andrew Drips to Joseph V. Hamilton, November 4, 1843, to David D. Mitchell, October 15, 1843, to Pierre Chouteau, Jr., and Company, November 1, 4, 20, 1843, to Pratte and Cabanné, November 1, 1843, to Honoré Picotte, October 31, 1843, to William Laidlaw, November 1, 1843, and to Sinclair Taylor, October 29, 1843, Honoré Picotte to A. Drips, October 29, 1843, and Sinclair Taylor to A. Drips, October 28, 1843, Drips (Andrew) Papers, *ibid*. On Mitchell's removal, see Thomas Hart Benton to Pierre Chouteau, Jr., January 10, 22, 30, 1844, Benton Family Papers, MoSHi.

Chouteau in January that in the previous autumn the Union Fur Company steamer *New Haven* had carried alcohol, and a lot of it, to Forts George and Mortimer, that Pratte and Cabanné owned a large liquor supply, that dealers were bringing additional fire-water overland from Minnesota to the Missouri, and that the American Fur Company would lose the Blackfoot and Assiniboin trade unless four to five hundred gallons reached the Upper Missouri posts in the spring. Every day Drips spent in the Indian country without finding evidence to destroy the Union Fur Company or Pratte and Cabanné was a day of lower profits for Pierre Chouteau,[39] and as long as traders representing three or four companies competed for upriver robes and furs, the Indians, previously dependent upon American Fur Company agents, took advantage of the competition and behaved in a free and insolent manner.[40]

When the ice broke on the Upper Missouri after the winter of 1843–44, mackinaws stuffed with robes and furs left the trading posts for St. Louis, where the companies busily collected supplies for shipment upriver. Ebbetts, Cutting, and several companions reached St. Louis on May 8 via steamboats from Weston. They had descended the Missouri in four mackinaws from Fort George, but once on the lower river, they had transferred to faster steam transportation. Three of the mackinaws floated into St. Louis on May 22, but the third sank in the Missouri with a loss of 150 bales of robes. Two months later, three additional Union Fur Company mackinaws reached St. Louis, carrying two dozen men and 550 packs of robes and furs from the Yellowstone.[41] The American Fur Company had anticipated, incorrectly, that Cutting's winter

[39] Honoré Picotte to Pierre Chouteau, Jr., and Company, January 4, 1844, Chouteau Family Papers, MoSHi; Andrew Drips to Thomas H. Harvey, Early (?) 1844, Letters Received, OIA, RG 75, NA.

[40] Thomas H. Harvey to T. H. Crawford, October 8, 1844, 28 Cong., 2 sess., *SD No. 1*, p. 438.

[41] Thomas H. Harvey to J. Arrott, July 15, 1844, Letters Received, OIA, RG 75, NA; *St. Louis New Era*, May 9, 22, 1844; *DMR*, May 10, 22, July 16, 1844; *St. Louis Democrat*, May 23, 1844, Transcript in Dale Morgan Collection, CSmH.

trade of 1843–44 would be poor, since his "people . . . [were] not to sell . . . goods [upriver] except at a fair profit" and were required to follow a tariff (or company price list) "with strict orders not to deviate from the prices therein stated."[42]

The Union Fur Company, encouraged by the Upper Missouri robe returns of the previous winter, outfitted a 126-ton steamer, the *Frolic*, and sent it upriver in July, but on the way up, many of her men deserted or simply refused to obey orders. Eventually, however, the boat unloaded passengers and freight at the Cheyenne, above Fort George, but low water prevented her from going up to Fort Mortimer and the Yellowstone. The shallow channel held throughout the summer and fall, and early in November, the captain and crew abandoned the *Frolic* for the winter (she was berthed at Fort George) and set out downriver in mackinaws. A few miles above Weston, one mackinaw hit a snag and sank. A Negro hand was lost, but the other *voyageurs* dragged themselves onto a sand bar and from there to the shore, where they rejoined their traveling companions and took passage on a packet to St. Louis. Since the *Frolic* had failed to reprovision adequately Union Fur Company posts above Fort George, Cutting's winter trade on the Yellowstone and Upper Missouri was weakened considerably and he was forced to supply his posts by land from Fort George or, possibly, from the Platte.[43]

Meanwhile, on April 30, the steamer *Nimrod*, newly built for the Upper Missouri trade, slid away from her moorings in St. Louis. She took advantage of the great spring flood of 1844, completed a record round trip to Fort Union, and tied up in St. Louis "through a window in J. E. Walsh's warehouse"—the flood was still under way—at about the time the *Frolic* left. The *Nimrod*, although nearly twice as large as the opposition boat, drew less water, was constructed of the "staunchest material . . . in [a] neat,

[42] Honoré Picotte to Pierre Chouteau, Jr., and Company, January 4, 1844, Chouteau Family Papers, MoSHi.

[43] *Weekly Reveille* (St. Louis), December 9, 1844; *St. Louis New Era*, December 2, 1844. For vessel tonnage figures, see the steamboat licenses recorded in License Books (Steamboats), Port of St. Louis Custom House Records, FRC, KC.

substantial and workmanlike manner," and was propelled by the engine and boilers taken from the *Trapper*.[44] Captain Sire commanded the *Nimrod*, ably supported by La Barge as pilot and John Durack, formerly of the British navy, as first mate. One hundred and twenty trappers elbowed one another for space on the cargo-crowded vessel and for a closer view of two French aristocrats, the "Comte d'Otrante, son of the famous [Joseph] Fouché" (Napoleon's Minister of Police), and "the Comte de Peindry." The two noblemen, who had "met by accident . . . and had little to do with each other," were totally unlike. Otrante was traveling for pleasure and surrounded himself with servants and the impedimenta of travel in the grand style. Peindry was a quiet, rather strange individual who deferred to Otrante as his superior, was "said to be a noted duelist," and, when he hunted ashore, frequently failed to return to the boat on time.[45]

At Council Bluffs, the *Nimrod* met a falling channel above the reach of the great flood and encountered an Indian agent, a former Methodist minister, who insisted upon thoroughly searching the boat for alcohol. According to La Barge, the Company's illegal firewater, packed in barrels of flour marked for delivery at Bellevue, was landed and stored in a warehouse. The agent, who then was permitted to search the boat, found no illicit spirits, but, still suspicious of the American Fur Company's alcoholic habits, stationed a lookout to watch the boat and retired for the night. In the early hours of the morning, the crew reloaded the *Nimrod* with the flour barrels of liquor from the warehouse. The lookout, however, awoke just as the cargo was aboard and whistled for the Indian agent. La Barge grabbed an ax, cut the line holding the boat ashore, and backed the *Nimrod* into the river. At that point the agent appeared on the levee, demanded to know what had happened, and was told the line had broken. The following day he learned that the flour barrels were gone and, realizing he had

[44] *DMR*, April 30, 1844. See also *Niles' National Register*, July 27, 1844; *St. Louis New Era*, July 10, 1844; Sire's Log Books, MoSHi; Chittenden, *Early Steamboat Navigation*, I, 154–55, 163.
[45] Quotations from Chittenden, *Early Steamboat Navigation*, I, 155–56.

been duped, reported the American Fur Company to the Indian Office, but the federal authorities lacked the proof and witnesses necessary to take the Company to court.[46]

The remainder of the *Nimrod's* journey was relatively uneventful, except for La Barge's capture and release by a Pawnee war party and a wind-, hail-, and rainstorm that broke all the glass on one side of the boat, flooded the cabins with water, and, unless La Barge exaggerated in his account of the tempest, piled up hailstones, some "as large as turkey eggs . . . to the depth of a foot." The pilothouse was toppled, literally blown away by the wind, and was replaced by a temporary skin roof. Captain Sire, however, seemed more disturbed by wood than weather. He discovered that at least two large woodpiles, cached along the river in 1843 for use by the *Nimrod* of 1844, had been taken by the crew of the *New Haven*, "conduct which [he] did not expect of Mr. Cutting."[47]

The *Nimrod* brought to St. Louis 1,250 packs of robes, approximately 20 packs of furs, and a quantity of buffalo tongues and meat. The tongue market had improved since 1841, when kegs of improperly packed and inadequately salted tongues rotted away on the eastern market. Better packing of fresh tongues and gourmet demand for dried tongues created, by the mid-forties, a flourishing market for them in St. Louis and the East.[48]

Also aboard the *Nimrod* when it returned to St. Louis in July, 1844, was a small menagerie: six buffalo, one to three beaver, an elk, and a grizzly bear, "all alive and apparently in excellent condition," destined, probably, for Pierre Chouteau's animal collection.[49]

Boats returning to St. Louis from the upper river brought the latest news of business conditions in the Indian country. In 1844,

[46] *Ibid.*, 156–59.   [47] *Ibid.*, 160, 164–65; Sire's Log Books, MoSHi.
[48] Ramsay Crooks to Pierre Chouteau, Jr., and Company, November 2, 1841, American Fur Company Papers, NHi; *DMR*, June 27, 1843; Abel, *Chardon's Journal*, 253 (n. 226).
[49] *DMR*, July 10, 1844; *Weekly Reveille*, July 15, 1844; *St. Louis New Era*, July 10, 1844.

the American Fur Company vessels carried downstream with them the most recent inventories of the upriver posts: Fort Clark, in late spring, stocked $5,927.24 in goods on hand and Fort Pierre, in comparison, $30,137.41.[50] The boats also brought down the latest business problems from the Upper Missouri posts. Was the "worthless" cook at Fort Pierre to be replaced? Were there enough tailors, smiths, and carpenters at the trading posts? Why did the upriver agents dislike Spanish and German hired hands? Was it best to pay an upriver-post employee as his salary fell due each month or was it best, as some agents advised, to wait several months until the man was less tempted to desert? What effect was the small amount of illicit alcohol reaching the Upper Missouri from the Minnesota country having on the fur trade? Would the fur trade suffer from the Secretary of War's recent order abolishing traffic in engraved medals? Trade medals were prized by the Indians, and symbolized to them the close association between the traders and the federal government.[51] And to what extent should the Company expand the self-sufficiency of each post? Some post industries (haymaking, charcoal burning, gardening, and limited grazing) were necessary to support a strong robe and fur trade, but what would happen to the fur trade if these became too large? And so early each winter, when the Missouri River closed to water commerce, the American Fur Company and each opposition fur concern in St. Louis reviewed the latest intelligence on the upriver trade—intelligence brought downriver on fur boats during the summer—and formulated business policies for the coming year.

Chouteau, Cutting, Pratte, and Cabanné all knew that the number of traders engaged in the Upper Missouri fur business had increased in 1843 and 1844 and might continue to grow. Unsettled conditions in Oregon, plus the booming overland migration to

[50] Pierre Chouteau, Jr., and Company Inventories, Upper Missouri Outfit, 1844, American Fur Company Ledger JJ, MoSHi.

[51] Andrew Drips to David D. Mitchell, January 2, 1844, and to Fulton Cutting, October 12, 1844, Drips Family Papers, CU-B.

the Columbia Valley, had focused the nation's attention upon the far Northwest. In May, 1844, the Pennsylvania Legislature had chartered an Oregon Fur Company, capitalized at $100,000.[52] As yet the new company had not inaugurated trade in the Northwest, but it might do so in 1845, and if other companies followed suit, the upper river would become the trade territory of a half-dozen competitors instead of two or three. Pierre Chouteau was determined, however, that the American Fur Company would not lose control of the upper river, not to the Union Fur Company, nor Pratte and Cabanné, nor Pennsylvania patriots, nor anyone else. If the St. Louis *Weekly Reveille* was correct and "the required animals abound[ed] still in numbers every way sufficient to maintain the trade"—and the American Fur Company had no reason to disagree with the literary weekly—the contest to hold the Upper Missouri trade might be decided in 1845.[53]

[52] *Laws of the General Assembly of the Commonwealth of Pennsylvania, Passed at the Session of 1844,* 175–76.
[53] *Weekly Reveille,* August 5, 1844.

CHAPTER FOUR

"Notorious for their misconduct"

WINTER, 1844–45, hugged the Upper Missouri in a chill embrace. Traders and Indians alike sought the warmth of roaring fires, buffalo robes, and blankets. But little snow fell on the high plains, and the buffalo fled the dark, burned-over prairies surrounding Fort Pierre and moved in large herds from the ice-filled Missouri eastward into the land of the Minnesota Sioux. At the upriver posts, although bourgeois kept order as best they could amongst weather-bound traders, Indian women, halfblood children, and mongrel dogs, winter quarrels were common, fists flew, and knives, even bullets, sometimes followed. In St. Louis and the East, fur-trade investors, who passed the winter safe from Upper Missouri threats to life and limb, worried, nonetheless, about the trade. Would insufficient snow on the high plains mean low-water navigation in the summer of 1845? Some investors said yes. Some old trappers disagreed, however, and said the summer channel of the Missouri was set by melting mountain snow plus late spring rain. But, even if the river ran high in 1845, would the Dakota Sioux hunt as far east as the buffalo herds had moved? Late reports from London brought discouraging news that beaver prices were low and likely to fall.[1] If the beaver market remained poor and few robes were made, then 1845 would be a disastrous year in the Upper Missouri trade. Although the American Fur Company was pleased by James K. Polk's recent election as President and the coming inauguration of a Democratic administration, fur and robe

[1] Curtis M. Lampson to Pierre Chouteau, Jr., and Company, January 18, 1845, Chouteau Family Papers, MoSHi; *DMR*, April 28, 1845; *Weekly Reveille*, May 5, 1845; *Arkansas Intelligencer* (Van Buren), May 17, 1845; *Niles' National Register*, July 5, 1845.

returns did not reflect political returns. And, as Benjamin Clapp noted in a letter to Andrew Drips in January, 1845, Polk's victory was "a matter of little moment" to the American Fur Company, since the Company believed that everything in Washington would "go about right whichever side" won.[2]

In April, 1845, Chouteau renewed the Company's license to trade at nearly all Upper Missouri locations listed in the license of 1844. The Company's answer to competition remained simple and direct: uphold a strong, far-reaching upriver trade against all comers. By mid-May, the annual American Fur Company express couriers had reached St. Louis with last-minute supply requests from the posts in the Indian country, and early mackinaw shipments of robes and furs were in transit downriver from Forts Union and Pierre.[3] Chouteau outfitted the steamboat *General Brooke,* under Captain Sire, with supplies and men for the Yellowstone and Upper Missouri; shortly before noon on May 22, the steamer swung into the shallow channel of the Mississippi and headed for the mouth of the Missouri and the long, arduous trip to the upper river. The *General Brooke* reached Fort Union on July 2, departed two days later on a rising river, and landed five hundred packs of buffalo robes at St. Louis on the eighteenth. The old trappers were correct; the early summer channel of the Missouri, built high by spring rain and mountain snow, permitted the steamboat to make the round trip in new record time of fifty-seven days. Before the end of the summer, additional shipments of American Fur Company robes and furs—at least three mackinaw loads—landed in St. Louis.[4]

Company profits fell in 1845, as Chouteau anticipated, but the business survived the temporary setback from the poor beaver-buffalo market and met successfully unexpected expenses in the East. The great New York City fire of July 19 destroyed Chou-

[2] Benjamin Clapp to A. Drips, January 6, 1845, Drips Family Papers, CU-B.

[3] *DMR,* April 28, May 5, 1845; *St. Louis New Era,* June 9, 1845; *Weekly Reveille,* May 12, 1845.

[4] Sire's Log Books, MoSHi; *DMR,* May 23, July 19, 1845; *Weekly Reveille,* July 21, 1845.

teau's eastern office at No. 40 Broadway. Insurance covered the building and equipment, valued at $20,000 to $25,000, but did not cover records burned and the value of business lost while the office was rebuilt and refurnished. In St. Louis, the Company operated on a more normal schedule during 1845, except for minor accidents (in late June, "a stone cutter had his leg crushed . . . by the falling of a cap stone" at Chouteau's warehouse) and one unusual incident. John C. Frémont, in St. Louis early in June hiring men for a California expedition, climbed an "old rickety fence" opposite the Planters House to address a crowd of several hundred prospective recruits. The crowd surged forward, Frémont and the shaky fence fell, and an Irishman, thinking a fight had started, dashed to Frémont's assistance, screaming "Fair play! fair play! and be d—d to yez—don't you see the man's down?" Near by, the men at the American Fur Company office, afraid the crowd would get out of hand, sent over an oxcart. Frémont climbed aboard and finished his speech on wheels.[5]

Despite lower upriver profits in robes and furs and the loss of eastern property in 1845, the year was outstanding for the Company. Both the Union Fur Company and Pratte and Cabanné withdrew from trade on the Upper Missouri, leaving the American Fur Company master of the Dakotas and eastern Montana. Union Fur Company profits in the Upper Missouri trade, always small, had shrunk in the face of mounting upriver expenses. In a last desperate effort to strike at both Drips and the American Fur Company, Cutting had written the Superintendent of Indian Affairs at St. Louis on September 16, 1844, charging that Drips was a Chouteau tool and should be dismissed as Indian agent. Drips said the charge was motivated by "malice and revenge" because he had stopped Union Fur Company liquor trade on the Yellowstone River during the winter of 1843–44. Cutting feared, Drips added, that he would halt the Union Fur Company's illegal alco-

[5] Quotation from *Weekly Reveille*, June 9, 1845. See also *DMR*, July 30, August 1, 1845; *Saint Louis American*, July 1, 1845. The following year, in July, a Chouteau warehouseman fell dead, while on duty in St. Louis, from "effects of the sun" (*Saint Louis American*, July 7, 1846).

hol traffic on the Missouri in 1845.[6] Thomas Harvey, St. Louis Indian Superintendent, forwarded Cutting's statement to the Indian Office in Washington, where the Commissioner exonerated Drips but suggested that he replace his interpreter, an American Fur Company man, with some other less controversial assistant. Benjamin Clapp wrote Drips that the American Fur Company was pleased with the decision of the Indian Office, and strongly advised Drips that he comply with the Commissioner's suggestion to hire a new interpreter. Clapp's letter, now in the Bancroft Library, indicates clearly that the American Fur Company still considered Drips to be one of its employees.[7] Since Cutting's attack on Drips had failed, the Union Fur Company investors had no choice but to seek an agreement with Pierre Chouteau. By mid-May, 1845, Cutting and Ebbetts had sold "their entire stock" on the Upper Missouri to Chouteau and had set out for St. Louis, leaving behind on the Missouri "upwards of fifty men—a mongrel set of halfbreeds and white men, the greater part," according to Drips, "notorious for their misconduct."[8]

The steamboat *Frolic*, "high and dry" at Fort George over the winter of 1844–45, attempted to leave for St. Louis on May 9, carrying seven hundred packs of robes and furs, but was forced back to the post by low water. After most of the cargo was transferred to mackinaws, the *Frolic* took advantage of a rise in the river and reached St. Louis by May 27, five days after the *General Brooke* left for the upper river. The *Frolic* was "pretty well used up" by her twelve months in the Indian country and cost the Union Fur Company, in leasing fees, far more than Cutting had anticipated.[9] Forts George and Mortimer, Cutting's principal up-

6 Fulton Cutting to T. H. Harvey, September 16, 1844, and A. Drips to T. H. Harvey, April 6, 1845, Letters Received, OIA, RG 75, NA.

7 T. H. Crawford to T. H. Harvey, December 13, 1844, and Benjamin Clapp to A. Drips, January 6, 1845, Drips Family Papers, CU-B.

8 Chittenden, *Fur Trade*, I, 372 (n. 7); *Missouri Reporter* (St. Louis) June 6, 7, 1845, Transcript in Dale Morgan Collection, CSmH.

9 *DMR*, May 28, 1845; *Saint Louis American*, May 28, 1845; *Gazette* (St. Joseph), May 16, 1845; *Missouri Reporter*, May 28, 1845, Transcript in Dale Morgan Collection, CSmH.

river posts, abandoned when the Union Fur Company sold out to Chouteau, reverted to the Indians. A band of Sioux who moved into Fort George temporarily prevented the American Fur Company from burning the post, and the wooden debris left behind at Fort Mortimer was consumed as fuel by the *General Brooke* and other steamboats plying the upper river.[10] Old dilapidated trading posts were excellent sources of wood for river vessels, and many an abandoned upriver fort was dismantled (to the chagrin of historians) to feed a hungry steamboat boiler.

But why did the Union Fur Company fail after four years' competition with the American Fur Company on the Upper Missouri? Granted that the American Fur Company possessed the power, prestige, and political connections of an entrenched monopoly and that perhaps no competitor could stand against it for long, the principal cause of the Union Fur Company's failure lay in its own inexperience in the fur trade. Few of its agents were tried and tested fur traders. Instead, through inexperience, they made costly mistakes, too many of them. They hired disreputable men; they relied heavily upon liquor as a trade item; they overextended their lines of trade—to the Yellowstone and to the Missouri above Fort Union; they failed to send annual steamboats to the Missouri early enough to ride the spring rise to the Yellowstone; at times they traded naïvely, at times shrewdly, but never within a pattern consistent enough for the Indians; and they never decided who was in command of the company. Was it the reckless, defiant John Ebbetts, or the aristocratic gentleman Fulton Cutting? Inexperience shattered the Union Fur Company, and the American Fur Company swept up the pieces.

Before the end of 1845, the American Fur Company, revitalized by victory over the Union Fur Company, consolidated its power amongst the squabbling traders at Council Bluffs and happily watched the demise of the house of Pratte and Cabanné on both

[10] Anthony R. Bouis to Honoré Picotte, August 31, 1845, Ft. Pierre Letter Book, 1845–1846, MoSHi; Sire's Log Books, MoSHi.

the Platte and the Upper Missouri.[11] By December, no important opposition to the American Fur Company remained on the upper river. One indication of the Company's reasserted upriver power could be seen on the left bank of the Fishhook Bend in the Missouri approximately fifty miles above old Fort Clark. At that location, two old hands in the Fort Clark trade—Francis Chardon, newly arrived from the Blackfoot country, and Canadian-born James Kipp, who spent nearly four decades in the fur trade and fathered children by both Indian and white wives—helped the Mandans build a palisaded village (Like-a-Fishhook Village) and constructed a fort near by. The Mandans, decimated by the smallpox epidemic of 1837, had abandoned their villages near Fort Clark and had joined their close relatives, the Hidatsas, at the Fishhook Bend. Chardon and Kipp first christened the new Mandan-Hidatsa trading post Fort James (after Kipp), then renamed it Fort Berthold for either Pierre or Frederick Berthold, St. Louis business associates of the American Fur Company.[12]

The deep stream of criticism of Andrew Drips's conduct of Indian affairs dried up at the source when the Union Fur Company and Pratte and Cabanné withdrew from the Upper Missouri. Drips secluded himself as much as possible from the public eye during the winter of 1845–46, having successfully defended himself against Cutting's attack with sworn statements from Sarpy and McKenzie that he was never an American Fur Company partner. The following April, Drips was removed from Office, however, and a new agent, Thomas P. Moore of Kentucky, whom Charles Larpenteur branded a "great drunkard," was appointed to fill the vacancy. Moore, who accepted the job "in consequence

[11] *St. Louis New Era,* June 9, 1845; Honoré Picotte to James Kipp, December 18, 1845, Ft. Pierre Letter Book, 1845–1846, MoSHi.
[12] G. Hubert Smith, "Archeological Work at 32ML2 (Like-A-Fishook Village and Fort Berthold), Garrison Reservoir Area, North Dakota, 1950–1954," *The Plains Anthropologist,* No. 2 (December, 1954), 28–29. Fort Clark continued to operate, with a reduced inventory, to serve an estimated six hundred Arikaras living near by.

of ruinous losses sustained . . . as surety for a defaulter, and with the hope of introducing [his] son into active business," wrote the American Fur Company requesting information on the Upper Missouri Indian situation and assured Chouteau he was convinced that the American Fur Company wished him to perform his duties faithfully![13] Two months later—and two months wiser—he wrote the Commissioner of Indian Affairs that the Indian country was soggy with illicit alcohol, that spies watched his every move, and that only a detachment of dragoons could keep the liquor traders out of the Dakotas.[14]

Moore sent the second letter from St. Louis, where he waited to board the American Fur Company's annual steamboat to the Upper Missouri. The city was packed with Oregon-bound emigrants, speculators and traders anticipating war with Mexico (declared May 13, the day before Moore sent his note to the Commissioner), supply-buying, news-seeking farmers, and westering gentleman travelers, including young Francis Parkman. Parkman, who hired a guide at the office of the American Fur Company, later launched his brilliant literary career with the journal he kept of his western tour in 1846. The "several gentlemen of the Fur Company" who had offered to furnish Parkman a guide did so by taking time from a busy spring schedule.[15] The ice on the Upper Missouri crumbled earlier than usual in 1846, and pessimistic observers of river conditions once again predicted low water above the Platte because little snow had fallen in the mountains during the winter. American Fur Company clerks and partners in St. Louis rushed to outfit the *General Brooke* for a second year of trade to the high Missouri. The first mackinaw loads of robes and furs were expected momentarily from Forts Union and

[13] Thomas P. Moore to Pierre Chouteau, Jr., and Company, March 21, 1846, Chouteau Family Papers, MoSHi. See also A. Drips to T. H. Harvey, June 1, 1845, and sworn statements of John B. Sarpy and Kenneth McKenzie, July 1, 1845, Letters Received, OIA, RG 75, NA; William Medill to A. Drips, April 2, 1846, Letters Sent, OIA, RG 75, NA.

[14] Thomas P. Moore to William Medill, May 14, 1846, Letters Received, OIA, RG 75, NA.

[15] Francis Parkman, *The Oregon Trail*, 11.

Pierre, and to add to the confusion, the incoming mail brought complaints from H. H. Sibley at Mendota, in the Minnesota country, that American Fur Company traders from the Upper Missouri were disregarding Company orders and trading east of the Dakotas.[16]

Few mackinaws reached St. Louis in 1846, however, since the Company took advantage of the improved Lower Missouri packet service and transferred mackinaw cargoes to steamboats between Fort Leavenworth and Glasgow for faster downriver shipment. On May 23, the *Tobacco Plant* landed at St. Louis with 909 packs of robes and "a few furs" taken on at Glasgow from four American Fur Company mackinaws whose crewmen had "become so refractory from intoxication, after getting into the settled portion of the country, that it was impossible almost to control them." Although two Company mackinaws tied up at St. Louis the following week with cargo from Council Bluffs, the heaviest upriver shipments did not appear until July, when the steamer *Balloon* put ashore 15 or 16 men and the cargo of two Company mackinaws from Fort Pierre and the *Tributary* landed 56 men under James Kipp from Fort Union and 1,800 packs of robes and furs (the cargo of seven or eight mackinaws). The last Company mackinaw of the season unloaded cargo at St. Louis on November 12 after a difficult six weeks' trip from Fort Pierre.[17]

Along with the July robe and fur shipment aboard the *Balloon* came an accused murderer, Victor Baraser, bound in irons, to be handed over to the marshal of the United States Circuit Court for the District of Missouri. Baraser was charged with shooting and killing instantly Napoleon McGuffin on May 25 "at a point or place between Fort John and Fort Pierre." The jurors selected to

[16] *Weekly Reveille*, February 9, 1846; Henry H. Sibley to Pierre Chouteau, Jr., and Company, April 21, 1846, Chouteau Family Papers, MoSHi; Honoré Picotte to F. A. Chardon, March 12, 1846, and to Pierre Chouteau, Jr., and Company, May 17, 1846, Ft. Pierre Letter Book, 1845–1846, MoSHi.

[17] *St. Louis New Era*, May 25, June 1, July 4, 22, 25, November 13, 1846; *Saint Louis American*, July 25, November 13, 1846; *DMR*, July 7, 25, 1846; *Weekly Reveille*, July 13, 1846.

try the case failed to agree on a verdict and were discharged. At that point, however, Baraser changed his plea from not guilty to guilty, threw himself upon the mercy of the court, and was sentenced to a fine of one dollar and a term of twelve months in the St. Louis County Jail. So much for murder on the Upper Missouri.[18]

Three weeks after the *Balloon* carried Victor Baraser to justice, the *Tributary* docked with news that the American Fur Company vessel *General Brooke*, under Captain Sire, had reached the Yellowstone country. At high noon on May 23, when the *General Brooke* had left St. Louis with Indian Agent Moore aboard, she was loaded heavily with trading goods, a "large supply" of powder and lead, and approximately 100 traders and trappers. The upriver trip was an easy one, and the crew of the vessel cast lines ashore at Fort Union on July 5. The downriver trip proved more difficult, however, since the channel was low, but Captain Sire brought his boat back to St. Louis on August 6, despite shallow water and thieves who took the cords of wood he had piled near the Vermillion. Sire's cargo included 450 packs of robes; 20 packs of assorted furs; 1,300–1,400 salted buffalo tongues; the stuffed carcass of a grizzly bear larger than an ox, shot by Alexander Culbertson as it was "pulling down" a buffalo bull caught emerging from the river; and an assortment of live animals—a buffalo calf, an elk, and a young grizzly. Culbertson, Chardon, and Honoré Picotte, all passengers on the steamboat, reported that the upriver tribes were quiet following a winter of hostilities during which the Arikaras had troubled Fort Pierre and the Blackfeet had killed eight people along the Yellowstone.[19]

Early in June, while the *General Brooke* steamed upriver to Forts Pierre and Union, the St. Louis press announced that a new company had formed to engage in the fur trade of the Yellow-

18 *DMR*, July 4, 1846; File of *U.S.* v. *Victor Baraser*, Criminal Case No. 410, Records of the United States Circuit Court, District of Missouri, FRC, KC.

19 Sire's Log Books, MoSHi; *Saint Louis American*, May 25, June 8, August 6, 1846; *DMR*, July 7, August 14, 1846; *Weekly Reveille*, June 1, August 10, 1846; *St. Louis New Era*, May 25, August 7, 1846.

stone and Upper Missouri valleys. Rumors had buzzed through the St. Louis business community for several weeks before the *General Brooke* departed and the American Fur Company had known they were true—a new fur company was forming—but Chouteau failed to keep the firm from filling the vacuum left on the upper river by the failure of the Union Fur Company and Pratte and Cabanné. All of its leaders, Alexander Harvey, Charles Primeau, Anthony R. Bouis, and Joseph Picotte, were former American Fur Company men. On July 6, they took out a license to employ eighteen men and $15,748, under the company name of Harvey and Primeau, at two principal trading posts in the Indian country: near Bad River close to Fort Pierre, to tap the Sioux trade, and about forty miles from the mouth of the Marias, to reach the Blackfoot trade. Harvey, Robert Forsythe, a St. Louis businessman whose deceased sister was Bouis' former wife, and David D. Mitchell, by now thoroughly out of sorts with the American Fur Company, stood bond for the new opposition. Some St. Louisans called the new partnership "Harvey, Primeau and Company," the "St. Louis Fur Company," or even the "Union Fur Company," borrowing the term from the old opposition, but titles meant little to the informally organized group led by Harvey. Any convenient title could designate opposition.[20]

Harvey resembled a tall, well-built storybook hero. He was strong, bold, and brave, as heroes should be, but his fiery temper marred an otherwise "fair and reasonable" character and pushed him into trouble. As a young man he had worked as a saddler's apprentice in a St. Louis shop, but saddlery was not to his liking; he quarreled with the shop's owners and signed up with the American Fur Company for Upper Missouri adventure. Eight years later, in 1839, when Chouteau fired him for accumulated ill-tempered outbursts, he left Fort McKenzie in a huff and hiked down the snow-clogged Missouri Valley to St. Louis. Chouteau,

[20] Trading License of Harvey and Primeau, July 6, 1846, Letters Received, OIA, RG 75, NA; *St. Louis New Era*, June 24, 1846; *Saint Louis American*, June 24, 1846.

amazed and impressed by Harvey's daring midwinter trip, rehired him and sent him back upriver in the spring. Once again in the fur country, Harvey sought out his enemies (those who had complained of him and caused his recall) and beat them up one by one. One adversary, a Spaniard named Isadore Sandoval, threatened to shoot Harvey on sight. Harvey cornered him behind the counter of the store at Fort Union and when Sandoval refused to leave the store to fight, shot and killed him on the spot and dared the Spaniard's friends to avenge the murder. Later, when Harvey returned to Fort McKenzie, he allied himself with Chardon, supposedly killed, in cold blood, an Indian who had stolen a milch cow from the post, and, along with Chardon, instigated the open attack on the Blackfoot party before the gates of the fort in February, 1844.[21]

By the spring of that year, Harvey was *persona non grata* to many in the American Fur Company, and his enemies, including a new one, Chardon, lurked everywhere on the upper river. When Fort McKenzie was abandoned, he moved to new Fort Chardon. Ten miles below that post in the summer of 1845, he met Alexander Culbertson, James Lee, Jacob Berger, and Malcolm Clark ascending the Missouri with a keelboat of supplies from Fort Union. Harvey boarded the boat on August 16 and offered to shake hands with Clark, Berger, and Lee, three of Chardon's friends, but they refused, turned on him with a hatchet, a rifle butt, and a pistol, and "did beat wound and ill treat" him on the head, right hand, and body until his life was "despaired of." Harvey stumbled off the boat, pulled himself on his horse, and fled to Fort Chardon, where he ordered his men to close the gates to Culbertson's party, but when Culbertson approached the fort, he was admitted, since he represented the Company and was not one of Harvey's many enemies. He paid Harvey the wages due him and saw him paddle off to Fort Union, where Harvey swore revenge

[21] Larpenteur, *Forty Years*, I, 167–70, 219–20; Chittenden, *Fur Trade*, II, 692–95; Bradley, "Affairs," *CHSM*, III, 214, 218, 221, 227, 231; McDonnell, "Forts Benton and Sarpy," *CHSM*, X, 302 (n. 281).

on the American Fur Company, then continued downstream to St. Louis.[22]

He reached Missouri when the Union Fur Company and Pratte and Cabanné were vacating the upper-river trade and almost immediately charged Lee, Berger, and Clark with plotting to kill him. Thomas Gantt, United States District Attorney for Missouri, heard Harvey's story and presented it to the Circuit Court, and in April, 1846, a grand jury indicted the three men. The American Fur Company tried desperately to quash the charges before an indictment was delivered and to rehire Harvey for the Blackfoot trade, but he pressed the indictment and the St. Louis Superintendent of Indian Affairs directed Drips to order Lee, Berger, and Clark "out of the Indian Country forthwith." Harvey demanded that five Upper Missouri American Fur Company traders— Archembeau, Bernabé, Crenier, Robert (or Robar), and one other —be called to St. Louis to witness his charges, but the Company, knowing the five did not wish to go (and not wanting them to testify), quickly assigned them to distant duties. On April 6, 1847, the District Attorney refused to prosecute further, probably for lack of adequate evidence, and the three defendants were freed of the indictment.[23]

Chardon was ordered out of the Indian country along with Lee, Berger, and Clark because Harvey had accused him of selling alcohol to the Indians, and in the midst of the flurry over Harvey's story, Chouteau turned on Drips for failing to prevent the Harvey-Chardon controversy from reaching the Superintendent of Indian Affairs, whereupon Drips lost his job as Indian agent. Harvey's charge that the American Fur Company was guilty of trafficking in liquor with the Indians was not the first ever made

22 Chittenden, *Fur Trade*, II, 696–97; File of *U.S.* v. *James Lee, Jacob Berger, and Malcolm Clark*, Case No. 393, Records of the United States Circuit Court, District of Missouri, FRC, KC.

23 File of *U.S.* v. *James Lee, Jacob Berger, and Malcolm Clark*, Case No. 393, Records of the United States Circuit Court, District of Missouri, FRC, KC; T. H. Harvey to A. Drips, March 13, 1846, Drips Family Papers, CU-B; Honoré Picotte to Alexander Culbertson, Late 1845 or Early 1846, and to John B. Sarpy, December 1, 1845, Ft. Pierre Letter Book, 1845–1846, MoSHi.

against the Company, but Harvey's charge was the first to send Chouteau, his partners, and agents into the courts to defend themselves against the federal government. Three years earlier, in the summer of 1843, a young lawyer and American Fur Company employee, James Arrott, Jr., had sworn in a letter to the Secretary of War that Superintendent Mitchell and all Indian agents under his jurisdiction were indebted to Chouteau for their political jobs; that Company agents had told the Upper Missouri Indians that the French owned the United States and that Americans were French "slaves"; that the Company had given arms and ammunition to the Sioux to war on other tribes; that the Company had murdered Indians and Americans "in cold blood"; and that the Company carried liquor to the Indians, stored it in Indian country, and bartered and sold it to the red men. Commissioner of Indian Affairs T. Hartley Crawford favored an investigation of Arrott's blistering statement by a competent military man, but the affair was turned over to new St. Louis Indian Superintendent Thomas Harvey and tabled indefinitely, despite Arrott's persistent letters to the Secretary of War and even to the President. The only action—and it was legislative, not investigative—that Superintendent Harvey supported was a plan, advocated by various Indian agents, to stiffen the penalties for liquor traders who violated the federal statutes. Prison sentences in addition to fines were needed to punish the guilty, and finally, in 1847, Congress imposed sentences of one to two years in addition to fines.[24]

On June 5, 1846, District Attorney Gantt proceeded against the Company in the United States Circuit Court for the District of Missouri. He stated to the court that it was "not accurately known who compose[d] the firm of Pierre Chouteau Junior & Co.," but that he had requested and received from Superintendent Thomas Harvey, after a preliminary examination held before

[24] James Arrott, Jr., to James M. Porter, August 11, 1843, and to President John Tyler, October 12, 1843, and T. H. Crawford to James M. Porter, August 28, 1843, and to James Arrott, Jr., October 9, 1843, Special File No. 70, OIA, RG 76, NA; Richard W. Cummins to David D. Mitchell, October 1, 1843, 28 Cong., 1 sess., *SD No. 1*, p. 405.

Harvey in March, the Company's license bonds for the period 1842 through 1845 and from those and his knowledge of business associations in St. Louis he had made an educated guess that Chouteau's principal associates and sureties were Sarpy; McKenzie; Clapp; Sylvestre Labadie, a wealthy St. Louis miller and another of Pierre Chouteau's many influential cousins; and New England–born Joshua B. Brant (his second wife was Senator Benton's niece), who had resigned from the army in 1839 after a quarter-century of military service to enter St. Louis business and politics. Gantt sued the partners specifically for two Company bonds of 1842 (each of $2,000) and three of 1843 (two of $3,000 and one of $5,000) to trade at Forts Pierre and Union and their dependencies and for one bond of 1844 and one of 1845 (each of $5,000) to trade at Fort McKenzie and dependencies. The United States asked a total judgment of $25,000 for at least 4,300 gallons of illegal alcohol carried into the Indian country and traded there.[25]

On August 4, two months after Gantt filed the initial seven suits, he brought "declarations in debt" of $800 each against four Company agents—Chardon, Culbertson, Kipp, and Honoré Picotte—for distributing alcohol to the Indians in violation of the Indian Intercourse Law of 1834. A twelfth and last suit, also for $800, was filed on September 12, 1846, against Captain Sire for commanding the steamboat *Nimrod*, in 1844, when it carried "several hundred gallons of alcohol into the Indian Country."[26] The more information Gantt gathered against the American Fur Company, the more convinced he became "that the Company and its agents [were] for a long time past reaping exorbitant profits from the most flagrant violations of the law" and that Chouteau was attempting "to stifle testimony" by offering "advantageous

[25] Quotation from Thomas Gantt's Report to the Solicitor of the Treasury, June 6, 1846, SOT, RG 206, NA; Thomas Gantt's Report to the Solicitor of the Treasury, October 30, 1846, *ibid.*; T. H. Harvey to William Medill, May 12, 1846, Letters Received, OIA, RG 75, NA.

[26] Thomas Gantt's Report to the Solicitor of the Treasury, October 30, 1846, and Thomas Gantt to the Solicitor of the Treasury, August 6, 1846, SOT, RG 206, NA.

engagements" to those fur-trader witnesses who would leave St. Louis for the Upper Missouri before the twelve cases were heard.[27] Meanwhile, the Company entangled the government in legal spider webs, the first of which was spun in the summer of 1846 when Chouteau, Sarpy, McKenzie, Clapp, Labadie, and Brant refused to accept the writs of the court. For the next nine months, the case bogged down in its own mounting complications.

The liquor suits constituted one half of Alexander Harvey's revenge; the new opposition fur company, planned originally at Fort Pierre by Harvey, Primeau, Bouis, and Joseph Picotte when Harvey was on his way downriver to St. Louis, formed the other half. St. Louis–born Charles Primeau had joined the American Fur Company as a clerk in 1831. When he left the Company fifteen years later, he was the respected head of an Indian family, a dependable interpreter, and an experienced robe and fur trader. Anthony R. Bouis, also of St. Louis, was a member of the Bouis-Vásquez family of Indian traders. He was in the prime of life in 1846, a "kind hearted, generous" man "of highly cultivated intellect."[28] Joseph Picotte, the fourth partner, was a nephew of the French-Canadian trader Honoré Picotte (Chouteau's right-hand man at Fort Pierre). Honoré implored Chouteau to "try and make some arrangements with" the new opposition—stop them from going up the Missouri in the spring of 1846—but Harvey and his friends would not be stopped, and Uncle Honoré had to bear his nephew in opposition.[29] Harvey, Primeau, Bouis, and Picotte possessed the fur-trade experience that Ebbetts, Kelsey, and Cutting had lacked, and experience paid dividends on the Upper Missouri. The new partners also had the financial support of Robert Campbell of St. Louis, and that made the dividends even more valuable.

To fur-trade investors in St. Louis and the East, Campbell represented anti-Chouteau capital in its purest form. Born in Ulster, Campbell had sought and found health and fortune in the Rocky

[27] Thomas Gantt to the Solicitor of the Treasury, September 12, 1846, *ibid.*
[28] *DMR*, January 28, 1860.
[29] Honoré Picotte to Pierre Chouteau, Jr., and Company, June 16, 1846, Ft. Pierre Letter Book, 1845–1846, MoSHi.

Mountain–Upper Missouri fur trade of the twenties and thirties. After several years in fur partnership with William L. Sublette, who died in 1845, Campbell had gone into business on his own and built a flourishing outfitting house serving Indian-country traders. He was prominent in Missouri banking, insurance, and land development, cultivated important friends in eastern commercial and political circles, and was regarded, even by his adversaries, as a man who understood the western Indian and his problems. Campbell's business drafts were as good as gold in the Indian country (better than United States Treasury drafts according to one army officer on the Upper Missouri in 1855), and from his Main Street wholesale dry-goods and Indian-goods store in St. Louis, barrels and boxes of Upper Missouri supplies and trade goods poured to outfit Harvey, Primeau and Company. In exchange, Campbell marketed the firm's robes and furs.[30]

Fifty thousand dollars in merchandise, most of it from Campbell and enough of it to outfit Harvey, Primeau and Company for at least one season's trade, piled up on the St. Louis water front in June, 1846, and was rolled or carried aboard the steamer *Clermont No. 2*. Harvey hired forty-five men (fifty more were to be engaged later along the river); sold a tourist ticket to Charles P. Cassilly, a Cincinnati merchant who was willing to tolerate trappers, mules, and packing cases aboard the crowded little boat in order to see the Upper Missouri; and on July 7, ordered Captain Daniel G. Taylor (Taylor also was a budding politician who later served as mayor and city treasurer of St. Louis) to shove off for the upper river. Since the Missouri was extremely low, Harvey wasted little time on unnecessary stops—only at Council Bluffs to allow the Indian agent to search the boat for alcohol (at Fort Pierre, Agent Moore also searched the boat for liquor) and at the Vermillion to take on a group of Indians, including Primeau's Indian wife and his two children—before reaching the Great Bend. The *Clermont No. 2* landed below the bend, where Harvey exchanged gifts and speeches with the Sioux, and again immediately above

[30] *DMR*, October 17, 1879; *Daily Morning Missourian* (St. Louis), July 4, 1846.

93

the great river loop to put ashore traders and goods for Fort Bouis (Defiance), to be built at the mouth of Medicine Creek. Above the bend, buffalo were scarce on the river plains, and long stretches of burned grass outlined the water's edge. Three hundred miles below Fort Union, forty or fifty "very troublesome" Sioux opened fire upon the boat, but, fortunately, none aboard was hit by the leaden balls ricocheting off the superstructure. A few days later, Harvey, having directed Captain Taylor to unload supplies and about fifteen men at a timbered bottom below Fort Union, joined his traders ashore and hurriedly set to work to build mackinaws to carry his outfit up the Missouri to the Blackfoot country near the Marias. As soon as Harvey and his party had landed, the steamer swung out into the channel and headed downriver toward St. Louis. At Antelope Island, she grounded—stuck so fast that the crew worked two weeks, "by sparring and forming a channel," to free her. Finally, on September 20, the long-overdue *Clermont No. 2* reached St. Louis.[31]

Before winter came, Harvey transported his outfit via mackinaw from the Yellowstone to the Blackfoot country and constructed a small log fort (Robert Campbell) on the north bank of the Missouri above the mouth of the Marias and just below the site where the American Fur Company built Fort Clay (Benton) early the following spring. Harvey, Primeau and Company opened trade in competition with Chouteau near each of the American Fur Company's principal upriver posts. In addition to sponsoring trade at Fort Campbell (for the Blackfeet) and at Fort Bouis (for the Sioux), the opposition sent an outfit, in 1848–49, to tap the Crow trade along the Yellowstone; repaired Fort Mortimer (for the Assiniboin trade) and reassigned the old name, Fort William, to the newly reoccupied post; and placed goods at the Mandan-Hidatsa villages. Each partner (Harvey, Primeau, Bouis,

[31] "Journal of Daniel G. Taylor" by Steamer *Clermont*, 1846, MS, Steamboats Envelope, 1800–1859, MoSHi; *St. Louis New Era*, June 24, July 8, September 21, 1846; *Saint Louis American*, June 24, 1846; *DMR*, July 7, September 21, 1846; *Saint Louis Daily Union*, September 21, 1846; *Weekly Reveille*, September 28, 1846; Larpenteur, *Forty Years*, I, 228.

and Picotte) assumed command of one of the new key posts, or outfits, channeled robes and furs through Campbell in St. Louis, and received in return supplies and assistant traders shipped up-river annually from Missouri. Harvey, "chief worker and organizer" of the opposition, presided over Fort Campbell until his accidental death in 1854 and married into the Piegan band which traded at the fort.[32]

Within a week after the *Clermont No. 2* steamed into St. Louis, the American Fur Company sold its Upper Missouri vessel, the *General Brooke,* to John and Joseph La Barge for $12,000. The La Barges immediately entered the steamboat in the Lower Missouri packet trade; then Joseph traveled to Cincinnati to supervise the building of a new boat, the *Martha,* a "fine . . . staunch" 180-ton, two-engine steamer with four-inch bottom planks and a "scant two feet" of draft. Early in 1847, Joseph moved the *Martha* to St. Louis, added the cabin and machinery, and by May was ready to pilot her, under lease to the American Fur Company, to the upper-river posts. The new boat was Chouteau's answer to Harvey's threat to capture the trade of the Indian country. Since the winter of 1846–47 was unusually cold on the Upper Missouri —in St. Louis, "connoisseurs in furs" spoke of the superior pelts, "as connoisseurs in wine do the great vintages," that low temperatures produced—the superiority of the *Martha* over any vessel Harvey might lease gave the American Fur Company added advantage over the opposition in the valuable trade promised for 1847.[33]

The American Fur Company and the opposition seldom paid attention to the contradictory reports on the fur trade that reached St. Louis in 1846 and 1847. Elijah White, the controversial (American) Indian agent in Oregon, wrote his friends in the East that in his section of the country the few remaining beaver had

32 McDonnell, "Forts Benton and Sarpy," *CHSM,* X, 298 (n. 268), 303; Bradley, "Affairs," *CHSM,* III, 247.
33 Quotation from Palliser, *Solitary Hunter,* 58. See also Chittenden, *Early Steamboat Navigation,* I, 177; *Weekly Reveille,* September 28, 1846; *Saint Louis Daily Union,* March 24, 1847.

"fled to the mountain streams, and the sea otter to the sea." His remark was published, as was an Illinois farmer's "laudable and patriotic" demand that the American beaver be domesticated and protected from extinction. J. D. B. DeBow, the editor of a widely read New Orleans review, took a position alongside White and the farmer: yes, the beaver had been "very nearly exterminated" and the fur trade was "of little value." Yet trappers and travelers along the Platte said the beaver hunt was good and getting better, and pamphleteers in St. Louis pointed to the Upper Missouri as the highway of a flourishing fur trade. Some of the reports were sufficient, if heeded by fur dealers, to demoralize the Missouri River trade, but the two major companies knew that the information they received from their own agents at the upriver posts was more reliable and indicated that the robe and fur trade would remain profitable for some time. Independent traders (Jacques Marten, who defied the American Fur Company and traded between the Vermillion and the Beaver in 1846, and John Shaw, who traded near the ruins of Fort George in the winter of 1845–46) evidently agreed with the larger fur companies, and no sudden exodus of independent traders from the Upper Missouri occurred.[34]

The first traders who arrived in St. Louis in the spring of 1847 said that upriver fur men "had generally done well" over the severe winter, "having sold most of their goods."[35] Soon, however, the guarded optimism of the early reports gave way to statements of "unprecedented success" in the winter's trade.[36] Nevertheless,

[34] *Cherokee Advocate* (Tahlequah, Indian Territory), February 5, 1846; *The Farmers' Cabinet and American Herd-Book*, Vol. XI (August 15, 1846), 25; *The Commercial Review of the South and West*, Vol. II (December, 1846), 383; "Diary of Virgil K. Pringle, 1846," *Transactions of the Forty-eighth Annual Reunion of the Oregon Pioneer Association* (1920), 290; *The Commerce and Navigation of the Valley of the Mississippi*, 30; Trading License of Jacques Marten, July 1, 1846, Letters Received, OIA, RG 75, NA; *St. Louis New Era*, May 18, 1846; *Weekly Tribune* (Liberty, Missouri), September 19, 1846.

[35] *St. Louis New Era*, April 30, 1847. See also *Saint Louis Daily Union*, April 30, 1847.

[36] *Niles' National Register*, June 19, 1847.

cautious St. Louis fur dealers preferred to wait upon the actual returns from the Upper Missouri before pronouncing 1846–47 a true vintage season. By late spring, however, "a very great" quantity of robes and furs was piling up in St. Louis, and the earlier optimism seemed fully justified. The packet *Tributary* landed on June 21 with 750 packs of robes and 54 packs of furs from Fort Pierre, taken aboard near St. Joseph from three American Fur Company mackinaws, and with two Harvey, Primeau and Company mackinaw cargoes (515 packs of robes and 7 packs of furs), also loaded on below St. Joseph, in charge of Joseph Picotte from Medicine Creek.[37] Late in July, the Lower Missouri steamers *Amaranth* and *Haydee* docked in St. Louis with approximately 1,300–1,400 packs of American Fur Company robes (the cargo of several mackinaws) from Fort Union and the Yellowstone. An additional 240 packs had disappeared into the river when one of the mackinaws hit a snag, swamped, and sank just below St. Joseph. "There were several hands on board, who barely made their escape by jumping overboard, and getting hold of [the] snag until they were taken off."[38]

The year's largest robe and fur shipment reached St. Louis on the Company steamboat *Martha*. On May 15, after the vessel had been inspected, properly licensed, outfitted with a crew, and loaded with fur men, trade goods, and Indian annuities, Captain La Barge had taken her to the upper river. He was accompanied by Gideon C. Matlock, the new Upper Missouri Indian agent replacing Thomas P. Moore, who resigned after one year's experience with the "bitter" rivalry and intense jealousy rampant in the Indian country.[39] Although Matlock was a former Company employee, as agent he took a pro-Indian stand and pleaded with his superiors in the Indian Office for stronger liquor regulations and

[37] *DMR*, June 22, 1847; *St. Louis New Era*, June 22, 1847.

[38] Quotation from the St. Joseph *Gazette*, July 16, 1847. See also *DMR*, July 22, 1847; *Saint Louis Daily Union*, July 22, 1847; *Weekly Reveille*, July 26, 1847; *St. Louis New Era*, July 21, 1847.

[39] T. P. Moore to T. H. Harvey, September 21, 1846, 29 Cong., 2 sess., *HED No. 4*, p. 292.

greater understanding of Indian problems.[40] The trip to the Yellowstone was relatively placid for the *Martha*. She unloaded men and supplies at the river posts and before the end of June headed downstream after only a 24-hour stop in stormy weather at Fort Union. In St. Louis, however, the Company heard rumors that the *Martha* had sunk near Council Bluffs. The local press reported that several passengers and crewmen had drowned and that part of the cargo was a total loss. The rumors were unfounded, luckily, and on the evening of July 8, the *Martha* pulled up to the St. Louis levee with an estimated 1,300–1,500 packs of robes, 280 packs of furs, 96 sacks of buffalo tongues, a large stack of beef hides, and a small animal collection consisting of fawns, mountain dogs, birds, bear cubs, and, taken from a narrow riverbank where they were caught between the boat and a steep bluff, a herd of buffalo calves. Menageries and circuses played St. Louis regularly during the forties, and any animals brought into the city from the Upper Missouri, if not placed in private collections, could be sold to the traveling shows.[41]

One of the passengers leaving the *Martha* at St. Louis, threading his way through bales of robes and caged animals, was a Catholic missionary, Jesuit Father Nicholas Point, returning from years of work in the Oregon country. Father Point had labored in the mission field opened by Father Pierre Jean De Smet in the Flathead Indian area. Father De Smet, a short, stocky, impressive-looking missionary with an abundance of zeal, had founded a handful of northwestern missions between 1840 and 1846. He was known throughout the Upper Missouri country as a genial, cheerful frequent visitor, an able peacemaker between whites and Indians, and an accomplished missionary-fund raiser in both Europe

[40] G. C. Matlock to T. H. Harvey, October 17, 1847, 30 Cong., 1 sess., *SED No. 1*, pp. 848–53. Larpenteur, *Forty Years*, II, 416, called Matlock a "drunken gambler" who cavorted with Mormon women.

[41] *St. Louis New Era*, July 9, 10, 1847; *Saint Louis Daily Union*, July 10, 1847; *Weekly Reveille*, July 12, 1847; *DMR*, July 8, 1847. For circus and menagerie advertisements, see *DMR*, May 29, 1845, May 21, 1847, September 5, 1848, June 16, September 10, 1852, July 6, 1853.

and America. He was charmed with the hospitality of American Fur Company fur posts and the consistent "cordiality . . . politeness . . . overflowing kindness . . . [and] charitable liberality" of the Company's Upper Missouri traders.[42] Father Point returned to St. Louis with similar pro-Company feelings. He had observed, he said, that Chouteau's posts were ruled by mild American Fur Company agents and that daily work schedules for post employees were "very moderate." Some posts, "out of good will," administered daily to dozens of sick and invalid Indians, and Company traders at Forts Lewis and Clay (Benton)—and even opposition traders at Fort Campbell—had contributed to his fund to open a Blackfoot Indian mission. Could any missionary expect more?[43]

Two months before Father Point reached St. Louis, he had witnessed the demolition of Fort Lewis and the building of Fort Clay in an attractive, fertile location convenient to Indian trade. Building materials from Fort Lewis, floated downriver on Company barges, were used to construct the high palisades of the new post. Father Point left Fort Clay aboard a mackinaw on May 21, dined at Fort Union (he enjoyed well-sugared coffee with the meal) early in June, and a few days later boarded the *Martha* for St. Louis. Captain La Barge, as ordered by Chouteau, refused to allow the missionary to pay passage on the downriver trip, and the Jesuit returned a full purse to the Church when he ended his Indian-country work. Later, when he explained to his superiors the missionary prospects in the Blackfoot land, he noted that, after some reflection, he doubted that all the upriver fur agents favored Indian missions, and said that on at least one occasion he had misplaced his confidence in an American Fur Company bourgeois; but he believed that Chouteau and the Harvey, Primeau and Company suppliers were "exceedingly sympathetic" to the Church

[42] Father Pierre Jean De Smet, *Oregon Missions and Travels over the Rocky Mountains in 1845–46* (ed. by Reuben G. Thwaites as Vol. XXIX of *Early Western Travels, 1748–1846*), 369.

[43] Father Point, "Journey," *Mid-America*, XIII, 238–39; Garraghan, "Nicholas Point," *loc. cit.*, 51–52 (and n. 8).

and were a "source of consolation" in his mission.[44] By the 1840's the American Fur Company, as well as the opposition companies, had learned the value of missionaries to the Upper Missouri fur trade. They knew that the trade might better operate as it pleased on the Missouri, on the one hand, if, on the other, it received public praise from missionaries; and they realized also that missionaries might bring peace to the warring river tribes, and peace would bring more stability to the fur trade. And so the traders co-operated with the missionaries, publicly sang their praises, carried their mail free of charge, and improved the public image of the fur business. Since many of the Upper Missouri traders were Catholics, the fur posts served "as the nuclei of later . . . parishes" and gave the Catholic church an early start in the religious life of the Dakotas and Montana.[45]

Four days after the *Martha* returned to the port of St. Louis, the small steamer *Lake of the Woods*, a new light-draft boat fitted with the boilers and machinery of the old *New Haven*, left the city with $40,000-$50,000 in supplies and fifty to sixty men for Harvey, Primeau and Company's upriver posts. The opposition, encouraged by a successful winter trading season and substantial returns in the spring, had renewed its license and plunged into another year of Indian-country competition. The *Lake of the Woods* discharged freight at several points below the Great Bend. The Indians who gathered to watch upriver steamboats unload tried to hide their wonder at the white man's "fire boats," but seldom completely covered up their astonishment,[46] and the *Lake of the Woods* was no exception.

At Fort Bouis, missionary Father Augustin Ravoux, who was visiting the tribes along the Upper Missouri, boarded the steamer. Father Ravoux's first missionary tour to the Missouri Valley from

[44] Garraghan, "Nicholas Point," *loc. cit.*, 52-53 (and n. 9), 58-61.

[45] Sister M. Claudia Duratschek, *The Beginnings of Catholicism in South Dakota*, 18; Father Christian Hoecken to Father Pierre Jean De Smet, December 11, 1850, *Collection de Précis Historiques*, Vol. 7 (1856), 572-76.

[46] *DMR*, May 8, 1847; *St. Louis New Era*, July 12, 1847; *Weekly Reveille*, April 3, 1847; Palliser, *Solitary Hunter*, 206.

the Minnesota country in 1845 had taken him to Catholic French
and Indian families settled at the mouth of the Vermillion. Two
years later, in the spring of 1847, under permission from the Bishop
of Dubuque, he returned to the Missouri for three months to con-
vert Sioux, Mandans, and Hidatsas and to baptize the children of
Catholic families. Accompanied by a small Indian band, he traveled overland from Mendota, Minnesota, via Traverse des Sioux
and Lac qui Parle, to Fort Pierre, where he "was received kindly"
by the American Fur Company garrison and met Indian Agent
Matlock. The missionary, assisted by two Company interpreters,
preached to the Sioux at the fort (he noted that "they listen to the
word of God with respect and attention") and in near-by Indian
camps, celebrated Mass in the fort on two Sundays before congre-
gations of twenty-five or thirty, and baptized dozens of halfblood
children.[47]

After ten days at Fort Pierre, Father Ravoux moved downriver
to the opposition post, Fort Bouis, and preached to forty Sioux
families. Although he was welcomed warmly by the garrison of
the fort and urged to remain for the summer, he refused the request, since he planned to go upriver on the *Lake of the Woods* to
continue the missionary work begun the year before by Father
George A. Belcourt at the Mandan-Hidatsa villages close to Fort
Berthold. The previous June, 1846, Father Belcourt, attached to
the Red River country, had joined the annual métis hunting caravan into the buffalo plains northeast of Fort Berthold. In mid-July,
when the caravan—short of food, plagued with measles and
dysentery, and under constant threat of Sioux attack—passed east
of Fort Berthold, Father Belcourt and a half-dozen hunters visited
the fort to buy medicine to relieve the "violent distemper" of the
main hunting party. The Mandans and Hidatsas welcomed him as
a distinguished visitor, and the clerk of the post "with much polite-

47 Father Augustin Ravoux to Bishop Loras of Dubuque, August 4, 12, 1847,
The United States Catholic Magazine and Monthly Review, Vol. VII (1848), 19,
25–26, 84–85; Sister Mary Aquinas Norton, *Catholic Missionary Activities in the
Northwest, 1818–1864*, 86–87; *Father Augustin Ravoux, Reminiscences, Memoirs
and Lectures*, 15, 19, 21, 25–26.

ness . . . shared with him the medicine of the fort." Before the day was over, the missionary baptized a dozen children and preached to a crowd of Mandans and Hidatsas gathered in a chief's lodge. Then, during the night, he and his métis companions, escorted by fifteen warriors, slipped away from Fort Berthold to elude the prowling Sioux, and carried their precious medicines back to the buffalo caravan. Although Father Belcourt wrote his superiors immediately upon returning to Red River and volunteered to undertake new missions to the Missouri River Indians, permission was never granted. Meanwhile, he sent a Chippewa halfblood interpreter to winter with the Mandans-Hidatsas in 1848-49, and in 1851, the Church permitted Father Albert Lacombe to accompany a hunting party to Fort Berthold, but Father Belcourt himself never returned to the Missouri. Father Lacombe's party included approximately one hundred métis dressed in brightly colored "semi-European, semi-Indian" costumes embellished with "tobacco pouches, girdles, knife cases . . . and [all] elaborately decorated with glass beads, porcupine quills, feather quills, etc." At Fort Berthold, the missionary reproached the garrison for living sinfully with Indian women and refused "to sleep in the same room" with a young Protestant trader.[48]

Four years before Father Lacombe's visit to Dakota, however, Father Ravoux preached at Forts Pierre and Bouis. On August 17, 1847, he was settled comfortably in a small cabin of the steamboat *Lake of the Woods*, headed upriver (five days above Fort Bouis), when, suddenly, the vessel rammed a snag near the mouth of the Cheyenne and two steam pipes burst from the impact. Fire broke out, smoke poured from the boat, and the passengers ran to the stern to abandon the steamer before the gunpowder in her cargo

[48] Father George A. Belcourt to Bishop Loras of Dubuque, January 5, 1849, *The United States Catholic Magazine and Monthly Review*, Vol. VIII (1849), 313-16; Father Belcourt to the Archbishop of Quebec, August 6, 1846, *Rapport sur les Missions*, Vol. 7 (July, 1847), 70-76; Father Louis Pfaller, *The Catholic Church in Western North Dakota, 1738-1960*, 14-15; Father James M. Reardon, "Father Lacombe, the Black-Robe Voyageur," *Acta et Dicta*, Vol. V (July, 1917), 93-95; Kurz, *Journal*, 82-83.

blew up. Fortunately, the fire was doused and none abandoned ship, but two men were scalded when the pipes split and blew up the main-cabin floor, which was above the boilers. One of the injured, severely burned over most of his body, died six hours after the accident and was buried on the riverbank. Alexander Harvey, who evidently joined the boat at Fort Bouis after descending the river from Fort Campbell, realized that the boilers were damaged seriously, transferred men and supplies to a keelboat (the keel was in tow to carry goods above the mouth of the Yellowstone), and continued upstream slowly to Fort Campbell. The *Lake of the Woods*, repaired temporarily, turned back to St. Louis. At the Great Bend, a Sioux war party appeared on the east bank and beckoned the steamer to land. Her captain, warned previously that the Indians were dangerous, pretended to seek a landing—he rang the steamer bell, took soundings, and edged closer to the bank—but, instead, moved the boat downriver past the Sioux, out of their range of fire, and on to safety. After brief stops at the Vermillion and the Mormon camp at Council Bluffs, the vessel limped into St. Louis on September 5, and Father Ravoux disembarked.[49]

Harvey's upriver keelboat trip from the Sioux country above Fort Bouis was an endurance contest for man and craft. Gale-force winds and early snow slowed the boat's progress, and the river clogged with ice in the first week of November. Under the circumstances, Harvey abandoned the keelboat, shifted his expedition to horses bartered from the Indians, and finally reached Fort Campbell in late November or early December. After a few days' rest, he and two or three companions broke their way back down the Missouri Valley through deep snow. At the Yellowstone, an Assiniboin war party robbed Harvey's band and left them to the

[49] Father Augustin Ravoux to Bishop Loras of Dubuque, August 12, 1847, *The United States Catholic Magazine and Monthly Review*, Vol. VII (1848), 84–85; Norton, *Catholic Missionary Activities*, 86–87; Ravoux, *Reminiscences*, 28–29; Father Augustin Ravoux to Bishop Loras of Dubuque, July 2, September 21, 1847, MSS, Dubuque Diocesan Archives, Catholic Chancery Office, Dubuque, Iowa; *Weekly Reveille*, September 13, 1847; *DMR*, September 6, 1847.

mercy of the land. Luckily, the Mandans and Sioux were more merciful than the Assiniboins that winter and supplied the white men with food, pack dogs, and mules. They abandoned all of the animals in short order, however, since the deep snow supported only travelers on snow shoes. Eventually, after a "long and cold trip," including at least five foodless days, Harvey and his friends found sustenance at the Mormon encampment at Council Bluffs and, refreshed, continued on downriver to Liberty, Missouri, where they boarded the river packet *Bertrand*. At St. Louis, late in March, 1848, they told their story of midwinter passage from the Falls of the Missouri and predicted that the upriver "buffalo trade had been pretty good" during the winter.[50]

Both Harvey and the American Fur Company had ended the year 1847 in good financial condition. Roustabouts unloaded the last shipment of American Fur Company robes at St. Louis (three mackinaw loads from Fort Pierre) from the steamer *St. Peter's* late in October. The national robe market flourished, beaver was in demand again—Lampson agreed to rush a large supply from England to New York City, labeled "nutria" to avoid the higher American tariff on beaver skins—and the early cold weather heralded a second excellent upriver winter trade. Although the American Fur Company liquor suits still hung fire in the Circuit Court as plaintiff and defendant jockeyed for legal position, Superintendent Thomas Harvey remained in charge of Indian affairs in St. Louis, despite attempts by anti-Company politicians to remove him; Andrew Drips was back in Company service as a full-fledged employee; and the immediate future of the Upper Missouri fur trade looked promising.[51]

[50] *St. Louis New Era*, March 30, 1848; *Weekly Reveille*, April 3, 1848; *DMR*, March 30, 1848; *Saint Louis Daily Union*, March 31, 1848.

[51] Curtis M. Lampson to John F. A. Sanford, October 2, 1847, Chouteau Family Papers, MoSHi; *St. Louis New Era*, October 22, 1847; *Weekly Reveille*, October 25, 1847; *DMR*, October 22, 1847.

CHAPTER FIVE

"Still the heroes of the day"

THE TWO-YEAR WAR with Mexico had ended in the Treaty of Guadalupe Hidalgo, and the resources of the Southwest, from the Río Grande to the Pacific, awaited development. The President, members of Congress, and editors—virtually everyone with a pen, a podium, or a pulpit—expounded on the merits or demerits of New Mexico and California and stirred the public to action. The Upper Missouri country, hundreds of miles from the southwestern magnet of national interest, remained isolated from the great events of the day. John Marshall discovered gold at Sutter's Mill in January, 1848, but few Argonauts crossed the Upper Missouri country on their way to California. The Compromise of 1850 gave territorial status to New Mexico and Utah, but the words of the Omnibus Bill touched the high Missouri only in a general way. Slavery was not an issue in the land of the Teton Sioux, the Blackfeet, and the Assiniboins. Francis Chardon, who died at Fort Berthold in 1848, owned a Negro slave, Black Hawk, but none of the fur traders seemed to care. The American Fur Company and the opposition adjusted, without protest or celebration, to post–Mexican War peacetime trade in isolation, as usual, on the upper river.[1]

Chouteau notified his Upper Missouri agents that the American Fur Company had reorganized in the spring of 1848, according to the familiar pattern of periodic stock redistribution. Honoré Picotte, who had entered the fur trade about 1820, married the daughter of a Teton Sioux chief, and became bourgeois at Fort

[1] Copy of F. A. Chardon's Will of April 20, 1848, Fur Trade Papers Envelope, MoSHi.

Pierre in 1842 when Jacob Halsey, the old bourgeois, was killed accidentally, was replaced by Culbertson as principal upriver agent. James Kipp was given a share in the Upper Missouri Outfit, and the Company sanctioned an increase in the number of upriver wintering posts and outfitted the steamboat *Martha* to provision the upper river in 1848. When the *Martha* left St. Louis on May 9 (the earliest date, in four years, for an upriver voyage), Joseph La Barge again held the wheel in the pilothouse, and mixed in with the crew and common traders were Indian Agent Matlock and at least three Company leaders, J. B. Sarpy, Honoré Picotte, and Alexander Culbertson.[2]

Alexander Harvey, in St. Louis during the spring following his harrowing land and water descent from Fort Campbell, gathered men and supplies for the upriver opposition trade and talked to District Attorney Gantt about the liquor suits. Harvey preferred life in Indian country to life in St. Louis—his partners, however, thoroughly enjoyed visits to that city—and he was "irked" by the legal and commercial problems that called him downriver in 1848. Anxious to complete his onerous duties, he renewed the opposition trading license in April, with sureties from Campbell and the well-educated St. Louis iron merchant, banker, and philanthropist James E. Yeatman.[3] On June 1, Harvey left aboard the steamboat *Bertrand* with supplies and trading goods for the upriver posts. After ascending the Missouri to a point fifty miles above the mouth of the Yellowstone, where Harvey transferred his Blackfoot and Crow goods to smaller craft, the vessel turned back down the Missouri and put into St. Louis late on July 24. Levee roustabouts carried hundreds of bales of Harvey, Primeau and Company

[2] Pierre Chouteau, Jr., and Company to A. Drips, August 18, 1848, Drips (Andrew) Papers, MoSHi; *DMR*, May 10, 1848; *Saint Louis Daily Union*, March 10, 1848; *St. Louis Daily New Era*, March 9, 1848.

[3] Thomas Gantt to the Solicitor of the Treasury, August 11, 1848, Letters Received, OIA, RG 75, NA; T. H. Harvey to William Medill, April 19, 1848, Clark (William) Papers, KHi; Record of Trading License of Harvey, Primeau and Company, April 17, 1848, Volume Entitled "Licenses for Indian Trade," OIA, RG 76, NA.

robes and furs ashore from the *Bertrand* and stacked them in the warehouse belonging to Robert Campbell and his nephew, and new junior partner, William.[4]

The upriver voyage of the *Martha* was, in comparison to that of the *Bertrand*, decidedly hectic. When the *Martha* landed at Colin Campbell's American Fur Company post at the mouth of Crow Creek below the Great Bend on June 13, hundreds of Yankton Sioux warriors assembled on the riverbank. Warned by Agent Matlock four months earlier that they had no annuities coming, some of the Indian warriors were determined to seize the boat and cargo. Approximately twenty-five or thirty Sioux moved toward the boat; some fired shotguns, others dispersed the crew and attempted to put out the fire in the boat's boilers. One shot whizzed past Culbertson and the clerk of the boat as they stood on the guardrail facing the Indians, tore through two staterooms behind them, and killed a crewman atop the guard near the pantry on the far side of the steamboat. Matlock offered immediately to go ashore to pacify the Indians before the skirmish became a pitched battle between the eighty armed men on the *Martha* and the yowling Sioux. Accompanied by an interpreter, he met the Yanktons in Colin Campbell's trading house, told them that Sarpy was preparing them a feast and many presents, and asked them to cease the attack on the boat. As soon as Matlock had quieted the tribesmen, Sarpy ordered the *Martha* away from the landing and upriver to safety.[5]

After the Indians finished their feast in the trading house, Matlock addressed them and, in turn, heard several chiefs detail Yankton grievances against white traders. Old Chief Smutty Bear said that the young warriors had ignored the counsel of the elders and

[4] *Weekly Reveille*, July 31, 1848; *Saint Louis Daily Union*, July 26, 1848.

[5] G. C. Matlock to T. H. Harvey, June 16, 1848, Letters Received, OIA, RG 75, NA; *Weekly Reveille*, July 17, 31, 1848; *DMR*, July 15, 1848. Joseph La Barge, in his memoirs (Chittenden, *Early Steamboat Navigation*, I, 178–83), mistakenly places the attack in 1847 and claims that the Indians seized half the boat and drove his cowardly passengers and crew to perches atop the paddle wheels. According to La Barge, he saved the boat when he aimed a cannon at the Indians crowded together in the main cabin.

planned to storm the boat but that the attack started prematurely—a common error in an Indian attack—before all the warriors had gathered on the bank. He also revealed that competing traders had encouraged the Indians to steal horses and other property from each other and to kill each other, and he stressed that the attack on the boat was the idea of anti-Chouteau (presumably Harvey, Primeau and Company) traders who said that although the *Martha* was loaded with Indian annuities, the Indians would receive none unless they seized the boat. When Smutty Bear finished his indictment, he demanded that the old traders be removed from the Indian country and that new ones be sent in. Deeply moved by the pleas of the Yankton chiefs, Matlock wrote the Indian Office a full report of the attack on the boat and the meeting in the trading house. He accused Colin Campbell (a "perfect nuisance . . . void of principle") of inciting the Indians to robbery and murder and charged Harvey's traders with planning the attack on the *Martha*. Matlock, who admitted that his first impression of some Upper Missouri traders had been favorable, had soon learned that law-abiding traders were rare and that the Indians were abused by all trading companies. Although he was uncertain of his power to revoke trading licenses, he intended, nevertheless, to act against both the American Fur Company and the opposition in the Yankton Sioux area.[6]

Before the end of June, Matlock revoked the Yankton Sioux trading licenses of the two fur companies and sent a report of his deed to Washington for approval of the Indian Office. Then he took passage on the *Bertrand*, bound downriver from the Yellowstone, and when he reached St. Louis, told newspaper reporters that he was prepared to battle dishonest traders who held out "delusive prospects to the Indians" and fashioned a "state of threatening discontent" in the Indian country.[7] Neither the Amer-

[6] G. C. Matlock to T. H. Harvey, June 16, 1848, Letters Received, OIA, RG 75, NA.

[7] Quotation from *Weekly Reveille*, July 31, 1848. See also G. C. Matlock to Harvey, Primeau and Company, June 19, 1848, and to Pierre Chouteau, Jr., and Company, June 19, 1848, Letters Received, OIA, RG 75, NA.

ican Fur Company, under suit for liquor violations, nor Harvey, Primeau and Company, under suspicion in the Indian Office because of Harvey's questionable character, dared forcefully to contradict Matlock before the Indian Office. Instead, both companies quietly removed their old traders from the Yankton country. Late in September, Agent Matlock, once again on the Upper Missouri, informed his superiors that, although he was still suspicious of Harvey, he was satisfied with the American Fur Company "as it now stands under the new organization" and, presumably, was willing to see trade reopened at the Yankton camps.[8]

The *Martha*, having completed her round trip to Fort Union in sixty-five days, tied up at St. Louis on July 14, ten days before the *Bertrand* returned, and unloaded over 1,700 bales of robes, approximately 260 packs of furs, and thousands of salted buffalo tongues. In addition to the Upper Missouri returns brought to St. Louis in July on the two steamboats leased by the fur companies, the Missouri River packet *Amelia* landed in May with a cargo (800 bales of robes) taken on at Weston from two Harvey, Primeau and Company mackinaws under Joseph Picotte. A third opposition mackinaw in Picotte's fleet, loaded with 100 packs of furs, had sunk above Council Bluffs. In mid-June, the packet *Mandan* reached St. Louis with 1,833 packs of robes for several consignees, and later in the month, an American Fur Company mackinaw, "heavily laden with furs," went down in the snag field at St. Joseph. One trader, a member of the Picotte family, drowned in the accident.[9]

Those passengers and crewmen who returned to St. Louis aboard the *Martha* gave the newspapers the outline of the Yankton Sioux attack on the vessel, and when Matlock arrived on the *Bertrand* ten days later, he satisfied the public appetite with additional details. Unfortunately, the 27-year-old Boston artist Wil-

[8] G. C. Matlock to T. H. Harvey, September 25, 1848, 30 Cong., 2 sess., *HED No. 1*, pp. 469–70.

[9] *DMR*, July 15, 1848; *Weekly Reveille*, May 22, June 19, July 3, 17, 1848; *Saint Louis Daily Union*, May 23, 1848; *St. Louis Daily New Era*, June 14, 1848; St. Joseph *Gazette*, June 9, 23, 1848.

liam Henry Tappan, who departed St. Louis in May on the *Martha* to collect scientific specimens and to draw "natural objects" in the West, left the vessel at the Platte before it reached the Great Bend of the Missouri and missed the opportunity to sketch the Indian attack. Tappan, who later designed the seal of Washington Territory, was not, of course, the only artist to sketch along the Missouri in the 1840's. Young Alexander H. Murray of Scotland, an American Fur Company employee, carefully sketched Forts Union, Pierre, Mortimer, and George in 1844-45 before he deserted the Upper Missouri country to join the Hudson's Bay Company at Fort Garry, located at the confluence of the Assiniboine and Red rivers.[10]

The latest inventories from the upriver posts of the American Fur Company and the opposition, brought downstream aboard the *Bertrand* and the *Martha*, were mulled over by the officers of the fur companies in St. Louis. Each year they decided whether or not to send small amounts of emergency supplies to the upriver posts before the winter set in.[11] Since some of the traders who returned to St. Louis by steamer or mackinaw each summer headed back to the upper river in September or October, they could be required by the fur companies, if necessary, to escort pack trains of supplies to the upriver posts. During the forties, James Kipp was frequently entrusted with the American Fur Company's autumn pack train to the Indian country. His train usually made up at Independence, the jumping-off place for both the Santa Fe and Oregon trails, but some trains made up at least as far north as St. Joseph, where fur men "crowded the streets and public houses of the town," bought and sold mackinaws whose robe and fur cargoes had been shipped downriver in packets, and "still the

[10] *DMR*, May 11, 1848; Louise Rasmussen, "Artists of the Explorations Overland, 1840-1860," *Oregon Historical Quarterly*, Vol. XLIII (March, 1942), 61; Alexander H. Murray, *Journal of the Yukon 1847-48* (ed. by L. J. Burpee), Introduction. See also the reproductions of Murray's sketches of Forts Union, George, Pierre, and Mortimer in *Forest and Stream*, January 25 and February 8, 1908.

[11] American Fur Company Ledger LL, MoSHi. The inventory for 1849 totaled $45,166.70 for Forts Pierre, Union, Benton, Berthold, Alexander, and Clark and Vermillion Post; for 1850, the total was $51,316.77 for the same seven locations.

heroes of the day ... took great delight" in their manly triumphs.[12]

By early November, 1848, the autumn pack trains were on their way to the fur posts, the last summer cargoes of Upper Missouri robes and pelts were stacked in fur warehouses in St. Louis and the East, and the investors in the trade watched the Taylor-Cass presidential contest end in a narrow victory for Zachary Taylor, the Whig candidate. His success in November gave Democratic partisans a dismal winter and the promise of a spring filled with the battle cries of patronage. The American Fur Company knew that a new Whig regime would move into the Indian Office and that new political eyes would look into fur-trade business in the Indian country. Chouteau believed the time ripe to negotiate with Harvey, Primeau and Company to forge a single and more powerful fur organization on the Upper Missouri, one capable of presenting a united front against any Whig efforts to pry into the Indian-country trade. Chouteau, anxious to draw up an agreement with the opposition during the winter, ignored Agent Matlock's "serious charges" against Harvey, as well as the many anti-Harvey rumors circulated by American Fur Company men, and proposed a united firm—but Robert Campbell and Harvey said no.[13]

The year 1849 looked like a trouble-filled one for the American Fur Company: a Whig was in the White House; Harvey had refused to sell out (the American Fur Company again encouraged its employees to circulate tales detrimental to the opposition), and the unusually cold and snowy Upper Missouri winter of 1848–49 killed herds of Company cattle and horses, cut communications between the river-valley posts, and forced the traders at Fort Pierre to live on corn instead of wild game. "Every thing looks gloomy ... we have nothing to eat ... things have not been managed properly," wrote clerk William D. Hodgkiss (a New Yorker who had entered the fur trade under Bonneville in the thirties and

[12] Quotation from Kurz, *Journal*, 30–31. See also Thomas Gantt to the Solicitor of the Treasury, August 11, 1848, Letters Received, OIA, RG 75, NA, and Palliser, *Solitary Hunter*, 59–60.

[13] Robert Campbell to William Medill, February 9, 1849, Letters Received, OIA, RG 75, NA.

held a share in the American Fur Company Upper Missouri Outfit in the fifties and sixties) in a letter of January, 1849, from Fort Union to his superiors. His complaint was only one of several carried into St. Louis by the spring express from the upriver posts. Many Company agents were dissatisfied with each other and suspected that the opposition traded superior goods, especially beads, tobacco, and guns. The Company, however, disregarded most of the complaints, since many were unsubstantiated, as usual, and others were aggravated by the hard winter.[14]

Chouteau was more concerned with the government annuities due the Yankton and Santee Sioux in 1849 than he was with disgruntled upriver Company bourgeois. Many of the Sioux, starving as a result of the severe winter, desperately needed annuities and threatened the food supplies of Company and opposition posts alike. The sooner annuities reached the Indians, the safer all Sioux-country posts would be. Chouteau bid $5,360 to supply and carry the annuities to the tribes, and David D. Mitchell, whom the Whigs reappointed Superintendent of Indian Affairs in St. Louis in place of Thomas Harvey, accepted the bid, let the contract, and indicated to the American Fur Company, by his co-operative attitude, that the Indian Office at St. Louis was not becoming an anti-Chouteau stronghold.[15] When Mitchell replaced Harvey, Agent Matlock was succeeded by a subagent, William S. Hatton of Tennessee, who protested that his salary was insufficient, his expense account inadequate, and his character subject to attack by any disgruntled trader.[16] Nevertheless, he reported to Mitchell that "the law of Congress prohibiting the introduction of ardent spirits into the Indian country has . . . been strictly observed." He charged that prices of Indian trade goods were unjustly high,

[14] W. D. Hodgkiss to A. Drips, January 30, 1849, Drips (Andrew) Papers, MoSHi; James Kipp (?) to Pierre Chouteau, Jr., and Company, February 12, 1849, and numerous other letters of February and March, 1849, in the Ft. Pierre Letter Book, 1849–1850, MoSHi; Deposition of Joseph Urbin, May 15, 1849, Chouteau Family Papers, MoSHi; *Saint Louis Daily Union*, March 20, 1849.

[15] David D. Mitchell to William Medill, May 11, 1849, Letters Received, OIA, RG 75, NA.

[16] Larpenteur, *Forty Years*, II, 417.

however, and requested funds to build an agency so that he would not be compelled to find shelter by traveling from trading post to trading post, "thus causing a great degree of jealousy among the different traders."[17]

Hatton's observations on the Upper Missouri liquor trade were, evidently, as accurate as any for the period between 1846, when the liquor suits began, and the early fifties. Throughout the early forties, the American Fur Company had shipped, as regularly as possible, moderate supplies of alcohol to the upriver posts, but when the bonds of the Company were placed in suit in the spring of 1846, Forts Union and Lewis were extremely short of alcohol for the Assiniboin and Blackfoot trade, despite Honoré Picotte's promise to James Kipp in the previous December that enough "grog" would be delivered upriver for the spring trade. In the fall of 1846, Father De Smet estimated that the liquor traffic on the Upper Missouri was at a standstill. He was correct, since neither the American Fur Company nor the opposition dared to ship much liquor by the Missouri River route until the liquor controversy in the court simmered down. The American Fur Company looked to Minnesota for an emergency supply of alcohol for the Upper Missouri, but H. H. Sibley advised Chouteau that it was "altogether out of the question" to transport alcohol across the Minnesota country from Mendota to the Missouri posts. He said it might be feasible, however, in light of the government crackdown on the liquor trade, to supply the Upper Missouri by cart from "the British Colony at Red River, where there [were] several private stills."[18]

The dozen liquor suits against the American Fur Company and

[17] First quotation from William S. Hatton to David D. Mitchell, October 5, 1849, 31 Cong., 1 sess., *SED No. 1*, p. 1075; second quotation from William S. Hatton to David D. Mitchell, October 20, 1850, 31 Cong., 2 sess., *SED No. 1*, p. 74.

[18] Quotation from H. H. Sibley to Pierre Chouteau, Jr., and Company, February 23, 1846, Chouteau Family Papers, MoSHi. See also Bradley, "Affairs," *CHSM*, III, 246; Chittenden and Richardson, *Father de Smet*, II, 595; Honoré Picotte to James Kipp, December 18, 1845, to J. A. Sire, March 10, 1846, and to Pierre Chouteau, Jr., and Company, March 10, 1846, Ft. Pierre Letter Book, 1845–1846, MoSHi.

its agents were continued time and again, "at costs of defendants," from one session to another of the Circuit Court, District of Missouri, during 1847 and 1848. While Company officials applied behind-the-scenes political pressure on the Indian Office, Chouteau's lawyers searched for a compromise solution to the suits and delayed them in court by well-chosen legal technicalities. Witnesses for the government failed consistently to appear before the court. "Several very important" ones died between 1846 and 1848, others were enticed into American Fur Company service and assigned to trading posts far beyond the reach of a court summons, and at least one, "taken with the small-pox," was too sick to testify. District Attorney Gantt believed, correctly, that the Company planned to delay the cases as long as possible, that it was guilty of the charges against it, and that its trading licenses should be revoked once it was found guilty by the court. In May, 1848, Gantt took depositions in St. Louis from Alexander Harvey and two other witnesses for the government and asked that the Treasury reimburse Harvey for the expense of his overland trip, undertaken at Gantt's request, from Fort Campbell to St. Louis in the winter of 1847–48. Gantt's impression of Harvey was decidedly favorable—contrary to the impression held by so many of the fur traders.[19]

During the summer of 1848, Chouteau's political pressure on the Indian Office paid dividends. The Commissioner of Indian Affairs seemed "liberally disposed" toward the Company, "less vigorous" in tone than previously, and Senator Benton anticipated "no further trouble" for the Company.[20] By August, Gantt was under heavy fire from Company advocates, who charged him with

[19] Thomas Gantt to the Solicitor of the Treasury, May 30, 1848, and Reports of Thomas Gantt to the Solicitor of the Treasury, May 25, 1847, and April 21, 1848, SOT, RG 206, NA; Pierre Chouteau, Jr., and Company to A. Drips, April 24, 1847, Drips (Andrew) Papers, MoSHi; Thomas Gantt to the Solicitor of the Treasury, April 25, 1848, Letters Received, OIA, RG 75, NA.

[20] Thomas H. Benton to Pierre Chouteau, Jr., and Company (?), June 23, 1848, Chouteau Family Papers, MoSHi.

"zeal far beyond the discharge of any official duty" and "feelings of personal hostility" toward Pierre Chouteau's interests.[21] J. F. A. Sanford, in a letter to the Commissioner, branded Gantt a "heated partisan," more a "private enemy" of the American Fur Company "than . . . an officer anxious for the public good." Gantt defended himself as best he could under the barrage, but it was obvious that the Company had won the ear of his superiors and that he could not prevent a compromise in the liquor suits.[22]

On December 5, 1848, Chouteau wrote Commissioner William Medill and asked him if the government would consider a compromise proposition in the liquor contest. Chouteau feared that if the suits were prolonged, the American Fur Company would be denied future trading privileges on the Upper Missouri, and he noted to the Commissioner that the Company wished to avoid further court costs. His letter referred to the "conflicting testimony of . . . witnesses," to Harvey's "bad character," and placed the burden of guilt upon Chardon (who had died and could not defend himself) and upon other "obnoxious" Company employees who might have violated the liquor law, but "not under [Company] instruction."[23] A month later, Chouteau wrote to Gantt and to Superintendent Harvey offering $5,000 plus court costs as a reasonable settlement to cover American Fur Company bonds for the period 1843–46. Commissioner Medill had agreed earlier to exclude the Company bond of 1842 from specific charges and had asked Chouteau, Gantt, and Superintendent Harvey to work out the details of a final settlement. Chouteau argued that the government was partially responsible for the upriver liquor traffic, since the Indian Intercourse Law of 1834 was a "dead letter" before Harvey took office; stressed that the Company was

[21] Thomas Gantt to the Solicitor of the Treasury, August 11, 1848, Letters Received, OIA, RG 75, NA.
[22] John F. A. Sanford to William Medill, May 9, 1848, *ibid.*
[23] Pierre Chouteau, Jr., and Company to William Medill, December 5, 1848, *ibid.* The "Cases Decided List" of October 12, 1848 (SOT, RG 206, NA), notes that the suit against Chardon had been dropped because of the defendant's death.

115

"the right arm of the government on the upper Missouri"; and pressed for a conclusion of the controversy before Commissioner Medill left office.[24]

Although Gantt estimated that the government stood to gain more than $7,500 if the suits were taken to trial, he also sensed that he had lost control of the cases, and recommended to the Commissioner that the government compromise at possibly $7,500 plus costs, since the Company had confessed its guilt to some extent. Superintendent Harvey, naïvely convinced that the Company had learned to respect the Indian laws and unwilling to throw the upriver tribes upon the mercy of other traders should the American Fur Company lose its trading rights on the Upper Missouri, endorsed Chouteau's rather than Gantt's interpretation of a reasonable compromise. Before the end of January, 1849, the Secretary of War approved a compromise sum of $5,000 plus court costs—the Chouteau solution—and ordered Gantt to settle the cases in the April term of the Circuit Court. Chouteau assured Gantt that the Company respected the District Attorney's "sense of duty" shown in the cases and hoped that the suits had created no "unpleasant feelings" between the fur company and either the District Attorney's or the Superintendent's offices![25]

Renewal of the Company's trading license on February 15, 1849, shortly after Chouteau learned that the Indian Office had instructed Gantt to accept a $5,000 compromise, indicated that the government was not vindictive toward the American Fur Company and was prepared, at least publicly, to place all Upper Missouri trading ventures on an equal level. Chouteau's cousin

[24] Pierre Chouteau, Jr., and Company to T. H. Harvey and Thomas Gantt, January 12, 1849, Letters Received, OIA, RG 75, NA.

[25] Thomas Gantt to T. H. Harvey, January 13, 1849, *ibid.;* T. H. Harvey to William Medill, January 15, 1849, Clark (William) Papers, KHi; Pierre Chouteau, Jr., and Company to Thomas Gantt, February 12, 1849, Chouteau Family Papers, MoSHi; William Medill to the Solicitor of the Treasury, January 30, February 24, 1849, and Thomas Gantt to the Solicitor of the Treasury, February 12, 1849, SOT, RG 206, NA. The cases were finally settled (in court) on April 4, 1849 (see Complete and Final Record, United States Circuit Court, District of Missouri, Vol. 3, 1841–1850, pp. 401–50, and Files of Cases No. 433 and 443–53, FRC, KC).

(and Sarpy's son-in-law), Frederick Berthold, and William Waddington, a wealthy St. Louis real estate broker, stood surety on the trading-license bond. By the second week in May, Chouteau, with trading license in hand, liquor suits compromised, and the Indian-annuity contract won, ordered the steamboat *Martha* stocked with supplies for the high-river posts. Few onlookers gathered on the levee to watch the loading, however, since a cholera epidemic, spread by steamboat passengers and other travelers, was sweeping up the Mississippi from the South. Incoming mail, freight, and peltries were piled high on the St. Louis water front, since only a few brave dock workers dared touch newly arrived cargo. Nevertheless, American Fur Company hands defied the cholera epidemic and loaded the *Martha*. Late on the evening of May 17, when the vessel stood ready to depart, wind-whipped fire joined pestilence, turned the levee and fifteen blocks of the business district into a midnight inferno, and destroyed the *Martha* and her cargo (total value of boat and cargo, fully insured, amounted to $40,000), including sixty gallons of liquor that Superintendent Mitchell had allowed the Company to ship for medicinal purposes to counteract the cholera.[26]

Before the smoke of the holocaust had cleared away, Company agents were searching for a boat to replace the *Martha*, but few vessels remained intact from the flames and days passed before the Company found and leased the 151-ton steamer *Amelia*, loaded her, and sent her upriver under Captain D. Finch, accompanied by Agent Hatton and the Indian annuities. The *Amelia* left St. Louis on June 9, and after "considerable difficulty and toil" and a brief stop at the Vermillion, reached Colin Campbell's trading house below the Great Bend. The Sioux, afraid that Agent Hatton would turn the annuities over to the traders at Fort Pierre for distribution at Company discretion, "knocked the heads out of

[26] David D. Mitchell to Pierre Chouteau, Jr., and Company, May 12, 1849, and a reference by Pierre Chouteau, Jr., and Company to the cholera in St. Louis, May 14, 1849, Chouteau Family Papers, MoSHi; Volume Entitled "Licenses for Indian Trade," OIA, RG 76, NA; *The Western Boatman*, Vol. I (June, 1849), 395.

[three] barrels of hard tack [sent ashore], which they threw into the river; then they horsewhipped the [crewmen who were loading wood] away from the woodpile, and placed a guard at the line."[27] Without invitation, the chiefs climbed aboard the *Amelia* and demanded that the annuities be unloaded there rather than at Fort Pierre. Agent Hatton, frightened by the red men, distributed coffee and biscuits to the assembled chiefs and ordered the annuities unloaded. The following morning, the *Amelia* headed upriver, and Hatton, after a brief visit with the Sioux, traveled overland to Fort Pierre, where he reboarded the boat for the Yellowstone. Early in August, the vessel, loaded with the upper-country returns, passed downriver from Fort Union to Council Bluffs, where the cargo of robes and furs was transferred to a packet for St. Louis. At Council Bluffs, the *Amelia* took on new cargo for the Company, dashed back upriver to unload her freight at Fort Pierre and to pick up the post's returns, and steamed quickly downriver, reaching St. Louis on the evening of September 14.[28]

Several eminent visitors accepted the hospitality of the Sioux-country posts during the summer of 1849. Colonel Aeneas Mackay, Deputy Quartermaster at St. Louis, accompanied by John Robertson, a minister on a pleasure trip from Scotland, stopped at Fort Pierre "to look out a situation to establish a military post."[29] Another traveler, Dr. John Evans, an associate of David Dale Owen of the United States Geological Survey, studied the geology "over a much larger tract" of the Bad Lands than he had anticipated, examining the area "in consequence of facilities afforded to him by the Fur Company, both in passing rapidly from point to point, on the river, and afterwards in procuring the means of land

27 Quotation from Larpenteur, *Forty Years*, II, 282–83. See also *St. Louis Daily New Era*, September 15, 1849.

28 A. Culbertson to Pierre Chouteau, Jr., and Company, August 2, 31, 1849, and W. D. Hodgkiss (?) to Malcolm Clark, November, 1849, Ft. Pierre Letter Book, 1849–1850, MoSHi; William S. Hatton to David D. Mitchell, October 5, 1849, 31 Cong., 1 sess., *SED No. 1*, pp. 1072–73; *St. Louis Daily New Era*, September 15, 1849; *DMR*, September 15, 1849.

29 W. D. Hodgkiss (?) to James Kipp, August 31, 1849, Ft. Pierre Letter Book, 1849–1850, MoSHi; *DMR*, September 26, 1849.

travel, which he otherwise could not have obtained."[30] Perhaps the most unusual summer visitor, however, was the French soldier of fortune M. E. De Girardin, employed as an artist in Dr. Evans's party, who commented freely upon the "inveterate hate" existing between the two principal fur companies and the willingness of each to do the other "harm." At Fort Pierre, the Company agent graciously honored Dr. Evans and De Girardin with a "most excellent dinner" of buffalo, corn bread, and pemmican. Later, the traders prepared Evans's party Upper Missouri crepes suzette over large bonfires kindled in the center of the post yard. Two violinists, atop a barrel, fiddled for the crowd, and "everyone danced and drank"—each guest with a bottle of whiskey in hand (to ward off the cholera)—"brawled and enjoyed themselves."[31]

In addition to the two cargoes of robes and pelts carried out of the Indian country aboard the *Amelia* in the summer of 1849, the American Fur Company in St. Louis received at least three other shipments from the upper river. On June 3, the steamer *St. Ange,* built by Joseph La Barge, brought down 1,098 packs of robes and 125 packs of skins and furs transferred to the vessel at St. Joseph from four Company mackinaws. Six weeks later, the packets *St. Croix* and *Mustang* together unloaded over 1,200 packs of robes (mackinaw cargoes from the St. Joseph transfer point) at the St. Louis docks. In comparison, however, only one shipment, more than 600 packs of robes on the packet *Mary Blane,* reached St. Louis in July for "R. and W. Campbell" from Harvey, Primeau and Company. The remainder of the opposition returns from the Upper Missouri were brought into St. Louis early in August aboard the *Tamerlane.*[32]

The *Tamerlane,* owned by the Campbells, was a recently built

[30] David D. Owen, *Report of a Geological Survey of Wisconsin, Iowa, and Minnesota,* 194–95.

[31] M. E. De Girardin, "A Trip to the Bad Lands in 1849," *SDHR,* Vol. I (January, 1936), 56–58.

[32] *Weekly Reveille,* June 11, July 23, 1849; *DMR,* June 4, July 17, 1849; *St. Louis Daily New Era,* July 17, 1849; St. Joseph *Gazette,* June 29, 1849. See also several letters of June, 1849, in the Ft. Pierre Letter Book, 1849–1850, MoSHi.

(1846) light-draft steamboat, one of the "very strongest and best secured" double-engine boats on the Missouri River, and was thirty tons lighter than the *Amelia*. One hundred traders, passengers, and crewmen had left St. Louis with the *Tamerlane* when she headed upriver on June 16, piled high with freight for Harvey, Primeau and Company posts. A month later (July 21), the vessel unloaded cargo at Fort William, then edged upriver a few miles above the mouth of the Yellowstone and put ashore freight to be carried to Fort Campbell in smaller boats. On July 23, the *Tamerlane* started downriver, met the *Amelia*, and took Agent Hatton aboard, but landed him at the Great Bend, where he found land transportation to the Vermillion. Although thirty men were stricken with cholera while the *Tamerlane* ascended the Missouri, only one man died of the plague; yet the *Amelia* lost nine to the cholera, and more than two dozen traders deserted the boat along the river. The clerk of the *Tamerlane* reported, when the boat docked in St. Louis on August 8, that a "good deal" of cholera existed in the Platte River Indian camps and that the Sioux had attacked the Hidatsa settlement adjoining Fort Berthold. The attack was repulsed, but the Sioux promised to return to harass the village and the fort.[33] By design and service, the *Tamerlane* seemed well suited to the upriver trade. Unfortunately, however, she struck a snag while on a routine Lower Missouri voyage in the fall of 1849, her hull broke in two, and she sank "nearly to her boiler deck," a total loss.[34]

By the end of the year, 1849, the American Fur Company had accumulated a substantial return in robes and furs and was no longer weighted down by the pessimism so evident in Company ranks earlier in the year. Harvey, Primeau and Company had made a much smaller return and the partners in the business, according to rumor, were quarreling. In the Sioux country, American Fur Company traders speculated that the opposition might give up

[33] William S. Hatton to David D. Mitchell, October 5, 1849, 31 Cong., 1 sess., *SED No. 1*, pp. 1072–73; *DMR*, August 8, 1846, August 9, 1849; *St. Louis Daily New Era*, August 9, 1849.

[34] *DMR*, October 17, 21, 1849.

during the winter, and in the Blackfoot country, five of Harvey's men deserted Fort Campbell "from want of food" and Malcolm Clark, at Fort Benton, gave them transportation downriver to American Fur Company posts. Although Company traders sensed dissension in opposition ranks, Harvey's trade at Fort William was holding strong, and experienced American Fur Company men along the river knew that they must continue to compete with the opposition as vigorously as ever over the winter of 1849–50.[35] Hodgkiss wrote that "the motto [at Fort Pierre] is now to get the Robe as cheap as possible and [make] our opponents pay as high as possible." He also reported to St. Louis that Company traders secretly carried large amounts of personal supplies to the upriver posts to avoid buying necessities at Company stores. Traders who refused to deal with Company stores were not only a threat to Company business but might at any time go over to the opposition and take their goods with them.[36]

Contrary to the expectations of some American Fur Company traders, the opposition survived the winter of 1849–50 and accumulated a large stock of robes, despite several Indian-trader skirmishes. Unusually mild weather in December, January, and February encouraged moderate barter in the Blackfoot country, but the Mandans and Hidatsas, swept by cholera carried upriver on the steamboats, brought in few robes or furs, and the Sioux were likely to return to the warpath in the spring. The average Upper Missouri trading post was unprepared for a long Indian siege, but since any post that served a particular tribe was regarded as fair plunder by all enemies of that tribe, most traders convinced the red men that trading posts were too strong to be taken by Indian assault, or resorted to fair trade and favors to replace fear

[35] W. D. Hodgkiss (?) to Joseph Desautel, November 16, 1849, Ft. Pierre Letter Book, 1849–1850, MoSHi; Malcolm Clark to A. Culbertson, November 5, 1849, and Edwin T. Denig to A. Culbertson, December 1, 1849, Chouteau Family Papers, MoSHi.

[36] Quotation from W. D. Hodgkiss (?) to Malcolm Clark, November, 1849, Ft. Pierre Letter Book, 1849–1850, MoSHi. See also W. D. Hodgkiss to Pierre Chouteau, Jr., and Company, February 14, 1850, Chouteau Family Papers, MoSHi.

with gratitude and, possibly, peace. Indians seldom openly attacked a post unless they were greatly superior in numbers to the garrison, yet a small war party might surround a fort for days, cut off the water supply of a post without a well, drive off stock, and pillage fields and outlying buildings. Parties of traders away from the posts "soon learned that the nature of their reception by any Indians met en route depended, not upon themselves [as much as it did] upon the conduct of the last party of white men with whom said Indians had had contact."[37]

Upriver intertribal warfare, the spread of cholera from Missouri (5,200 people died of it in St. Louis in 1849) to the Dakota country, and the slow but sure push of settlers into the Indian hunting grounds of Iowa and Minnesota were problems for the policy makers of the American Fur Company and the opposition to reflect upon in the new year, 1850. Three years earlier, the Potawatomi, Chippewa, and Ottawa Indians had moved from the new state of Iowa to lands west of the Missouri to make way for some of the tens of thousands of white settlers that Iowa soon claimed. North of Iowa, Congress created Minnesota Territory in 1849, with a western border running from the White Earth River south along the Upper Missouri to the Big Sioux. Although in earlier years the jurisdiction of Louisiana, Missouri, Michigan, and Wisconsin territories had extended as far west, Minnesota Territory was much closer than they to the Upper Missouri, and in due time its leaders might govern the area—contrary to the best interests of the St. Louis fur companies. For the moment, however, the St. Louis traders hoped that politicians in Minnesota would ignore the land of the Teton Sioux and that the cholera death rate on the upper river would drop in 1850.[38]

The first reliable news of the opposition's profitable winter trade reached St. Louis early in April, 1850, when two traders from Fort Bouis disembarked from the packet *Haydee* with ex-

[37]Quotation from Irene Paden, *The Wake of the Prairie Schooner*, 123. See also Kurz, *Journal*, 171–72; Father Point, "Journey," *Mid-America*, XIII, 240–41.

[38]Edward M. Douglas, *Boundaries, Areas, Geographic Centers and Altitudes of the United States and the Several States*, 195, 197, 206–207.

press dispatches for Robert Campbell and told the press that Harvey soon would send down four thousand packs of robes. Five weeks later, on May 13, Harvey and another trader, James Russell, arrived in St. Louis and told an amazing story of their dangerous descent from Fort Campbell in the Blackfoot country. They left the post on April 2, accompanied by two other traders, rowing a large skiff through high water and jagged, shore-bound ice. A few miles below the fort, they were summoned ashore by an Assiniboin-Crow war party, but they refused to land. The Indians fired a ball or two through the boat, but, fortunately, ended the barrage when Harvey called to some of the Crows, who recognized him. At Fort William, two additional traders joined the party. The six men pushed downriver through a three-day blizzard and barely avoided being lured ashore by a Sioux war party that had encamped at an old trading house. On May 1, approximately one hundred miles below Fort Bouis, where another trader had boarded the skiff, the boat was swamped in midriver by a heavy, unexpected wind. The men, thrown into the icy water, lost all their equipment and struggled to hold onto the water-filled craft. One man, who swam for the shore, drowned in the wild water. Two others, numbed by the bitter cold, lost their grip on the boat and sank from sight, and a fourth, shoved across the keel of the skiff by his companions, was carried away by the strong current.[39]

After several minutes in the ice-glazed water, the three survivors pushed the skiff atop a bar. One man, unable to find shelter on the wind-swept island, died a few feet from the river's edge. Harvey and Russell crawled into a hollow in the sand, where they dried out and revived. When they were able to walk, they bailed out the boat, paddled it—with an oar broken in two—from the bar to the main shore, and kindled a fire with a steel which had accidentally hooked onto the boat. Later, as they paddled downriver, they found a sack and a bottle of coffee and Harvey's trunk. Above the Vermillion, they met three of Harvey's mackinaws,

[39] *DMR*, April 5, May 14, 1850.

123

took on supplies and two men, and continued to Liberty, Missouri, where they transferred to a packet. Harvey recuperated in St. Louis, renewed his trading license, and talked over business prospects with the Campbells.[40] A few weeks later at Fort Pierre, Joseph Picotte told American Fur Company traders that Bouis and Primeau were "heartily sick of their association with Harvey" and had planned to dissolve the partnership in 1850, but had learned, when Harvey arrived on the upper river early in July, that they were bound to the firm for another year.[41] Perhaps Picotte's story of dissension in the opposition was true, perhaps false (since the American Fur Company always encouraged such rumors), yet true or false, the tale did not shatter the agreement built by Harvey, Primeau, Bouis, and Picotte.

Harvey returned to the Indian country aboard the new steamboat *St. Ange*, a rather plush vessel with 32 staterooms. On June 13, the steamer, filled with approximately 150 tons of freight and 75 Mountain Men, had shoved away from St. Louis for the upper river. La Barge piloted her to the Yellowstone (on July 8) and back to St. Louis (on July 19) in a record 36 days. Three or four men died of cholera during the voyage (two of them, however, were "addicted to drinking" and may have succumbed to cirrhosis of the liver instead of the plague), but otherwise the trip was as dull as the daily menu of beans, salt pork, hominy, corn meal, and, when available, wild game.[42] Only a small cargo of robes and furs reached St. Louis on the *St. Ange*, since most of the opposition-company returns of 1850 were shipped downriver by mackinaw, to be picked up by packets between Council Bluffs and St. Joseph. One of the three opposition mackinaws that Harvey and Russell met near the Vermillion in early May sank 60 miles above Council

[40] *Ibid.*, May 14, 1850; Volume Entitled "Licenses for Indian Trade," OIA RG 76, NA.

[41] Quotation from W. D. Hodgkiss (?) to Pierre Chouteau, Jr., and Company, July 13, 1850, Ft. Pierre Letter Book, 1849-1850, MoSHi.

[42] *DMR*, March 4, 18, 1849, June 8, 13, July 20, 1850; *St. Louis Daily New Era*, June 4, July 20, 1850; *Weekly Reveille*, June 17, July 22, 1850; *Saint Louis Daily Union*, July 20, 22, 1850; St. Joseph *Gazette*, July 17, 1850; Branch, *Hunting the Buffalo*, 112.

Bluffs later in the month, but the cargo of the other two boats was put aboard the steamer *Saranac* at Council Bluffs and delivered safely in St. Louis. Additional cargoes of robes and furs, divided about equally between the American Fur Company and the opposition, were unloaded in St. Louis from the packets *Pocahontas, Saluda, Robert Campbell*, and *Robert Fulton* before the end of the summer.[43]

The American Fur Company chartered the steamboat *El Paso* (260 tons) at $1,200 per month to carry its 1850 expedition to the upper river. The loyal, experienced Company riverboatman John Durack steered the vessel away from the St. Louis levee at noon, May 11, and ran her upriver through days "generally cool and pleasant, with occasionally a severe gale or heavy rain." Cholera was aboard the crowded boat, however, and cut the passenger list by at least a half-dozen before the vessel reached Fort Pierre. The channel, unpredictable as usual, led the *El Paso* onto two sharp snags. The first crushed the boat's blacksmith shop and carried the bellows overboard; the second splintered three or four beams in the hold and held the boat fast until crewmen, in a yawl, chopped away the forest in the channel. Peaceful Indian bands visited the boat at points along the river, and after short stops at Forts Pierre, Clark, and Union, Captain Durack took advantage of an unusually deep channel to land the remainder of the freight eight miles above the mouth of Milk River. There a passenger nailed a hastily lettered sign to a tree to commemorate the day, June 20, 1850, when the *El Paso* landed at the highest point ever reached, to that date, by a steamboat on the Missouri[44]

After the freight was unloaded at the mouth of the Milk River—left in charge of ten men, who cordelled it to Fort Benton in a

[43] *Saint Louis Daily Union*, May 22, 30, June 3, 1850; *Weekly Reveille*, May 27, June 3, 1850; *St. Louis Daily New Era*, May 22, July 5, 1850; *St. Louis Intelligencer*, July 1, 6, 1850; *DMR*, May 17, September 23, 1850; *Daily St. Louis Times*, July 6, 1850.

[44] Quotation from *St. Louis Daily New Era*, July 8, 1850. See also *DMR*, April 30, May 7, 15, July 7, 8, 1850; *Weekly Reveille*, May 13, 1850; *St. Louis Intelligencer*, July 8, 1850; *Daily St. Louis Times*, July 8, 1850; *St. Joseph Gazette*, May 17, 1850.

smaller boat—the steamer turned downriver past large herds of buffalo, deer, and elk to Forts Union and Pierre, and on July 6, reached St. Louis with a cargo of robes, furs, and elk horns. The 56-day round trip took at least a week longer than the Company expected, however, because upriver woodcutters had failed to stack sufficient cords at key landings along the Missouri. Since the lower river was extremely shallow during the month of July, some St. Louis observers predicted that the *El Paso* and *St. Ange* would be forced to wait on the upper river for an autumn rise or might even spend the winter in the Indian country. Nevertheless, and fortunately for both fur companies, the steamers challenged the low channel and reached St. Louis, the *St. Ange* ahead of and the *El Paso* slightly behind schedule.[45]

On the Upper Missouri, chief Company agent Alexander Culbertson replaced Fort Alexander on the Yellowstone with a new post, Fort Sarpy, and started to rebuild Fort Benton in adobe. Fort (John B.) Sarpy, named after the Company partner (some traders, however, preferred to call it by the name of the older post, Fort Alexander, or even to combine the names into Fort Alexander Sarpy), was built during the warmer months of 1850 on the north bank of the Yellowstone just below the mouth of the Rosebud. Kentuckian Robert Meldrum, son of a Presbyterian circuit rider, was placed in charge of the new fort. He was an experienced American Fur Company trader, an authority on the Crows' language and customs, and had commanded Fort Alexander before it was torn down. "Round Iron," as the Crows called Meldrum, had intermarried with them, survived a number of intertribal battles, and was the perfect Company man to continue the dangerous Crow trade.[46] When Meldrum was settled at Fort Sarpy, Culbertson took advantage of mild autumn weather and reconstructed Fort Benton in the Blackfoot country. Part of the

[45] W. D. Hodgkiss (?) to Pierre Chouteau, Jr., and Company, June 30, 1850, Ft. Pierre Letter Book, 1849–1850, MoSHi.

[46] McDonnell, "Forts Benton and Sarpy," *CHSM*, X, 282–83 (n. 145), 284–85 (n. 153); Jessie T. Teal to C. N. Kessler, February 21, 1918, Montana Manuscripts Collection, CLUC; Bradley, "Affairs," *CHSM*, III, 261.

old log post was dismantled and rebuilt with slabs of adobe ("doughboys" measuring six by fifteen inches)—the technique borrowed from the Spanish in the Southwest—made from wild grass mixed with Missouri River bottom mud. Adobe buildings were definitely superior to log structures, were fire resistant, gave better defense against Indian attack, defied rot, and were cool in summer and warm in winter. Other Upper Missouri posts, notably Forts Campbell and William, in addition to Fort Benton were built or rebuilt with adobe in the forties, fifties, and sixties, proof that practical architectural ideas circulated on the fur frontier.[47]

Culbertson not only gave considerable time, in 1850, to trading-post construction, but eagerly assisted his young half-brother, Thaddeus, a Princeton divinity student who was collecting scientific specimens in the Indian country. Thaddeus Culbertson was not the first amateur or professional scientist to find interesting the animals, plant life, and geology of the Upper Missouri country, but he was the first to work over the area with the assistance of a close relative in the fur trade who knew the countryside in detail and believed scientific collecting important. The geology of the Bad Lands and the upper river, particularly, caught the attention of scientists in the years before the Civil War, when the study of geology and paleontology advanced significantly, both nationally and internationally. Nicollet reported to Congress that when he toured the Upper Missouri in 1839, he received from fur traders valuable specimens of "the larger mammiferae," but did not bring them downriver because of poor transportation.[48] Between 1843 and 1845, however, Alexander Culbertson picked up fossils and bones in the Bad Lands and gave a few of them to his father, Joseph Culbertson, for presentation to the Academy of Natural

---

[47] McDonnell, "Forts Benton and Sarpy," *CHSM*, X, 3, 37, 40, 75–76, 246 (n. 6); Bradley, "Affairs," *CHSM*, III, 264. Adobe building and rebuilding at Fort Benton continued until 1860, at a total cost of $10,000. See George F. Weisel (ed.), *Men and Trade on the Northwest Frontier as Shown by the Fort Owen Ledger*, xxxviii.

[48] "Report to Illustrate a Map of the Upper Mississippi," 28 Cong., 2 sess., *HED* No. 52, p. 41.

Sciences of Philadelphia and, presumably, to Dr. Hiram A. Prout, a St. Louis physician and mineralogist. In an 1847 issue of *The American Journal of Science and Arts*, Dr. Prout described one of the specimens, "a Fossil Maxillary Bone of a Paleotherium," from the Bad Lands and directed the attention of scientists to the Upper Missouri country.[49]

"Due chiefly to the fossils that the fur traders began to bring from the hills and to the descriptions of them that appeared in scientific journals," Dr. John Evans surveyed the geology of the Bad Lands between 1849 and 1851;[50] the American Fur Company offered Dr. Prout free transportation upriver to continue his study of paleontology, since "the members of the [fur] company . . . [were] very ready to do anything to promote collections" on the Upper Missouri; and the Dakota country was recognized as a vast storehouse of fossils.[51] Thaddeus Culbertson, anxious to go west to overcome a persistent cough, relied upon his half-brother Alexander and the American Fur Company to give him most of the assistance he needed to visit the Bad Lands. Cousin Ferdinand Culbertson, also an Upper Missouri trader, and the entire Culbertson family in Pennsylvania encouraged Thaddeus to make the trip, and Professor Spencer F. Baird of the Smithsonian contributed two hundred dollars (Alexander paid for all additional expenses) toward the cost of the journey, expecting in return a collection of natural-history specimens for the national museum. The two Culbertson brothers left St. Louis aboard the packet *Mary Blane* on March 19, 1850, landed at St. Joseph, and proceeded overland, on a route generally parallel with the Missouri, to Fort Pierre. From the fort they moved westward for a three-week collecting tour in the Bad Lands, then returned to the river, where

[49] Hiram A. Prout, "Description of a Fossil Maxillary Bone of a Paleotherium, from near White River," *The American Journal of Science and Arts*, Vol. III, Second Series (1847), 248.

[50] Thomas A. Rickard, *A History of American Mining*, 203.

[51] Quotation from Thaddeus Culbertson to S. F. Baird, March 16, 1850, Spencer F. Baird Private Letters, DSI. In 1853, Dr. Prout said his medical practice in St. Louis was too "lucrative" to permit him to ascend the Missouri on a collecting trip. See Hiram A. Prout to James Hall, April 27, 1853, Hall (James) Papers, NLA.

they boarded the *El Paso,* which was bound upstream to the mouth of Milk River. On the return trip, Alexander left the steamer at Fort Union, but Thaddeus continued downriver to St. Louis and on to the East, where he died, late in August, of consumption.[52]

Although Professor Baird was shocked by Thaddeus' sudden death, he was extremely satisfied with the collection of Dakota animal skulls, skins, and skeletons, as well as plants, that the young collector had given the Smithsonian. Two years later, Professor Joseph Leidy, the eminent anatomist and paleontologist, described many of the fossil mammals and reptiles, gathered so carefully by the Culbertsons and Dr. Evans, in one of the outstanding scientific papers of the day. Meanwhile, in 1851, Professor Baird edited and published, as an appendix to the Smithsonian Institution's fifth annual report, a copy of a portion of the journal Thaddeus Culbertson kept on his trip to the Bad Lands. The journal (Baird called it the most valuable Upper Missouri report since Lewis and Clark) referred favorably to the American Fur Company and gave Chouteau good reason to patronize science on the upper river.[53]

A few months after Thaddeus Culbertson had returned to his death in the East, Baird sent hearty personal thanks to the American Fur Company and to its agent, Edwin Denig, for the assistance given the Smithsonian; the Board of Regents of the Smithsonian, under a resolution made by Jefferson Davis, voted official thanks to the Company and to Alexander and Ferdinand Culbertson, Denig, and traders Charles E. Galpin (of Fort Pierre) and Schlegel (of Vermillion Post) for their co-operation in Thaddeus' work.[54] Actually, many of the animal specimens presented to the Smith-

[52] Culbertson, *Journal,* 1–14.

[53] S. F. Baird to Ferdinand Culbertson, February 15, 1851, and to A. Culbertson, March 24, 1851, February 15 (?), 1852, Spencer F. Baird Letters Written, 1 and 2, DSI. See also Joseph Leidy, "Description of the Remains of Extinct Mammalia and Chelonia, from Nebraska Territory," in Owen, *Report,* 539–72.

[54] S. F. Baird to Pierre Chouteau, Jr., and Company, March 27, 1851, and Joseph Henry to A. Culbertson, March 26, 1851, Spencer F. Baird Letters Written, 1, DSI.

sonian were collected and prepared by Denig at Fort Union. When Audubon visited the Upper Missouri in 1843, Denig assisted him in collecting animal specimens and Indian curiosities and gave him a detailed written account of the history of Fort Union. After Audubon's visit, Denig collected many natural-history specimens and in 1850 offered fatherly advice about collecting to Thaddeus Culbertson when the young scientist stopped at Fort Union. With Baird's encouragement, Denig, Alexander Culbertson, and a few friends continued to collect on the Upper Missouri during the fifties and forwarded box after box of fossils, bones, stuffed animals, and animal skins to museums in St. Louis and the East.[55]

[55] S. F. Baird to Edwin T. Denig, March 24, 1851, March 31, 1855, *ibid.*, 1 and 2; Edwin T. Denig to A. Culbertson, December 1, 1849, Chouteau Family Papers, MoSHi; "Fifth Annual Report of the Board of Regents of the Smithsonian Institution," 32 Cong., 1 sess., *SMD No. 1*, p. 42.

CHAPTER SIX

"Rapacity, envy and sickly emulation"

PIERRE CHOUTEAU'S SON, Charles Pierre, had returned to St. Louis in 1845 after three years' service in the London office of the American Fur Company. Charles was an energetic, well-educated, rather handsome young man, "perfectly polite . . . quiet . . . very discreet" as a friend later said, who assumed, as his father grew older, greater responsibility in Pierre Chouteau, Jr., and Company. In 1850, for the first time, Charles stood surety on the Company's Upper Missouri trading license, and, since he had studied the rudiments of engineering, took a personal interest in navigation problems faced by steamboat pilots on the upper river.[1] He learned thoroughly the complexities of the Company's Indian-country business and the endless details of the day-by-day conduct of the St. Louis office. He saw how the Company, interwoven as it was into the fabric of the entire St. Louis business community, touched small artisans—blacksmiths and carpenters—who fashioned beaver traps, tomahawks, and barrels for the robe and fur trade; steamboatmen; local furriers who traded in finished fur products; and auctioneers, who might, unless watched closely, send runners into "all the thoroughfares leading to the City" to buy up all the deer "skins coming to Market at high rates . . . for the express purpose of selling them" at an exorbitant profit.[2] By the late fifties, after a dozen years of training, Charles knew the

[1] Quotation from White, *Morgan Journals*, 199. See also Beckwith, *Creoles*, 58–59.
[2] Quotation from Fur Dealers Agreement of January 8, 1851, Chouteau Family Papers, MoSHi. See also *DMR*, March 12, 1851, August 19, 1853; St. Louis business directories for the years 1850–59.

fur business and replaced his father, almost entirely, in Company affairs.

Inventories at upriver posts remained high throughout the early fifties (approximately $112,300 for 1854 alone) and few old partners voiced an opinion in Company policy. Sanford withdrew from the business in 1851, and both Sire and Sarpy died within the next six years. Fewer and fewer "relics of the old set" of Mountain Men and *voyageurs* remained active in the upper-river trade, and none exercised authority in the St. Louis office of the Company. The principal upriver agents—Culbertson, Kipp, Denig, Hodgkiss, Malcolm Clark, Charles E. Galpin, and Andrew Dawson—held small portions, amounting to a half or a full share each, of the Upper Missouri Outfit of the Company and received annually a percentage of the profit of the Outfit proportionate to individual shares. The agents did not hold shares of stock in Pierre Chouteau, Jr., and Company, however, although the Company held substantial shares, usually eight of twelve, in the annual Upper Missouri Outfit.[3]

Culbertson, Kipp, Denig, and Hodgkiss were "of the old set" only by liberal interpretation of the term, and Clark, Galpin, and Dawson were never members of that exclusive group. Malcolm Clark was born on a frontier military post and attended West Point, where William Tecumseh Sherman, his classmate, remembered him as a "remarkably bright, open-hearted, and high-spirited young man." Instead of following a professional military career, however, Clark sought adventure in the Texas Revolution and about 1840, entered the American Fur Company trade on the Upper Missouri. He served the Company, except for a brief period as an independent trader, until the mid-sixties, when he retired to a ranch in Montana. Clark, known to the Indians by several names ("Four Bears" for his grizzly-killing prowess and "The

[3] Pierre Chouteau, Jr., and Company Inventories, Business Agreements, and Share Distribution Lists, 1851–1854, Chouteau Family Papers, MoSHi; St. Joseph *Gazette*, February 2, 1853.

White Lodge Pole" for his height and fair skin), intermarried with the Blackfeet and fathered a brood of halfblood children.[4]

Andrew Dawson, who hailed from Scotland, joined the American Fur Company as "a good accountant" in the late forties, was soon promoted to chief trader at Fort Clark, and then, for ten years, ruled Fort Benton. Although a "genial and hospitable host," he was a heavy drinker and in 1858 fell into the cellar at Fort Benton and gradually lost the use of his lower limbs. Six years later, he retired to Scotland with his sons and died there in 1871, as the *Glendive* (Montana) *Times* candidly remarked, "detested by himself and everyone surrounding him." Charles E. Galpin wandered into the Dakota country in 1839, married into the Sioux Nation, and traded along the Missouri River for thirty years, first with the American Fur Company and later as an army sutler and storekeeper on an Indian reservation.[5]

By the early 1850's, daily life at Upper Missouri posts had settled into a monotonous pattern, into a design repeated from the Vermillion to the Falls of the Missouri. The Company bourgeois and chief clerks formed the upper echelon of trading-post society and oversaw salaries, prices, and charges. They—and their guests—ate at the first table, where the best food was served, lived in the most comfortable quarters available at each post, and received from $800 to $2,000 per year in salary plus a share of yearly up-river profits proportionate to their share in the Outfit. Post hunters, who received approximately $400 per year, and workmen (or craftsmen), such as blacksmiths (paid $180–$250 per year), ate the poorer food at the second table, yet ranked ahead of boatmen

[4] Larpenteur, *Forty Years*, II, 241 (n. 5); McDonnell, "Forts Benton and Sarpy," *CHSM*, X, 253 (n. 30); Charlotte O. Van Cleve, *Three Score Years and Ten*, 148–55; Malcolm Clark's Daughter to N. P. Langford, n.d., Typescript, MnHi.

[5] The quotation from the *Glendive Times* appears in Michael A. Leeson, *History of Montana, 1739–1885*, 194. See also McDonnell, "Forts Benton and Sarpy," *CHSM*, X, 266 (n. 42), 305 (n. 282); Weisel, *Fort Owen Ledger*, 164 (n. 1); W. D. Hodgkiss (?) to F. A. Chardon, December 18, 1847, Ft. Pierre Letter Book, 1847–1848, MoSHi.

and assistant workmen who drew $120–$180 per year and ate, directly from the pot, the poorest (or third-class) diet, frequently consisting of "buffalo meat, very odorous" cooked in a "large kettle which was always half full of bouillon three or four days old."

The hunters, workmen, and boatmen were usually in debt to the Company for items bought from the post store. At Fort Union in 1851, coffee, brown sugar, and soap each sold for one dollar per pound, meat cost twenty-five cents per pound, biscuits were seven for a dollar, and calico brought a dollar a yard. The rare frugal employee who ate the post food, owned his own bedclothes or returned those he borrowed from the supply room, craved no luxury goods, made his own clothing or repaired carefully what he possessed, and avoided the Indian women who wanted trinkets from the Company store might save money in the trade.[6]

The average employee, with no stake in the Company and little chance of a salary increase or promotion, was inefficient and avoided work. Since many of the clerks and agents quarreled and drank heavily, they set poor examples for Company employees, and lax discipline encouraged violence. Holiday celebrations, at Christmas and on the Fourth of July, easily evolved from a feast and dance into a drunken brawl, but the sound and feel of post life—fleas and mosquitoes, squealing halfblood children, complaining Indian wives, dirt, smallpox and cholera—could drive even the most even-tempered and understanding trader to the bottle. If a negligent or drunken agent or clerk failed to watch the storeroom, an employee or a visiting Indian might steal valuable merchandise or make off with some of the more unusual furnishings of the post, such as the fireworks, surgical tools, or magic lantern and slides at Fort Union. Trading goods—mirrors and bells from Leipzig; clay pipes from Cologne; beads from Italy; cloth from France; guns and blankets from England; and tools, clothing, firearms, and a great variety of bric-a-brac from American manu-

[6] Quotation from Constant R. Marks (ed.), "Autobiography of Louis Dace Letellier," *SDHC*, Vol. IV (1908), 222. See also Kurz, *Journal*, 129, 234–37; Pierre Chouteau, Jr., and Company Contracts with Employees, May 11–21, 1852, Chouteau Family Papers, MoSHi.

facturers—filled the post supply room and tempted the Indians and the poorly clothed, housed, and fed garrison.[7]

The Indians who visited a post to trade, beg, or leave sick, lame, old, and crippled tribesmen to be cared for by the traders might steal livestock from the fields adjoining the fort, as well as merchandise from the storeroom and furnishings from the post living quarters. In 1850–51, both Forts Benton and Union were stocked with horses, mules, cattle, pigs, oxen, and, at Fort Benton, even a cat. The trading-post cattle that survived hungry traders, thieving Indians, marauding wolves, alkali poisoning, deadly wild plants, and bovine overindulgence in green willows proved to fur traders who left the trade to squat on the public domain that cattle ranching was feasible on the upper river; and the livestock industry of the northern plains took its start in the modest herds belonging to Indian traders.[8]

The winter of 1850–51 was particularly trying for the traders cooped up in Indian-country posts. Smallpox raged "with great severity" in the Sioux camps near Forts Pierre and Bouis, hundreds of Indians died, and by spring, the epidemic had edged downriver to the Poncas and Sacs and Foxes. Cholera, along with smallpox, drove Indian bands from the Missouri Valley to refuge in the Black Hills and to isolated camps, where they threatened to kill any contaminated stranger approaching. Under such circumstances, the winter trade of 1850–51 was poor in the region between the White and Little Missouri rivers. By fall, 1851, the worst of the two epidemics, smallpox, was over and Fort Pierre was again healthy, but at Forts Berthold and Clark, the Indians still died of a severe influenza-type infection and of another kind with choleric symptoms. By then, the traders, who blamed each other for the spread of disease, had vaccinated thousands of panic-

[7] Inventories of Forts Benton, Union, and Alexander in the Chouteau Ledgers, MoSHi; Kurz, *Journal*, 234; Ray H. Mattison, "The Upper Missouri Fur Trade: Its Methods of Operation," *NH*, Vol. 42 (March, 1961), 24–25.

[8] Inventories of Forts Benton, Union, and Alexander in the Chouteau Ledgers, MoSHi; Paden, *Prairie Schooner*, 205, 217, 238, 459; James H. Norwood to David D. Mitchell, September 16, 1852, 32 Cong., 2 sess., *SED No. 1*, p. 359.

stricken Indians for smallpox and had doctored scores of others with whiskey and whatever medicine was on hand, receiving in return neither thanks nor gratitude. Instead, the Indians held the traders responsible for the epidemics and in some instances forced them temporarily to close trading posts under threat of assault.[9]

Alexander Harvey and five or six opposition traders stepped ashore in St. Louis from the steamer *Sacramento* on May 21 and reported additional bad news from the Upper Missouri. Harvey said that when he left Fort Campbell in a small mackinaw in mid-April, after a mild winter, buffalo were so scarce around the head-waters of the Missouri that the Blackfeet and Crows were starving, and the Missouri above the Platte, he said, was extremely low and unfit for steamboat navigation. His company had taken at least seven thousand robes in the winter trade with the Sioux, however, and he fully intended to remain in the fur business. He immediately outfitted a steamboat for a summer trip to the upper river, despite his remarks about the shallow channel, and renewed his trading license with surety from the Campbells and James Christy, a St. Louis wholesale grocer who, although born and raised in Philadelphia, had trained himself as a merchant in a frontier store at Liberty, Missouri.[10]

On July 1, Harvey and more than one hundred of his employees left St. Louis aboard the chartered steamer *Robert Campbell* (just in from St. Joseph with the season's first robe shipment from the Upper Missouri), carrying two hundred tons of freight to the opposition's upriver posts. Harvey intended, if the channel permitted, to take the vessel at least as high as the mouth of Milk River and possibly beyond, but the Missouri remained low throughout the summer and Harvey unloaded his Blackfoot freight at the mouth of the Yellowstone and sent the steamer back to St. Louis on a slight rise. On the way downriver, the boat met

[9] *DMR*, April 28, August 3, October 14, 1851; *Saint Louis Daily Morning Union*, April 28, 1851; *Frontier Guardian* (Kanesville, Iowa), April 18, 1851.

[10] *DMR*, May 22, 1851; *Saint Louis Daily Morning Union*, May 22, 1851; David D. Mitchell to C. E. Mix, July 1, 1851, and Correspondence Relating to Harvey's Licenses of 1850, 1852, and 1853, Clark (William) Papers, KHi.

a severe storm early in August, a few miles below Fort Pierre, and lost both chimneys in the heavy wind. The storm ripped through a large section of the valley above the mouth of the Platte and littered the muddy banks of the Missouri with broken trees for hundreds of miles. The steamer's cargo, one hundred packs of robes and a few skins, was undamaged in the tempest, however, and the boat tied up safely in St. Louis on August 17, fifteen days from the Yellowstone. No smallpox or cholera occurred on board the *Robert Campbell* during the round trip, but one crewman, John Blass, who fell ill on the way upriver and, against his will, was put ashore near Fort Berthold, where he remained with the Indians "a long time," later sued the *boat* for his "great pain, injury and damage."[11]

The opposition's small Upper Missouri return unloaded from the *Robert Campbell* was supplemented during the summer with cargoes of robes and furs landed in St. Louis from the river packets *Alton* and *El Paso*. Two other packets, the *Saranac* and the *Duroc*, each reached the St. Louis levee with robes and furs for both the American Fur Company and the opposition. As usual, the packets had taken on the cargoes from mackinaws near St. Joseph or Council Bluffs, and at least one mackinaw had struck a snag, sank, and lost most of its cargo just short of the transfer point. Dozens of traders and mackinaw *voyageurs* landed in St. Louis on the robe-laden packets and spread the latest rumors of the Upper Missouri epidemics: four to six thousand Indians, but only two whites, they said, had died of the cholera![12] Every bit of upriver news was printed immediately by the newspapers, and in one instance, someone, perhaps an eager reporter, "clandestinely tore off, and carried away the memoranda attached to the [*Duroc's*] manifest

11 *DMR*, July 2, August 18, 1851; *Saint Louis Daily Morning Union*, June 9, July 2, August 18, 1851; *St. Louis Intelligencer*, June 9, 30, July 2, August 18, 1851; Samuel A. Bennett (reporter), *Reports of Cases Argued and Determined in the Supreme Court of the State of Missouri*, XVI, 266–67.

12 *Saint Louis Daily Morning Union*, June 21, 26, July 3, 1851; *DMR*, July 3, 12, 1851; *St. Louis Intelligencer*, June 3, July 12, 1851; *Jefferson Inquirer* (Jefferson City, Missouri), June 7, 1851.

containing news brought by Mr. Papin and others from the upper Missouri."[13]

When the steamer *St. Ange*, rechartered by the American Fur Company for upriver service during the summer of 1851, pulled up to the St. Louis levee on July 27, three weeks in advance of the *Robert Campbell*, her passengers told the newspapers of the boat's extremely difficult round trip to the Yellowstone. Shortly after the *St. Ange* had left St. Louis on June 7 under Captain La Barge, encumbered with a "heavy cargo" of freight and passengers, including Dr. Evans (the geologist), Fathers De Smet and Christian Hoecken, Frederick Berthold, and Mrs. La Barge (supposedly "the first white female" ever to risk a steamboat trip to the mouth of the Yellowstone), cholera struck the boat and rode with it on high water to the Indian country.[14] The Lower Missouri was flooded from bluff to bluff for miles above the mouth of the river, and Captain La Barge, despite dangerous floating debris, was forced by the powerful current to proceed full steam up the chocolate-colored waterway. By the time the boat reached Bellevue, five were dead of cholera and several others seriously ill. Father De Smet, feverish and sick unto death (not of cholera, however), lay confined to his bunk, but Dr. Evans and Father Hoecken, missionary to the Nez Percés, worked tirelessly to comfort the sick and dying—at one time sixty were sick—aboard the floating hospital. Before sunrise on June 19, Father Hoecken, exhausted by overwork, was suddenly stricken with cholera and died a few hours later. That evening, the *St. Ange* anchored at the mouth of the Little Sioux, and in a torchlight service the crew and passengers buried the missionary in "a temporary grave . . . dug in a beautiful forest." Then, to fight the spread of the epidemic, Captain La Barge renovated the boat: unloaded and aired it while the passengers camped on the prairie a few days. Later, on the boat's downriver trip, the crew exhumed Father Hoecken's re-

---

[13] *St. Louis Intelligencer*, June 21, 1851.

[14] Quotation from St. Joseph *Gazette*, June 18, 1851. See also *Saint Louis Daily Morning Union*, June 6, 1851.

mains, over the objections of some passengers, and they were reburied in the Jesuit novitiate at Florissant, Missouri, near St. Louis.[15]

A few days' journey above Father Hoecken's "temporary grave" near the Little Sioux, the trader Schlegel, out of sorts with the American Fur Company because it had forbidden him to sell whiskey to the Indians around the Vermillion, boarded the boat with his Indian wife as it ascended the river and after becoming intoxicated on board, left the vessel to open a Ponca trading post near the Niobrara (L'Eau qui Court) River. On July 4, the *St. Ange* landed at Fort Pierre—by then the cholera epidemic (death toll: fourteen or fifteen) on the boat was over—and unloaded freight for the post. Four days later, the vessel stopped at Fort Clark, where, according to Captain La Barge, White Shield, the Arikara chief, met Father De Smet on the steamboat and asked the missionary to send rain for the drought-stricken Indian corn crop. Father De Smet instructed the chief to return to his lodge and assemble his village elders. When the Indians had gathered, the missionary went to the lodge and prayed for rain. Late in the afternoon, after the red men had feasted aboard the boat, a heavy thunderstorm struck the area, convincing the Indians of Black Robe's medicine.

From his station on the boat, Rudolph F. Kurz, a budding artist and new Company employee, less interested than the missionary in corn crops and rainfall, scanned the post and the Arikara village and "had an interesting view of about 50 girls and women bathing" in the Missouri. "As they thought themselves well concealed," he explained, "they were sportive and animated in a natural way. There were several dainty figures among them—so slender yet round, so supple yet firm. How they splashed and romped behind the partly submerged tree that they thought

[15] Quotation from Chittenden, *Early Steamboat Navigation*, I, 192. See also Chittenden and Richardson, *Father de Smet*, II, 638–44; *Saint Louis Daily Morning Union*, June 2, 6, July 31, 1851; *DMR*, June 21, 1851; Father Pierre Jean De Smet to the Society, January 16, 1852, *Annales de la Propagation de la Foi*, Vol. XXIV (1852), 236–42.

screened them from observation."[16] Kurz disembarked at Fort Berthold, a few miles above the Ree Post, to take up his duties with the Company. Although he was born in Switzerland, at the age of twenty-eight he had traveled to the New World to observe the "romantic life of the American Indian" and the forests, prairies, and wild animals of the American West. He remained on the upper river in Company employ for a year, painted and sketched almost continually, and kept a long, detailed, and very candid journal, in German, of his experiences. His account, later translated into English and published in part, is an outstanding narrative of life at the Upper Missouri posts, particularly at Forts Berthold and Union, in the fifties.[17]

While on the upper river, Kurz painted portraits of Pierre Chouteau, Jr., Joseph Picotte, and Denig, and used Denig's live-animal collection and natural-history specimens (Indian trinkets and stuffed quadrupeds and birds) at Fort Union as models for sketches. He and Denig exchanged ideas on religion, morals, and Indian ethnology and speculated upon the effect of the fur trade on the development of the Upper Missouri country, and Kurz included in his journal considerable information on Indian language, customs, and history. Denig read widely in books and newspapers, shipped upriver on Company steamers, controlled tactfully the heterogeneous group of men under his command at Fort Union, and, encouraged by his friend Father De Smet, prepared a report on the Assiniboins which the missionary incorporated in a published volume (1863) on western missions. Denig also assembled an Assiniboin vocabulary, published in 1854; prepared a short article on medicine amongst the Crees, published the following year; and wrote two lengthy manuscripts, one on the Assiniboins, completed in 1854 and published in 1930, and another on several Upper Missouri tribes, finally published in 1961. Denig's vast Indian experience and scholarly objectivity qualified

[16] Quotation from Kurz, *Journal*, 69–72. See also Chittenden, *Early Steamboat Navigation*, I, 196–98.

[17] Kurz, *Journal*, Foreword.

him better, as John C. Ewers of the Smithsonian notes, "than any other man of his generation to write on the history and ethnology of the Indian tribes of the Upper Missouri." Much of what we know in this generation of the mid-nineteenth-century "buffalo-hunting Indians of the Upper Missouri . . . has been derived from the descriptions of their customs written by those practical businessmen—the fur traders."[18]

After brief stops at Forts Berthold and Union, the *St. Ange* reached the mouth of Poplar River. Since the mid-July channel of the Missouri was too low to allow Captain La Barge to go upriver beyond that point, he unloaded freight destined for the Blackfoot country, then swung the steamer around and rode the current downriver to St. Louis, carrying a large cargo of robes and furs and new Indian-country curiosities: spherical stones from Cannonball River and a caged wild songbird resembling an Old World finch.[19] Father De Smet, who disembarked at Fort Union, accompanied Alexander Culbertson and thirty Indians in a small wagon and cart train overland from the Yellowstone to Fort Laramie to attend a scheduled September meeting between St. Louis Indian Superintendent Mitchell and the northern Plains tribes.

The Great Council, held at Horse Creek below Fort Laramie, began on September 8 and broke up nine days later. Thousands of Indians—Sioux, Assiniboins, Crows, Mandans, Arikaras, Cheyennes, Arapahos, and Hidatsas—encamped in the valley adjoining the treaty ground. Upper Platte River Indian Agent Thomas Fitzpatrick, a former Mountain Man, had personally carried the council invitation to many of the tribes, and assisted Superintendent Mitchell in negotiating the agreement. When Mitchell first

---

[18] Denig, *Five Indian Tribes* (Ewers), xiii, xxxii. Denig also kept records of the weather at Fort Union and sent some of his meteorological observations to Washington (see Weather Bureau Records for Fort Union, August, 1853–June, 1854, NA). Other fur traders—F. G. Riter, for example—supplied the government with additional meteorological data.

[19] *DMR*, July 31, 1851; *Saint Louis Daily Morning Union*, July 31, 1851; *St. Louis Intelligencer*, July 31, 1851; St. Joseph *Gazette*, July 30, 1851.

proposed the meeting to his superiors in Washington in 1849, he stated that a treaty clearly defining tribal boundaries might reduce both intertribal warfare and Indian-white conflict. Increasing migration over the Oregon Trail had caused dozens of incidents between whites and Indians along the overland route and had provoked increasingly louder outcries for concentration of the tribes in well-defined areas. Early in 1851, the Congress, in answer to Mitchell's request and with strong support from the Indian Office and from Senator David R. Atchison of Missouri, appropriated $100,000 to cover the cost of treaty making on the Platte.[20]

On September 17, Mitchell, Fitzpatrick, and chiefs representing all of the assembled tribes, except the Shoshonis, signed a treaty in the presence of Father De Smet, who drew the official map of the newly established tribal boundaries, B. Gratz Brown, editor of the St. Louis *Daily Missouri Republican*, and Mitchell's dragoon escort. Although many of the tribesmen brought together in council (the largest Indian meeting ever held) were "hereditary enemies," they were also anxious "to prove the sincerity of their peaceful and friendly intentions," and, accordingly, "interchanged daily visits . . . smoked and feasted together; exchanged presents [and] adopted each others children."[21] The treaty promised the tribes $50,000 in annuities per year for fifty years in exchange for peace, well-defined tribal boundaries, unmolested white passage along the Platte route, the right of the United States Army to place military posts along the overland trail, and Indian "restitution . . . for any wrongs committed after the ratification" of the treaty.[22] Shortly after the document was signed and the Indians received wagonloads of presents, the meeting broke up and the tribes dispersed to their hunting lands—the Sioux to the Dakota country

[20] Alban W. Hoopes, *Indian Affairs and Their Administration . . . 1849–1860*, 201–203; Ewers, *Blackfeet*, 205–207; LeRoy R. Hafen, "Thomas Fitzpatrick and the First Indian Agency of the Upper Platte and Arkansas," *MVHR*, Vol. XV (December, 1928), 379–80.
[21] David D. Mitchell to Luke Lea, November 11, 1851, in Hoopes, *Indian Affairs*, 204.
[22] *Ibid.*

above the Platte; the Mandans, Arikaras, and Hidatsas to a triangle east of the Yellowstone; the Assiniboins to the country west of the Yellowstone; the Cheyennes and Arapahos to the hills between the Arkansas and the North Platte; and the Crows to the region west of Powder River. The Blackfeet, represented at the council by Alexander Culbertson and Father De Smet, had been assigned hunting grounds in the mountains above the headwaters of the Missouri.

The Senate disregarded the fifty-year annuity provision written into the treaty and reduced it 80 per cent, to ten years with a five-year extension possible at the President's discretion. Only three of the tribes, the Cheyennes, Arapahos, and Sioux, accepted the amendment, but the government considered the treaty in force amongst all signatory Indians and paid annuities for approximately fifteen years.[23] Although the treaty brought little peace to the Platte Valley and northern plains, it extended and increased the annuity business on the Upper Missouri and threw the American Fur Company and its adversaries into thirteen years of hotter-than-ever competition for the annual government contracts.[24] Mitchell returned to St. Louis to preside over the superintendency —officially re-entitled the "Central Superintendency" in 1851— for nearly two more years and to struggle with the American Fur Company over the yearly contracts. In the summer of 1852, he asked the American Fur Company and Harvey, Primeau and Company to bid on carrying $20,000 in annuities upriver from St. Louis. Robert Campbell, unwilling to risk a steamboat on the low midsummer channel of the Upper Missouri, declined to bid for Harvey, Primeau and Company, but Chouteau, equally as unwilling as Campbell to send a boat upriver, agreed to make the necessary goods available to the tribes from Company supplies at upriver posts, and the Superintendent was compelled by circum-stances to accept the high prices set by Chouteau on Company

[23] *Ibid.*, 205; Hafen, "Thomas Fitzpatrick," *MVHR*, XV, 381.

[24] Chester L. Guthrie and Leo L. Gerald, "Upper Missouri Agency: An Account of the Indian Administration on the Frontier," *Pacific Historical Review*, Vol. X (March, 1941), 53.

goods. Although Mitchell learned a lesson (the earlier the annual contract was let in the spring, when the river was usually high and steamboats ready to go upriver, the better the chance for competitive bidding), he learned also that the American Fur Company intended to control the large annuity traffic of the future as it had the small upriver annuity traffic of the past, and would rely more and more on annuity-contract profits to help balance out any losses sustained in the robe and fur trade. The Company won the Upper Missouri annuity contracts, not only in 1852, but in all but four succeeding years through 1864. Nevertheless, competition for the contracts gradually cut hauling costs from St. Louis to the upriver distribution points (frequently Company posts) over the thirteen-year period from $8.50 per one hundred pounds to Fort Pierre in 1853 to $2.00–$3.00 by the sixties, and from $11.50 per one hundred pounds to Fort Union in 1853 to $2.50 in 1861, but the haulers still turned a good profit.[25]

Mitchell returned to Missouri from the Fort Laramie council at about the time the last bales of robes and furs from the Upper Missouri trade of 1851 were stacked in warehouses along the St. Louis levee. A few weeks later, the upper river clogged with ice, and the traders at snow-covered posts along the riverbanks discussed the prospects of the winter trade and the future of the American Fur Company and the opposition. In November, Rudolph Kurz noted in his journal that Joseph Picotte of the opposition lived "in a state of continual provocation because the United States government [took] no notice of his company and . . . always [upheld] the greater corporation." Kurz believed that opposition profits were "inconsiderable" and that only the Campbells were making money from Harvey's business.[26] In January, 1852, Honoré Picotte wrote Andrew Drips from Fort Pierre that Har-

[25] R. and W. Campbell to David D. Mitchell, July 26, 1852, David D. Mitchell to Pierre Chouteau, Jr., and Company, July 26, August 3, 1852, to Luke Lea, August 3, 1852, and to R. and W. Campbell, July 26, 1852, and Pierre Chouteau, Jr., and Company to David D. Mitchell, July 27, 1852, May 4, 1853, Letters Received, OIA, RG 75, NA.

[26] Kurz, *Journal*, 234.

vey's company was out of trade goods and heavily in debt to Robert Campbell. A few weeks later, when the opposition suspended payments, rumors circulated in St. Louis and in the upper-river posts that Harvey and his partners were on their last legs.[27]

Business observers agreed that only Robert Campbell could save the opposition, but would he risk outfitting Harvey in 1852 after the mediocre opposition return of 1851? Harvey, who was determined to keep the opposition alive at all costs, left Fort Campbell with two of his children early in April, 1852, and stepped ashore in St. Louis five weeks later. He placed the children in boarding school and closeted himself with Campbell to talk over the prospects of the tottering opposition. Weeks passed, and by late June, Joseph A. Sire of the American Fur Company, alert to any evidence in St. Louis of opposition preparation of a new upriver outfit, wrote Pierre Chouteau that no such preparation was under way. Sire was apprehensive, however, that Campbell had made some sly deal in Washington, or with eastern investors, to back Harvey. In the meantime, since business was business, the Company marketed (at a 50 per cent handling charge) a large part of Harvey's 1851 robe and fur return according to a previous agreement made between Chouteau and Campbell. Then, on July 29, Harvey, with Campbell's surety, renewed his license. Although he employed fewer traders for the coming year, his company's structure remained essentially unaltered, and Campbell, evidently encouraged by the early returns of 1852, supported him.[28]

Except for an unexpected cold snap in March, the winter of 1851–52 was mild on the Upper Missouri; the tribes were healthy, although some lacked adequate food; and the river, when the ice gave way in April, surged fifteen feet above its normal banks and carried the season's first mackinaws downstream on a high, fast

[27] *Ibid.*, 305–306; Honoré Picotte to A. Drips, January 3, 1852, Drips (Andrew) Papers, MoSHi.

[28] Joseph A. Sire to Pierre Chouteau, Jr., May 26, June 24, 25, 1852, Chouteau Family Papers, MoSHi; Volume Entitled "Licenses for Indian Trade," OIA, RG 76, NA; McDonnell, "Forts Benton and Sarpy," *CHSM*, X, 265 (n. 41).

crest. Alexander Culbertson and Harvey each announced, when they landed in St. Louis on May 17 from different steamboats, that the mackinaw fleets were afloat for the Lower Missouri. During the first two weeks in June, the initial upriver cargoes (all belonging to the opposition), transferred, as usual, from mackinaws to packets on the lower river, reached the St. Louis levee aboard the *Banner State* (one mackinaw load), the *El Paso* (three mackinaw loads), and the *Highland Mary No. 1* (three mackinaw loads). Late in June, the first American Fur Company cargo arrived on the *Honduras*, and before the end of summer, the *St. Ange* brought in two loads for the Company and the *Isabel* brought in one load each for the Company and the opposition. Harvey, Primeau and Company sent approximately 16,000 robes and 450 beaver skins from the Upper Missouri to St. Louis during the 1852 season, but the return, although valued at $50,000, was considerably less than that of the American Fur Company.[29]

Having renewed his trading license late in July, Harvey returned to the upper river (he spent the winter of 1852–53 at Fort Campbell) by packet to Council Bluffs and from that point by interlocking overland trails. Although stories persisted in St. Louis during the late spring of 1852 that Campbell was outfitting a steamer to ascend the Missouri to the opposition posts, apparently no boat was sent upriver that year.[30] The American Fur Company, as usual, chartered a boat—the *Banner State*—under "a powerfully built man," Captain John Gunsollis, a "first class [although illiterate] pilot ... quarrelsome and dangerous when under the influence of liquor."[31] Gunsollis piloted the *Banner State* away from St. Louis about June 8, completed the round trip to Fort Union in seven and a half weeks, and tied up his mud-splattered boat in St.

[29] *DMR*, May 17, June 1, 14, 15, 25, 26, July 27, 30, August 10, 28, 1852; McDonnell, "Forts Benton and Sarpy," *CHSM*, X, 231–32.

[30] *DMR*, May 23, 30, 1852, June 11, 1853.

[31] Quotation from the information file of Ruth Ferris, curator of the River Room, MoSHi. See also *DMR*, May 23, 1852, January 12, 1863. La Barge, in his memoirs (Chittenden, *Early Steamboat Navigation*, I), said that he took the *Sonora* upriver for the American Fur Company in 1852, but his dates are frequently inaccurate.

FORT BENTON
from a sketch by Gustavus Sohon

Courtesy Historical Society of Montana

Fort Berthold on the Upper Missouri
by William Cary

Courtesy Thomas Gilcrease Institute of American History and Art

FORT GEORGE
from a drawing by Alexander H. Murray

Courtesy Library of Congress

FORT MORTIMER
from a drawing by Alexander H. Murray

Courtesy Library of Congress

FORT PIERRE
from a drawing by Alexander H. Murray

Courtesy Library of Congress

FORT UNION
from a drawing by Alexander H. Murray

Courtesy Library of Congress

A MACKINAW BOAT WITH CORDELLE

Courtesy Missouri Historical Society

Buffalo Crossing the Missouri
by William Cary

Courtesy Thomas Gilcrease Institute of American History and Art

Louis on July 30 with 1,400 bales of robes and furs and a new shipment of Upper Missouri wildlife. The trip was uneventful except for a minor accident, which tore apart a section of the vessel's starboard guard, and a week spent grounded on a bar on the return trip.[32]

The merchandise for the Blackfoot trade, unloaded from the *Banner State* at Fort Union, was reshipped upriver to Fort Benton on a flat-bottomed barge. Louis Letellier, a young French-Canadian carpenter and boatbuilder employed by the American Fur Company, traveled upriver on the barge and many years later told his story of the trip, a trip similar to those made by other barges and many men during the 1840's and 1850's. In 1852, Malcolm Clark commanded the barge, and the "equipage," in addition to Letellier, consisted of a pilot, a tailor, a cook, four hunters, twenty-five laborers (who tugged the cordelle each day from sunrise to sunset), and a dozen Indian women! The riverbanks were so heavily overgrown with trees and wild rose bushes that two men chopped a path for the cordelle men through the heavier growth. Narrow, mud-filled ravines which cut across the towpath also hindered the men on the rope, and whenever the Missouri's channel swung to the opposite bank, the cordelle men plunged into the strong current and struggled across the river. Two men drowned during the trip in 1852, and a Blackfoot war party unexpectedly appeared one day when the boat was tied up, climbed aboard, and forced Clark to accept as passengers a group of nine young Indians, "boys of twelve and fifteen years of age," and to rescue a tribesman with an injured leg left by the war party a few miles upriver. Clark found the injured red man—snatched him from the claws of an approaching grizzly bear—and nursed him back to health aboard the barge. The Indian boys feasted on the boat's provisions for three days and "decamped one night taking with them [the] hunters' best horses." Fortunately, since elk, bear,

---

[32] *DMR*, July 31, 1852; *Saint Louis Daily Evening News*, July 30, 1852; *St. Louis Intelligencer*, July 31, 1852; *Glasgow* (Missouri) *Weekly Times*, June 10, 1852.

and buffalo fed in large herds along the river and the water was full of fish, the hunters kept the crew and passengers from starving. At the first dangerous rapids, just below Judith River (and by then the barefoot cordelle men were dressed in the torn-rag remains of their original clothes), Letellier and the crew felled cottonwood trees, cut them into inch-thick boards, and built a small barge to lighten the load of the larger one. The two craft continued upriver slowly, but eventually, after sixty-six days on the way from Fort Union, landed at Fort Benton and were unloaded by the post hands.[33]

Part of the merchandise taken from the barges was destined to be distributed as annuities to the Blackfeet under the agreement made between the Company and the Indian Office during the summer, and as a result of the Treaty of Fort Laramie, Alexander Culbertson and the other Company agents knew that the expanding upriver annuity business would demand more and more attention from the fur traders and from Upper Missouri Indian agents. But at least for the moment, in the fall of 1852, there was no agent on the upper river. Subagent Hatton had left Fort Pierre in April, 1851, after a brief career in the Indian country, returned to his home at Nashville, and requested reappointment to another, less taxing job in the Indian Service. Culbertson feared that if a strong agent did not appear soon on the Upper Missouri, the Red River métis would increase the "considerable quantities" of liquor they were trading illegally in American territory to the Hidatsas, Assiniboins, and Crees in exchange for robes and furs which normally went to the American Fur Company.[34]

James H. Norwood, "for the benefit of his health [more] than anything else," had filled temporarily the job relinquished by Hatton,[35] but one winter (1851–52) at Fort Pierre in the Sioux country, convinced him that he would "have little influence with the Indians, and do but little towards preventing the intercourse

[33] Marks, "Letellier," *SDHC*, IV, 227–30.

[34] A. Culbertson to David D. Mitchell, 1852, Central Superintendency Field Papers, OIA, RG 76, NA.

[35] *Frontier Guardian*, October 31, 1851.

laws from being violated" unless the Indian Office provided him better transportation, more than one interpreter, an agency independent of the trading posts, and dragoon protection.[36] Early in 1852, he fled the dull routine of the upper river and forgot his frustrations in the social life of the tiny settlements springing up between Council Bluffs and Sioux City. In September, 1852, he was murdered at Sergeant's Bluff (near Sioux City), struck on the head with the "butt end of a rifle," and his death left the upper river without an Indian agent until Robert B. Lambdin was appointed to the post two months later. Lambdin, however, was agent in name only, avoided the upper river, and was replaced in the spring of 1853 by Alfred J. Vaughan (at $1,500 a year), who had served as agent to the Osages, Iowas, and Sacs and Foxes. Vaughan was a "jovial," hard-working, hard-drinking agent who understood Indians and by holding onto the Upper Missouri Agency for four years gave it, at last, the authority it lacked under his many predecessors.[37]

In the spring of 1853, the new Democratic administration under Franklin Pierce, elected the previous fall, turned out scores of Whig appointees in the Indian service, including Lambdin, who was replaced by Vaughan (a loyal Democrat); Superintendent Mitchell, succeeded by Alfred Cumming; and Indian Commissioner Luke Lea, who was followed by George W. Manypenny. Pierce's victory not only ended the last Whig administration in the history of American politics, but again brought the American Fur Company into intimate political contact with the national government. Cumming and Vaughan assumed their new duties in April at the end of a very severe, snowy winter on the high plains. The Upper Missouri Indians had hunted little and traded less during the cold months, and the American Fur Company had lost

[36] James H. Norwood to David D. Mitchell, September 16, 1852, 32 Cong., 2 sess., *SED No. 1*, pp. 359–60; James H. Norwood to Luke Lea, June 26, 1852, Letters Received, OIA, RG 75, NA.

[37] George W. Manypenny to A. Vaughan, April 25, 1853, Letters Sent, 1846–1864, OIA, RG 75, NA; McDonnell, "Forts Benton and Sarpy," *CHSM*, X, 272 (n. 82); Larpenteur, *Forty Years*, II, 417.

numerous cattle at upriver posts. Early in May, Culbertson and Colin Campbell and their Indian wives arrived in St. Louis, verified to the press the earlier reports of a miserable winter in the Dakotas, and told a detailed story of mules frozen in their tracks and trading posts surrounded by mountainous white drifts.[38]

Before the end of May, the first mackinaws of the season floated downstream past the Vermillion and the Big Sioux with cargoes belonging to the American Fur Company and the opposition, and by late July, at least four packets—*Patrick Henry*, *F. X. Aubrey* (two trips), *Highland Mary No. 1*, and *Bluff City*—had carried those cargoes from Council Bluffs or St. Joseph to the St. Louis wharves.[39] Harvey, who landed in St. Louis on the *Highland Mary No. 1* early in the morning of June 9 after a long mackinaw trip from Fort Campbell to Council Bluffs, contradicted some of the statements about the winter trade given the press by Culbertson and Colin Campbell a few weeks earlier, and mentioned an unusually large winter robe trade with the Blackfeet. He outfitted immediately the 254-ton steamer *St. Ange*, chartered by Robert Campbell under Captain P. E. Hannum, for the annual voyage to the opposition's Upper Missouri posts. Late in the summer, Campbell and Edward Walsh, a St. Louis flour-milling tycoon, investor in river traffic, and close friend of former Senator Benton, backed the bond on Harvey's new license. Meanwhile, on July 7, the *St. Ange* steamed away from the levee, reached the mouth of the Yellowstone a month later, and returned to St. Louis on August 27 with over 1,300 packs of robes and a few furs.[40]

In comparison to the opposition return brought in on the *St. Ange*, the American Fur Company steamer *Robert Campbell* docked on July 25 with better than 3,000 packs of robes and furs.

[38] St. Joseph *Gazette*, March 23, 1853; *Weekly Tribune*, April 22, 1853; *DMR*, May 7, 1853.

[39] *DMR*, May 21, 29, June 10, July 22, 25, 1853; *Daily Missouri Democrat* (St. Louis), July 14, 1853.

[40] *DMR*, June 11, July 8, August 29, 1853; *Daily Missouri Democrat*, August 29, 1853; "Reports of Explorations and Surveys . . . 1853–5," 36 Cong., 1 sess., *HED No. 56*, p. 87.

That cargo, together with the small robe and fur shipments received during the summer from river packets, brought the Company's total 1853 return to approximately $112,000. The *Robert Campbell* had been leased by the Company late in April, 1853, at $30 a day, after extensive improvements in dry dock had lightened the vessel and increased cargo capacity. As a result of the "material alterations," the steamer carried 300–400 tons of freight and well over 100 passengers when it left St. Louis on May 21, flying a banner emblazoned "P. Chouteau." Captain Gunsollis commanded the steamer, and Culbertson and Sarpy accompanied the boat to represent the Company. The passenger list included not only the names of Indian Agent Vaughan, in charge of $30,000 in annuities; John C. Tevis, a St. Louis merchant on a health-seeking trip to the upper river; a New York City physician; and a public official from Kanesville, Iowa, but referred to young William Nicholas of Nassau, a German prince, and his four-man entourage; two scientists bound for the Bad Lands; and a military party headed for Fort Union.[41]

The two scientists, Fielding Bradford Meek and Ferdinand Vandeveer Hayden, were sponsored by the eminent New York paleontologist James Hall. Meek, a frail young man from Indiana, had worked with the United States Geological Survey of the Territories and had later joined Professor Hall's staff. Hayden, also young, and ambitious for a career in natural science, was Hall's protégé at the Albany, New York, medical school and lived in Hall's home while completing his medical training. In 1852, Meek and Hayden, both busily at work in Hall's laboratory, read of Dr. Evans's recent survey of the Bad Lands and asked Hall to sponsor them on a collecting trip to the Dakota country. Hall was uncertain about the venture until the Smithsonian offered to pay for quality fossils collected; then he agreed to finance the trip and

[41] Upper Missouri Returns for 1853, Chouteau Family Papers, MoSHi; Leasing Agreement of April 26, 1853, between Edds and Boyd and Pierre Chouteau, Jr., and Company, Chouteau Family Papers (Uncatalogued), MoSHi; *DMR*, September 7, 1852, July 26, 1853; St. Joseph *Gazette*, June 1, 1853; *Daily Missouri Democrat*, May 23, 1853; *Saint Louis Daily Evening News*, May 23, 1853.

asked the American Fur Company to assist the two young scientists.[42] Chouteau was becoming more and more interested in science on the Upper Missouri and had authorized Company steamers to transport animal-preserving materials (alcohol and arsenic) to upriver posts. Alexander Culbertson had just sent the Smithsonian several fossils of the Dakota Eocene period, rivaling, as the Institution reported, the "celebrated" deposits in the "basin of Paris," and Denig was preparing to donate to the Smithsonian the skeleton (the Institution called it an outstanding mammal skeleton) of a female gray wolf from the Yellowstone. And so the Company, as Hall anticipated, was willing to help the two young collectors, Meek and Hayden.[43]

Supplied by Hall with letters of introduction to the scientific, religious, and business leaders of St. Louis, Meek (Hall appointed him superior partner in the venture because of his age and experience) and Hayden journeyed west from New York in the spring of 1853. In St. Louis, Culbertson advised them on the proper outfit for their upriver trip and offered to sell or rent them Company equipment at reasonable rates. Although they found the Company co-operative, they soon realized that others in St. Louis strongly opposed their plans. Former Major and outstanding West Point graduate Isaac I. Stevens, appointed by President Pierce to survey a transcontinental railroad route from the Upper Mississippi to Puget Sound—one of many surveys recently authorized by Congressional appropriation—stopped in St. Louis for a brief visit during the spring of 1853 on his way north to St. Paul. A man of considerable prestige and influence, Stevens was re-

[42] George P. Merrill, *The First One Hundred Years of American Geology*, 501; John M. Clarke, *James Hall of Albany*, 244–46; "In Memoriam—Fielding Bradford Meek," *The American Journal of Science and Arts* (March, 1877), 169–71; Charles A. White, "Biographical Memoir of Ferdinand Vandeveer Hayden, 1839–1887," *National Academy of Sciences Biographical Memoirs*, Vol. III (1895), 399.

[43] Quotation from "[Sixth] Annual Report of the Board of Regents of the Smithsonian Institution," 32 Cong., 1 sess., *SMD No. 108*, p. 19. See also "Seventh Annual Report of the Board of Regents of the Smithsonian Institution," 32 Cong., 2 sess., *SMD No. 53*, pp. 54–55.

sponsible not only for the northern railroad survey, but was headed west to take up his duties as governor and ex officio Superintendent of Indian Affairs for Washington Territory. While in St. Louis, he arranged with the American Fur Company to carry a party under command of Lieutenant A. J. Donelson and a quantity of supplies upriver on the *Robert Campbell* to Fort Union to meet his main party, which was moving west from St. Paul. Dr. Evans of the Bad Lands survey and Benjamin F. Shumard, another noted geologist, both attached to the Donelson party, planned to geologize in the Indian country during the summer of 1853 and resented sharing the Dakotas with Meek and Hayden.[44]

Stevens was offended when he learned that Hall intended to send two young scientists up the Missouri, and joined Evans and Shumard to oppose Hall's plan. Meek and Hayden, in turn, appealed to George Engelmann of St. Louis, a leading scientist and one of Hall's good friends, and to the renowned Jean Louis Agassiz of Harvard, who was in St. Louis at that time lecturing before the local scientific society, to intervene with the Stevens group. Engelmann and Agassiz explained to Stevens and Evans that Hall's young men would not disrupt the Upper Missouri survey. Evans agreed reluctantly that Engelmann and Agassiz were correct—there were enough fossils for hundreds of collectors in the Bad Lands—but Stevens refused to aid the Meek-Hayden venture. Engelmann and Agassiz then advised Meek and Hayden to join the government party, but they were as adamant as Stevens and decided to go upriver without "official" co-operation.[45] "I was deeply pained to witness the spirit of rapacity, envy and sickly emulation evinced by most of the persons interested" in the Bad Lands project, Engelmann wrote Hall on May 23. "There is a

44 James Hall to F. V. Hayden, May 9, 1853, in Merrill, *American Geology*, 696; James Hall to George Engelmann, March 27, 1853, Engelmann (George) Papers, MOSB; James Hall to Father Pierre Jean De Smet, May 9, 1853, and to Pierre Chouteau, Jr., May 9, 1853, Meek (Fielding B.) Papers, DSI-M.

45 F. V. Hayden to James Hall, May 16, 1853, and F. B. Meek to James Hall, May 19, 1853, in Merrill, *American Geology*, 697–99.

want of the true spirit of science, the pure love for science in all this."[46]

When the *Robert Campbell* headed upstream, the feuding geologists, Evans, Shumard, Meek, and Hayden, were all aboard, crammed in with traders, Indian wives, Donelson's men, the Prince's tour group (few, if any, of whom, Hayden remarked, appeared "to have any taste for natural history"), and a mountain of freight. Despite the jam-packed condition of the boat, none fell ill on the trip, and morale was high. On May 24, however, a fire broke out in a pile of barrels stacked in the bow, and the passengers, fearing an explosion, ran to the stern and prepared to abandon ship. Fortunately, Sarpy kept cool, doused the flames, and restored order aboard the steamer. Since the river was high, fast, and full of snag-making debris, the boat tied up each night, and the scientists took advantage of the stops to gather botanical specimens by lantern light and to fill bottles full of unusual insects attracted, along with myraids of mosquitoes, by the glow of the large evening campfires.[47]

Above Council Bluffs, occasional Indian parties gathered on the riverbanks, but the red men were quiet and friendly and the passengers aboard the steamer tossed them crackers and bread. At the Vermillion, however, the Yankton Sioux saluted the boat noisily with several rounds, and Agent Vaughan and an interpreter ventured ashore briefly to distribute parcels of food, powder, and shot to a crowd of "really fine looking" warriors accompanied by women, children, and "a troop of gaunt, wolfish looking dogs." A week later, shortly after a heavy windstorm (possibly a tornado) nearly sank the steamer, Meek, Hayden, Evans, and Shumard stepped ashore at Fort Pierre and collected their horses, carts, guides, and interpreters, all supplied by the Company, before starting west in two separate groups. Meek and Hayden collected specimens in the Bad Lands for approximately three weeks, then

[46] George Engelmann to James Hall, May 23, 1853, in Clarke, *Hall*, 247–49.
[47] F. B. Meek to James Hall, May 22, 25, 28, June 2, 1853, Hall (James) Papers, NLA; see also Merrill, *American Geology*, 699–705.

returned to the East to distribute a large number of choice fossils and hundreds of plants to the scientific community. Hall and Meek studied the invertebrate remains, and Joseph Leidy the vertebrates. But Hayden preferred field work to laboratory study, severed his association with Hall, and returned to the upper river in 1854 to roam the valleys of the Missouri and Yellowstone for two years, traveling alone on foot or moving in company with fur traders.[48]

Meanwhile, aboard the *Robert Campbell,* tied up below Fort Pierre in June, 1853, two hundred Sioux met to feast and hold council with Vaughan and Sarpy. An old chief, who "looked upon [Sarpy] as one [only] a little inferior to the Great Father," presented him with a beautiful buffalo robe, and the council ended in good will. Nevertheless, some tribesmen had refused to meet Vaughan at Fort Pierre for their annuities and threatened to prevent the steamer from ascending the river above the Arikara settlement.[49] No Indian attack materialized, however, and the vessel churned upriver to a point seven miles above the mouth of Poplar River, where low water forced Sarpy to order ashore the Blackfoot freight, to be hauled by keel to Fort Benton, and Lieutenant Donelson's party disembarked to reconnoiter the north bank of the Missouri. Once the men and material were ashore, the *Robert Campbell* headed downriver, took on robes and furs at several Company posts, fought a bar-filled channel, and in late July, amidst shouts from shore and the squawks and yowls of penned animals aboard, edged up to the St. Louis levee.[50]

On August 1, Stevens' overland party, then 48 days (715½ miles) on the trail west of St. Paul, approached Fort Union from

[48] *DMR*, September 14, 1853; F. B. Meek to James Hall, June 2, 11, 19, 1853, Hall (James) Papers, NLA. The Academy of Natural Sciences of Philadelphia holds some seventy Hayden letters for the years 1854–62 alone. The collection should be valuable to any biographer of F. V. Hayden who may wish to write a detailed study—more detailed than that given here—on his early western career.

[49] F. B. Meek to James Hall, June 19, 1853, Hall (James) Papers, NLA.

[50] *DMR*, July 26, 1853; "Reports of Explorations and Surveys . . . 1853-5," 36 Cong., 1 sess., *HED No. 56*, pp. 79–82.

the east. Lieutenant Donelson, his examination of the region between Poplar River and the fort complete, and Denig welcomed the main party to the post, and the Company threw a champagne supper for the leaders of the expedition. Both the American Fur Company and the opposition, which was based at Fort William, the lower fort (old Fort Mortimer), "zealously co-operated" with Stevens and placed at his disposal "animals . . . guides, hunters, and . . . information in regard to the country." While he supervised the re-equipping of his party and absorbed Indian lore from Culbertson—"a man of great energy, intelligence and fidelity"—his men were outfitted "pleasingly with moccasins, gloves etc." by the Indian women at Fort Union. John Mix Stanley, artist of the expedition, painstakingly made daguerreotypes of the post Indians, and Dr. George Suckley, survey-party naturalist and physician, sent downriver, on the opposition steamboat *St. Ange*, a shipment of specimens for Professor Baird at the Smithsonian. Stevens had requested Baird to supervise as best he could, from the Museum of Natural History in Washington, the field work of the expedition. Baird eagerly accepted the challenge and used his good offices to further co-operation between the American Fur Company and the Stevens survey.[51]

After ten hectic days of preparation, the expedition was ready to push on to the Rockies, accompanied as far as Fort Benton by Culbertson and a band of friendly Blackfeet. On September 1, twenty-three days from the Yellowstone, the guns of Fort Benton saluted Stevens' arrival, and the post traders gave the survey party the hospitality of the fort. Stevens reported to his superiors that in three weeks at the post (he left it on September 22), his party "made warm and fast friends of all the inhabitants," and, he added, "I ascribed it mainly to one reason, that they felt that beneficial

[51] Hazard Stevens, *The Life of Isaac Ingalls Stevens*, I, 345–46; S. F. Baird to Pierre Chouteau, Jr., and Company, April 4, 1853, Spencer F. Baird Private Correspondence, Letters Written, DSI; Journal of George Suckley, 1853, DSI-M; "Reports of Explorations and Surveys . . . 1853–5," 36 Cong., 1 sess., *HED No. 56*, pp. 78–82, 86.

results would flow from the expedition, and they saw that every man was thoroughly in earnest in furthering it."[52] Stevens was partially correct. The Company knew it was politically dangerous to oppose the survey, and since it was to be made, the Company agreed to sell it supplies and equipment at reasonable profit and to enhance its own business reputation through co-operation with a great national project.

Alexander Culbertson and his Blackfoot wife personally assisted the survey—and so further entrenched the American Fur Company in Stevens' good graces—by accompanying the expedition through the dangerous Indian country between Forts Union and Benton and by assembling at Benton, on September 21, a council of Blackfoot leaders to hear Stevens' plea for peace and brotherhood in the Upper Missouri country. The council was a success, and Stevens hoped to hold a much larger meeting later if he could win Congressional support. On October 1, approximately ten days after he left Fort Benton for the West, Culbertson started downriver for St. Louis and the East. He had promised Stevens to pass the winter in Washington lobbying for Congressional and Indian Office backing for a large Upper Missouri Indian meeting. Although Culbertson remarked that the job was the "most distasteful proceeding of his life," he influenced Congress, nevertheless, to appropriate $10,000 for Stevens' treaty-making plan.[53]

The Company stood to gain as much as Stevens from a treaty that would bring peace to the warring tribes along the upper river, and Culbertson was convinced, correctly, despite his "distasteful" winter in Washington, that the federal government would in the future seek his advice many times in Blackfoot Indian affairs. But for the years immediately ahead, a railroad along the route of the Stevens survey seemed remote to fur traders, who knew, as the

[52] "Reports of Explorations and Surveys . . . 1853–5," 36 Cong., 1 sess., *HED No. 56*, p. 117.

[53] Quotation from Bradley, "Affairs," *CHSM*, III, 270–71. See also Ewers, *Blackfeet*, 208–11; Stevens, *Life of Stevens*, I, 350, 431; McDonnell, "Forts Benton and Sarpy," *CHSM*, X, 240–42 (n. 2).

veteran bourgeois James Kipp said, that the fur trade was tied to the riverboat and that the "way business" for any railroad was unlikely to "ever be heavy" as long as the Dakotas and Montana supplied more buffalo and beaver than grain and livestock to the world market.[54]

[54] St. Joseph *Gazette*, August 10, 1853.

CHAPTER SEVEN

"Under the influence of Christian civilization"

A BUSINESS RECESSION, the second in six years, struck the nation in 1854, shook the fur market, and forced the American Fur Company and the opposition to keep sharp watch over the Upper Missouri trade. Fortunately, the economic setback was short lived. Business conditions improved before the end of the year and triggered a boom that lasted until overspeculation in banking, credit, and railroading caused a major panic in 1857. Between recession and panic, during the prosperous years of the mid-fifties, the Chouteaus soberly examined the Indian-country trade and the changes under way in the western fur market. Although the St. Louis Chamber of Commerce no longer mentioned the western fur trade in its annual reports, the Upper Missouri robe and fur business was still lively and profitable, and if it was less important to the total commerce of St. Louis, it was surely more significant to the commerce of several towns along the lower river. Each year, Kansas City merchants handled thousands of buffalo robes and smaller skins sent to market by "hundreds" of hunters, and cut into the profits reaped from independent trappers and hunters by the older companies led by the Chouteaus and their associates.[1]

Although the St. Louis–based fur companies adjusted their policies to compete with the new fur dealers along the lower river, the St. Louisans knew that in due time (five years, ten years —who could say?) the merchants between Kansas City and the settlements in the land of the Yankton Sioux would hold a large

[1] *Weekly Tribune*, September 10, 1858.

159

share in the fur trade and that the new river towns northwest of St. Louis would outfit traders and send robes and furs to market via rail lines reaching east across northern Missouri and central Iowa. A few traders complained that fur posts located on old overland trails were becoming supply stations for emigrant parties and that it was disgusting to see former fur traders selling goods to emigrants, but most of the old traders seemed willing, whenever the fur trade died out in a particular region, to pre-empt land in the area, graze stock, raise crops, and perhaps run a sawmill or keep store for a living. They, their Indian wives, and their half-blood children and grandchildren constituted the first families of many river communities between Council Bluffs and Fort Randall, and embellished the Missouri Valley's folklore with tales of Indian wars, illicit whiskey, buffalo herds stretching as far as the hunter could see, disastrous epidemics, and the glories of the fur trade.[2]

By the mid-fifties, the Lower Missouri Valley was speckled with tiny settlements, some predominantly halfblood, some not, between St. Joseph and the lower Sioux country. The Congress, under pressure from land speculators, railroad promoters, slavery antagonists, and bona fide settlers anxious to take up land ceded by tribes west of the Missouri, organized the two popular sovereignty territories of Kansas and Nebraska in May, 1854. All land west of the Missouri as far as the Continental Divide and between the fortieth parallel (Kansas' northern border) and the Canadian boundary line—the bulk of the Upper Missouri fur country—was placed under the formal jurisdiction of Nebraska, and the eventual settlement of the entire area moved one step closer to reality. Omaha, site of the new Nebraska territorial capital, claimed two to three thousand inhabitants by early 1857 and, along with sister towns (Nebraska City, Brownville, Bellevue, Florence, and Plattsmouth), tapped a heavy flow of river traffic and overland

[2] Howard R. Lamar, *Dakota Territory, 1861–1889*, 32–33; Willoughby M. Babcock, "The Fur Trade As an Aid to Settlement," *NDHQ*, Vol. VII (January and April, 1933), 91–92.

parties bound from Iowa to the western country.³ North of Omaha, settlers founded Sioux City in 1855 and soon infiltrated the Yankton lands to mingle with the Indian–halfblood–fur trader society in the region west of the Big Sioux River. By the time the inflated national economic bubble burst in 1857, the Upper Missouri, fortress of the robe and fur trade, was under siege from settlers banging on the southeast door.

Further consolidation of power within the American Fur Company in the hands of Pierre and Charles Chouteau accompanied the conflict in the fifties between the Company and the many Lower Missouri fur dealers. When Joseph Sire died in 1854, his capital in the Company (a 26 per cent interest) was removed, and when John B. Sarpy died in 1857 (he had been inactive in Company affairs for two or three years prior to his death), his share, also 26 per cent, ended. Pierre Chouteau, interested, as he said, in continuing the business, not for himself, but for his family, offered a share in the Company to his son-in-law, former army surgeon Dr. William Maffitt. Maffitt gracefully declined, and Pierre, unwilling at that point completely to finance the Company personally, suggested to his son Charles and to Alexander Culbertson that unless some division of investment in the firm were arranged, the Company should unite with the opposition, or, as a last resort, "sell all." Before the end of the year, however, after Pierre Chouteau, Jr., and Company had suspended payments briefly because of the Panic of 1857, the Upper Missouri Outfit received sufficient support (presumably from the Chouteaus, in co-operation with the leading upriver agents) to continue, year by year, until 1865.⁴

Both the recession and Sire's death in 1854 disrupted Company

³ Norman A. Graebner, "Nebraska's Missouri River Frontier, 1854–1860," *NH*, Vol. 42 (December, 1961), 218–22; Herbert S. Schell, *History of South Dakota*, 65–66.

⁴ Files of Estates of Joseph A. Sire, No. 4292, and John B. Sarpy, No. 4974, Records of the St. Louis Probate Court, St. Louis; Pierre Chouteau, Jr., to William Maffitt and Charles P. Chouteau, April 20, 1857, and to William Maffitt, April 24, 1857, Chouteau Family Papers, MoSHi; Pierre Chouteau, Jr., to Charles P. Chouteau and A. Culbertson, April 28, 1857, Chouteau Family Papers (Uncatalogued), MoSHi; *Weekly Tribune*, October 9, 1857.

management and handicapped Culbertson's efforts, following his return to the Upper Missouri from Washington, to bolster trade. Upriver Company expenses were heavier in 1854 "than [in] any former year," and Culbertson "was determined not to" throw away goods "to break down a few lousy [opposition] traders."[5] Strict economy was his watchword for the year, and better discipline at all Upper Missouri trading posts his goal. When he reached Fort Benton on September 28, he feasted the garrison and treated it to a ball, but observed next morning that "little or no work" was under way and that "intemperance" was "noticeable" in at least two men, who had "made a sorry display of their reasons" at the previous night's festivities.[6] If the upriver posts were to ship more than seventy thousand robes to St. Louis the following spring, and so surpass the trade of 1853 and 1854, Culbertson believed the post employees would have to pay closer attention to their duties. The annual payroll at Fort Pierre alone totaled $30,-000, and the Company could ill afford abnormally high upriver expenses during the recession. Fortunately for Culbertson, most trading posts were orderly and well kept during the mid-fifties, with the notable exception of Fort Sarpy on the Yellowstone, commanded by an agent whose motto was "obey orders if you break [the] owners," where violence and prostitution prevailed and the Indians stole goods regularly from the supply room. Eventually, in May, 1855, the Company abandoned and burned "badly Forted" Sarpy and, except for an unsuccessful attempt late in the fifties to operate a new post, Fort Sarpy II, south of the Yellowstone near the mouth of the Big Horn, entirely gave up year-round, on-the-spot trade in the dangerous Crow country.[7]

Meanwhile, in 1854, the Company chartered the steamboat *Sonora* under Captain Joseph La Barge to carry the year's supply

[5] A. Culbertson to C. E. Galpin, September 6, 1854, Chouteau Family Papers, MoSHi.

[6] McDonnell, "Forts Benton and Sarpy," *CHSM*, X, 1.

[7] Quotation from *ibid.*, 133. See also *ibid.*, 108, 126, 282–83 (n. 145); St. Joseph *Gazette*, March 22, 1854.

of trade goods to the Upper Missouri posts. The six-week round trip to the Yellowstone, made between June 3 and July 17, was fast, safe, and reasonably profitable—1,496 bales of robes and over 300 packs of furs—for the American Fur Company.[8] At least four additional shipments (a perfectly normal trade) of upriver robes and furs, some consigned to the Company and some to the opposition, reached St. Louis aboard Lower Missouri packets before the end of the season.[9] By comparison, Company and opposition robe and fur shipments on lower-river packets fell off at least 50 per cent between 1855 and 1857, since the St. Louis fur men had learned that it cost less to fill up, with seasonal returns, all available space on the steamers returning from the annual trips to the upper river than it did to ship mackinaw cargoes by commercial packets from transfer points on the lower river.

Two days before the *Sonora* left St. Louis for the Yellowstone, the new 226-ton *Genoa*, "built expressly for the Missouri trade," slid away from the levee, bound upriver to the opposition posts.[10] Captain Joseph Throckmorton, an old hand in the river trade, commanded the steamer under charter to Robert Campbell, who, together with wholesale grocer John P. Helfenstein (one-time chief clerk to Sublette and Campbell and always an anti-Chouteau businessman), had renewed the opposition license the day before the boat sailed. The decks of the light-draft vessel were covered with Harvey, Primeau and Company freight; passenger gear; and piles of Indian annuities, watched carefully by Indian Agent Vaughan, who regretted that Robert Campbell had received the annual contract from the Indian Office. Although Campbell had underbid the American Fur Company and had won the contract fairly, Vaughan feared that Campbell and the opposition traders would fail to furnish adequate Upper Missouri storage space for the annuities, lacked the distribution service necessary to channel the goods to the tribes, and might "hurry [him] every foot of the

---

[8] *DMR*, May 31, June 3, 27, July 18, 1854.
[9] *Ibid.*, May 8, June 16, July 6, 8, 1854. [10] *Ibid.*, May 26, 1854.

way" on the voyage. Vaughan admitted later, however, that Campbell delivered the goods to the tribes in good order and without any clash with the Indians. On the way upriver, whenever the *Genoa* landed at a Sioux camp, the Indian chiefs stationed guards at the gangplank to prevent inquisitive tribesmen from boarding the vessel, and order prevailed in the distribution of annuities.[11]

Vaughan landed at Fort Pierre on June 22, met in council with six or seven Sioux bands, and, after eating a few pieces of dog meat (the Indian delicacy prepared for honored guests), gave out the annuities. A few days later, he distributed the Arikara goods at Fort Clark and the Hidatsa goods at Fort Berthold. On July 5, the *Genoa* unloaded at Fort William (Mortimer) before turning downriver to St. Louis, and Vaughan held an Indian council, with traders from both Fort William and Fort Union in attendance, in an open field between the two posts. He then loaded the remaining annuities aboard a keelboat heading for the Yellowstone and accompanied the cargo to Fort Sarpy, the annuity distribution center in the Crow country. Meanwhile, the *Genoa* had raced back to St. Louis in thirteen days, landing on July 15, two days before the *Sonora*, with a small cargo of robes and furs.[12]

Alexander Harvey—according to the anti-Chouteau St. Louis *Daily Missouri Republican*, "a brave, an honest, and a kind-hearted man"—died at Fort William on July 20, two days after Vaughan left the post for the Yellowstone. Harvey, who had fallen ill at Fort Campbell earlier in the summer, had floated downriver via keelboat to the post at the mouth of the Yellowstone and along the way willed his estate, to be administered by Robert Campbell, to his two daughters. Since Harvey was the driving force in the upriver opposition business, his death left Harvey,

[11] Quotation from A. Vaughan to George W. Manypenny, April 11, 1854, Letters Received, OIA, RG 75, NA. See also A. Vaughan to A. Cumming, July 3, 1854, R. Campbell to A. Cumming, April 10, 22, 1854, and Pierre Chouteau, Jr., and Company to A. Cumming, April 10, 1854, *ibid.*; *Daily Missouri Democrat*, July 14, 1854.

[12] A. Vaughan to A. Cumming, October 19, 1854, 33 Cong., 2 sess., *HED No. 1*, pp. 287–93; *DMR*, July 16, 1854.

Primeau and Company at least temporarily disorganized and with less influence in the Indian camps.[13] His surviving partners, Primeau, Bouis, and Picotte, under Campbell's pressure, renewed the opposition trading license in 1855 in the name of "J. Picotte and Company" and for two years competed, disharmoniously, with the American Fur Company.[14]

Throughout the mild winter of 1854–55, the buffalo herds avoided the river valleys and the robe trade decreased. In the spring, the Upper Missouri, short of melted snow water, flowed alarmingly low, and, as if to compound natural handicaps to the new season's trade, the Sioux were in a mood for war. Agent Vaughan, at St. Joseph early in May, reported that many upriver tribes were hostile, and rumors circulated along the lower river that the Indians had burned Fort Pierre and seized Fort Laramie. When Culbertson and John C. Tevis of Fort Union landed in St. Louis on May 18, they confirmed that the Sioux were restless. A Yankton band had detained Culbertson's party two days on the way downriver and had threatened to kill all white men.[15] Late in June, American Fur Company traders from Forts Benton and Sarpy told the St. Louis press that the Crows and Blackfeet had fought each other intermittently all winter and spring and that early in May a large Sioux war party had attacked a group of seven white traders between Forts Union and Sarpy. In the melee, two of the whites were wounded and all were robbed and left naked and defenseless. When the Sioux dispersed, the traders struck out for Fort Sarpy. Along the way, one man killed a young buffalo calf with a stone, and the party lived on the animal's meat and blood until they stumbled into the fort. Five days later, the Sioux reappeared and surrounded the fort, but rode away after

[13] File of Estate of Alexander M. Harvey, No. 4888, Records of the St. Louis Probate Court, St. Louis; *DMR*, September 19, 20, 1854. The author of *Back-Trailing on the Old Frontiers* stated (p. 19) that at least amongst the Blackfeet, however, Harvey was remembered "as the worst white man" the tribe knew "in the fur trade days."

[14] Volume Entitled "Licenses for Indian Trade," OIA, RG 76, NA.

[15] *DMR*, May 19, 1855; *St. Joseph Commercial Cycle*, May 11, 1855; *Weekly Tribune*, May 11, 1855.

smoking and talking with the bourgeois in charge.[16] Clearly, the Indians, even those as far south as western Iowa, "were very troublesome" in the spring of 1855 and "determined upon taking white scalps"; the robe trade promised to fall far below normal; and, although the streams once again swarmed with beaver, the price on beaver skins was low.[17]

Campbell and Picotte, who reorganized Harvey, Primeau and Company following Harvey's death, had cut the Upper Missouri opposition force from thirty to fourteen traders and instead of chartering a steamer to supply the upriver posts in 1855, sent goods by land. The American Fur Company, however, selected the "neat and very light draught steamer" St. Mary to make the annual upriver voyage, in this instance a maiden voyage, starting in the rain on June 6, under supervision of Captain La Barge, Charles Chouteau, and Alexander Culbertson. Indian Agent Vaughan was aboard with the annuities. Joseph Picotte had bid for the annuity contract, but lost, and Campbell, sensing political chicanery, had demanded to see copies of all papers relating to the award.

The upriver trip was slow, yet surprisingly peaceful, and late on July 11, the St. Mary reached Fort Union, where the most eminent passenger aboard, Georgia-born Superintendent of Indian Affairs at St. Louis (and later Governor of Utah Territory) Alfred Cumming, transferred his supplies and Indian goods to keelboats that started up the Missouri toward Fort Benton on July 17. Then he joined Culbertson's party and followed the overland route (generally paralleling the Missouri) west to Fort Benton to council with the Indians. Vaughan, rather than attend the Indian meeting, distributed Assiniboin annuities at Fort Union, shipped the Crow annuities up the Yellowstone on a Company mackinaw (the Sioux stopped the boat and forced its crew to turn back to Fort Union), and then moved down the Missouri to Fort Clark

[16] A. Vaughan to A. Cumming, September 12, 1855, 34 Cong., 1 sess., SED No. 1, pp. 394–95; DMR, June 30, 1855; McDonnell, "Forts Benton and Sarpy," CHSM, X, 123–26.
[17] Weekly Saint Louis Pilot, May 19, 1855. See also DMR, May 21, 1855.

to council with recalcitrant tribesmen who had broken a promise to meet Superintendent Cumming at the Arikara camp on his way upriver.[18]

On August 3, the *St. Mary*, three weeks from the Yellowstone on a low channel, landed in St. Louis to a barrage of welcoming cannon. Throngs of people, some eager for late upriver news of Indian hostilities, some attracted by a big pile of large antlers stacked on the boat's hurricane roof, boarded the vessel, while others remained ashore to watch the bales of robes and furs (2,250 of them) go ashore into the Company warehouse. Captain La Barge, the round trip complete, turned in to the Company his formal report on cargo and crew—one crewman drowned and one deserted on the voyage—but it was late in the season before a candid upriver trader, Andrew Dawson, told Pierre Chouteau that the Company had suffered "inconceivable trouble in getting" supplies to Fort Benton that year and so summarized the conduct of the fur trade in the mid-fifties: inconceivably troublesome.

Two weeks after the *St. Mary* tied up at St. Louis, the Cumming-Culbertson party reached Fort Benton, where they joined Governor Isaac Stevens from Washington Territory. Stevens, who had originally planned the council for 1854, was irked by the year's delay, by the War Department's discontinuation of his northern railroad survey, and by Cumming's appointment as senior commissioner to the Indian council. Early in the afternoon of October 16, the meeting opened in a cottonwood grove near the junction of the Missouri and the Judith, rather than at Fort Benton, since the keelboats from Fort Union had landed cargoes of Indian presents at the mouth of the Judith.[19]

[18] A. Cumming to George W. Manypenny, June 4, July 13, 1855, A. Vaughan to John Haverty, September 12, 1855, Pierre Chouteau, Jr., to A. Cumming, May 28, 1855, and Joseph Picotte to A. Cumming, May 29, 1855, Letters Received, OIA, RG 75, NA; A. Vaughan to A. Cumming, September 12, 1855, 34 Cong., 1 sess., *SED No. 1*, pp. 394–95; *DMR*, May 31, June 2, 1855.

[19] Andrew Dawson to Pierre Chouteau, Jr., and Company, October 10, 1855, Chouteau Family Papers, MoSHi; *Daily Missouri Democrat*, August 4, 1855; *DMR*, August 4, 1855. See also the manuscript journal of Edwin A. C. Hatch in

Peace and friendship prevailed amongst the Indians at the meeting, and in less than two days the commissioners signed a "Treaty with the Blackfoot Nation." By the terms of the agreement, dated October 17, the boundary of the Blackfoot country was set and the Indians agreed to allow white men peacefully to live in and pass through the Blackfoot region. In return, the United States government granted the Blackfeet an annual sum of $20,000 for ten years and promised to establish an agency in the Blackfoot country—Cumming opposed the plan, but Stevens favored it—to educate the Indians in the three R's, farming, and various crafts. As soon as the treaty was signed and the Indians had received their gifts, the commissioners parted company. Cumming headed downriver, Stevens turned west, and the fur traders who had assisted the commissioners scattered to the trading posts to hole up for the coming winter.[20]

The Blackfoot council helped restore order temporarily between the warring tribes along the Upper Missouri above the mouth of the Yellowstone, but to the south, in the land of the Sioux, whites and Indians continued to clash along the overland trail through the Platte Valley. General William S. Harney, dispatched to the Sioux country by the United States Army, campaigned west along the Platte in the late summer of 1855, defeated the Oglalas at Ash Hollow, then turned northeastward from Fort Laramie across the Teton Sioux territory, and on October 19 settled his command in uncomfortable winter quarters at Fort Pierre. The old post, previously "most inviting" to travelers, had deteriorated rapidly during the early fifties (the American Fur Company was undecided whether to abandon it or repair it), and

---

the Newberry Library, Chicago. Hatch was appointed agent to the Blackfeet on March 3, 1855. His journal covers the period June 6, 1855, to June 5, 1856, and contains information concerning his upriver voyage aboard the *St. Mary* (in 1855), the Indian council at Judith River, and life at various Upper Missouri fur posts. Professor Martin Ridge of the History Department of San Diego State College is editing the Hatch journal for publication.

[20] Ewers, *Blackfeet*, 213–22; McDonnell, "Forts Benton and Sarpy," *CHSM*, X, 38–49; Hoopes, *Indian Affairs*, 112–15.

when the army moved in, the soldiers, certain that Peter the Hermit must have chosen the dreary site for a fort, sang in disgust around their campfires: "Oh, we don't mind the marching, nor the fighting do we fear,/ But we'll never forgive old Harney for bringing us to Pierre./ They say old Shoto built it, but we know it is not so/ For the man who built this bloody ranch is reigning down below."[21]

General Harney, however, was not to blame for the army's acquisition of Fort Pierre from the American Fur Company. Early in the spring of 1855, the War Department had outlined the Sioux campaign and ordered Harney to concentrate men and supplies at Forts Kearny and Laramie and at a point, to be selected by the Department, on the Upper Missouri near Fort Pierre. The U.S. Army Quartermaster at St. Louis, under orders from the Quartermaster General, investigated the condition of Fort Pierre and reported late in March that according to John B. Sarpy of the American Fur Company, the post was unfit to be a large military depot. The Chouteaus, however, contradicted Sarpy's statement shortly after it reached Washington, pressured the Quartermaster General himself, and on April 14, sold Fort Pierre—the Company's white elephant on the upper river—to the army for the exorbitant sum of $45,000. Early in July, when the first infantrymen landed at the fort from the steamer *Arabia* out of St. Louis, officers inspected the site, pronounced it in miserable shape, and estimated it would cost the government $22,000 to restore the post. The Chouteaus had promised, in the April agreement, to repair the fort at Company expense if the army found it in poor shape, but the Chouteaus did not intend to foot the repair bill; they argued that they had saved the government the higher cost of building an entirely new supply depot, and finally, after some delay, talked the government into paying the full purchase price.[22]

21 Wilson, "Old Fort Pierre," *SDHC*, I, 263–64.
22 *Ibid.*, 278–81; Kingsbury, *Dakota Territory*, I, 63–64; Memorandum of Agreement between the United States Army and Pierre Chouteau, Jr., and Company, April 15, 1855, and Joseph La Barge to Pierre Chouteau, Jr., and Company, 1855, Chouteau Family Papers, MoSHi.

Trader Charles Galpin, under orders from the Chouteaus, transferred Fort Pierre to the military in July and moved those Company employees remaining at the post to a grassy, well-wooded campsite approximately four miles above Chantier Creek. At first, the Sioux were "greatly alarmed" to see the army at Fort Pierre and believed that the military had forcibly driven the traders away, but when they learned that Galpin had pitched camp near by, they quieted down, or as Indian Agent Vaughan thought, were cowed by the "presence of troops in the [Upper Missouri] country . . . [who] caused many of the refractory [Indians] to be taken with fear and trembling."[23]

A few of Harney's men received new assignments in the East before winter, including Lieutenant George T. Balch, who left the post for St. Louis with a "very valuable collection of fossils and petrifactions collected in the mauvaise terres" which he planned to lend to the Military Academy.[24] Most of Harney's command, however (twelve hundred men), spent the cold months in uncomfortable, inadequate shelter in or near Fort Pierre. Lieutenant Thomas W. Sweeny wrote home that the "cottages" at Fort Pierre were "worthless" shells "so thin and light that they have to be propped up on the leeward side, for fear of being blown down."[25] But let another army man, Augustus Meyers, testify in detail to the winter: "Our experience since we arrived at Fort Pierre had been very trying through the incompetency or carelessness of some one in authority. We were ill prepared for the rigors of so severe a climate as to clothing, food, quarters and

[23] Quotation from A. Vaughan to C. E. Galpin, September 29, 1855, Chouteau Family Papers, MoSHi. See also A. Cumming to George W. Manypenny, June 18, 1855, and John Haverty to George W. Manypenny, June 30, 1855, Letters Received, OIA, RG 75, NA; "Explorations in the Dacota Country, in the Year 1855," 34 Cong., 1 sess., SED No. 76, pp. 36-37.

[24] Lt. George T. Balch to a "Beloved Friend," October 21, 1855, CU-B. However, no record exists in the archives of the Military Academy—at least for the period 1855-60—to verify that Lieutenant Balch's collection was ever received at West Point.

[25] Lt. Thomas W. Sweeny to his Brother (?), December 10, 1855, Sweeny Papers, CSmH.

medical stores. Men died from exposure and from scurvy and many animals succumbed to starvation. Officers and soldiers suffered alike. The miserable huts in which we lived during the winter were unfit for stables. We almost froze in them, and when the spring came, the mud roofs leaked like sieves."[26]

In the spring, Harney held a council with the Sioux at Fort Pierre and issued several directives to strengthen his shaky military hold on the Upper Missouri. All unauthorized persons were ordered to leave the Indian country, whites were forbidden to live in Indian camps, and the fur companies were required to furnish the army up-to-date lists of employees. The traders, antagonized by the restrictions, ignored them whenever possible.[27] By late spring, Harney's subordinates had surveyed several sites between Fort Pierre and the Niobrara River to the south for the location of a permanent military post, since Fort Pierre was pitifully inadequate. They found a desirable site for a post on the west bank of the Missouri approximately thirty miles above the mouth of the Niobrara, and in June, construction of Fort Randall, the first permanent military post on the Upper Missouri, commenced at that location. Before the end of the year, most of Harney's men had moved from the Fort Pierre area to the new post, set on a natural terrace some one thousand yards above the Missouri. A handful of troops garrisoned Fort Pierre through the winter of 1856–57, but in spring, when navigation opened on the river, they loaded their stores on a steamer from St. Louis, evacuated the post, and moved downriver to join the main command at Fort Randall.[28]

Under contract to the army, Charles Galpin of the American Fur Company leveled much of Fort Pierre, transported portions of the dismantled post to Fort Randall, and put the remainder of

[26] Augustus Meyers, "Dakota in the Fifties," *SDHC*, Vol. X (1920), 169.

[27] General Harney's Circulars of February 20 and March 1, 1856, Chouteau Family Papers, MoSHi.

[28] Kingsbury, *Dakota Territory*, I, 65–66; Linda W. Slaughter, "Fort Randall," *CHSND*, Vol. I (1906), 425; Charles E. DeLand, "Basil Clement (Claymore)," *SDHC*, Vol. XI (1922), 350.

the old fort to his own use. Then the Indians plundered the skeleton of Fort Pierre; snow, wind, and rain ruined what was left of it; and the army, after one attempt to repair part of the post, decided, in disgust, that it was useless to waste money on the rundown fort. Meanwhile, in 1857, Galpin replaced his temporary trading camp near Chantier Creek with a 125-foot-square stockaded post named in his honor and built on the west bank of the Missouri approximately two to three miles above Fort Pierre. Within two years, however, Galpin closed his namesake post and a half-mile below it erected a new one, Fort Pierre II, perhaps in part from building materials taken from the old post. The new fort, almost as large as the old, resembled "a somewhat irregular [stockaded] quadrilateral" with a large open center but, if recent excavation is correct, without bastions. The lack of defensive bastions at the new post suggests that by the late 1850's, the American Fur Company either believed that the Fort Pierre region was free of Indian danger or, as a result of cost or other considerations, decided not to add protecting blockhouses. Two openings provided access to the fort, buildings were constructed of rough-hewn cottonwood, and the new post was intended, evidently, "to be a full replacement of the old post . . . and not merely another secondary post."[29]

The American Fur Company built Fort Pierre II not only to replace the old, irreparable post but to re-establish lagging Company trade in the Sioux country, for the Indian menace on the Upper Missouri had diminished after Harney's campaign and the robe and fur trade had improved following the business difficulties of the mid-fifties. A few weeks before Harney's command moved to Fort Randall in the spring of 1856, the steamer *Genoa* from St. Louis picked up the season's first robe and fur shipment, for Picotte and Company, from three mackinaws near the Great

[29] Wilson, "Old Fort Pierre," *SDHC*, I, 361–62; G. Hubert Smith, "Fort Pierre II (39ST217), a Historic Trading Post in the Oahe Dam Area, South Dakota," *Bureau of American Ethnology River Basin Survey Papers*, XVIII, 117–22.

Bend of the Missouri.[30] The shipment, a substantial one, proved to the St. Louis fur companies that the recent severe, snowy Upper Missouri winter had not damaged the trade and that prospects were good for the coming year. The American Fur Company once again outfitted the *St. Mary*, piloted by Captain La Barge, for the annual run to the Yellowstone country. Charles Chouteau, Culbertson, a newspaper correspondent who sent stories signed "S," and Indian Agent Vaughan, with the annuities, all witnessed the voyage. The Chouteaus underbid their competitors—three of them—and won the annuity contract, although one eager competitor, John Shaw, a steamboat captain backed by Campbell, pledged himself to carry the Blackfoot annuities by steamer all the way to Fort Benton, since the army, for military reasons, wished to learn whether or not the Upper Missouri was navigable to that place.[31]

The *St. Mary* sailed for the Upper Missouri on June 7, riding a swollen channel that held her above snags and bars. On the trip upriver, Vaughan distributed annuities and held brief Indian councils at riverside landings between the Great Bend and Fort Union. Although some tribesmen objected to traveling long distances to Old Fort Pierre to receive the annuities Vaughan deposited there for them, most of the Indians along the river were friendly, peaceful, and co-operative. Some of the soldiers in the small, "worn and torn" garrison at Old Fort Pierre, however, were more troublesome than the Indians. Despite orders to the contrary from their officers, they bought liquor from the *St. Mary* and were "thrashed by . . . voyageurs" from the vessel in a drunken fight. A few days later, as the steamer neared Fort Clark, the passengers celebrated the Fourth of July with a sunrise volley, innumerable short speeches, and a champagne supper given by Charles Chouteau. Buffalo, the first seen on the trip, watched the

[30] *Daily Missouri Democrat*, June 7, 1856; *DMR*, June 7, 8, 1856.

[31] John Shaw to A. Cumming, March 31, 1856, and to George W. Manypenny, April 14, 1856, and Pierre Chouteau, Jr., and Company to A. Cumming, March 31, 1856, and to George W. Manypenny, May 14, 1856, Letters Received, OIA, RG 75, NA.

THE MISSOURI FUR TRADE, 1840-1865

boat from the riverbanks above Fort Berthold, and the hunt was on. Chouteau, a mate, and several crewmen put out in a yawl and captured three calves, and for days the passengers and crew shot swimming buffalo from the moving steamer. Three Indians aboard butchered one of the buffalo red man fashion "by cutting the skin along the back" and turning it "down on both sides." Then they "cut off the flesh from the hump, shoulders and rump" and when they reached the skeleton, turned the animal over and removed "the contents of the cavities." The tastiest "portions of the stomach and its *continuation* were eagerly seized . . . and eaten raw, first, however, they dipped them in the blood that stood in pools upon the deck; the marrow of the bones and the brain they also ate in the same manner."[32]

On July 10, the *St. Mary* reached Fort Union, where Captain La Barge put ashore the Assiniboin annuities and landed a party from Old Fort Pierre under command of Lieutenant Gouverneur K. Warren of the Topographical Corps, a dashing young West Pointer attached to Harney's command. During July and August, 1855, Warren had mapped, with chain and compass, the new military reservation surrounding Old Fort Pierre. He favored the permanent establishment of a strong military force at forts in the Sioux country and respected American Fur Company traders for the accurate information they gave him about sections of the Upper Missouri he had not visited. On his second expedition west, in 1856, he and his party had collected natural-history specimens and sketched the course of the Missouri River from the mouth of the Platte to Old Fort Pierre while traveling upriver on the steamer *Genoa* from St. Louis. After a brief stop to report to Harney, they had boarded the *St. Mary*. From Fort Union, in August, Warren's party, under orders from Harney to gather military and scientific information, examined the Yellowstone Valley below Powder River and early in the fall, as they floated down the Missouri on a mackinaw boat to Sioux City, the valley of that

[32] *DMR*, August 9, 1856; A. Vaughan to A. Cumming, September 10, 1856, 34 Cong., 3 sess., *SED No. 5*, pp. 628-29.

stream as well. In 1857, Warren investigated the Black Hills and collected seven maps of the region drawn by Mountain Men, including Culbertson and Colin Campbell. His excellent, copiously illustrated reports, published by the federal government, contained information on the animal and plant life, soil, geology, and geography of the Bad Lands–Upper Missouri country and demonstrated the value of co-operation between fur traders and the Topographical Engineers.[33]

After Warren's party went ashore at Fort Union in mid-July, 1856, the *St. Mary* continued upriver. Captain La Barge hoped to take the vessel two to three hundred miles above the Yellowstone, but the channel fell and he swung the boat around within ten miles of the point, just above the mouth of Milk River, reached by the *El Paso* in 1850. Before the *St. Mary* turned homeward, Chouteau landed both the goods consigned to the Blackfoot trade and the Blackfoot annuities—in charge of Edwin A. C. Hatch of Minnesota, the new Blackfoot Indian agent (appointed March 3, 1855), who had boarded the *St. Mary* at Fort Union—and instructed the men sent ashore to build mackinaws as soon as possible to cordelle the goods to Fort Benton. Then the steamboat hurried downriver to St. Louis to unload, on July 29, its Upper Missouri cargo: robes and furs, scientific specimens, and Charles Chouteau's latest collection of wild animals.[34]

As Pierre Chouteau gradually retired from active direction of the American Fur Company during the fifties, his son Charles not only assumed his father's business responsibilities, but continued the elder Chouteau's patronage of science. In January, 1856, Charles Chouteau and fourteen friends founded the Academy of Science of St. Louis, a successor organization to the older Western Academy of Natural Science. For over forty years Chouteau participated actively in the new academy, contributed numerous

[33] G. K. Warren to the Chief of the Topographical Bureau, September 15, 1855, May 24, July 13, October 4, 1856, Letters Received, 1855–1856, Topographical Bureau, RG 77, NA; Emerson G. Taylor, *Gouverneur Kemble Warren*, 30–31; Carl I. Wheat, *Mapping the Transmississippi West, 1540-1861*, IV, 56.

[34] *Daily Missouri Democrat*, July 30, 1856; *DMR*, August 9, 1856.

Upper Missouri natural-history specimens to the institution's museum, and sponsored several of his Upper Missouri associates (Culbertson, Galpin, Hodgkiss, Dawson, Kipp, Denig, Vaughan, and Frederic F. Gerard) for corresponding membership in the Academy.[35] Before the May meeting of the Academy, the executive board, on Chouteau's motion, voted to supply upriver American Fur Company posts with "suitable antiseptics . . . for the preparation of specimens in Natural History," and a St. Louis neurologist, Dr. Charles W. Stevens, accompanied Chouteau to the Upper Missouri aboard the *St. Mary* to collect specimens for the Academy. Six days after the *St. Mary* returned to St. Louis, Chouteau and Stevens jointly presented the Academy with fossils, animal skulls, and Indian curiosities. Stevens, in Indian Agent Vaughan's name, also gave the Academy a supplementary collection of skulls, fossils, and stuffed animals, and Benjamin Shumard contributed, for Charles Galpin, a new species of fossil shell from the Cheyenne River Valley.[36]

Late in the fall of 1856, Ferdinand V. Hayden (he had returned to the Missouri in 1854 following his earlier work with Meek in the Bad Lands) addressed the Academy on his recent upriver experiences. During his two years in the Indian country (1854–56), he had traveled without charge on American Fur Company boats and had sent his collections, also free of charge, via Company steamers to St. Louis, where Chouteau forwarded some to the East, as Hayden directed, and stored others until the young scientist returned from the upper river to examine them. Culbertson, who greatly admired Professor Baird of the Smithsonian and knew that Baird supported Hayden's project, gave Hayden all possible assistance on the Upper Missouri, and Charles Galpin, Company

[35] "Minutes of the Academy of Science of St. Louis," and "History of the Western Academy of Natural Science," Typescripts, MOSA. The "Minutes" also appear, in slightly altered content, in *Transactions of the Academy of Science of St. Louis*, Vol. I (1856–60).

[36] Quotation from "Minutes of the Academy of Science of St. Louis," MOSA. See also F. V. Hayden to S. F. Baird, July 11, 1856, Spencer F. Baird Private Letters, DSI.

bourgeois at Old Fort Pierre, "treated [Hayden] like a brother" and offered him financial support. Since Galpin possessed "a pretty good practical knowledge" of geology, he appreciated Hayden's work, but other upriver traders viewed the young scientist as a burden to the Company, despite Hayden's willingness to earn his keep by teaching the halfblood children at Old Fort Pierre and by carrying express messages from post to post.[37]

Hayden realized that he could not adequately repay the Company for supplies and protection and seriously considered accepting Galpin's offer of financial help. Chouteau, however, agreed to put up the money Hayden needed if Hayden and Vaughan (he was an amateur scientist as well as an Indian agent, supplied the Smithsonian with natural-history specimens, and was assisting Hayden's work) turned over to him approximately one-fourth of the specimens they collected. Hayden and Vaughan accepted Chouteau's offer and presented a portion of their collection to him in the spring of 1856; he, in turn, later placed it in the museum of the St. Louis Academy. The remainder of the Hayden-Vaughan collection found its way into eastern hands, and several choice items—fossils, skins, skulls, and animals preserved in alcohol —reached the Smithsonian. Hayden's work on the northern plains continued between 1857 and 1860, first in association with Lieutenant Warren, then in partnership once again with Meek, and finally in the ranks of Captain William F. Raynolds' military reconnaissance of the Yellowstone and Upper Missouri. After the Civil War, Hayden, always ambitious, always a political opportunist, returned to the West to command an extensive federally sponsored land survey of Nebraska and Wyoming, one of the so-called "Four Great Western Land Surveys."[38]

[37] F. V. Hayden to S. F. Baird, May 19, 24, 1854, February 9, April 6, May 10, 1855, Spencer F. Baird Private Letters, DSI; F. V. Hayden to George Engelmann, November 11, 1854, April 5, July 10, 1855, Engelmann (George) Papers, MOSB.

[38] F. V. Hayden to S. F. Baird, July 10, 1855, January 20, 1856, Spencer F. Baird Private Letters, DSI; "In Memoriam Charles Pierre Chouteau," *Transactions of the Academy of Science of St. Louis*, Vol. XI (1901), xxi–xxii; *Tenth Annual Report of the Board of Regents of the Smithsonian Institution*, 61.

In the days immediately following Hayden's speech to the St. Louis Academy in mid-November, 1856, navigation on the Missouri closed for the winter season and the Congress of the United States, in joint session, certified James Buchanan's presidential victory. His election continued Democratic control in Washington, to the satisfaction of the American Fur Company, but, as usual, brought job reshuffling in the Indian Office. James W. Denver replaced George W. Manypenny as Commissioner; John Haverty succeeded Alfred Cumming as Central Superintendent at St. Louis and, in March, 1858, was followed by Alexander M. Robinson; Alexander H. Redfield was given Vaughan's position as Upper Missouri agent; and Vaughan, in May, 1857, took over the Blackfoot Agency, previously held by Edwin A. C. Hatch and briefly by John H. McBrayer, who did not serve when appointed. While Buchanan formulated the outlines of his new administration during the winter of 1856–57, the Chouteaus carefully took the national political pulse, as they had on so many previous occasions, ran the St. Louis office of the American Fur Company on a business-as-usual basis, and authorized extensive midwinter remodeling of Fort Berthold. In January, however, James Kipp confirmed, in a letter to St. Louis from Fort Union, that a persistent rumor which had been bandied about for several months was true: smallpox was indeed raging in the Assiniboin-Crow country and the Indians blamed the opposition for bringing the epidemic to the plains.[39]

According to Vaughan and the Company's Upper Missouri agents, shortly after the steamer *Clara*, under Captain John Shaw, left St. Louis on July 14, 1856, with freight for the upriver opposition posts, smallpox broke out on the boat. The Captain refused to land the victims at lower-river posts, and as the vessel moved upriver, putting ashore supplies at Picotte and Company posts,

[39] Samuel E. McElderry to Pierre Chouteau, Jr., and Company, February 25, 1857, and James Kipp to Pierre Chouteau, Jr., and Company, January 29, 1857, Chouteau Family Papers, MoSHi.

smallpox infected the Arikaras, Mandans, Hidatsas, and Assiniboins and during the winter spread to the Crows, the Blackfeet, and the Red River métis. Kipp estimated that three hundred Assiniboins had died by late January, 1857, and that thousands of Indians had contracted the dreaded disease. On September 12, the *Clara* had returned to St. Louis from the mouth of the Yellowstone with three hundred bales of robes for Robert Campbell, but Captain Shaw reported to the press only that the upper river was low and navigation difficult. He preferred not to mention the smallpox.[40]

Both red and white men on the Upper Missouri ranked 1856 as a memorable year—memorable for the pestilence, certainly, but memorable also for the unusual visitors who passed through the country. In April (two months before Shaw took her to the Yellowstone) when the *Clara* made a round trip between St. Louis and Old Fort Pierre, she carried, in addition to government supplies, American Fur Company freight, and military passengers, a "jolly" party of young French nobles and their wives on a pleasure trip to the Sioux country. Two months later, in mid-June, the American Fur Company vessel *St. Mary*, bound upriver with a cargo of post supplies and Indian annuities, landed at Bellevue and took aboard the Reverend Elkanah D. Mackey and his wife Sarah, Presbyterian missionaries to the Blackfeet. Earlier that spring in St. Louis, Culbertson had "extended . . . every courtesy and encouragement" to the Mackeys in their mission and, aboard the boat, put the facilities of the Company at their disposal.[41] Since he had originally informed the executive committee of the Board of Foreign Missions of the Presbyterian Church, U.S.A., the Mackeys' sponsor, that the Blackfeet needed a mission and "felt a sincere desire to see [the Indians] brought under the influence of

[40] *Ibid.*; *DMR*, June 15, September 13, 1856; A. Vaughan to A. Cumming, October 27, 1856, 34 Cong., 3 sess., *SED No. 5*, pp. 636–37.

[41] Walter Lowrie, "North-Western Indian Missions," *The Home and Foreign Record of the Presbyterian Church in the United States of America*, Vol. VII (August, 1856), 240. On the voyage of the *Clara*, see *DMR*, April 21, June 12, 1856.

Christian civilization," he held himself responsible for the missionary couple's safety on the upper river.[42]

The Mackeys were warmly welcomed to the Indian country by Mrs. Culbertson, who boarded the boat at Fort Pierre, and Andrew Dawson, who joined them at Fort Clark and seemed pleased to see Presbyterians on the Upper Missouri. From Fort Union, Culbertson and the Mackeys journeyed overland in a wagon party (a three-week trip) to Fort Benton. There, on Sunday, August 17, a small "but very attentive" congregation, according to Indian Agent Hatch, heard "the sound of protestant divine service."[43] Although Catholic missionaries, such as Father Jeremiah F. Trecy, who was with the traders on White River between Fort Randall and the Great Bend in October, 1856, regularly visited the Upper Missouri in the fifties and regarded Fort Benton as a mission site as early as 1855, Protestant missionaries were rare in the area. The last Protestant missionary on the upper river—the Mackey's immediate predecessor—was the Reverend Stephen R. Riggs (sponsored by the American Board of Commissioners for Foreign Missions), who, accompanied by Alexander G. Huggins, a missionary farmer, had visited Fort Pierre sixteen years earlier. With baggage loaded upon two horses and a cart, the two men left the Lac qui Parle, Minnesota, mission on September 2, 1840, joined a westward-moving hunting party of friendly Indians, and reached Fort Pierre two weeks later. The traders at the post gave Riggs and Huggins "all the assistance in their power," but Riggs doubted that the fur men favored Protestant missionaries. Nevertheless, the Teton Sioux encamped around the post asked Riggs to establish a mission near Fort Pierre and told him that "their hearts were glad because light had come to them from the east." Since his Indian guides were anxious to return to Minnesota, he abandoned his

[42] *The Twentieth Annual Report of the Board of Foreign Missions of the Presbyterian Church of the United States of America*, 26.

[43] Diary of Edwin A. C. Hatch, June 7–October 13, 1856, Typescript, MnHi; E. D. Mackey, "Blackfeet Indian Mission," *The Home and Foreign Record of the Presbyterian Church in the United States of America*, Vol. VII (September, 1856), 271.

work at Fort Pierre after four days and rejoined his Minnesota mission. Although he recommended to his superiors that a Protestant mission be founded on the Upper Missouri, his request was rejected and a generation passed before his son, Thomas Riggs, built a Protestant mission near Old Fort Pierre.[44]

The Mackey's missionary career in Montana was, unexpectedly, almost as brief as Riggs's service at Fort Pierre. In September, 1856, the Mackeys accompanied Agent Hatch to the Judith River, where the Blackfoot annuities were distributed, and asked Lame Bull, the Blackfoot chief, for permission to set up a mission in his country. Lame Bull and his fellow chiefs agreed to the request, but Mrs. Mackey, pregnant, lonely, and unhappy in the wilds of Montana, fell ill before a mission could be founded and "it was at length necessary" for the missionary couple to return home to Maryland before heavy snow blocked the Upper Missouri country. During the winter of 1856–57, Mackey reported favorably to the Presbyterian Board of Foreign Missions on the Blackfoot mission plan and stressed that he was willing to return to the Indian country to open a school the following spring. The Board, however, preferred to wait until the government appropriated funds for Blackfoot Indian education and rejected Mackey's offer.[45]

The best-publicized visitor on the upper river in 1856 was not Reverend Mackey, however, but a wealthy, Oxford-educated baronet from northern Ireland, Sir St. George Gore, who reached Fort Union in the summer following a two-year game hunt in the

[44] Stephen R. Riggs, *Mary and I,* 64; Henry W. Casper, *History of the Catholic Church in Nebraska,* 83; *The Missionary Herald,* Vol. XXXVII (April, 1841), 180, 185; Stephen R. Riggs to David Green, November 9, 1840, ABCFM, MS 141: No. 64, Ayer Collection, ICN; Father J. F. Trecy to Bishop James M. O'Gorman, August 4, 1859, O'Gorman Papers, Archdiocesan Archives of the Catholic Church, Omaha. Lawrence B. Palladino, in his *Indian and White in the Northwest* (p. 331), noted that in October, 1855, Father James Croke, a Catholic missionary from Oregon, visited Fort Benton and baptized seventeen halfblood children belonging to Canadians attached to the post.
[45] *The Home and Foreign Record of the Presbyterian Church in the United States of America,* Vol. VIII (January, 1857), 13; *The Twentieth Annual Report of the Board of Foreign Missions of the Presbyterian Church of the United States of America,* 27; Ewers, *Blackfeet,* 195, 222–23.

high plains and northern Rockies. Sir George—most of his contemporaries dropped the "Saint" (and properly so)—traveled grandly, with more than two dozen vehicles piled high with supplies and camping comforts, a large herd of stock, and approximately forty men. Both Culbertson and Vaughan protested Sir George's hunting excesses and interference in Indian affairs, but the nobleman continued to wander freely in the Upper Missouri country until he appeared at Fort Union and asked Culbertson for transportation downriver. The two argued over cost, and Sir George, in a rage, burned most of his vehicles and supplies in front of the fort, tossed the warm metal remains into the river, sold or gave away his livestock, and floated downriver on two rickety flatboats to spend the winter at Fort Berthold. In the spring of 1857, he returned to St. Louis with a large collection of animal trophies for his home in Ulster. Many years later, Buffalo Bill Cody referred nostalgically to Sir George as "a sportsman among a thousand," but some of the Baronet's western contemporaries thought the "Irish Butcher" was a game hog.[46]

Along the Upper Missouri, the tribes remained quiet, traders bartered for more robes and furs than usual, and heavy snow piled up during the winter of 1856–57. In April, Sir George assembled his equipment to return to civilization from Fort Berthold, President Buchanan's appointees took up their jobs in the Indian Office, and boats bearing the year's first upriver fur returns floated down the Missouri toward the port of St. Louis. One of the early boats carried Joseph Picotte, who landed in St. Louis in mid-April, from Fort Campbell, located near the headwaters of the Missouri. Within three days of his arrival, he formally announced that the old opposition was dissolved. Since Harvey's death in 1854, Picotte had led the opposition on the Upper Missouri and had, until early 1857, rejected all propositions to join the Chouteaus or to dissolve Picotte and Company. But under pressure from Bouis,

[46] Clark C. Spence, "A Celtic Nimrod in the Old West," *Montana: The Magazine of Western History*, Vol. IX (April, 1959), 56–66; Henry Boller to his Father, May 20, 1858, Boller Papers, NdHi.

one of his principal traders, who was anxious to collect $10,000 owed him by the organization and "to quit the [Indian] country," Picotte decided to refuse Chouteau's latest offer, made early in the spring of 1857, to unite the two companies and end the old opposition. Picotte then talked to Campbell, who agreed to dissolve the business (at a cost of approximately $18,000) if Picotte consented to advise, for one year, a new Campbell-backed opposition beginning in the summer of 1857. Picotte said yes, and Campbell assembled a large outfit. Actually, Picotte and Company had been wrecked by three years of disagreement between Picotte, Bouis, Primeau, and Campbell and was finally overcome by the Chouteaus' competition. The American Fur Company had prevailed—another competitor fell apart—and figuratively, if not literally, bought out the remains of the opposition, only this time someone else, Robert Campbell, paid the bill.[47]

The new opposition, a loose coalition of businessmen, included Campbell, who continued to supply the opposition Upper Missouri posts from St. Louis; Picotte, who advised the traders in the field as he had promised; Primeau, who remained on the upper river as a trader; and Frost, Todd and Company. Daniel Marsh Frost, a former army colonel, had opened a St. Louis mercantile house in 1853 and three years later, in the summer of 1856, formed a partnership at Sioux City with another army veteran (Mary Todd Lincoln's cousin), John Blair Todd, and two Iowa men, Lewis H. Kennerly and Edward G. Atkinson. Todd, a man of great political talent, was appointed post sutler at Fort Randall before the end of the year, and Frost, who had served as post sutler at Old Fort Pierre while Harney's command was billeted there, was named civilian custodian of the post and stayed on to trade with the Indians when the army moved down to Fort Randall. Although Frost and the American Fur Company quarreled

[47] W. D. Hodgkiss to Pierre Chouteau, Jr., and Company, April 14, 1857, William Maffitt (?) to Pierre Chouteau, Jr., and Company, May 6, 1857, Chouteau Family Papers, MoSHi; William Maffit to Pierre Chouteau, Jr., and Company, May 14, 18, 1857, Pierre Chouteau, Jr., and Company Letter Book, 1856–1860, MoSHi; *DMR*, May 17, 1857.

over their respective rights at Old Fort Pierre, the shrewd army veteran held a bona fide government license (first issued in 1856 and reissued in 1857 with Campbell and David Mitchell as sureties) to trade with the Upper Missouri tribes, and the American Fur Company dared not brand him an unlicensed trader.[48]

By late May, 1857, Campbell and Frost, Todd and Company, with Picotte's assistance, had formulated the new anti-Chouteau alliance and had chartered the steamer *Twilight*, recently built in Louisville by Captain Shaw at a cost of $45,000, to carry the annual outfit to the Upper Missouri. On May 31, the light-draft steamer started upriver from St. Louis with more than four hundred tons of freight—fortunately, the boat's bottom planks were unusually strong—seventy Indian traders, and thirty passengers who enjoyed all the comforts of richly carpeted, satin-curtained cabins. At Fort Randall, Captain Shaw landed freight for the army garrison and took aboard the Hidatsa Indian Chief Four Bears and his family. Indian Agents Vaughan and Redfield, aboard the boat with the annuities (Campbell and Shaw had won the contract for 1857), discussed tribal problems with the Hidatsa leader and set him ashore a few days later.[49] Not far from Four Bears' village, however, Redfield witnessed the most memorable event of his upriver trip. About midnight, under a bright moon that outlined the crooked channel of the river, "the boat ran into an immense herd of Buffalo, which were swimming across the river." Before the vessel stopped, he said, "we could plainly feel the wheels strike against them; on going out we found the boat entirely surrounded by the poor, frightened creatures, struggling and panting in the strong current of the river."[50]

The *Twilight* reached Fort William on July 5 and unloaded

[48] Lamar, *Dakota Territory*, 37; Wilson, "Old Fort Pierre," *SDHC*, I, 290; Kingsbury, *Dakota Territory*, I, 116; Norman Thomas, "John Blair Smith Todd, First Dakota Delegate to Congress," *SDHC*, Vol. XXIV (1949), 181.

[49] *DMR*, April 28, June 1, 1857; A. H. Redfield to John Haverty, September 9, 1857, 35 Cong., 1 sess., *SED No. 11*, pp. 411–17.

[50] A. H. Redfield to John Haverty, September 9, 1857, 35 Cong., 1 sess., *SED No. 11*, pp. 416–17.

freight for the opposition; steamed upstream to the mouth of the Poplar to unload supplies for Fort Campbell and annuities, in Vaughan's care, for the Blackfeet; and promptly turned around and headed back to St. Louis. Agent Redfield, who remained at Fort William to arrange delivery of the Crow annuities before returning to St. Louis, met Malcolm Clark early in August when Clark passed through on his way from the Red River settlements to the Blackfoot country to take command of Fort Campbell for the opposition. Clark, at Fort Campbell, and Primeau, assigned by the opposition to Fort William, made up the so-called "Clark, Primeau and Company" subsidiary of the opposition and competed (with Campbell's support) against the American Fur Company until 1860. Meanwhile, on July 21, the *Twilight* tied up at the St. Louis levee. Captain Shaw told the press that the return trip was rapid and without incident, but de-emphasized the fact (perhaps his pride got the better of him) that he had unloaded, in addition to a large cargo of robes and furs for the opposition, the latest shipment of wild noisemakers—birds, buffalo, wolves, and wild dogs—for collectors.[51]

In anticipation of the dissolution of Picotte and Company and of stronger opposition from Campbell, the American Fur Company had sent the *Spread Eagle*, with Captain John La Barge (Joseph's brother) in the pilothouse and Culbertson and Charles Chouteau at his side on deck, to the Yellowstone three weeks in advance of the *Twilight*. Carrying $70,000 in Company freight, army supplies, and a handful of passengers, including Leo Dinkler, a St. Louis taxidermist sponsored by Charles Chouteau and the Academy of Science of St. Louis, the *Spread Eagle* completed the round trip to the upper river in forty-nine days (May 9–June 26) and brought into St. Louis five thousand packages of robes and furs for the Company.[52] Chouteau and Dinkler presented the

[51] *Ibid.*, p. 419; A. Vaughan to A. Cumming, August 20, 1857, *ibid.*, pp. 408–409; McDonnell, "Forts Benton and Sarpy," *CHSM*, X, 265 (n. 41); *DMR*, July 21, 22, 1857; *Daily Missouri Democrat*, July 22, 1857.

[52] *DMR*, May 9, 10, June 27, 1857; William Maffitt to Pierre Chouteau, Jr., May 10, 1857, Pierre Chouteau, Jr., and Company Letter Book, 1856–1860, MoSHi.

Academy with "beautiful specimens of Natural-Historical objects" collected on the voyage, and the following spring, Chouteau gave the Academy a 30.5-pound meteorite found near Old Fort Pierre. Unfortunately, the museum of the Academy burned several years later, and only the meteorite, out of all the natural-history specimens on display from the Upper Missouri, survived the blaze.[53]

[53] Quotation from "Minutes of the Academy of Science of St. Louis," MOSA. See also *Transactions of the Academy of Science of St. Louis*, Vol. I (1856–60), 711.

CHAPTER EIGHT

"For Fort Benton or bust"

THE PANIC OF 1857, ignited in August by the failure of the Ohio Life Insurance Company of Cincinnati, increased unemployment in eastern industrial towns and damaged middle western grain growers, but largely bypassed the South and the Upper Missouri country. For the time being—from the early fall of 1857 until the spring of 1858—St. Louis fur men held their cash in hand a little tighter, watched the market a little closer, and waited for the economic storm to clear. Fortunately, before the end of 1858, the tempest subsided and general prosperity returned. Alexander Culbertson took advantage of the national business lull and American Fur Company reorganization following Sarpy's death to reconsider his role in the fur trade. He had accumulated a large bank account during the previous decade and had purchased a farm near Peoria, Illinois. In the winter of 1857–58, while visiting in St. Louis and the East (the Secretary of the Interior asked him for his views on the Blackfeet, and Culbertson replied that he favored federal support of a Blackfoot farm and manual-labor school under provision of the Treaty of 1855), he arranged to retire partially from the fur trade. He bought additional acreage near Peoria where he built a manor house, *Locust Grove*, and, to indulge his wife, pitched a tipi on the lawn. Until 1862, however, he made regular trips to the Indian country, continued to speak with some authority in Upper Missouri affairs, and enjoyed little of the solitude he sought at his Illinois estate.[1]

During the spring of 1858, while Culbertson negotiated with

---

[1] C. E. Mix to A. Culbertson, March 2, 6, 1858, Letters Sent, OIA, RG 75, NA; McDonnell, "Forts Benton and Sarpy," *CHSM*, X, 241–42 (n. 2).

the Chouteau's, the season's first *voyageurs* and fur traders, with mackinaw cargoes from the Upper Missouri, drifted downstream behind the last large chunks of broken river ice and landed at towns between Sioux City and Omaha. Most of the traders were Company or opposition employees, but a few were free traders: independent men who disliked all fur companies and preferred, as others had preferred before them, to trade alone. One independent, the French Creole Louis Dauphin, had quarreled with both the American Fur Company and the opposition. He traded with the Indians at several locations between the Poplar and Milk rivers from the late fifties until the Sioux killed him in the mid-sixties, and shipped dugout loads of robes and furs down the Missouri to market in St. Louis. Canadian-born Augustin Hamell, one of Dauphin's contemporaries, was not a free trader but built tiny posts along Milk River and the Marias for the American Fur Company. Hamell's houses and Dauphin's posts—all small, crude, and impermanent structures—helped keep the fur trade alive, nonetheless, in the forties and fifties between the Yellowstone and the Falls of the Missouri.[2]

The first robe and fur shipments of the season, sent downriver by free trader Dauphin and agents employed by the American Fur Company and the opposition, reached St. Louis at about the time (early May) that Culbertson finished his business conversations with the Chouteaus and stepped aboard the steamer *Spread Eagle* to join his old friends Kipp and Dawson on the annual upriver voyage. The vessel, under general command of Charles Chouteau and Captain John La Barge, was well manned by an excellent engineer with attentive assistants"; an "amiable" second clerk serving under chief clerk Pierre M. Chouteau, a cousin to the Company owners; an "honest, candid" carpenter; and an "industrious mate." A half-dozen "ugly, uninteresting" women; a dozen "large, bald and warlike" Yankton Sioux, most of them

[2] "Floating on the Missouri—IV," *Forest and Stream*, Vol. LVIII (March 8, 1902), 183; McDonnell, "Forts Benton and Sarpy," *CHSM*, X, 261–62 (n. 27A), 292 (n. 212).

dressed in tribal regalia, returning to the upper river from "business of great importance" (treaty talks) in Washington; fifty to sixty traders and *voyageurs*, "mostly gumbo French"; and a miscellaneous lot of passengers, each paying $150 for the round trip, filled the boat to capacity. Charles Chouteau's friend and fellow amateur naturalist Dr. Thomas Kennard, scion of a wealthy, socially prominent Maryland family, had signed on as a boat surgeon. He wrote a detailed account of his free trip—sponsored by Chouteau—to the high Missouri and later donated to the Academy of Science of St. Louis minerals and fossils gathered on the voyage.[3]

On a "dismal and dreary" May 15, the *Spread Eagle* pulled away from the St. Louis levee in a torrential rain. For most of the upriver voyage, the weather remained cold, rainy, and windy, with occasional hail, and many of the woolen-clad passengers gathered frequently about the cabin stoves. Others took comfort in bottled heat, including three of the Sioux, who disturbed the peace aboard the steamer on the third night afloat. A few days later, however, the Yanktons left the vessel near the Vermillion, and tranquillity returned until the boat approached the Great Bend, where two or three Dakota Indian women ran along the bank and threatened to fire on the steamer. Captain La Barge steered the vessel away from the armed women, but a short time later when he landed to wood, two Indians "in almost perfect nudity" rushed aboard. Again the Captain and crew prevented a dangerous incident, and the *Spread Eagle* pushed on to the Sioux encampment (170 lodges) at Old Fort Pierre. The steamer landed; Chouteau talked with the chiefs and treated them to coffee and crackers; and the following morning, after the last Company freight had been unloaded and stored in the low, buffalo-skin-lined log and mud warehouse at Fort Pierre II, Captain La Barge ordered his German hands to cast off. A few Sioux warriors, for reasons best known to them, fired empty cartridges point blank at the crewmen. In the confusion

---

[3] Quotations from *DMR*, June 29, 1858. See also *ibid.*, May 15, 16, 1858; "Minutes of the Academy of Science of St. Louis," MOSA.

that followed, an interpreter advised Chouteau to give the Indians another feast. Chouteau took the suggestion, and the boat departed peacefully.[4]

Between Forts Pierre II and Berthold, sand bars clogged the channel and slowed the boat's progress, but there were few Indian incidents. One afternoon, however, two dozen Mandans and Arikaras "stealthily" boarded the boat at a wooding lot and proudly presented Culbertson a letter—gibberish to the Indians—from Hodgkiss at Fort Clark, warning the vessel that the red men were out to steal horses. Again Chouteau threw an impromptu feast of fat meat and bread, and the Indians withdrew full and happy. A few days later, on June 1, a crewman toppled into the river and was swept under the boat when the steamer struck a bar, but someone threw him a bucket on a line, and while he hung onto the improvised life preserver—and passengers dashed about the deck screaming—Captain La Barge and a few hands put out in a yawl and rescued him. At Forts Clark and Berthold, the boat landed briefly to unload Company goods. Only a few Indians, Arikaras, welcomed the steamer at Fort Clark, but at Fort Berthold a large number of Hidatsas lined the bank.[5]

Above Fort Berthold, Chouteau distributed corn to sixty-five lodges of starving Assiniboins, and on June 10, he feasted a large gathering of Blackfeet, Crees, Hidatsas, and Assiniboins at Fort Union after Mrs. Culbertson and the traders had reconciled, at least temporarily, the collection of traditionally antagonistic tribesmen. The following day, the *Spread Eagle*, towing two large mackinaws, headed up the Missouri toward Milk River, but early on the twelfth, one mackinaw got caught between the boat and the shore, was crushed, and was cut adrift. When the steamer reached a point fifty miles below Milk River, Chouteau, unwilling to push ahead against a contrary channel, ordered ashore all supplies and passengers bound for Fort Benton. Then the *Spread Eagle* fired three salutes from its cannon and turned downstream while the men ashore loaded the Fort Benton freight on the macki-

[4] *DMR*, June 29, 30, 1858.　　　　　[5] *Ibid*.

naw *Black Feet Star*. At Fort Union, the crew of the *Spread Eagle* buried ten-year-old Alexander Chompagne, who had died aboard the boat. Culbertson's "old intimate friend" Father Thomas Scanlon of St. Joseph, Missouri (the priest was interested in Black-foot missionary work and, evidently, had accompanied the steamboat on the upriver trip), performed the burial service. Immediately afterwards, the *Spread Eagle* sailed from Fort Union with approximately 1,700 packs of robes and furs; took on additional Company cargo at Forts Berthold, Clark, and Pierre II; and, despite difficult sailing near the Great Bend, added a large shipment of government freight at Fort Randall.[6] On June 28, La Barge steered the battered, overburdened steamer into port at St. Louis, and as soon as the cargo was unloaded, Chouteau sent the vessel to dry dock to be cleaned, repaired, and "furnished with an entire new cabin, of an elegant get-up . . . a handsome office, elegant pantry, roomy promenade, and extensive list of passenger apartments."[7]

The eventful 1858 voyage of the *Spread Eagle* was matched, almost incident by incident, by the "exceedingly agreeable and expeditious" round trip of the opposition vessel *Twilight*, commanded by Captain Shaw in agreement with Campbell and Frost, Todd and Company. Loaded with opposition freight and Indian annuities and stripped of carpets, mirrors, and draperies, the *Twilight* stood ready to leave St. Louis on the morning of May 23. An unusually large crowd lined the levee—normally somewhat deserted because business was still a bit slow in May, 1858. On the hurricane deck of the boat, Frost called the roll of *voyageurs*, or, rather, screamed to be heard above the singing French Canadians; the last passengers straggled aboard; and a couple of local landlords searched the vessel for delinquent boarders. Finally, in a cloud of black smoke, the *Twilight's* sidewheels turned, steam

[6] *Ibid*.; McDonnell, "Forts Benton and Sarpy," *CHSM*, X, 244–45 (n. 3); Manuscript File on the Reverend Thomas Scanlon, Pius XII Library, St. Louis University, St. Louis.

[7] Quotation from *Daily Missouri Democrat*, September 29, 1858. See also *DMR*, June 29, 1858.

roared from the boat's escape pipes, a cannon resounded, a crew-man played *Yankee Doodle* and *Oh! Susannah* on the steam cal-liope set astern, and everyone aboard, on the shore, and on boats tied up near by cheered as the *Twilight* swung away into a high, debris-filled river.[8]

Two miles above St. Louis, the boat took on a shipment of gun-powder, and a short distance below St. Charles, Frost, having supervised the proper storage of cargo and livestock, disembarked. At Jefferson City, Indian Agent Vaughan and several other pas-sengers boarded the vessel while the steam calliope filled the town with music; then the boat pushed upriver. The crew, under Cap-tain Shaw (master), consisted of two pilots (one was a "devotee of Shakespeare, quoting or reciting page after page of his Trage-dies without interruption of his duties at the helm"), two engi-neers, cooks, clerks, cabin boys, deck hands, and approximately seventy-five "stout laboring" woodcutters.[9] The all-male pas-senger list included fur traders and *voyageurs* under contract to Frost, two Lutheran missionaries, an artist, two English sports-men, a young Harvard graduate traveling for his health, a dozen sight-seers (tourism on the Upper Missouri picked up consider-ably in the fifties and gave steamboatmen a new source of reve-nue), and six young boys chaperoned by Indian Agent Redfield (father to one of the boys) and his brother. Redfield "was a staid, straight-laced gentleman," but Vaughan, his "frolicsome" Indian Service colleague, as usual "patronized [the] bar late into the night and when asked of his health in the morning would say 'Erect on my pasterns, bold and vigorous.' " But Redfield had good reason to be "staid." Whenever the boat landed in an uninhabited place, the boys in his party—his charges, his responsibility—explored

8 Henry Boller to his Mother, May 22–23, 1858, Boller Papers, NdHi; A. M. Robinson to C. E. Mix, May 8, 15, 1858, Letters Received, OIA, RG 75, NA; A. Vaughan to A. M. Robinson, September 10, 1858, 35 Cong., 2 sess., *SED No. 1*, pp. 429–30; Boller, *Among the Indians*, 12–15.

9 Henry Boller to his Mother, May 22–23, 1858, Boller Papers, NdHi; W. B. Napton, *Over the Santa Fe Trail in 1857*, 76–77.

ashore, competed in shooting matches, and splashed in the river, unmindful of Indians.[10]

At Sioux City, where Frost, Todd and Company ran a store, the *Twilight* loaded on an additional twenty tons of opposition freight. Five days later, on June 6, when the boat, its calliope blaring, landed at the Yankton Sioux settlement, the Indians "were seized with . . . panic" and fled the riverbank until the calliope stopped. Then they reassembled near the boat, and Carl Wimar, the artist on the *Twilight*, photographed with a crude box camera (an ambrotype) "several groups" of half-frightened Indians. Aboard the steamer, Agent Redfield treated with the Sioux chiefs, listened carefully to their grievances against white settlers in the area, and promised to make amends. By the time the boat pulled away from the Yankton settlement and continued upstream toward Fort Randall, the passengers realized that whenever the vessel touched an Indian village, all aboard were in danger of attack. At Fort Randall, their fears were relieved, however, when Major H. W. Wessells hurriedly led approximately forty soldiers aboard to convoy the boat upriver, yet the *Twilight* stayed at the fort long enough for the regimental band to entertain the visitors and for the "exceedingly courteous" officers to give the passengers a tour of the ten-acre military quadrangle. The passengers, certainly, felt safer with the soldiers aboard the steamboat, but the crew was unimpressed with the boys in fatigue uniforms and called the troopers "useless saviors."[11]

Above Fort Randall, the upper Yankton Sioux at the Great Bend, overawed by sight of the soldiers, accepted Agent Redfield's annuities quietly. Nevertheless, the eight bands of Teton Sioux at Old Fort Pierre were decidedly more hostile than the Yanktons and took their large pile of goods without pleasure or

[10] Quotation from Napton, *Santa Fe Trail*, 77. See also A. H. Redfield to John D. Caton, May 12, June 14, 1858, Photostats, SdHi.

[11] Henry Boller to his Mother, June 14, 1858, Boller Papers, NdHi; Napton, *Santa Fe Trail*, 84; *DMR*, July 11, 1858; Perry T. Rathbone, *Charles Wimar, 1828–1862*, 19.

gratitude. Big Head's band of Sioux entirely ignored the meeting at Old Fort Pierre and met the boat on June 16 well above the old trading post. Hundreds of Big Head's tribesmen assembled on the riverbank, howled angry protests at the military escort, fired shots of welcome closer than usual to the boat (some bullets hit the wheelhouse), and galloped their mounts back and forth along the water's edge. Under close military surveillance—Major Wessells held tight rein on his command aboard the steamer and posted guards day and night throughout the upriver trip—Agent Redfield feasted the angry Sioux, distributed annuities, and restored order temporarily.[12]

On shore, during the prolonged council between Redfield and the Sioux leaders aboard the boat, young Wimar attempted to take a candid photograph of a Sioux medicine man, but gave up the plan when the Indian drew an arrow. Since Wimar dared not photograph Big Head's band or even sketch them in pencil or pastels, he traded with them for a bow and a quiver of arrows. They picked his pockets in return, but his loss was small in comparison to the artistic value he placed upon the Indian curiosities he gathered. Although he had visited the Upper Mississippi Valley in 1849, the thin, dark, German artist was making his first trip up the Missouri in 1858 and hoped to improve his painting by close study of Indian objects. He stored the "artifacts, handicrafts and raiment" that he collected on the Missouri in his cluttered St. Louis studio and used the material to illustrate further the sketches he made in the field. The finished canvases were "bold, free, expanded" works of art unlike his earlier "tight," properly academic painting at Düsseldorf.[13]

On June 19, at rat-infested Fort Clark, Captain Shaw anchored the *Twilight* offshore to avoid the Arikaras, who were nearly destitute and likely to rob the vessel. When Redfield offered the Indians their annuities, they angrily fired their guns at his feet

[12] Henry Boller to Col. F. Boller, June 23, 1858, and to David Ranken, June 26, 1858, Boller Papers, NdHi; Napton, *Santa Fe Trail*, 85, 87–88; Rathbone, *Wimar*, 20–21; *DMR*, July 11, 1858.

[13] Rathbone, *Wimar*, 18.

(one shot close enough to leave powder burns on his clothes) and only reluctantly, after a five-hour council, accepted the goods. Both the Arikaras and the Sioux believed the annuity provisions of the 1851 Treaty of Fort Laramie to be inadequate, and Redfield judged that only the superior force aboard the *Twilight* saved the vessel from Indian assault. The following day, when the steamer reached Fort Berthold, however, the few Hidatsas and Mandans present—most were out hunting buffalo—accepted their annuities with thanks, and Wimar, hidden behind a curtain, photographed the Indians.[14]

On the lower edge of the Hidatsa-Mandan village (Like-a-Fishhook Village) immediately below Fort Berthold (the American Fur Company post which stood on the upper edge of the village), Frost, Todd and Company workmen were building a new opposition trading post in the summer of 1858, named Fort Atkinson in honor of Edward G. Atkinson, "the resident partner [of the opposition] in the Indian country." Fort Atkinson, larger than Fort Berthold, rose around the dilapidated remains of a small trading post previously operated at that point by Harvey, Primeau and Company. When completed, the new fort, 120 feet square, was protected by a sixteen-foot timbered stockade and two towers. The one-story buildings inside the wall were white-washed, and the chief trader's house, a "cosy and comfortable" dwelling, boasted two cottonwood bedsteads covered with robes and gaudy calico curtains. On the Fourth of July, the men at Fort Berthold opened their jugs of illicit whiskey—some brought up-river secretly, some brought in from Red River—to celebrate Independence Day; the men at Fort Atkinson, who were not too busy with construction, joined in; the village Indians included themselves in the festivities, "brandishing weapons and uttering terrific yells"; and for a week red men and white men caroused together. Later in 1858, at Christmastide, "the Big Medicine day

---

[14] A. H. Redfield to C. E. Mix, June 14, 21, 1858, Letters Received, OIA, RG 75, NA; Boller, *Among the Indians*, 28; Rathbone, *Wimar*, 23; *DMR*, July 11, 1858.

of the whites," both posts feasted the Indians with roasts, puddings, and pies. In return, the Indians gave the traders small gifts, and again the rival traders and the tribesmen enjoyed "a regular frolic" until dawn, when the last celebrant gave up from too much dancing and feasting. By the end of the year, the men at the two posts lived in a pattern of friendly competition and enjoyed exchanging visits, celebrating holidays together, and, generally, making Upper Missouri life more bearable.[15]

Meanwhile, the *Twilight* had steamed upriver from the Hidatsa-Mandan village to Fort William, where Redfield told the Assiniboins assembled there to move over to Fort Union, a safer location, to receive their annuities, and Malcolm Clark ordered the opposition post abandoned. Clark, who had spent the previous winter at Fort Campbell and had returned to St. Louis early in May, 1858, in time to talk over opposition business problems with Campbell and Frost before ascending the Missouri on the *Twilight*, knew that the Assiniboins were too frightened of the Sioux to receive their annuities at Fort William, and he therefore planned to build a new post farther up the Missouri. On June 22, Clark quickly loaded the *Twilight* with the stores from Fort William, and the boat proceeded to Fort Union the same day to disembark the Assiniboin and Crow annuities in good time from St. Louis, despite the loss of precious time to a falling channel; sand bars; two accidents to the boat's steering gear; frequent stops for wood; and the many delays occasioned by Indian war parties, councils, and general tribal contrariness.[16]

After a few hours at the American Fur Company post, Captain Shaw directed the *Twilight* up the Missouri to a landing point on the north bank of the river approximately five miles by water above the mouth of the Big Muddy. There he landed the Blackfoot annuities, and Agent Vaughan set out overland to gather the

---

[15] Henry Boller to his Father, December 1, 1858, and to his Sister, May 23, 1858, Boller Papers, NdHi; Boller, *Among the Indians*, 75–76, 78–79, 253–54.
[16] *DMR*, May 8, July 11, 1858; Boller, *Among the Indians*, 39–40.

Blackfeet together to receive their yearly goods. Clark sent ashore opposition supplies from Fort William and immediately began to build Fort Stewart (or Stuart) for the Assiniboin-Crow trade. On June 25, the *Twilight*, calliope blasting, turned downstream. She landed briefly at Fort Union to take on ice, then steamed downriver, stopping along the way to receive robes and furs at opposition posts. At the Arikara village, Captain Shaw hired Indian women to carry bales of robes, atop their heads and shoulders, from the warehouse to the boat. The women took the heavy duty in stride while the Arikara men watched and smoked. After loading quartermaster freight at Fort Randall, the heavily laden *Twilight* avoided unnecessary stops and churned along the lower river to reach St. Louis on July 10.[17]

Indian Agent Redfield, who remained at Fort Union when the *Twilight* descended the Missouri, contracted with Culbertson for the American Fur Company to carry up the Yellowstone the Crow annuities of both 1857 (they had been stored at Fort William) and 1858. On July 6, Redfield, accompanied by Wimar, the two Lutheran missionaries from the *Twilight*, and a band of Company *voyageurs* and traders, started up the Yellowstone on two mackinaws. Three weeks later, near the mouth of Powder River —after constant cordelling by the *voyageurs* in cold, rainy weather along almost impassable riverbanks—Redfield, ill with fever, was forced to return to Fort Union on the smaller mackinaw while the larger craft continued upriver to the Yellowstone post. Redfield's associate, Henry W. Beeson, escorted the annuities to Fort Sarpy II, distributed them, and returned to Fort Union with Wimar. On September 1, Redfield, Wimar, and a half-dozen

---

[17] A. Vaughan to A. M. Robinson, September 10, 1858, 35 Cong., 2 sess., *SED No. 1*, p. 430; E. G. Atkinson to C. E. Mix, March 26, 1859, Letters Received, OIA, RG 75, NA; "Report of Colonel Raynolds," 40 Cong., 2 sess., *SED No. 77*, pp. 113–14; Napton, *Santa Fe Trail*, 96–97; *Daily Missouri Democrat*, July 12, 1858; *DMR*, July 11, 1858. Fort Stewart (or Stuart) was named in honor of Lieutenant Colonel Adam D. Steuart, who had resigned as Deputy Paymaster of the U.S. Army in 1855.

companions left Fort Union in a mackinaw and rowed and floated their way downstream until they met the packet *Omaha*, in mid-October, and boarded it for St. Louis.[18]

Jacob J. Schmidt and Moritz Braeuninger, the Lutheran missionaries, had gone to the Yellowstone country carrying a license, issued by Agent Redfield, permitting them to live one year with the Crows. Through Redfield's influence with Captain Shaw, the missionaries received either free or very inexpensive passage to Fort Union on the *Twilight* (they conducted morning and evening services aboard the steamer on the way upriver), and Culbertson allowed them to travel free of charge with the Redfield-Wimar party up the Yellowstone to Fort Sarpy II. The American Fur Company provisioned Schmidt and Braeuninger on the mackinaw voyage upriver and permitted them to stay at the Crow post. But Fort Sarpy II was unappealing to most visitors. In 1859, Captain William F. Raynolds praised the well-defended fifteen-foot cottonwood stockade of the post and the defensive loopholes at the top of the wall, yet he called the fort "a decidedly primitive affair." The missionaries found life intolerable at the post, where, according to them, vice prevailed and the traders accorded them little consideration. Since the 1,500 Crows encamped near the post were unusually friendly to the missionaries, the two men borrowed Indian horses and spent two months traveling and learning enough of the Crow language to "make themselves understood to a certain extent." Having promised the Indians that they would return the following year, Schmidt and Braeuninger left the Crow country early in October and by late November reached Lutheran Iowa Synod headquarters at St. Sebald, Iowa.[19]

The Synod decided immediately to sponsor a more permanent

---

[18] A. H. Redfield to A. M. Robinson, September 1, October 12, 1858, 35 Cong., 2 sess., *SED No. 1*, pp. 436–44; A. H. Redfield to Alfred B. Greenwood, May 25, 1859, Letters Received, OIA, RG 75, NA; Rathbone, *Wimar*, 23–24.

[19] "Report of Colonel Raynolds," 40 Cong., 2 sess., *SED No. 77*, p. 50; A. H. Redfield to A. M. Robinson, September 1, 1858, 35 Cong., 2 sess., *SED No. 1*, p. 443; Henry Boller to his Mother, May 31, 1858, Boller Papers, NdHi; Albert Keiser, *Lutheran Mission Work Among the American Indians*, 99–100; Erwin G.

Crow mission and outfitted Schmidt, Braeuninger, and four associates to return to the Indian country. In July, 1859, the mission party left Iowa and traveled overland to Deer Creek, near Fort Laramie, where they planned to meet the Crows. When the Indians failed to appear, two missionaries returned to Iowa for additional supplies while the others constructed winter shelter on Deer Creek. The following year, after Braeuninger was killed by the Sioux on Powder River, the Synod ordered the mission to remain at Deer Creek. But mission life near Fort Laramie was dangerous, and in 1867, the Synod, short of money for missionary work, voted to close the Deer Creek station.[20]

Within a month after Redfield and Wimar boarded the packet *Omaha* and Schmidt and Braeuninger set out from the Crow country for St. Sebald, in 1858, Upper Missouri navigation closed for the year. In St. Louis, the Chouteaus and the opposition, as in so many years past, reviewed the season's trade and planned for the new year. The opposition had worked hard on the Upper Missouri in 1858 and had earned a good return in robes and furs. Daniel Frost, leader of the opposition partnership, was a driving, no-excuses-allowed type of business organizer—"just such a man as you would expect a graduate of West Point to be." *Voyageurs* and traders who signed on with the opposition knew that Frost would refuse to pay them if they broke their contracts and that he was no more lenient than the American Fur Company. In 1858, while he presided over the busy, sometimes "fairly besieged" St. Louis office of the opposition and outfitted the upriver posts with goods from Campbell and other merchants, his partners ran company business above Sioux City and kept him informed by express of upriver conditions.[21]

Fritschel, "A History of the Indian Mission of The Lutheran Iowa Synod" (Typescript, Bachelor of Theology Thesis, Wartburg Theological Seminary, Dubuque, Iowa), p. 154.

[20] Fritschel, "Indian Mission," pp. ii–v.; Keiser, *Lutheran Mission Work*, 101–102.

[21] Quotation from Henry Boller to his Father, May 17, 1858, Boller Papers, NdHi. See also Henry Boller to his Father, May 18, 19, 1858, *ibid.*; Boller, *Among the Indians*, 262.

Actually, by late 1858, Frost, Todd and Company was more interested in Dakota land speculation than it was in the Upper Missouri robe and fur trade. Since the partners held an Indian trading license, controlled the sutlership at Fort Randall, operated the largest wholesale house in Sioux City, and, in 1857, had placed trading posts on the James River and in other strategic locations in the lower Yankton Sioux country, they were well prepared to plunge into Dakota land manipulation. Early in 1858, Todd led a delegation of Yankton Sioux, who represented only a portion of the tribe, to Washington, D.C., to sign, on April 19, a treaty whereby the Yanktons ceded a triangular plot of land between the Big Sioux and Missouri rivers and withdrew to a reservation in exchange for $1,600,000 in annuities payable over fifty years. Since white squatters on the newly ceded land were permitted to purchase choice parcels at low prices, Frost, Todd and Company (through the Upper Missouri Land Company) claimed several excellent townsites, especially around the new settlement and future territorial capital of Yankton.[22]

Although Frost, Todd and Company was deeply involved in Dakota land deals by the winter of 1858–59, the partners continued to oppose the American Fur Company in the Upper Missouri fur trade and fought doggedly, but unsuccessfully, to win the Indian-annuity contract awarded the American Fur Company in March, 1859, for two years rather than the usual one. Previously, in June, 1858, Captain Joseph Throckmorton, the highly regarded Missouri River pilot, had asked the Indian Office to award him a four-year contract, covering the period 1859–62, to transport annuities to the Upper Missouri. In exchange, he promised to build a comfortable yet light-draft steamer to carry them from St. Louis to Fort Benton and to all annuity distribution points in between. Direct steamer service to Fort Benton would end the slow, laborious keelboat transportation of Blackfoot annuities above the Yellowstone–Milk River region. Alexander Robinson,

[22] Kingsbury, *Dakota Territory*, I, 117, 120; Lamar, *Dakota Territory*, 37–38; Schell, *South Dakota*, 70–71.

Superintendent of Indian Affairs in St. Louis (the office was moved to St. Joseph before the end of 1859), believed Captain Throckmorton's proposal sound. Since it would undoubtedly save the government money by assuring ready transportation at set rates and might prove the Missouri, and perhaps even the Yellowstone, navigable to steamers above Fort Union, Robinson, in a December, 1858, letter to the Commissioner of Indian Affairs, endorsed Throckmorton's plan.[23]

When Charles Chouteau learned of Robinson's action, he sent a private proposal, similar to Throckmorton's, to the Indian Office. A few weeks later, on March 26, 1859, Edward Atkinson, representing Frost, Todd and Company, also bid on the annuity contract. He criticized the Indian Office for allowing Chouteau to submit a private bid and added, in his letter, that opposition interests would be "greatly injured" if the government persisted in special favors to the American Fur Company. The Commissioner, however, had recommended to the Secretary of the Interior, two weeks before Atkinson's bid was even submitted, that Chouteau be awarded the contract and the Secretary had concurred on March 14. Although the contract was awarded politically, the American Fur Company bid was lower than either Throckmorton's or the opposition's—and lower than Captain Shaw's winning bid of 1857. Charles Chouteau intended to win the battle with the Upper Missouri, a battle joined by the American Fur Company a quarter-century before, and to send a steamer, *à la Throckmorton*, to conquer the river all the way to Fort Benton.[24]

The value of American Fur Company robe returns for 1857–58 was average (approximately $300,000), the domestic robe market was slow, and the European market still suffered from the dis-

[23] J. Throckmorton to C. E. Mix, June 2, July 12, 1858, and to Jacob Thompson, August 7, 1858, and A. M. Robinson to James W. Denver, December 8, 1858, Letters Received, OIA, RG 75, NA.

[24] Pierre Chouteau, Jr., and Company to C. E. Mix, March 12, 1859, J. Thompson to C. E. Mix, March 14, 1859, and E. G. Atkinson to C. E. Mix, March 26, 1859, *ibid*.

ruption of the recent Crimean War and was overstocked with skins. If market conditions failed to improve in 1859 and 1860, St. Louis fur men were threatened with a large surplus of robes on hand, since the Upper Missouri hunt was above average in the winter of 1858–59. Should the American Fur Company open dependable steamer traffic between St. Louis and Fort Benton, however, any seasonal decrease in Company profit from poor fur and robe returns could be offset by revenue earned from carrying passengers, Indian annuities, non-Company freight, and military supplies and men to Fort Benton. Thus in 1859, the Upper Missouri carrying trade assumed new significance to the Chouteaus and the opposition.[25]

Charles Chouteau seldom gambled with the prestige of the American Fur Company, but by accepting the two-year annuity contract, he also accepted the challenge of steamboat navigation to Fort Benton; and to reduce the odds against the Company, he needed a small, light-draft vessel to fight the shallow, broken channel of the Missouri above the mouth of the Yellowstone. Fortunately for the Company, after searching the boatyards, Chouteau found the ideal steamer, the 165-foot stern-wheeler *Chippewa*, owned by Captain M. H. Crapster, a Baltimore physician who had drifted from medicine to steamboating. Crapster agreed to take the "small, staunch" boat upriver as a tender to the larger, heavier *Spread Eagle*, commanded, as usual, by Captain John La Barge, and Chouteau immediately outfitted both steamers for the voyage. Approximately sixty cabin passengers and eighty "deckers," mostly Company employees, left St. Louis, to the sound of cannon, shortly before noon on May 28 aboard the heavily freighted *Spread Eagle*. In addition to Chouteau and Culbertson, the vessel carried other distinguished travelers: Hayden, the American Fur Company's favorite scientist, was on his way upriver, again free of charge; John Pearsall, a taxidermist spon-

---

[25] *Annual Statement of the Trade & Commerce of St. Louis for the Year 1858*, p. 39; Price Report by Ramsay Crooks' Son and Company, 1859, McKenzie Papers, MoSHi.

sored by the Smithsonian (he also traveled free of charge because Professor Baird had promised to give Chouteau, for the Academy of Science of St. Louis, the "greater bulk" of whatever natural-history specimens Pearsall collected); a 22-year-old world traveler, big-game hunter, and "good fellow" who adapted himself well to whatever society he was in, Lord Richard–De Aquila Grosvenor, second son of the Marquis of Westminster; one of Chouteau's "very agreeable and pleasant" colleagues in the Academy, the young St. Louis physician (and, on this voyage, boat surgeon in exchange for free passage) Elias J. Marsh; and Carl Wimar, the painter.[26]

At Leavenworth, Kansas, the *Spread Eagle* took on mules, additional freight, and several new passengers, including Jim Bridger, the renowned fur trader, guide, and Indian fighter, and Lieutenant Henry E. Maynadier of the U.S. Army Topographical Engineers. Upriver, at St. Joseph, Indian Agents Vaughan (he had descended the Missouri from Fort Benton earlier in the spring) and Bernard S. Schoonover, who had recently replaced Redfield as Upper Missouri agent when Redfield was appointed Yankton agent, boarded the boat. Captain William F. Raynolds (Topographical Engineers) also joined the vessel at St. Joseph. He was in charge of an army expedition to reconnoiter the Upper Yellowstone–Powder River region for possible wagon routes. His investigation of the Indians, geography, natural resources, and climate of Montana and Wyoming continued and broadened the earlier work of Gouverneur K. Warren in Nebraska and the Dakotas. A thirty-man military escort for Raynolds' party boarded the *Spread Eagle* at Fort Randall, and at Fort Pierre II, on June 18, Chouteau disembarked the army group—including Hayden, Jim Bridger, and Maynadier, who was Raynolds' second in

[26] *DMR*, May 4, 28, 30, August 22, 1859; F. V. Hayden to S. F. Baird, June 13, 1859, Spencer F. Baird Private Letters, DSI; S. F. Baird to C. P. Chouteau, March 31, 1859, Spencer F. Baird Letters Written, 18, DSI; C. P. Chouteau to S. F. Baird, April 21, 1859, Spencer F. Baird Letters Received, 1859, DSI; "Minutes of the Academy of Science of St. Louis," MOSA; "Journal of Dr. Elias J. Marsh," *SDHR*, Vol. I (January, 1936), 81–83.

command—and, according to the American Fur Company contract with the federal government, part of Raynolds' supplies. On June 28, the military party headed west from Fort Pierre II to Fort Sarpy II, where, late in August, the Company delivered to them the remainder of the supplies, shipped up the Yellowstone via mackinaw transportation from Fort Union.[27]

As long as Raynolds remained in the Indian country (another fifteen months), he and his subordinates were received hospitably whenever they visited an American Fur Company post. Robert Meldrum, Company bourgeois at Fort Sarpy II in 1859, helped Raynolds draw a map of the terrain between the Yellowstone and the Platte, and the following year when Maynadier stopped at Fort Benton for provisions, he was "courteously" received, given "pleasant" overnight accommodations, entertained at a dance in the expedition's honor, and generally showered with "unremitting . . . attention."[28] Other army surveying parties, such as the one under Lieutenant John Mullan that was laying out a military road from Walla Walla to Fort Benton, found upriver Company and opposition posts alike as hospitable to visitors in the late fifties as they were ten or twenty years earlier. In December, 1859, Mullan and his party spent a comfortable week at Fort Benton, then took shelter for the winter in an isolated mountain camp, and finally completed the survey, a major one by all standards, in the summer of 1861.[29]

At Omaha, shortly after Raynolds boarded the *Spread Eagle* for Fort Pierre II in mid-June, 1859, the steamer *Chippewa* (she had sailed from St. Louis on May 25, four days before her larger sister vessel) joined the *Spread Eagle* in tandem voyage. In comparison, however, to the previous year, when Indian troubles

[27] "Journal of Marsh," *SDHR*, I, 84–85; "Report of Colonel Raynolds," 40 Cong., 2 sess., *SED No.* 77, pp. 47–49.
[28] Elmer Ellis (ed.), "The Journal of H. E. Maynadier," *NDHQ*, Vol. I (January, 1927), 41–42; "Report of Colonel Raynolds," 40 Cong., 2 sess., *SED No.* 77, pp. 49, 110, 114.
[29] "Report on the Construction of a Military Road from Fort Walla Walla to Fort Benton," 37 Cong., 3 sess., *SED No. 43*, p. 147.

plagued the *Twilight,* the two American Fur Company vessels in 1859 experienced fewer tribal incidents on the way upriver. The Yankton Sioux, in full regalia, visited the boats below Fort Randall and feasted on coffee and hard bread. Although disappointed that Agent Redfield was not aboard the boats with Indian annuities, the Yanktons agreed to wait patiently for their goods when they learned that Redfield was on his way with the annuities aboard the packet *Carrier.* At Fort Pierre II, chiefs of five Teton Sioux bands objected to Raynolds' plan to march west across Indian country—the red men were irritated by the recent Yankton land cession—and swore they would not be responsible if Sioux warriors attacked the military party. Chouteau, Vaughan, and Galpin believed that the chiefs meant what they said and called a meeting aboard the *Spread Eagle.* After two days in council, the Indians agreed to grant Raynolds safe passage westward and to allow Vaughan to land the annuities, even though the tribesmen thought they were inadequate, and store them ashore for distribution.[30]

Between Forts Pierre II and Union, the tribes, for the moment more interested in hunting and raising corn than waging war, were friendly and received peacefully their annuities from Schoonover, the new Upper Missouri agent. Late in the evening of June 30, the two vessels reached Fort Union, and two days later, Captain Crapster, according to a previous agreement with the Company, sold Chouteau the *Chippewa* for $13,700. Crapster, the crew from the *Chippewa,* and three or four passengers from the *Spread Eagle* left the fort almost immediately after the sale and floated downriver on a mackinaw boat, through hot weather and abundant mosquitoes, to Sioux City, where they transferred to the packet *Carrier,* bound for St. Louis. The same day, July 2, that Crapster's party started downriver from the mouth of the Yellowstone, Agent Schoonover, with the Crow annuities in his care, joined a party under Meldrum of the American Fur Com-

[30] *DMR,* July 26, 1859; "Report of Colonel Raynolds," 40 Cong., 2 sess., *SED No. 77,* p. 18.

pany headed, via mackinaw, up the Yellowstone to Fort Sarpy II. Meanwhile, Chouteau loaded the *Chippewa* with 160 tons of freight, lashed a mackinaw to each side of the vessel, and on July 3, ordered Captain La Barge to pilot the small stern-wheeler up the Missouri to Fort Benton.[31]

Early on the Fourth of July, the *Chippewa* fired her guns as she passed Fort Kipp, a new, "very small" American Fur Company post located about six hundred feet from Fort Stewart (the opposition post) a few miles above the mouth of the Big Muddy. James Kipp, chief agent at Fort Union, had founded the new Company post, named in his honor, in the spring of 1859 to compete with the opposition for the Assiniboin trade. West of Forts Kipp and Stewart, the *Chippewa* churned slowly upstream atop a low, shifting channel. At Dauphin's Rapids, the crew cordelled the boat through a fast, treacherous current, and three days later, Chouteau released one of the mackinaws—damaged in the stern— and the following day released the second to reduce the drag on the steamer. Fortunately, by then the *Chippewa* was nearing the mouth of the Marias, had set a new record for navigation above Milk River, and could do without the mackinaw lighters. Chouteau ordered the boat to land at Old Fort McKenzie (Fort Brûlé) on July 17; after sounding the channel, he decided it was useless to continue upriver, and disembarked freight for Fort Benton, located a dozen miles upstream. Then, by land, he briefly visited Fort Benton, arranged for cordwood to be cut for steamer use the next season, and returned to Old Fort McKenzie, where he re-boarded the *Chippewa* and commanded Captain La Barge to head the vessel downstream.[32]

[31] Charles W. Schlieffarth to C. N. Kessler, March 2, 1919, Wimar Papers, MoSHi; *DMR*, July 26, 1859; "Report of Chas. P. Chouteau to the Secretary of War of a Steamboat Expedition from St. Louis to Fort Benton, 1859," *CHSM*, Vol. VII (1910), 253.

[32] "Journal of Marsh," *SDHR*, I, 105; *DMR*, July 26, 1859; "Report of Chas. P. Chouteau," *CHSM*, VII, 254–56; Chittenden, *Early Steamboat Navigation*, I, 219; A. Vaughan to A. M. Robinson, July 24, 1859, 36 Cong., 1 sess., *SED No. 2*, pp. 483–84.

On the way downriver, the steamer was damaged—nearly disabled—in the rapids and buffeted about by heavy winds above the Yellowstone. The Indians along the river remained quiet, however, game was plentiful for hunters from the boat, and at the mouth of White River, just below the Great Bend, the *Chippewa* overtook the *Spread Eagle* descending from Fort Union. They passed Sioux City together on August 9, but then the "somewhat dilapidated" and heavily loaded *Chippewa* slowed down to mud-crawl speed, and the *Spread Eagle* pushed ahead to land in St. Louis, her guns booming to wake up the levee, on the afternoon of August 16. The Company unloaded forty thousand robes and a "forest of antlers" from the vessel, and Dr. Marsh disembarked a collection of Indian artifacts, some given him by Andrew Dawson and Mrs. Culbertson at Fort Union. On August 20, the *Chippewa* finally arrived, and Chouteau announced proudly that a new highway had been opened to the Falls of the Missouri.[33] He sent the Secretary of War a detailed account of the upriver trip of the two vessels and predicted that "with suitable boats and the removal of boulders here and there obstructing the channel and forming the rapids," the Upper Missouri could "be made just as safe and easy [for navigation] as the Upper Mississippi and Ohio rivers." "I have no hesitation in affirming," he added, "that the trip from Saint Louis to Ft. Benton can be easily accomplished within thirty-five days."[34]

The extensive publicity given the voyage of the *Chippewa* and the *Spread Eagle* almost hid from public notice the fact that Frost, Todd and Company also sent a steamer to the Upper Missouri in the summer of 1859. In midmorning, June 4, one week after the *Spread Eagle* left St. Louis, the 399-ton *Florence*, commanded by Captain Throckmorton and probably with Malcolm Clark at his side as representative of the opposition, pulled away from the

---

[33] "Journal of Marsh," *SDHR*, I, 103–104; *DMR*, August 17, 22, 1859; *Sioux City* (Iowa) *Register*, August 11, 1859.
[34] "Report of Chas. P. Chouteau," *CHSM*, VII, 256.

levee. Packed with recruits for the garrison at Fort Randall, the vessel steamed upriver in excellent time (twenty-three days) to Fort Stewart ("in ... very bad condition"), near the mouth of the Big Muddy. On the way upriver, Captain Throckmorton landed supplies, including many "mysterious black bottles" (of liquor), at opposition posts and consulted with several bands of Indians. On the return trip, high winds punished the boat day after day and she grounded at least four times before reaching St. Louis on July 16 with approximately 25,000 robes, plus passengers and military goods from Fort Randall.[35]

When the *Florence* returned safely to port, Frost, Todd and Company evaluated the year's robe and fur return, studied market conditions, and after the American Fur Company vessels arrived in August, reconsidered future upriver trade in light of Chouteau's victory over the Upper Missouri. By early fall, Frost, Todd and Company concluded that, as anticipated, its stake in Dakota land, business, and politics far outweighed its interest in the upper-river robe and fur trade. On November 4, Frost, Todd and Company was dissolved by mutual written agreement, leaving the upriver trade to Clark and Primeau, its subsidiary since 1857. After the dissolution of the greater part of the opposition, both Frost and Todd turned their full attention to Dakota politics. During the winter of 1859–60, they campaigned vigorously for a Dakota territorial government, and eventually, in March, 1861, Congress created Dakota Territory, embracing the remains of Minnesota (admitted to the Union as a state in 1858) west of the Red River–Big Sioux line and all of Nebraska Territory north of the forty-third parallel. Congress placed the capital of Dakota Territory at Yankton, in the Missouri Valley near the mouth of the James, where Frost-Todd interests dominated, instead of in the valley of the Big Sioux, the epicenter of land development by Minnesota

---

[35] *Kansas City Daily Western Journal of Commerce*, July 16, 1859; *DMR*, May 22, June 4, July 18, 1859; Boller, *Among the Indians*, 342; Larpenteur, *Forty Years*, II, 307.

speculators who had contested with Frost and Todd for the site of the new capital.[36]

Frost, Todd and Company's withdrawal from the Upper Missouri fur and robe trade left the Chouteaus (Clark and Primeau were little more than nominal competitors with the American Fur Company) uncontested masters, once again, of the upriver trade. From their "substantial" St. Louis headquarters, the exterior adorned with huge elk antlers and gilded moose horns, old Pierre Chouteau and son Charles welcomed in the new decade of the sixties in command of the Upper Missouri. Despite the slow, steady push of settlement up the river above Omaha, the clamor for territorialism in Dakota, the presence of soldiers at Fort Randall, and the Raynolds and Mullan surveys at work in the Indian country, most westering Americans still sought their fortunes south of the Upper Missouri on farms in eastern Kansas and Nebraska, in the new Nevada mines, and in Colorado placer gold. As early as 1854, however, a few leading fur traders, particularly Culbertson and Frederic F. Gerard, had seen particles of gold taken from the mountains west of Fort Benton, but no gold rush had as yet swept into the northern Rockies. For the time being, spokesmen for the American Fur Company ignored the mineral prospects of Montana and Idaho (in the fall of 1859, Galpin asked the Academy of Science of St. Louis to memorialize Congress to support *Colorado* settlement) and waited for better proof that gold abounded above the Falls of the Missouri.[37]

The 1850's ended in a mild, pleasant, dry winter on the upper river. Buffalo herds moved unusually close to Fort Benton, the Blackfoot made a large hunt, most tribes were quiet, and the bits

[36] Articles of Agreement between Frost, Todd, and Atkinson, November 4, 1859, Typescript, SdHi; Schell, *South Dakota,* 72–77; Lamar, *Dakota Territory,* 43; Thomas, "John B. S. Todd," *SDHC,* XXIV, 188.

[37] "Minutes of the Academy of Science of St. Louis," MOSA; McDonnell, "Forts Benton and Sarpy," *CHSM,* X, 1, 246–47 (n. 8); *DMR,* July 26, 1859; *Daily Missouri Democrat,* December 24, 1859; *Freedom's Champion* (Atchison, Kansas), March 12, 1859.

of unimportant upriver news reaching St. Louis during the winter contrasted sharply with the post-mortems on John Brown, and Lincoln's no-compromise-with-slavery address at Cooper Union. A few interesting end-of-the-decade statistics on the fur trade appeared in middle western newspapers and periodicals and gave fur men food for thought. The value of Kansas City fur and robe exports had decreased since the mid-fifties—down to an average trade of $50,000 per year—and was expected to fall even more. Merchants in western Missouri were more interested in outfitting the Colorado gold rush and the farmers of Kansas and Nebraska than they were in buying and selling buffalo robes and beaver pelts. In St. Louis, fur dealers (big ones, such as the American Fur Company, and little ones, such as Lewis and Groshon and the New York and Philadelphia Fur Company) still held a backlog of robes, and the 1859 season had closed with estimated sales of $340,000 in robes and $209,000 in beaver and less choice skins from Arkansas, Illinois, and Missouri. None of the figures suggested, however, that the robe and fur trade was suffering a precipitate decline. On the contrary, end-of-the-decade statistics revealed there was still considerable life in the old industry.[38]

A few weeks after navigation opened on the Missouri in the early spring of 1860, the Chouteaus outfitted three steamers in St. Louis, the *Spread Eagle, Chippewa,* and *Key West No. 2,* for the annual upriver voyage. The Company had just paid $11,000 for the little *Key West,* since she drew only thirty-three inches of water when loaded with 180 tons and was suited ideally to the Missouri above Fort Union. About May 1, Charles Chouteau began to load the three boats, docked on the water front side by side, with Indian annuities, military freight, and Company goods. In addition to the crews of the three vessels and the usual number of Company traders and *voyageurs* and a few tourists and other passengers, the vessels were outfitted to carry approximately three

[38] *DMR,* April 30, May 2, 1860; *Daily Missouri Democrat,* December 24, 1859; *Kansas City Daily Western Journal of Commerce,* January 1, 1859, January 1, 1861; *Hunt's Merchants' Magazine,* Vol. XLII (May, 1860), 617; *De Bow's Review and Industrial Resources,* Vol. XXVIII (March, 1860), 330.

hundred officers and men (mostly raw recruits) of the United States Army, plus "a due allowance of laundresses." The American Fur Company had agreed, by contract with the War Department, to transport the military contingent and its freight to the head of navigation on the Missouri, presumably Fort Benton, where the small army planned to march west over Mullan's new military highway to Walla Walla.[39]

As the hour of sailing neared, a crowd jammed the levee to watch army representatives from Jefferson Barracks present Charles Chouteau with special flags for the expedition—one banner carried the picture of a buffalo hunt on one side and the motto "For Fort Benton or bust" on the other. Chouteau accepted the flags with appropriate comments, an army officer added a few remarks, and then Chouteau treated those participating in the ceremony to a "sumptuous repast" aboard the flagship *Spread Eagle*. "Wit and wine flowed freely" until the hour arrived for the three hundred troops to march aboard the three steamers. Then the guests, except for a few who remained atop the hurricane deck of the *Spread Eagle* as far as St. Charles, went ashore. Captain John La Barge immediately backed the *Spread Eagle* into the channel; the *Chippewa*, under Captain William H. Humphreys, joined her in mid-river; the *Key West*, under Captain Robert Wright, took her place in line; and late in the afternoon of May 3, "amid the roar of cannon" and cheers that "rent the air," the mountain fleet—one of the largest steamboat expeditions ever to sail for the Upper Missouri—steamed upriver.[40]

The channel was low, however, and navigation "tedious" until the river rose two to three feet near Fort Randall. Although one soldier fell overboard and drowned near Kansas City and a crewman drowned later on the voyage, the trip was otherwise free of major accidents. Hunters from the boats brought in abundant game, and the crew loaded on fresh vegetables at riverside land-

[39] *Daily Missouri Democrat*, April 25, May 1, 1860; Martin D. Hardin, "Up the Missouri and over the Mullan Road" (ed. by John E. Parsons), *The Westerners New York Posse Brand Book*, Vol. V (1958), 3.

[40] *DMR*, May 4, 1860; *Saint Louis Daily Bulletin*, May 4, 1860.

ings as far as Sioux City. Above that point, the Quartermaster issued antiscorbutics (pickles, dried vegetables, and whiskey) to the soldiers, and sold them to the crew and passengers. The monotony of daily travel was broken by card games, army band music, and occasional brawls, and a lieutenant was court-martialed for exchanging shots with the pilot of the *Key West*. The upriver Indians, overawed by the fleet, behaved peaceably toward the Indian agents and accepted annuities without incident. The tribesmen complained, nonetheless, of mistreatment by the government, and filled the summer of 1860 with bloody intertribal warfare. Two young eastern artists who accompanied the fleet, William Jacob Hays and "Mr. Terry" (probably W. Eliphalet Terry of Connecticut), both talented landscape painters, sketched the wildlife and trading posts along the river as the boats moved upstream toward Fort Benton and captured in their sketches some of the warlike mood of the Indians.[41]

On June 15, Chouteau quickly unloaded the Assiniboin and Crow annuities at Fort Union, and the fleet pushed up the Missouri on a high channel to the mouth of Milk River, where the *Spread Eagle* transferred its cargo to the two smaller boats. When the large boat was empty, Chouteau invited the principal army and fleet officers to board the vessel and proposed that Captain La Barge steer her upriver to a point a few miles above that reached by the *El Paso* in 1850. Captain La Barge, anxious to set a new Missouri River record for side-wheel steamers, piloted the flagship fifteen miles above El Paso Point, and Chouteau broke out bottles of champagne to celebrate the occasion. Then the *Spread Eagle* dropped downstream to rejoin her sister boats at Milk River. Captain La Barge took command of the *Key West*, Captain Wright transferred to the *Spread Eagle*, and the fleet divided: the two smaller boats headed upriver to Fort Benton, the flagship downriver to St. Louis. Ten days later, on July 2, the "fire canoes"

[41] Hardin, "Up the Missouri," *The Westerners . . . Brand Book*, V, 4; *DMR*, July 11, 1860; *The Crayon*, *Vol. VII* (July, 1860), 206; Robert Taft, *Artists and Illustrators of the Old West, 1850–1900*, 38–44.

Chippewa and *Key West* passed Old Fort McKenzie, the highest point reached the year before by the *Chippewa*, and "in great commotion" disembarked troops, freight, and Indian annuities at Fort Benton.[42]

Meanwhile, the *Spread Eagle* rapidly descended the Missouri and early in the morning of July 10, roused the St. Louis levee with a cannon salute and docked with 45,000 buffalo robes (from upriver American Fur Company trading posts) and a small shipment of wild animals. On July 26, Captain La Barge brought the *Key West* into port, and three days later, on the twenty-ninth, Captain Humphreys landed the *Chippewa*. The *Key West* carried robes and furs consigned to Campbell (under agreement between the American Fur Company and Clark and Primeau), a group of halfblood children to be enrolled in schools in St. Louis, and a few wild animals on "private account." The *Chippewa* carried only a small American Fur Company cargo, since she had burst her boiler near Milk River on the way up and Chouteau ordered her to return to St. Louis slowly and only partially loaded.[43]

By July, it was obvious to St. Louis businessmen that Clark and Primeau had no intention of sending an opposition steamer to the Upper Missouri in 1860. Rumors had persisted since early spring that Campbell was unwilling to risk the capital necessary to support Clark and Primeau in the trade and that the American Fur Company had consolidated with them. When the *Key West* landed with furs and robes consigned to Campbell, the rumors of consolidation multiplied, and by late summer, some of the details were known publicly. The story of the consolidation was simple. In the spring, Clark and Primeau had arrived in St. Louis from the upper river to outfit their partnership for the year ahead. Campbell, largely for financial reasons, was reluctant to support them. The Chouteaus offered Clark and Primeau jobs as upriver agents in the American Fur Company, and the two men agreed, under

[42] A. Vaughan to A. B. Greenwood, August 31, 1860, 36 Cong., 2 sess., *SED No. 1*, p. 306; *DMR*, July 11, 1860; *Daily Missouri Democrat*, July 27, 1860.

[43] *DMR*, July 11, 27, 1860; *Daily Missouri Democrat*, July 27, 1860; *Saint Louis Daily Bulletin*, July 30, 1860; *Sioux City Register*, July 7, 1860.

pressure, to consolidate with the giant. At first the Upper Missouri tribes were "greatly dissatisfied" with the consolidation, but became reconciled to it before the end of the summer. Once the opposition was removed from the Upper Missouri, the American Fur Company abandoned Fort Sarpy II (many of the Crows had moved north to the Missouri River) and started to close out trade at Fort Clark. Forts Stewart and Kipp also were abandoned (and burned almost at once by the Indians), and Fort Campbell, adjoining Fort Benton, was closed to trade—but not to Catholic missionaries serving the Montana-Idaho country, who used it intermittently, with American Fur Company approval, as a temporary mission site.[44] Father Joseph Giorda, an Italian Jesuit, wrote to Bishop James M. O'Gorman of Omaha in March, 1862, that three times a week and "twice on Sundays" he went up from Fort Campbell to "preach [to] the workmen" at Fort Benton, and throughout the Civil War years, relations between the American Fur Company and Upper Missouri Catholic missionaries remained extremely cordial.[45]

[44] McDonnell, "Forts Benton and Sarpy," *CHSM*, X, 263 (n. 31); Andrew Dawson to W. D. Hodgkiss, September 25, 1860, Dawson (Andrew) Papers, MtHi; Henry Boller to his Father, June 18, 1860, Boller Papers NdHi; "Journal of J. Hudson Snowden," 1860, MS, CtY-WA.

[45] Father Joseph Giorda to Bishop James M. O'Gorman, March 31, 1862, O'Gorman Papers, Archdiocesan Archives of the Catholic Church, Omaha. See also Palladino, *Indian and White*, selections on Father Giorda; Father Pierre Jean De Smet to Andrew Dawson, July 11, 1863, Dawson (Andrew) Papers, MtHi.

CHAPTER NINE

"Political troubles involving everything"

LATE IN THE SUMMER OF 1860, the American Fur Company was jolted by events that destroyed the shaky peace between Sioux and whites on the Upper Missouri and introduced a new opposition partnership into the robe and fur trade. At sunrise on August 22, when the watchman opened the gate at Fort Union, approximately 250 mounted Sioux charged the post. Before the Indians reached the pickets, however, the traders slammed the gate shut and, in great confusion, took to the walls to defend the fort. The traders in charge, Clark and Meldrum, ordered their men—a mere fifteen or so—to hold fire until Indian Agent Schoonover talked with the Sioux chiefs. Unfortunately, the Indians refused to listen to him. Instead, they killed two dozen cattle outside the walls; burned the outbuildings and tons of hay, cordwood, and building lumber; and fired two large mackinaws and cut them loose. Then about a dozen warriors attacked the pickets of the fort with hatchets and firebrands. At that moment the traders opened fire from the ramparts; one Sioux fell dead at the northwest corner, and the attackers, with two or three wounded, withdrew beyond the bluffs. Although the Indians did not renew the assault, the men in the fort were too frightened to venture beyond the gates for several days. The property loss to the Company resulting from the skirmish was said to be substantial, and downriver, the small, vulnerable eleven-man garrison at Fort Berthold under Frederick G. Riter, a refined Philadelphian who had entered the fur trade for his health, faced threat of a Sioux attack for the remainder of the summer.[1]

[1] B. S. Schoonover to A. M. Robinson, August 23, 1860, and Pierre Chouteau,

Above Fort Union, the Blackfeet were more peaceful than the Sioux below, and Andrew Dawson, agent at Fort Benton, wrote his superiors that the summer was busy but relatively quiet. By late September, he had forwarded forty thousand pounds of military supplies, under government contract, across the Rockies to support the soldiers who were marching west from Fort Benton over the Mullan Road to Walla Walla. He had also negotiated a contract (later canceled) to transport annuities from Fort Benton to the Flathead country and had continued to sell thousands of dollars' worth of supplies, including food, small tools, and whiskey, to Mullan's surveying parties. Two years later, in 1862, the American Fur Company even paid some of the men Mullan discharged, men who reached Fort Benton destitute. Clearly, by the mid-sixties, Fort Benton had become the outstanding upriver outfitting point for the military and civilians alike in the Montana Rockies.[2]

Dawson's report to the Company—that conditions at Fort Benton were normal in September, 1860—was well received in the St. Louis office but was overshadowed, nevertheless, by the trouble with the Sioux. In addition, the eastern market was overstocked with poor buffalo robes; an independent trader, Françoise La Framboise, was operating in the Teton Sioux country (Chouteau urged Primeau, new Company bourgeois at Fort Pierre II, to buy out La Framboise if necessary); and a new opposition partnership, Larpenteur, Smith and Company, had just formed. The Chouteaus anticipated "some annoyance" from the new opposition, although at first the Company had branded it a mere "abortion," and feared

Jr., and Company to A. M. Robinson, January 2, 1861, Letters Received, OIA, RG 75, NA; Pierre Chouteau, Jr., and Company to Charles Primeau, February 6, 1861, Chouteau Family Papers, MoSHi; White, *Morgan Journals*, 192, 198; "Journal of Snowden," CtY-WA.

[2] Pierre Chouteau, Jr., and Company to the Chief of the Topographical Bureau, June 6, July 2, 3, 7, November 8, 1862, Letters Received, 1862, Topographical Bureau, RG 77, NA; Andrew Dawson to W. D. Hodgkiss, September 25, 1860, Dawson (Andrew) Papers, MtHi; Bill of Pierre Chouteau, Jr., and Company to the United States, n.d., Chouteau Family Papers, MoSHi; Weisel, *Fort Owen Ledger*, 189.

that it might "create [further] dissatisfaction among the Indians,"[3] since "small, wiry . . . Gallic" Charles Larpenteur, formerly an American Fur Company man, was "very intelligent . . . proud . . . quick to resent an offense" and was one of the most experienced and tenacious Upper Missouri traders.[4] Old Jefferson Smith, a veteran of nearly thirty years in the fur trade, knew the Indians thoroughly, especially the Hidatsas, and had traded under both the American Fur Company and Joseph Picotte's earlier opposition. Although Larpenteur and Smith gave the new opposition their names and the benefit of their long trading experience, the business was shared with Henry A. Boller, the young son of a prosperous Philadelphia importer (Boller was formerly employed by Frost, Todd and Company at Fort Atkinson), and Robert H. Lemon, a clerk in Robert Campbell's St. Louis office.[5]

The new opposition organized in St. Louis in July, 1860. Boller raised $2,000 from his wealthy father, Smith contributed approximately $4,000, and Campbell, no longer under obligation to Clark and Primeau, sponsored Larpenteur's share in the outfit. Since the partnership was not finally "fairly organized" until mid-August (and by that time it was too late to outfit and send a steamer to the Upper Missouri), Boller and Larpenteur took what equipment was on hand and proceeded up the Mississippi by steamer to St. Paul, where they gathered eight wagons, stock, and additional men and equipment for an overland journey, around the Dakota Sioux, from Minnesota west via Pembina to the Upper Missouri. By early September, Smith and Lemon had joined Boller and Larpenteur at St. Paul and, in temporary quarters on the levee, made final arrangements for the overland trip. Even before the small wagon train set out on September 5, however, Smith and Larpenteur quarreled. Larpenteur fancied himself general super-

---

[3] Pierre Chouteau, Jr., and Company to Charles Primeau, October 14, 1860, February 6, 1861, Chouteau Family Papers, MoSHi.

[4] Charles Larpenteur, *Forty Years a Fur Trader on the Upper Missouri* (ed. by Milo M. Quaife), Introduction. All citations of Larpenteur's *Forty Years*, with the exception of this one, refer to the Coues edition.

[5] Boller, *Among the Indians*, Introduction; White, *Morgan Journals*, 156.

intendent of the "young men" in the party, resented Smith's advice, and on one occasion called Boller "a young blatherskite"— and possibly other things on other occasions. Smith, Boller, and Lemon, on their part, thought that Larpenteur was dishonest. As a result, within a year, internal dissension nearly destroyed the new company.[6]

West of Pembina, near the junction of South Antler Creek and Souris (Mouse) River, the wagon train divided. Smith and Boller took four wagons southward to the Hidatsas, where they hastily threw up a sod wintering post to compete with the American Fur Company traders at Fort Berthold. Larpenteur and Lemon continued west from the Souris to the Assiniboin country to reopen Fort Stewart. They found both Forts Stewart and Kipp in ruins and at first started to build a new post on the charred debris, but then decided to move up the Missouri about twenty-five miles to the mouth of Poplar River, where trade was better. There they put up Poplar River Post and settled down for the winter. To compete with Larpenteur and Lemon in the winter of 1860–61, Malcolm Clark, American Fur Company agent at Fort Union, sent traders to build a wintering post (Malcolm Clark's Fort) adjoining the opposition's new Poplar River Post.[7]

Early in the spring, Boller, after a disagreeable winter with the Hidatsas, traveled upriver to Poplar River Post to urge Larpenteur and Lemon to send their returns by land to St. Paul. Larpenteur and Lemon refused, however, and on April 5, Boller and Lemon started downriver to St. Louis in a large skiff. Smith joined them at Fort Berthold, but once in St. Louis, he hired on with the American Fur Company. In June, Lemon returned to the upper river to help Larpenteur bring down the Poplar River returns in a large mackinaw, and when they reached St. Louis early in August, they reorganized the opposition. Smith, of course, was dropped from the partnership, and Boller, despite Larpenteur's

---

[6] Larpenteur, *Forty Years*, II, 310–11; Boller, *Among the Indians*, xxiii–xxv.

[7] Larpenteur, *Forty Years*, II, 314–19; "Reminiscences of Antoine A. Juneau," Typescript, MtHi.

statement that the young man was allowed to retain a small share, evidently left the opposition, since "he had intended to dispose of his interest in the Company on reaching St. Louis." Robert Campbell and his brother Hugh, a prominent Philadelphia dry-goods merchant who moved to St. Louis in 1859, stood surety on the new opposition trading license in the name of Larpenteur, Lemon and Company.[8]

Once again, the opposition, now only Larpenteur and Lemon, gathered an outfit (seven wagons plus men and equipment) at St. Paul, and on September 14, the party headed overland to Poplar River Post. On the way, however, they heard a rumor that winter trade would be better at Old Fort Stewart. Unfortunately, they took the rumor—later proved false—at face value, built a temporary trading house at the site of Old Fort Stewart, and spent a miserably cold winter in the Indian country. By the spring of 1862, Larpenteur and Lemon were entirely out of sorts with each other, and when Lemon refused to agree to Larpenteur's plan to take trading goods up to Milk River, they decided to dissolve the partnership and sell out to a new opposition recently organized in St. Louis by the La Barge brothers and several associates. Lemon descended the Missouri to St. Louis. Larpenteur joined the new opposition, selected a site for a post (Fort Charles E. Galpin) on the north bank of the Missouri approximately a dozen miles above Milk River, and then returned to St. Louis briefly to close out the remains of the former partnership. Although each of the quarrelsome four, Larpenteur, Lemon, Boller, and Smith, had earned a modest profit in opposition to the American Fur Company, their partnership of 1860–62 was always weak and ineffectual and had provided little more than token opposition to the giant Company.[9]

Actually, the Upper Missouri Outfit of the American Fur Company was dislocated, in the winter of 1860–61, far more by secession—and then by the outbreak of the Civil War—than it was

---

[8] Boller, *Among the Indians*, xxvi–xxvii; Larpenteur, *Forty Years*, II, 321–24; Volume Entitled "Licenses for Indian Trade," OIA, RG 76, NA.

[9] Larpenteur, *Forty Years*, II, 329–42.

by the business tactics of Larpenteur, Lemon, Smith, and Boller. Lincoln's election in November, 1860; the secession of the first Southern state, South Carolina, a few days before Christmas; and the organization at Montgomery, Alabama, of a Confederate government the following February, 1861, created great confusion in all border slave states, particularly in their large business centers. The Chouteaus warned their upriver agents early in 1861 that "political troubles involving everything in a commercial way" created "the utmost distress" in St. Louis. Confusion in the robe and fur market, together with a fall in sales by robe dealers during the mild winter just ending, meant that much of the Upper Missouri return for 1860 (larger than that of 1859) was almost certain to pile up unsold in St. Louis warehouses. Market prospects for robes and furs in 1861 were poor, and when the war started in April, fur and robe traffic on the Lower Missouri was endangered by Union and Confederate military operations.[10]

Although most Missouri River steamboats were owned by Union supporters, many of the river pilots were Southern sympathizers and under suspicion by Federal authorities in St. Louis; and all vessels on the Lower Missouri were subject to attack by Confederate guerrilla bands (most of the irregulars infested the south bank of the Missouri between St. Louis and Kansas City), who fired upon steamboats and, whenever possible, seized their cargoes. Some vessels carried Union troops for defense, and many, including several fur-trade steamers, were protected by stacks of cotton bales and "equipped with shields of boiler iron, semicylindrical in form, enclosing the wheel, and capable of being moved so as to be adjusted to the changing course of the vessel." Yet in spite of guerrilla action that drove many packets from the lower-river trade, upper-river traffic in military supplies, troops, and gold seekers bound for the Idaho and Montana mines flourished from outfitting points above Kansas City, and fur-trade

---

[10] Quotation from Pierre Chouteau, Jr., and Company to Charles Primeau, February 6, 1861, Chouteau Family Papers, MoSHi. See also *Hunt's Merchants' Magazine*, Vol. XLIV (January, 1861), 103.

vessels continued regularly to enter and leave the port of St. Louis.[11]

Since the Chouteaus were slaveholders and ardent Democrats and were closely linked by family and business ties to many friends in the South, Unionists suspected them of disloyalty and were quick to find evidence of subversion at Upper Missouri American Fur Company posts. In August, 1862, the upper-river Indian agent wrote the Commissioner of Indian Affairs that "most" of the American Fur Company men at Fort Union were disloyal and dishonest and that a "discharged Union soldier" had told him that "they were all secessionists" at the trading post "and had threatened his life for the part he had taken in the" war.[12] Yet Alexander Culbertson was recommended to the Federal government, by one of his neighbors in Peoria, Illinois, as an ideal special agent to keep the Upper Missouri tribes loyal to the Union, and in February, 1864, Charles Chouteau himself swore a formal oath of loyalty to the Union! If the Chouteaus and most of their agents were secessionists—and, possibly, they were—they held their sentiments quietly, and the American Fur Company gave no significant aid or comfort to the Confederacy.[13]

On March 3, 1861, one day before Lincoln's inauguration, the outgoing Buchanan Administration accepted the American Fur Company bid to transport annuities to the upriver tribes. The Company insisted that the new contract covered a two-year period, 1861–62, similar to the previous contract's two-year length (1859–60), but the Republican administration, perhaps irritated by evidence that the Democratic Buchanan Administration had acted hastily to complete the new contract with the Democratic American Fur Company just one day before Lincoln took office, refused to consider the agreement binding beyond 1861.

11 Chittenden, *Early Steamboat Navigation*, II, 249–50.

12 Samuel N. Latta to William P. Dole, August 27, 1862, 37 Cong., 3 sess., *HED No. 1*, p. 341. According to the United States Census of 1860 for Missouri, Pierre Chouteau, Jr., owned five slaves.

13 T. H. McCulloh to Caleb Smith, September 5, 1861, and C. P. Chouteau's Oath of Loyalty, February 29, 1864, Letters Received, OIA, RG 75, NA.

Nevertheless, later in the spring, the War Department, on the Chouteau's request, ordered troops to board the Company steamboat at Fort Randall to escort the Indian annuities upriver.[14] By the end of the summer, as the Company anticipated, Lincoln had replaced many of the Buchanan men in the Indian Service with new appointees. William P. Dole took Alfred B. Greenwood's position as Commissioner; Harrison B. Branch moved into the office of Central Superintendent at St. Joseph; Walter A. Burleigh was given Redfield's Yankton Agency; John H. Charles, followed by Samuel N. Latta, replaced Schoonover in the Upper Missouri Agency; William Jayne was appointed governor and ex officio Superintendent of Indian Affairs for the new Dakota Territory and was followed in October, 1863, by Newton Edmunds; and Luther Pease, succeeded by Henry H. Reed in April, 1862, and then by Gad E. Upson in October, 1863, received the Blackfoot Agency. Before Lincoln's second inauguration in March, 1865, Mahlon Wilkinson was appointed to assume some of the burden of Latta's work on the Upper Missouri, Sidney S. Edgerton was sent west as governor and ex officio Superintendent of Indian Affairs for Montana Territory (created in 1864), and William M. Albin replaced Branch in the Central Superintendency.

The new Indian Service patronage appointees were generally unfavorable to the Democratic, and as many said, disloyal, American Fur Company. Protests against the Company by Indian agents in the field increased during the war and were more vehement than similar protests made by the "don't-care-a-damn" devotees of "the Whiskey bottle," as Boller once entitled one of them, under previous Democratic administrations. The new Republican appointees complained, as had their predecessors (Redfield, Schoonover, Vaughan, and others), that it was wrong for Upper Missouri agents to depend, as they did, upon the Company "for shelter,

14 A. M. Robinson to A. B. Greenwood, February 23, 1861, *ibid.*; W. P. Dole to Pierre Chouteau, Jr., and Company, April 5, December 20, 1861, Letters Sent, OIA, RG 75, NA.

food, transportation, protection, labourers, interpreters & in fact everything."[15] Even more specifically, by midsummer, 1862, Samuel Latta, the new, conscientious Upper Missouri agent, had heard and seen enough to believe that the Company used Indian agents and annuities to promote its own interests. He had learned in less than a year the truth of what independent traders and "squaw men" alike were saying: that the "whole system [was] rotten through and through" and that the annuities were not distributed to the Indians, but were "placed in the forts or posts of the Company" to be sold to the Indians for furs.[16] In a report to Commissioner Dole, Latta denounced the Company, perhaps unwisely, but well: "This old American Fur Company (so called) is the most corrupt institution ever tolerated in our country. They have involved the government in their speculations and schemes; they have enslaved the Indians, kept them in ignorance; taken from them year after year their pitiful earnings in robes and furs, without giving them an equivalent; discouraged them in agriculture by telling them that should the white man find that their country would produce they would come in and take their lands from them. They break up and destroy every opposition to their trade that ventures into their country, and then make up their losses by extorting from the Indians."[17] The Company protested and demanded Latta's removal from the Upper Missouri, but the Commissioner of Indian Affairs evidently knew, as did Latta, that the Chouteaus were political enemies who took "every opportunity to denounce" the Republican administration, and allowed Latta to remain in office.[18]

When Lincoln's crop of Indian Service appointees took office in the spring of 1861 (Latta was appointed later, in August), the

[15] A. H. Redfield to C. E. Mix, February 3, 1858, Letters Received, OIA, RG 75, NA; Henry Boller to his Father, August 30, 1859, Boller Papers, NdHi.

[16] White, *Morgan Journals,* 97.

[17] S. N. Latta to W. P. Dole, August 27, 1862, 37 Cong., 3 sess., *HED No. 1,* pp. 340–41.

[18] S. N. Latta to W. P. Dole, January 8, 1863, Letters Received, OIA, RG 75, NA.

American Fur Company outfitted the steamers *Chippewa* and *Spread Eagle* for the annual upriver voyage. On April 25, two weeks after the Confederate attack upon Fort Sumter, the *Chippewa* sailed under Captain Humphrey's command. One week later, on May 1, Captain John La Barge steered the *Spread Eagle* away from the port of St. Louis, "amid cheers, waving of handkerchiefs, booming of cannon," and pointed the vessel upriver to rendezvous with the *Chippewa* near Sioux City. There the boats met and sailed upstream together to the mouth of the Yellowstone, where the larger vessel turned back to St. Louis while the smaller carried freight and passengers on to Fort Benton.[19]

The upriver trip from St. Louis to Fort Union was a tourist's delight for many of the adventure seekers aboard the "very roomy and pleasant" *Spread Eagle*. Although politics was a main topic of conversation in the passenger lounge, political arguments did not disrupt the gaiety aboard the steamer. Some passengers played cards, others earned their sea legs at the bar, and many hunted ashore whenever the boat landed to wood or shot buffalo swimming in the river and littered the decks with trophies. Talented passengers—and some, unfortunately, not so talented—played the piano and melodeon in the after cabin, accompanied by flutes, violins, and banjos. For further diversion, dozens of men drilled on deck "in skirmishing, loading and firing" with rifles provided by Charles Chouteau, who was aboard the boat, from the Yankton annuities, and nearly every male passenger had his hair cut short—military style—as a joke. Beginning in 1862, however, passengers on the Missouri River steamers took military drill far more seriously in the face of immediate danger from Indians and Southern guerrillas along the river.[20]

As usual, the passenger list of the *Spread Eagle* carried a wide variety of interesting names. One party included W. F. Scholfield, a "good natured, bustling" elderly Englishman with "baggage

[19] *DMR*, May 2, 1861; *Daily Missouri Democrat*, April 26, 1861.

[20] John Mason Brown (ed.), "A Trip to the Northwest in 1861, Part I," *FCHQ*, Vol. 24 (April, 1950), 107; W. H. Schieffelin, "Crossing the Plains in '61," *Recreation*, Vols. II–III (1895), 397.

enough for a regiment and fire arms sufficient to arm a platoon of riflemen"; his wife; Miss V. Talbot, his protégée; and a small group of New York friends.[21] Three young easterners, William de la Montaigne Cary, W. H. Schieffelin, and E. N. Lawrence—all "awakened . . . [to] a desire for travel and adventure" by reading the Lewis and Clark journals and Cooper's novels—comprised another unusual party. Cary was a New York artist with a "keen eye for the picturesque and striking." He sketched the Missouri Valley landscape, wildlife, and Indian camp life as the *Spread Eagle* ascended the river and later incorporated the sketches into oil paintings.[22] Young John Mason Brown (the half-brother of Benjamin Gratz Brown, vice-presidential candidate on the Liberal Republican ticket of 1872) also sailed aboard the *Spread Eagle* and struck up a friendship with old "Sorrel top" Andrew Dawson, who was headed for Fort Benton.[23]

Low water and sand bars delayed the larger boat for eleven days just above Yankton, while the *Chippewa* waited, but when the river rose, the two vessels moved upstream together once again, without great difficulty, past Fort Pierre II. At the Arikara settlement near abandoned Fort Clark, Agent Schoonover encouraged the Rees to move upriver as soon as possible (they did, within the year) to join the Hidatsas and Mandans. On June 13, just as the *Chippewa* reached Fort Berthold, a cabin boy accidentally shot and killed another crew member. Agent Schoonover held an examining court and appointed John Mason Brown, who was a Yale man with a license to practice law, counsel for the United States. Although Brown "failed to make a case" in the unusual and legally questionable trial, he collected a pair of government bullet molds as his fee. Two days after the trial, the steamers landed at Fort Union, still a strong post, "though going to decay very rapidly."

[21] Brown, "A Trip in 1861," *FCHQ*, Vol. 24, p. 106; *DMR*, July 4, 1861.

[22] Schieffelin, "Crossing the Plains," *Recreation*, II–III, 395; George B. Grinnell, "Recollections of the Old West," *The American Museum Journal*, Vol. XVII (May, 1917), 339.

[23] John M. Brown to Andrew Dawson, March 15, 1863, Dawson (Andrew) Papers, MtHi.

The *Spread Eagle* discharged her freight, transferred most of her passengers to the *Chippewa*, took on thousands of buffalo robes, and on June 23, set out downriver for St. Louis on a mountain rise. She reached St. Louis on July 1, a record nine days and eight hours from the Yellowstone.[24]

As the *Spread Eagle* started downstream from Fort Union, Chouteau and Captain Humphreys pointed the heavily loaded and overcrowded *Chippewa* up the Missouri toward Fort Benton. At suppertime on June 23, as the stern-wheeler neared a curve in the river (Disaster Bend) a few miles below Poplar River, fire broke out in the forward hold near a large quantity of "ordinary black and giant" gunpowder, variously estimated at from 25 to 300 kegs, or perhaps 5,925 pounds, surrounded by a barricade of other goods. As smoke billowed from the hatches, "panic ensued" on the boat and "the women and some of the men lost their heads, and were with great difficulty prevented from jumping overboard." The chief engineer, the hero of the hour, ran the vessel close to the near-by low bank of the Missouri and, after some delay while a hawser was put out ahead, landed her. The passengers rushed ashore, few daring to save more than their firearms or the clothing they wore for fear that the *Chippewa* would explode at any moment, and found safety a quarter of a mile away in a grove of large cottonwoods. The crew, under Chouteau's shouted directions, scrambled ashore to join the passengers. According to one passenger, however, Captain Humphreys "had the instinct of self-preservation strongly developed . . . and as soon as the boat got within six feet of land he leaped like a wild man" for the bank.[25]

When all were ashore, the hawser burned, or was cut, the boat floated downstream about a mile to the opposite bank, and within

[24] Brown, "A Trip in 1861," *FCHQ*, Vol. 24, pp. 124–28; *DMR*, July 2, 1861.

[25] Brown, "A Trip in 1861," *FCHQ*, Vol. 24, p. 130; Schieffelin, "Crossing the Plains," *Recreation*, II–III, 397–98; Chittenden, *Early Steamboat Navigation*, I, 220–21; Kingsbury, *Dakota Territory*, I, 568–69; Frank L. Worden to Lyman Powers, December 24, 1861, in Albert J. Partoll, "Frank L. Worden, Pioneer Merchant, 1830–1887," *PNQ*, Vol. 40 (July, 1949), 201.

JOSEPH A. SIRE

Courtesy Missouri Historical Society

DANIEL M. FROST

Courtesy Missouri Historical Society

JAMES B. HUBBELL

Courtesy Minnesota Historical Society

JOSEPH LA BARGE

Courtesy Missouri Historical Society

DAVID D. MITCHELL

Courtesy Missouri Historical Society

FATHER PIERRE JEAN DE SMET

Courtesy Missouri Historical Society

THE REVEREND STEPHEN R. RIGGS

Courtesy Minnesota Historical Society

GENERAL ALFRED SULLY

Courtesy Minnesota Historical Society

an hour "she was burnt to the waters edge and then blew into ten thousand atoms the whole sinking in about 20 feet of water."[26] One deck hand was badly burned in the fire, and a pointer dog, last seen on the upper deck before the explosion, was lost. The following day, when the air was clear of burning debris, foraging parties from the cottonwood grove picked up containers of food along the riverbank (they were blown clear by the explosion), "and there was a wild scramble" by the passengers and Indians from a neighboring village for scorched blankets and strips of cloth blown into the brush. Only part of the $60,000 cargo—approximately $9,000 in merchandise consigned to Francis (Frank) L. Worden of Washington Territory and $5,500 in Blackfoot annuities—was insured.[27]

Some of the passengers evidently found shelter, on the night following the explosion, in a large cabin in a woodchoppers' camp a few miles below the wreck of the *Chippewa*. The following morning, Chouteau brought a mackinaw down from the American Fur Company post at Poplar River and, possibly, with additional canoes and rowboats, transported the cabin-class passengers (the women "showed great fortitude in the face of . . . hardships") downstream to Fort Union. Under orders from Chouteau, Andrew Dawson dashed to Fort Benton immediately after the disaster, gathered more than twenty ox-drawn wagons, and within six weeks had returned with them to Fort Union. There he packed the vehicles with supplies and "after many days of slow travel" delivered the goods at Fort Benton to sustain the post through the coming fall and winter. Artist Cary and his friends, stranded by the wreck of the *Chippewa*, enjoyed the hospitality of Fort Union —and watched the antics of a playful pet grizzly that guarded the enclosure, wrestled pigs, and frightened horses—until Dawson brought the wagons down from Fort Benton. Then the Cary party accompanied the wagon train upriver and were entertained

26 F. L. Worden to L. Powers, December 24, 1861, in Partoll, "Worden," *PNQ*, Vol. 40, p. 201.
27 *DMR*, July 9, 1861.

with horse races and other amusements by the men at Fort Benton for two weeks before the easterners set out for Walla Walla and the Pacific Coast.[28]

What caused the fire on the *Chippewa*? The best eyewitness account, by an American Fur Company employee aboard the boat, states that the vessel carried twenty-two barrels of illicit alcohol, hidden in the hold not far from the gunpowder. Deck hands stole alcohol from the barrels several times on the upriver trip and frequently were drunk. On June 23, shortly before the fire broke out, the witness saw a deck hand go into the hold and draw a pitcher of alcohol from a barrel. Later, the same hand returned to the hold, presumably for another containerful, but at that moment the witness went to the hurricane deck. There he heard the cry of fire and saw the deck hand emerge from the hold "enveloped in a sheet of flame." Statements made by others (some on the *Chippewa*) at the time of the accident or immediately thereafter support the eyewitness account of alcohol and fire and add that a deck hand took a lighted candle into the hold, where he either got drunk, tripped over the taper, and set the fire or allowed alcohol fumes to reach the candle and start the blaze.[29]

After Chouteau escorted the more important passengers from Disaster Bend to Fort Union, he hurried downriver and formally notified the Indian Office at St. Joseph of the explosion. On July 7, Superintendent Branch filed insurance claims for the 113,100 pounds of Blackfoot annuities destroyed on the *Chippewa*, and within two months the insurance companies holding the policies

[28] Brown, "A Trip in 1861," *FCHQ*, Vol. 24, p. 130; Schieffelin, "Crossing the Plains," *Recreation*, II–III, 15, 17, 53; William Cary to Charles N. Kessler, September 2, 1919, Typescript, Cary Collection, Thomas Gilcrease Institute of American History and Art, Tulsa.

[29] S. N. Latta to W. P. Dole, September 28, 1862, Letters Received, OIA, RG 75, NA; "Report on Steamboat Wrecks on Missouri River by Capt. H. M. Chittenden, Corps of Engineers," 55 Cong., 2 sess., *HR Doc. No. 2*, p. 3876; Leeson, *Montana*, 395; Chittenden, *Early Steamboat Navigation*, I, 221; Kingsbury, *Dakota Territory*, I, 568; Schieffelin, "Crossing the Plains," *Recreation*, II–III, 397; James and Granville Stuart, *Forty Years on the Frontier*, (ed. by Paul C. Phillips), I, 181.

on the goods paid the claims. Meanwhile, the Indian Commissioner accepted Chouteau's offer, made on July 20, to furnish annuities to the Blackfeet early the following spring from Company supplies at upriver posts (and repaid the Company for them two years later at 1861 prices rather than at the higher 1863 rates that the Company hoped to receive). In the fall of 1862, Agent Latta sent the Commissioner another of his lengthy indictments of the American Fur Company. He charged that the Company had taken, for its own use, the Assiniboin and Crow annuities of 1861! Latta demanded a thorough investigation and appended to his report the statement of an Upper Missouri trader who, in 1861, saw the Company unload at Fort Union the Assiniboin and Crow annuities from the *Chippewa*, before the explosion, and was told at that time by Charles Chouteau himself that the goods piled up at the fort were Assiniboin and Crow annuities. According to Latta, after the explosion the trader talked to Agent Schoonover at Fort Union and Schoonover admitted that he was pressed for money and had sold out to the Company; that Charles Chouteau had taken the Assiniboin and Crow goods to replace Company supplies, destined for Fort Benton, lost on the *Chippewa*; that the Assiniboin and Crow chiefs were told their annuities had gone down with the boat; and that the Company replaced the annuities, in the spring of 1862, with new goods shipped upriver before the government realized what had happened. Latta's lengthy protest, however, brought no federal investigation.[30]

In the months immediately after Charles Chouteau's return to St. Louis in July, 1861, the Union forces in Missouri, both military and civilian, gradually won control of the state. Loyalists overpowered the strong secession movement in St. Louis; General John Charles Frémont issued his controversial state-wide emancipation proclamation; and by spring, 1862, when old, partially blind Pierre Chouteau tottered into the American Fur Company's

[30] S. N. Latta to W. P. Dole, September 27, 28, 1862, and H. B. Branch to W. P. Dole, July 11, October 3, 18, 1861, Letters Received, OIA, RG 75, NA; W. P. Dole to Pierre Chouteau, Jr., and Company, August 10, 1861, October 18, 1862, March 19, 1863, Letters Sent, OIA, RG 75, NA.

downtown office to say good-by to his son Charles and the annual upriver expedition to the Upper Missouri, the lower river, although still under guerrilla attack, was no longer the scene of significant North-South clashes. During the winter, Charles Chouteau had finally allowed Andrew Dawson to unseat Culbertson (not that Culbertson minded very much, since he had partially retired anyway) as "king of the Missouri," and Charles Galpin, "a good friend, a bad enemy, a good business man and a perfect gentleman," left the American Fur Company to join the La Barges in opposition. In the spring, when navigation opened on the Upper Missouri, the first mackinaws to reach Yankton and Sioux City carried good news for fur traders—the river channel ran deep—and for gold seekers—the gold rush had spread from Idaho into Montana.[31]

Once again, in 1862, the American Fur Company selected two steamers, the large side-wheeler *Spread Eagle* and the smaller stern-wheeler *Key West*, to carry Company men and supplies, Indian annuities, and gold hunters to the upper river. The Company promised the prospectors, many of whom simply expected to "go over the ground and pick up the big chunks," that they could purchase horses, mules, wagons, and additional equipment to use in the Idaho and Montana mines (at a profitable markup for the Company, of course) at Fort Benton. Captain Humphreys commanded the *Key West* out of St. Louis on May 3, and a week later, on May 10, Captain Robert E. Baily (or Bailey), under close supervision of Charles Chouteau, piloted the *Spread Eagle* from port. Agent Latta sailed from St. Louis on the larger vessel with the Indian annuities, accompanied by Father De Smet, who said Mass every day in a small chapel that Chouteau, his former student, built for him aboard the boat. At St. Joseph and Sioux City, the *Spread Eagle* picked up additional passengers, including several who kept diaries, made reports on the river trip, or left

[31] Robert Morgan to Andrew Dawson, February 24, 1862, Dawson (Andrew) Papers, MtHi; *DMR*, May 7, 1862; *Dakotian* (Yankton, South Dakota), June 3, 1862; Helen A. Howard (ed.), "Diary of Charles Rumley from St. Louis to Portland, 1862," *Frontier and Midland*, Vol. XIX (Spring, 1939), 190.

memoirs of the voyage: Henry H. Reed, the new Blackfoot agent; Lewis Henry Morgan, the ethnologist; John O'Fallon Delaney, a young St. Louisan traveling in Father De Smet's party; and A. H. Wilcox. Other accounts were jotted down by two travelers who embarked in St. Louis, Jirah Isham Allen and James Henry Morley, and Father De Smet contributed his personal comments upon what was, as a result of the many records kept, one of the most extensively documented voyages to the Upper Missouri.[32]

Agent Reed exaggerated when he said the trip was safe, pleasant, and peaceful, but the river flowed high during the late spring, navigation was easier than usual (at least to Fort Union), good food was plentiful aboard the boats, and the Indians were quiet. On the *Spread Eagle*, Jon Postlewaite and his band entertained the passengers each evening, while Old Sam Johnson (Isaac Rea), combination bartender and "Ethiopian minstrel," divided his talents between the two boats. The passengers gambled, smoked, drank, argued—all in a cheerful way, however—and "formed a military company," commanded by John Mason Brown, who was returning to the upper river, to drill on the deck of the *Spread Eagle*. Buffalo shooting from the boats was excellent, the Hidatsas and some of the more friendly Sioux danced for the passengers at upriver landings, and ethnologist Morgan met Andrew Dawson and the Culbertsons on the voyage and they very willingly gave him details of Arikara and Blackfoot culture.[33]

On May 27, however, when the *Spread Eagle* landed freight and Indian annuities two miles above Fort Pierre II, the passengers experienced their first taste of Indian hostility. Although hundreds of Sioux gathered on the riverbank to receive presents, many of

[32] *DMR*, May 3, 4, 10, 11, 1862; Chittenden and Richardson, *Father de Smet*, II, 783; S. N. Latta to W. P. Dole, August 27, 1862, 37 Cong. 3 sess., *HED No. 1*, p. 336; E. Laveille, *The Life of Father De Smet, S.J.* (*1801–1873*), 310.

[33] Henry H. Reed to W. Jayne, October 1, 1862, 37 Cong. 3 sess., *HED No. 1*, pp. 322–23; John E. Sunder (ed.), "Up the Missouri to the Montana Mines: John O'Fallon Delany's 'Pocket Diary for 1862,' " Part I, *BMHS*, Vol. XIX (October, 1962), 8; *DMR*, July 8, 1862; White, *Morgan Journals*, 146–47, 156.

them seemed to be angry. The chiefs met in council with Chouteau and Agent Latta, but Latta had difficulty making himself understood through an interpreter, and few of the Indian leaders were friendly. The more belligerent chiefs accused Chouteau of cheating the Sioux for a long time and said that he carried arms and ammunition to their tribal enemies upriver. They denounced the Great White Father in Washington, refused to accept annuities, and threatened to destroy commerce on the Missouri. At that point the meeting ended abruptly, several passengers aboard the *Spread Eagle* rushed for their firearms, and the Indians hastily formed three lines along the bank opposite the boat and may have fired twenty or thirty high warning shots at the vessel. Since "fears were entertained about [the Indians'] hostile intentions," Chouteau, to avoid panic on the boat, sent boxes of gifts ashore to the Sioux. The Indians quieted down, and by the time the boat pulled away, at least one Sioux band, under Bear's Rib, had accepted annuities.[34]

At Fort Berthold, the Arikaras, Mandans, and Hidatsas lined the bank and offered robes and women in exchange for whiskey. One passenger thought the Indians an "intolerable nuisance," but the crew did a thriving business.[35] Chouteau and Latta held a peaceful council with the Indian chiefs, and the following morning, the *Spread Eagle* continued upriver right into a race—probably "the first ever run on the upper Missouri"—with the opposition steamer *Emily*, commanded by Captain Joseph La Barge. The race started when the *Emily* drove ahead to pass the *Spread Eagle*. After a neck-and-neck upriver contest for a little over a mile, the channel narrowed and the *Emily* swung into the other boat's path. The *Spread Eagle* rammed the opposition boat and broke a few of her starboard guards: three or four "staunchions forward of the wheel house." Captain La Barge grabbed a rifle and pointed it at

[34] Sunder, "Up the Missouri," *BMHS*, XIX, 12; Diary of James Henry Morley, 1862, Typescript, MtHi; "From St. Louis to Ft. Benton in 1862" (The Diary of Jirah Isham Allen), Typescript, MtHi; "Up the Missouri River to Montana in the Spring of 1862" (by A. H. Wilcox), Typescript, MtHi.
[35] "Up the Missouri River to Montana," MtHi.

Captain Baily on the *Spread Eagle* and several passengers on the Company boat seized their weapons and aimed them at the *Emily*, but before anyone opened fire, the boats separated and the *Emily* ran ahead upstream. La Barge believed that Chouteau and Baily had attempted "designedly" to sink the opposition steamer and later brought charges of reckless conduct against Captain Baily. The Captain lost his license temporarily and in his disgrace swore to La Barge, or so La Barge stated, that he had rammed the *Emily* under Chouteau's orders.[36]

On June 8 or 9 (the diarists disagree), the *Spread Eagle* landed at Fort Union. Lewis Henry Morgan visited the "rude, old fashioned" trading post and was amazed to see a tame young beaver being nursed by Indian women. The *Spread Eagle* remained at the fort only briefly, however, before continuing upriver, with the *Key West* trailing along behind. Since the channel remained "remarkably high," Chouteau decided to take the heavier *Spread Eagle*, in addition to the light-draft *Key West*, all the way to Fort Benton. On June 16, a few miles below the first rapids above Milk River, he transferred a quantity of freight from the smaller steamer to the larger one to allow the *Key West* additional power to overcome the rapids. Then they moved ahead by cordelle through one rapid after another—Bird's, Lone Pine, Dauphin's, Kettle, Dead Man's (Drowned Man's), and Kipp's, to mention a few—to within "sight of Ft. Benton," where four crew members drowned in the rough water before the boats reached the levee. The unexpected tragedy dampened the enthusiasm of the passengers, who otherwise were delighted to reach the head of navigation on the Missouri and the gateway to the mines.[37]

Late in the afternoon of June 22, the *Spread Eagle*, carrying

---

[36] *Ibid.*; Chittenden, *Early Steamboat Navigation*, II, 289–91; Sunder, "Up the Missouri," *BMHS*, XIX, 12; "From St. Louis to Ft. Benton," MtHi; *Sioux City Register*, July 5, 1862; "Diary of James Harkness, of the Firm of La Barge, Harkness and Company," *CHSM*, Vol. II (1896), 347.

[37] "Up the Missouri River to Montana," MtHi; "From St. Louis to Ft. Benton," MtHi; White, *Morgan Journals*, 167–68, 182; Sunder, "Up the Missouri," *BMHS*, XIX, 13–16.

approximately twenty crewmen and thirty passengers, turned downriver from Fort Benton, reached Fort Union three days later, and tied up close to the *Key West* (it had left Fort Benton on June 21). Company laborers quickly loaded both steamers with robes and furs, and on the following morning, the *Spread Eagle* set out for St. Louis. At Fort Pierre II, a sudden squall struck and drove her onto a dangerous sand bar, but she wiggled free and survived the blast intact. Eight days later, on July 7, she steamed up to the St. Louis levee and was joined the next day by the *Key West*.[38] In a few well-chosen words, Lewis Henry Morgan, a man who appreciated a good drink, summed up the average passenger's view of the *Spread Eagle* and its crew: "It is extremely well manned . . . the spirit among the officers and men is excellent . . . [and] Sam Johnson, the bar keeper, is an original genius."[39]

While American Fur Company clerks inventoried the returns from the *Key West* and the *Spread Eagle* and Charles Chouteau sent the steamers to the boatyard for renovation, Captain Joseph La Barge, who returned from the Upper Missouri on July 2 aboard the opposition boat *Emily*, brought charges against Captain Baily. The new opposition had formed in St. Louis during the previous winter of 1861–62. Joseph and John La Barge, James Harkness, Eugene Jaccard, and Charles E. Galpin each put ten thousand dollars into the company (other investors offered additional money, but the five partners rejected it for the time being) and bought the steamers *Emily* and *Shreveport*. Jaccard, a highly respected St. Louis merchant, agreed to handle the St. Louis end of the business; Harkness visited Washington, D.C., to establish friendly contact between the new company and the Indian Office and then sailed upriver on the *Emily* to open opposition trade near Fort Benton; Galpin, whose Indian wife was influential amongst the tribes, consented to oversee Missouri River trade between Fort Pierre II and the Milk River country; and the La Barges, of course, took command of the boats. Charles Larpenteur joined the opposi-

38 White, *Morgan Journals*, 182, 192, 197; *DMR*, July 8, 9, 1862.
39 White, *Morgan Journals*, 199.

tion later, in the spring of 1862, and Robert Campbell agreed to market whatever robes and furs the new company sent down to St. Louis. The prominent Missouri stove manufacturer, Giles F. Filley—he had helped organize the Free Soil (Liberty) party of 1848 and during the Civil War was an ardent Unionist and Lincoln supporter—stood bond for the new opposition (La Barge, Harkness and Company) and so crowned it with a halo of loyalty to the Union.[40]

The Chouteaus knew that the opposition was one of the most powerful ever raised against the American Fur Company, that the Unionist sentiments of its supporters would command favorable treatment from officials in the Indian Office, and that upriver competition would stiffen in 1862. Accordingly, Charles Chouteau outfitted the *Key West* and *Spread Eagle* as quickly as possible and started upriver with them early in May, but not early enough. The *Shreveport*, under Captain John La Barge, had sailed at noon on April 30. Armed with "two small brass field pieces" on the "forward deck," the light-draft *Shreveport* carried seventy-five cabin and a "goodly number" of deck passengers and a variety of opposition-company goods. Accidents harassed the passengers continually during the first week of the trip. One man was severely wounded by the farewell salute fired at St. Louis and was left behind to recover; another young man walked overboard in his sleep, but was rescued before drowning; and a third took "a run upon the river bank," but the bank collapsed and he was dragged from the river wet and muddy. The boat, however, except for a broken mud valve and a shattered rudder, stood up under the first days of travel better than the passengers![41]

At Yankton, "most of the members of the [new Dakota territorial] legislature [boarded] the steamer, and with common consent and enthusiasm, joined in drinking success to Capt. La Barge,

[40] Volume Entitled "Licenses for Indian Trade," OIA, RG 76, NA; Insurance Record Book of Robert Campbell, 1862–1864, Campbell Family Papers, MoSHi; Chittenden, *Early Steamboat Navigation*, II, 287–88.
[41] *DMR*, May 1, July 8, 1862; Francis M. Thompson, "Reminiscences of Four Score Years," *MM*, Vol. V, Supplement (1912), 141–42.

the *Shreveport,* the new trading company, and the expedition in general." Near Fort Pierre II, a handful of Sioux chiefs met the vessel and wished the new company success against the American Fur Company. Two days later, an Arikara war party boarded the boat, said they too were happy to see the opposition on the Upper Missouri, and entertained the passengers (some of whom sprawled on their stateroom floors in fear of an attack) with an impromptu war dance. By the time the *Shreveport* reached the mouth of the Yellowstone, late on June 2, Captain John La Barge had every reason to believe that many of the Indians and settlers along the upper river welcomed the new company.[42]

Since the channel was high and Captain La Barge was confident that his brother Joseph would soon arrive on the *Emily* and would pilot her well above the mouth of the Yellowstone, possibly all the way upriver to Fort Benton, he continued upstream on the *Shreveport.* On June 5, the *Shreveport* "lay all day" waiting for the *Emily* opposite Fort Charles, built in the fall of 1861 by either the American Fur Company or, more likely, by the tiny independent fur partnership of Bruguier and Booge, on the north bank of the Missouri near Elk Prairie (Little Dry) Creek approximately fifty miles, by land, above Old Fort Stewart. When the *Emily* failed to appear at Fort Charles, the *Shreveport* pushed on past Milk River and Bird's and Dauphin's Rapids. "Sunday, June 15th was a cold rainy day," Captain La Barge had given up hope for the *Emily,* and the *Shreveport* "lay at the foot of Dead Man's rapids." Suddenly, "a mighty yell went up," cannon boomed in the distance, and "the *Emily* with colors flying [came] around the point below."[43]

"Large, portly" Captain Joseph La Barge, Father De Smet's "intimate friend" and the "head and front of the La Barge interests," had embarked on the *Emily* from St. Louis late in the afternoon of May 14. The boat, built in 1859 under Joseph's direc-

[42] *DMR,* July 8, 1862; Thompson, "Reminiscences," *MM,* V, Supp., 143–45.

[43] Larpenteur, *Forty Years,* II, 333; Volume Entitled "Licenses for Indian Trade," OIA, RG 76, NA; *DMR,* July 8, 1862; Thompson, "Reminiscences," *MM,* V, Supp., 147–49.

tion and named in honor of his eldest daughter (and not, as rumored, for Mrs. Pierre Chouteau), carried at least three hundred tons of freight plus eighty-five cabin passengers, who paid one hundred dollars apiece, and fifty-three deckers. Except for a few invalids seeking better health on the Upper Missouri, most of the passengers were gold hunters—a few "whiskey loving," but most content to play chess, checkers, dominoes, and cards aboard the boat—traveling individually or in companies to the Idaho and Montana mines. Chancellor and Mrs. Joseph Gibson Hoyt of Washington University in St. Louis occupied quarters behind a temporary partition in the rear of the main cabin. The Chancellor suffered from tuberculosis. He was a Yale man, had taught courses in Greek language and literature for over twenty years, had served in the New Hampshire constitutional convention of 1851, and was ascending the Missouri under orders from his physician. On the way upstream, he struck up a cordial acquaintance with the Reverend John Francis Bartlett, a Welsh minister with "rare powers of adaptation," who conducted Sunday services aboard the boat and was headed for evangelical work at the mines.[44]

Generally, the voyage to Fort Union was quiet, although slower than anticipated because of "many severe wind storms." At St. Joseph (about one-third of the town stood in ruins from military action), a crowd of people flocked to the levee to see the *Emily;* at Fort Randall, the vessel took on "two wagon loads of ice"; and at the Sioux camp near Fort Pierre II, Captain La Barge traded a load of groceries for robes and Charles Galpin presided over a "talk" with a dozen Indian chiefs aboard the boat. A few days later, the *Emily* overtook the American Fur Company boats at Fort Berthold and engaged in the highly controversial race with

[44] F. H. Garver, "Reminiscences of John H. Charles," *Proceedings of the Academy of Science and Letters of Sioux City, Iowa, 1905–06,* Vol. II (1906), 60; Chittenden, *Early Steamboat Navigation,* I, 240; *DMR,* September 19, 1859, May 15, November 27, 1862; Thompson, "Reminiscences," *MM,* V, Supp., 150; "Diary of James Harkness," *CHSM,* II, 343, 346; *Daily Missouri Democrat,* July 8, 1862; Laveille, *Father De Smet,* 230; Samuel T. Hauser to his Sister, May 24–June 17, 1862, CtY-WA.

the *Spread Eagle*, then ran ahead of Chouteau's steamer and passed the mouth of the Yellowstone on June 8, still six days behind the *Shreveport*. Finally, a week later, after the *Emily*, "trembling under [a] heavy head of steam," had passed the first two great rapids above Milk River, "the pilot announced that he saw the smoke of the *Shreveport*." A few minutes later the boats stood side by side, and for an hour the passengers and crew visited back and forth. Then most of the men went ashore to stand "in the mud and rain" to lighten the *Emily* while she steamed upstream through Dead Man's Rapids and "dropped a line to the *Shreveport* and helped her over."[45]

Two days later, on June 17, the boats reached the rapids within two miles of Fort Benton, but the *Emily*, too weak to fight the current and tow the *Shreveport* upstream at the same time, "passed up" to the fort above the rapids, "dropped a hawser" to the other vessel, and pulled her up. After a brief stop at the American Fur Company post—the La Barges wished to impress upon the Company that the opposition steamboat *Emily* was the *first side-wheeler* to reach Fort Benton—Joseph La Barge took the *Emily* upriver past Old Fort Campbell (Malcolm Clark and his family had moved into the adobe ruins) to a point one and one-half miles above Fort Benton, where he "began to unload her Cargo." On June 18, the *Emily* departed for St. Louis, but Jaccard, Filley, and Harkness, all of whom had ascended the river to witness the birth of the new opposition, laid out a new timber and adobe post, Fort La Barge, near the bank where the *Emily* had landed above Fort Benton, assisted by the officers from the *Shreveport* and a crowd of passengers from the *Shreveport* and the *Emily*.[46] Dr. J. H. McKellops, a St. Louis dentist, presided over the ceremonious founding of Fort La Barge, "and brief speeches,

[45] "Diary of James Harkness," *CHSM*, II, 345–49; Thompson, "Reminiscences," *MM*, V, Supp., 151, 153, 158; Samuel T. Hauser to his Sister, May 24–June 17, 1862, CtY-WA; Howard, "Diary of Charles Rumley," *Frontier and Midland*, XIX, 190–91.

[46] "Diary of James Harkness," *CHSM*, II, 349–50; Thompson, "Reminiscences," *MM*, V, Supp., 160; Robert Vaughan, *Then and Now*, 233.

under the quiet stars, amid the white tents of the gold seekers dotting the bottom lands, were made by Rev. [Bartlett] . . . and others, and the whole affair passed off pleasantly, with hearty cheers for the new fort, the captain, the Union, and the old flag waving."[47]

Two days after the celebration, a group of opposition leaders, their wives, and children paid a visit to the Falls of the Missouri. "Madam La Barge and Margaret Harkness . . . ran to the point from which the first glimpse could be had, and [were] the first white women to have seen the Great Falls."[48] During the summer, construction of Fort La Barge proceeded, aided by lumber cut from the first steam sawmill in Montana, carried upriver in sections aboard the *Shreveport* and the *Emily*, and erected on the site of the new fort. Meanwhile, the *Emily* had returned at "railroad speed" to St. Louis, landed on July 2, took on new passengers and supplies for the mines, and headed back upriver to Sioux City. There she transferred her freight and passengers to the *Shreveport*, down from Fort La Barge, and returned to the lower river. The *Shreveport*, in turn, left Sioux City on July 26, her sides barricaded and her pilothouse well armed to protect her from hostile Sioux, and three weeks later deposited her cargo and passengers at Milk River for land transportation to Fort La Barge and the mines. On August 20, she turned downriver to St. Louis, carrying gold seekers from the mines, $70,000 to $80,000 in gold dust, 165 packs of robes consigned to Campbell and the new opposition, and a collection of stuffed animals. She docked a month later, on September 25, but the St. Louis press, more interested in the latest war news than in the Upper Missouri, devoted little space to Captain John La Barge and his upper-river Argonauts.[49]

During 1862 and 1863, La Barge, Harkness and Company relied upon a half-dozen small new posts to oppose the American Fur Company at key locations along the Upper Missouri. Fort La

[47] *Daily Missouri Democrat*, July 8, 1862.

[48] "Diary of James Harkness," *CHSM*, II, 350.

[49] *Daily Missouri Democrat*, July 8, September 20, 27, 1862; *DMR*, July 3, September 27, 1862; *Sioux City Register*, May 24, July 26, August 2, 1862.

Barge competed with Fort Benton, and Fort Galpin, finally given up in 1864 after an Indian attack, tapped the trade of the Milk River country. Owen McKenzie's Post, built late in the summer of 1862 and abandoned a year later because of poor trade and Indian troubles, stood a few miles above the site of Old Forts Stewart and Kipp, where the Chouteaus supplied one of the Roulette brothers as a trader. Opposition traders also built a small post near Fort Berthold in September, 1862, and Françoise La Framboise, the independent trader who had competed with the American Fur Company in the Sioux country even before the new opposition formed, joined La Barge, Harkness and Company and built a tiny, crude opposition post, Fort La Framboise, three miles above Fort Pierre II. La Framboise, however, "was not a Competent man he did not have no manner and no education either and he was rough to command."[50]

Before the end of the year (1862), the Chouteaus took steps to strengthen their position in the Indian country and to prepare, rather unsuccessfully, for closer competition with La Barge, Harkness and Company. American Fur Company traders and carpenters from Fort Benton built Fort Andrew (Dawson) on the Missouri River approximately fifteen miles above the mouth of the Musselshell; and Fort Berthold was evacuated after a Sioux attack and a fire. The Company men stationed at Fort Berthold moved into the abandoned stockade of near-by Fort Atkinson, rechristened it Fort Berthold (II) in honor of its well-known predecessor, and settled down to near-normal trade. At Fort Pierre II, however, antagonism between the traders and the Sioux dimmed trade prospects for the coming year. Early in June, 1862, shortly after the *Spread Eagle* passed upriver, a hostile party of Sans Arcs (Teton Sioux) reached the post and killed Chief Bear's Rib because he was too friendly with the whites. Following the murder and, two months later, the great Sioux outbreak in Minne-

[50] Quotation from Charles P. Barbier, "Recollections of Ft. La Framboise in 1862 and the Rescue of Lake Chetak Captives," *SDHC*, Vol. XI (1922), 232–33; Wilson, "Old Fort Pierre," *SDHC*, I, 368 (n. 69); "Diary of James Harkness," *CHSM*, II, 358–59; Chittenden, *Early Steamboat Navigation*, II, 293.

sota, the Indian trade in the Dakota country was completely disrupted while the army campaigned against the Indians.[51]

Neither the American Fur Company nor La Barge, Harkness and Company earned a very large return in 1862 in the Upper Missouri Indian trade. Moreover, each company realized that much of its profit came from the carrying trade to Fort Benton. Fortunately, the carrying trade promised to increase in 1863, but the robe and fur trade was almost certain to decline again as a result of the outbreak of Indian hostilities in Minnesota and Dakota. Other events—the movement of wagon trains of gold prospectors and settlers into Montana and Idaho in the summer of 1862; Congressional passage of the Homestead Act and a trans-continental-railroad bill a few months after the opening of the overland telegraph line late in 1861; and the expansion of the Idaho-Montana mining frontier—suggested that the old Upper Missouri fur and robe trade might soon be inundated by settlement.

[51] Herbert O. Brayer, "The Western Journal of Edward Shelley," *The Westerners Brand Book* (Chicago), Vol. XIII (January, 1957), 88; Smith, "Archeological Work at 32ML2," *The Plains Anthropologist*, No. 2, p. 29; Smith, "Fort Pierre II," *Bureau of American Ethnology River Basin Survey Papers*, XVIII, 102–105.

CHAPTER TEN

"Tired and out of spirits"

THE MINNESOTA SIOUX, confined, by treaty with the United States, to a long, narrow reservation fronting upon the south bank of the Minnesota River, had swallowed their pride long enough. Most of them resented the restrictions of reservation life, disliked the Indian agents sent to govern them, and refused to live by the plow and the white medicine man's religion. In August, 1862, while inexperienced local militia garrisoned the frontier posts of southwestern Minnesota to replace the regulars called away to the Civil War, a party of Sioux killed a handful of whites at Acton, and the incident quickly led to a general Indian attack upon settlers in the Minnesota River Valley. As the alarming news of the uprising spread into Iowa and Dakota, hundreds of settlers fled scattered, defenseless farms and tiny towns to take refuge at Fort Randall, in the Yankton Agency, or in Sioux City. Militiamen gathered for emergency duty. Settlers abandoned Sioux Falls, and the Indians fired the town. Most of the tribes along the Missouri from the Vermillion to Fort Benton soon showed hostility, and "most of the Indian traders on the river" anticipated "serious difficulty" with at least the Sioux before Christmastide.[1] "Companies of . . . miners," returning to the Lower Missouri by mackinaw and canoe from the gold fields above the Falls of the Missouri, were "shamefully treated . . . some of them severely wounded, and others robbed of their entire effects" by marauding war parties. River traffic above Omaha was disrupted thoroughly weeks before freezing temperatures closed the stream to com-

[1] Robert H. Jones, *The Civil War in the Northwest*, chap. II; *Dakotian*, October 28, 1862.

merce for the winter, and traders, messengers, and settlers using
the roads and trails in the Dakota country traveled under threat
of ambush.[2]

In command of the Department of the Northwest, General
John Pope, fresh from defeat at the Second Battle of Bull Run,
ordered General Alfred Sully (the eminent artist Thomas Sully
was his father, and the General himself dabbled in water-color
paintings of western forts) to move up the Missouri River, in
1863, to engage the Sioux, who were retreating west before Minnesota forces under General Henry H. Sibley. Although delayed
by supply problems and low water in the Missouri, Sully's command moved upriver during the summer of 1863 and in early
September defeated the Sioux at White Stone Hill between the
James and Missouri rivers. The Indians, however, were not
permanently beaten by the Sully-Sibley pincers movement, and,
pending a new campaign against the tribes in 1864, Sully sent two
companies of the Sixth Iowa Cavalry to build a fort, Old Fort
Sully, on the east bank of the Missouri close to the head of Farm
Island and within seven miles of Old Fort Pierre. In July, 1866,
when the garrison abandoned Old Fort Sully "because of the un-
healthy character of the site," the army put up a new camp, a
second Fort Sully, thirty miles north of the old post.[3]

At the beginning of the Sioux uprising in 1862, the Chouteaus
offered the army "all accommodations necessary for quartering
troops and storing supplies" at upriver American Fur Company
posts. Later, General Pope requested that the Chouteaus furnish
General Sully information on the Sioux and told the American
Fur Company that the army planned to build four Dakota-
country posts to control the subjugated tribes. Naturally, the
Chouteaus resented the army's plan, since Company power on the
Upper Missouri was certain to diminish under regular military
surveillance. But the American Fur Company was, even then,

[2] Territorial Council of Dakota, *Report of the Select Committee on Indian
Affairs, December 29, 1862,* 6.

[3] United States War Department, Surgeon General's Office, *A Report of
Barracks and Hospitals,* 388.

suspected of subversion, and the Chouteaus dared not lobby strongly against the army proposal.[4]

Meanwhile, in the spring of 1863, despite Indian hostilities in Dakota Territory, the American Fur Company and La Barge, Harkness and Company outfitted and sent steamboats upriver. Although the Indian Office had allowed the American Fur Company to transport the Upper Missouri Indian annuities in 1862— the Office had finally, yet reluctantly, accepted the Company argument that the annuity contract of 1861 also covered 1862— Indian Commissioner Dole and his superior, Secretary of the Interior Caleb B. Smith, refused to grant the Company any special favors when the government called for bids on the 1863 annuity contract. La Barge, Harkness and Company underbid the American Fur Company and four minor contestants and won the contract. The American Fur Company protested the decision, but Commissioner Dole wrote the Chouteaus on March 19 that he considered the question closed. By early April, the opposition steamers *Shreveport* and *Robert Campbell* were tied up at the St. Louis levee ready to receive freight and passengers for the Indian country. During the winter, carpenters had lengthened the *Shreveport* twenty feet, added staterooms and new engines, and lightened the draft of the vessel in preparation for heavy duty on the shallow upper river.[5]

After waiting approximately three weeks for the Indian annuities to reach St. Louis from the East, the opposition decided that Captain John La Barge should proceed upriver in command of the *Shreveport*, while his brother Joseph, in charge of the *Robert Campbell*, would continue to wait in St. Louis for the belated arrival of the Indian annuities. Early in the evening of

4 "Expedition from Fort Abercrombie to Fort Benton," 37 Cong., 3 sess., *HED No. 80*, p. 3; Gen. John Pope to Pierre Chouteau, Jr., and Company, April 6, 1864, in R. N. Scott *et al.* (eds.), *The War of the Rebellion: A Compilation of the Official Records of the Union and Confederate Armies*, Series I, Vol. XXXIV, Part III, 69-70.

5 Special File No. 243, OIA, RG 75, NA; W. P. Dole to Pierre Chouteau, Jr., and Company, November 18, 20, 1862, March 19, 1863, Letters Sent, OIA, RG 75, NA; *DMR*, February 20, April 3, 1863.

April 20, the *Shreveport* sailed for the mines with approximately eighty passengers and one hundred tons of freight. The Missouri was low and full of sand bars, and the vessel lost time from adverse winds, but reached Sioux City without encountering any lower-river guerrilla bands. At Fort Randall, the Missouri rose, and the *Shreveport* steamed upriver on a higher channel past the small garrison at Fort La Framboise and the ruins of Old Fort Clark—"a pile of stones," a rubbish-filled icehouse, and an overgrown burial ground. The Arikaras, Mandans, and Hidatsas at Fort Berthold were peaceful, afraid of Sioux attack, and pleased to hear from Captain La Barge that the army planned to fight the hostiles. On June 8, the steamer passed the mouth of the Yellowstone and two days later reached McKenzie's Post, where Captain La Barge evacuated McKenzie and his men (during the winter, the Sioux had attacked the post, killed two traders, and stolen their livestock) and carried them upriver to safety at Fort Galpin.[6]

Above Milk River, the *Shreveport* passed a seven-man party of miners, with a jackass, a grizzly bear (presumably small!), and two dogs, all in one small boat, on their way downstream to civilization. The channel of the Missouri grew shallower and shallower as the steamer moved upriver, and finally, on June 20, at the foot of Bird's Rapids, Captain La Barge landed his passengers and cargo and sent a messenger ahead to Fort La Barge to order mackinaws sent downriver to carry the freight up to the mouth of the Judith, where it could be forwarded by wagon to Fort La Barge and the mines. Once the passengers and cargo were safely ashore, the *Shreveport* turned downstream to meet and assist her companion vessel; took on robes and furs at Fort Galpin; passed two American Fur Company steamers struggling with the channel just above Fort Union; and at last, on July 2, met the *Robert Campbell*.[7]

After "annoying and even disastrous delay" caused by the late

[6] Boller, *Among the Indians*, 360–61; DMR, April 20, May 16, August 6, 1863.
[7] *DMR*, August 6, 1863.

arrival of the annuities, the *Robert Campbell* had sailed from the port of St. Louis on May 13, heavily loaded with freight and passengers, including Indian Agents Reed and Latta, the Culbertsons, and a military escort to protect the boat from Confederate raiders along the lower river. Navigation was extremely difficult on the skimpy channel, but after considerable struggle, the boat reached Fort Pierre II. Although the Sioux had warned Agent Latta in 1862 not to return to the upper river, he talked with the chiefs assembled at the fort and distributed annuities without incident. Captain La Barge, however, later said that Latta gave the Sioux "only . . . about two-thirds . . . of the goods" they were entitled to receive and that when the boat pulled away, the Indians followed the vessel upstream for hundreds of miles, "appeared and attacked the crew" at every woodpile, and frequently "fired into the boat."[8]

The *Robert Campbell* and the *Shreveport* met near the mouth of Heart River and proceeded up the Missouri together. On the afternoon of July 5, the *Shreveport*, in the lead, stopped to wood above Fort Berthold and was fired upon by a large Sioux war party. One arrow struck the *Shreveport* within two feet of Captain John La Barge as he directed the vessel from the bank into mid-channel. At that crucial moment the *Robert Campbell* steamed up and fired several cannon rounds at the Indians and drove them to cover. The boats continued upriver, and early on July 7, the *Shreveport* pulled close to a sand bar (Tobacco Garden Landing) below tiny Tobacco Creek, which empties into the Missouri from the north approximately halfway between Forts Berthold and Union. The channel of the Missouri ran near the south shore at that point and afforded hostile Indians an "ideal place to 'hold up' a boat." On the high south bank, a hunter from the *Shreveport* discovered tracks of a large war party in the

8 S. N. Latta to W. P. Dole, March 7, 1863, Letters Received, OIA, RG 75, NA; Kingsbury, *Dakota Territory*, I, 572–73; Chittenden, *Early Steamboat Navigation*, II, 299–302.

timber, returned to the boat, and warned the crew and passengers. Almost immediately the Indians, "mostly mounted," gathered on the bank, shouted to the boat that they were friendly, and asked the vessel to cross to the south shore.[9]

Just then the *Robert Campbell* rounded the bend in the Missouri and anchored alongside the *Shreveport* in the channel. The Indians screamed that they wanted to talk to Agent Latta and, if Joseph La Barge's memoirs are correct, demanded the remainder of the annuities denied them a few days earlier at Fort Pierre II. Latta agreed to meet a delegation of chiefs on the *Robert Campbell*, and the La Barges, after a few words together, sent seven crewmen in a yawl to bring the Indian leaders aboard the steamer. The Culbertsons, very suspicious of the Sioux, evidently advised against sending the small boat ashore, but the La Barges sent the boat in anyway while the passengers and crews aboard the two steamers watched from the shelter of bales and boxes of freight piled up on the decks. When the yawl landed, four Indians approached, shook hands with the rowers, and then, just as quickly, "sprang back & commenced the slaughter by shooting & stabbing." Three crewmen were killed instantly and one was wounded before the onlookers aboard the two steamboats opened fire with small arms and cannon. For three hours the whites fired volley after volley at the Indians scattered along the bank. The red men returned the fire sporadically and then withdrew from the battleground, leaving an estimated eighteen to thirty dead and wounded warriors. Meanwhile, the men in the yawl who survived the Indian attack rowed to the bar in the river, where three of them scrambled onto the sand and dashed to the steamboats. Then the steersman of the yawl, William Stinger, dragged the tiny boat and the three casualties in it through the shallow water to the *Robert Campbell*. Late in the afternoon, the two steamers cautiously headed upriver and when night came, anchored in

[9] *DMR*, August 6, 1863; Chittenden, *Early Steamboat Navigation*, II, 305–306; Larpenteur, *Forty Years*, II, 347; Boller, *Among the Indians*, 363–69.

midstream until dawn. By then the danger of Indian attack had passed, and the vessels continued safely to the mouth of the Yellowstone.[10]

The Missouri at the Yellowstone bar stood two feet deep in the channel—much too shallow to float the *Robert Campbell*—and the *Shreveport* was forced to make at least five trips to carry, bit by bit, the Indian annuities from the larger boat to the trading post, where Agent Latta distributed the Assiniboin annuities and stored the Crow goods in the American Fur Company warehouse for distribution at a later date. Agent Reed also put the Blackfoot annuities in storage for future distribution. The two steamers immediately turned back to St. Louis, but at Crow Creek, approximately eighty miles below Fort Pierre II, the commander of one of General Sully's units halted the boats and impressed the lighter craft (the *Shreveport*) into service to carry military freight up to the Fort Pierre area. The La Barges loaded the *Robert Campbell* with all of the opposition robe and fur returns (889 packs) collected on the upper river, exchanged commands, and the *Robert Campbell*, now under Captain John La Barge, steamed away from Crow Creek and docked in St. Louis on August 6. Captain La Barge immediately sent her to dry dock to be "generally overhauled and repaired" and to undergo "extensive additions to her cabin and upper works."[11] Meanwhile, the *Shreveport* hauled government freight between Leavenworth and Sioux City for three months and finally returned to St. Louis on November 11.[12]

The American Fur Company steamers *Nellie Rogers* and *Alone*

---

[10] C. J. Atkins (ed.), "Log of Steamer Robert Campbell, Jr., from St. Louis to Fort Benton, Montana Territory," CHSND, Vol. II (1908), 278; Kingsbury, *Dakota Territory*, I, 573; Boller, *Among the Indians*, 363–69; S. N. Latta to W. P. Dole, August 27, 1863, Letters Received, OIA, RG 75, NA; Larpenteur, *Forty Years*, II, 348–49; Chittenden, *Early Steamboat Navigation*, II, 307–13; DMR, August 6, 1863.

[11] Quotation from DMR, August 17, 1863. See also *ibid.*, August 6, 8, 1863; S. N. Latta to W. P. Dole, August 27, 1863, Letters Received, OIA, RG 75, NA; Chittenden, *Early Steamboat Navigation*, II, 317–18; S. N. Latta to W. P. Dole, September 27, 1863, 38 Cong., 1 sess., HED No. 1, p. 282.

[12] DMR, September 17, November 17, 1863.

made difficult voyages to the upper river in 1863, similar to the trouble-filled trips of the *Shreveport* and *Robert Campbell*. Both Company vessels, the *Nellie Rogers* under Captain Humphreys and the *Alone* under Captain Thomas Ray of Pittsburgh, sailed from St. Louis on a dangerously low channel on May 9 under the over-all command of Charles Chouteau, who switched from boat to boat on the tandem voyage. In addition to Company supplies and employees, the vessels carried gold seekers and freight for the many new mining camps west of Fort Benton. When the steamboats reached Fort Pierre II, the Sioux demanded gifts, and Chouteau appeased them with hardtack, bacon, sugar, and coffee. Between the Teton Sioux country and the mouth of the Yellowstone, several war parties observed the steamers from the riverbanks, frightened crewmen sent ashore for wood, tried to bribe Chouteau for presents, and took pot shots at the vessels, but no general Indian attack upon the boats occurred. Late in June, the *Nellie Rogers* reached the mouth of Milk River, unloaded freight for further shipment by pack animal and wagon to Fort Benton, and headed back toward the mouth of the Yellowstone. The *Alone* sailed upriver only as far as Fort Charles (recently abandoned), where Robert Meldrum, under Chouteau's orders, repaired the post and reopened it for trade.[13]

As the *Nellie Rogers* dropped downstream toward Fort Union, she stopped briefly at Roulette's Post, on the site of old Forts Stewart and Kipp. According to the statement of Eli W. McNeal, a passenger aboard the *Alone*, Roulette had cheated the Indians and the tribesmen had sworn revenge. When the *Nellie Rogers* reached Roulette's Post, Chouteau took on a cargo of furs and robes and smuggled Roulette aboard the steamboat. After the *Nellie Rogers* turned downriver from the post, the *Alone*, also bound downstream, arrived, took on some additional cargo, and tied up for the night on the south bank of the Missouri opposite the post. Shortly before midnight, an Assiniboin war party set the

[13] *Ibid.*, April 22, May 2, 10, 1863; Reminiscences of Eli W. McNeal, Typescript, MtHi.

249

post afire and killed the entire garrison—seven traders—who remained within the stockade. Captain Ray, fearful of an attack upon the *Alone,* ran the vessel upriver by firelight, anchored in midstream for the remainder of the night, and the next day continued upstream to Fort Charles. Later, when Assiniboin tempers had cooled, the *Alone* slipped down from Fort Charles past the charred ruins of Roulette's Post to Fort Union and on to Fort Pierre II, where the government commandeered her to carry military freight in Sully's Missouri River campaign. The *Alone* eventually reached St. Louis on November 4, two and one-half months after the *Nellie Rogers,* and was laid up for repairs. Chouteal had landed on the *Nellie Rogers* on August 16 with twenty thousand buffalo robes and a cargo of furs piled in every available space on deck and "filling nearly all" the vessel's staterooms. Despite the large return, he resented the seizure of the *Alone* and accused the Fort Randall quartermaster of "gross negligence" in handling military supplies for Sully's expedition.[14]

Chouteau and the officers and crew of the *Nellie Rogers* not only returned to St. Louis with a large robe and fur cargo and complaints about the army, but carried with them the story of a murder (cold blooded, according to rumor) aboard the *Nellie Rogers.* The distinguished-looking trader Malcolm Clark was aboard the *Nellie Rogers* at Milk River when his old enemy, Owen McKenzie, son of Kenneth McKenzie, the former American Fur Company leader, boarded the vessel. Owen McKenzie was "a splendid rider, first-rate shot," and an excellent hunter. Perhaps he was drunk when he boarded the boat, perhaps not, but he encountered Clark, "a man to be feared" when angry, in the hall leading from the main cabin. They may have quarreled briefly in the hallway, but whether or not they exchanged denunciations was of no consequence to the outcome. Clark, who knew McKenzie was a crack shot, pulled a pistol, fired three times, and killed his adversary, then claimed self-defense and fled the Milk

[14] Reminiscences of Eli W. McNeal, MtHi; *DMR,* August 16, 17, November 5, 1863; *Dakotian,* October 6, 1863.

River country for Fort Benton to avoid McKenzie's friends. Chouteau carried the murdered man's remains downriver aboard the *Nellie Rogers* and interred them at Fort Union, where Mc-Kenzie had spent so many years of his life. Clark became a rancher in Montana and was killed by his halfblood brother-in-law a few years later.[15]

By the time the American Fur Company steamer *Alone* and the opposition steamer *Shreveport* pulled up to the St. Louis levee in November, 1863, La Barge, Harkness and Company had started to disband. In his memoirs, Joseph La Barge claimed that Harkness was, from the beginning of the partnership, unfit to conduct opposition affairs, refused to serve as agent at Fort La Barge during the winter of 1862–63 when he was most needed at the new, strategically located post, and quickly grew "tired and out of spirits" with La Barge, Harkness and Company. When Harkness declined to remain at Fort La Barge, the opposition assigned Joseph Picotte to the post, but he took little interest in the job. In desperation, the partners appointed Robert Lemon to replace him, and when Lemon reached Fort La Barge, he found "Mr. Picotte drunk," the other traders at the post, their salaries unpaid, dissatisfied with the firm, and "everything going to ruin." Although Joseph La Barge charged that Lemon was not even as competent a trader as Picotte, Lemon clearly realized that he was in an impossible position at Fort La Barge in the late summer of 1863. He took the only sensible alternative to financial disaster and, on August 30, turned over for safekeeping to Andrew Dawson, the American Fur Company agent at Fort Benton, all opposition goods at Fort La Barge. In return, Dawson promised to pay the wages due the opposition traders at Fort La Barge and to carry up to Fort Benton the remainder of the freight left by the *Shreveport* at the foot of Bird's Rapids a month earlier. By failing to transport

[15] Chittenden, *Early Steamboat Navigation*, I, 233–34; Larpenteur, *Forty Years*, II, 352–53; McDonnell, "Forts Benton and Sarpy," *CHSM*, X, 293 (n. 219); Culbertson, *Journal*, 55 (n. 10); Joseph Culbertson to C. N. Kessler, October 5, 1919, Montana Manuscripts Collection, CLUC; "Up the Missouri River to Montana," MtHi; E. W. Gould, *Fifty Years on the Mississippi*, 423–27.

THE MISSOURI FUR TRADE, 1840–1865

all of the freight from the rapids to Fort Benton, La Barge, Harkness and Company had broken contract with various consignees. One of them, the firm of John J. Roe and Nicholas Wall, had sent wagons to pick up its freight at Bird's Rapids, and subsequently sued La Barge, Harkness and Company for $24,000 in damages. In 1865, the (territorial) Supreme Court of Montana decided in favor of the plaintiffs (Roe and Wall), and La Barge, Harkness and Company, then well into dissolution, paid the claim by auctioning off to the American Fur Company the sawmill, buildings, and robe and fur stock remaining at Fort La Barge. Joseph La Barge estimated, many years later, that the opposition lost at least $100,000 between 1862 and 1865 on the Upper Missouri, yet heavy property loss was only one bitter pill to swallow; the loss of much of that property to the American Fur Company was another.[16]

Although La Barge, Harkness and Company was wrecked by the end of 1863 and a large pile of robes and furs, carried to St. Louis aboard the *Nellie Rogers*, stood in the Chouteaus' warehouse, the future of the American Fur Company on the Upper Missouri remained in doubt. The Sioux were still at war in Dakota Territory, miners and settlers flocked into Montana and Idaho, and the old Indian trade at Fort Benton was giving way to new mining trade. Each soldier, miner, settler, and hostile Indian on the upper river, every army post and squatter colony along the Missouri between Fort Randall and Fort Benton threatened the life of the robe and fur trade. The Chouteaus realized that the American Fur Company could survive beyond 1864 only if the rush to the Montana mines ended, permanent peace returned to the Indian country, the army withdrew from the Upper Missouri, and the Civil War terminated quickly—all unlikely events.

Since the sooner the hostile Sioux were beaten by the army the sooner the Upper Missouri might be free of military interference,

[16] Bradley, "Affairs," *CHSM*, III, 285; Chittenden, *Early Steamboat Navigation*, II, 296, 324–29; Robert H. Lemon to La Barge, Harkness and Company, September 1, 1863, and Inventory of the Stock of Ft. La Barge, August 28, 1863, La Barge Collection, St. Charles County Historical Society, St. Charles, Missouri.

the American Fur Company renewed its pledge to the army, in the spring of 1864, to co-operate with General Sully in his Indian campaign. During the winter, the Sioux threatened Fort Union; attacked Forts Berthold and Charles; ambushed a Company supply train between Forts Union and Galpin; and completely overpowered another Company caravan between Forts Andrew and Galpin and carried off more than four thousand dollars' worth of goods. In March, in a letter to General Henry W. Halleck in Washington, D.C., the Chouteaus advised the army to concentrate upon subjugating the Sioux in the triangle of land between the Yellowstone and the Missouri, and opposed the army's plan to place four new permanent posts in the Dakota country and to open an overland emigrant route into the Yellowstone Valley. To facilitate General Sully's Sioux campaign, Charles Chouteau offered to provide steamers to carry supplies and soldiers up the Missouri and the Yellowstone as far as Clark's Fork, or even above that point if the channel permitted. He intended to prove that a military force could be transported by water up the Yellowstone and that future emigrants might utilize an all-water route, rather than one by land, across Montana to the Upper Yellowstone country.[17]

In March, General Sully, under orders from General Pope to proceed up the Missouri with a large infantry and cavalry force, negotiated with the American Fur Company in St. Louis for steamers to carry the expedition's freight as far as the Yellowstone. Charles Chouteau offered to transport the freight, under special contract, at four cents per pound, but the St. Louis quartermaster rejected Chouteau's offer to supply all of the vessels and the expedition floundered while General Sully chartered boats from various owners. Finally, in May, he ascended the Missouri, met units of his command at Sioux City and at Old Fort Sully, and

[17] Pierre Chouteau, Jr., and Company to Gen. H. W. Halleck, March 26, 1864, *War of the Rebellion: Official Records*, Series I, Vol. XXXIV, Part II, 743–44; Gen. Benjamin Alvord to the Assistant Adjutant General at San Francisco, February 25, 1864, and to Gen. Samuel R. Curtis, March 3, 1864, *ibid.*, Vol. L, Part II, 771, 776.

early in July laid out Fort Rice near the mouth of Cannonball River. Two weeks later, he led his expedition (approximately 2,400 soldiers plus 250 Montana-bound gold seekers) west from Fort Rice up the Cannonball, then north to Killdeer Mountain, where he defeated the Sioux on July 28, and on west across the Bad Lands of the Little Missouri River toward the Yellowstone. On August 12, two light-draft steamers carrying military provisions (one, the *Alone*, was certainly an American Fur Company boat, and the other, the *Chippewa Falls*, may possibly have been owned by the Company) met General Sully's expedition on the Yellowstone. A third vessel, the *Island City*, loaded with corn for the horses of the expedition, had sunk near Fort Union. Since military provisions were short, fodder for the animals dangerously low, and colder weather only a few weeks away, General Sully decided not to build a Yellowstone post, at least not that season, to protect the proposed overland emigrant route from the Missouri River to the Northwest.

Instead of lingering with his men on the Yellowstone or leaving a small garrison behind (and he had none to spare) to build a fort, he moved his entire command downstream to Fort Union, arranged to garrison the trading post for the winter, and pushed ahead down the Missouri. He assigned a company of the Sixth Iowa Cavalry to protect Fort Berthold and in mid-October returned safely with the remainder of his men to the Yankton–Sioux City area. Although General Sully did not beat the Sioux decisively in 1864 and failed to build a fort on the Yellowstone, he proved to the army, with the help of St. Louis steamboatmen, including the Chouteaus, that the Yellowstone was navigable for light-draft boats and that steamers could be used successfully, despite irritating complications, to support military campaigns on the Upper Missouri.[18]

[18] Jones, *Civil War in Northwest*, 84–89, 93; Lass, *Steamboating*, 27–31; Ray H. Mattison, "The Military Frontier on the Upper Missouri," *NH*, Vol. 37 (September, 1956), 168–69; Raymond L. Welty, "The Frontier Army on the Missouri River, 1860–1870," *NDHQ*, Vol. II (January, 1928), 90.

Meanwhile, in mid-March, the American Fur Company won, over one minor competitor, the contract for 1864 to carry annuities to the Upper Missouri tribes and, in addition, to the Flatheads west of Fort Benton. Charles Chouteau also complied with the government's request to carry Father De Smet, a peace emissary to the Indians, upriver on the Company boat, and the army agreed to furnish the American Fur Company steamer with two cannons, ammunition, and a thirty-man military escort. The Company outfitted a new $70,000 vessel, the 378-ton *Yellowstone* for the 1864 trip to the mountains, and at noon on April 16, Charles Chouteau ordered Captain William R. Massie to cast off from the St. Louis levee. The engines of the *Yellowstone*, however, were too weak to overcome the current of the Missouri easily and the boat was overloaded with freight. As a result, the vessel pushed upstream slowly, stuck on innumerable bars, and did not land at Fort Union until June 13. A week later, when the *Yellowstone* grounded at Cow Island below Bird's Rapids, Chouteau knew that the steamer could neither overcome the rapids below Fort Benton nor prove the Yellowstone navigable. He put ashore all freight and passengers destined for Fort Benton, and after a ten-day struggle with the Cow Island sand bar, Captain Massie freed the *Yellowstone* and headed her downriver.[19]

Chouteau anchored the boat at Fort Berthold on July 8 and accompanied Father De Smet to a council with the Sioux. None of the river tribes had attacked the vessel on the upriver trip, and the meeting was peaceful. Following it, the *Yellowstone* resumed her course to St. Louis and landed on July 21 with a cargo of 1,700

19 Memorandum of W. R. Massie, Typescript, Eugene Stephens Collection–IV, MoSHi; Pierre Chouteau, Jr., and Company to W. P. Dole, February 25, March 2, 30, 1864, Secretary of the Interior to W. P. Dole, March 5, 1864, and Elias L. Beard to W. P. Dole, March 2, 1864, Letters Received, OIA, RG 75, NA; W. P. Dole to Pierre Chouteau, Jr., and Company, March 18, 22, 25, 1864, Letters Sent, OIA, RG 75, NA; Gen. U. S. Grant to Gen. H. W. Halleck, April 9, 1864, *War of the Rebellion: Official Records*, Series I, Vol. XXXIV, Part III, 112; Henry H. Reed to W. P. Dole, 1864, and Father Pierre Jean De Smet to W. P. Dole, June 24, 1864, 38 Cong., 2 sess., *HED No. 1*, pp. 413–14, 421.

bales of robes and furs, collected from upriver Company trading posts, and several hogsheads of tobacco taken on at Lower Missouri landings. The entire voyage—interrupted only by sand bars and large herds of buffalo which at times filled the river, stopped the boat, and rocked it back and forth—was more peaceful than the Company had anticipated.[20]

Although La Barge, Harkness and Company had collapsed in 1863, the La Barge brothers continued to command boats on the Missouri River. In the spring of 1864, Joseph La Barge took the *Effie Deans*, "purchased expressly" for the mountain trade, upriver with freight and passengers for the mines. He intended also, while on the way to Fort Benton, to pick up the Crow and Assiniboin annuities that Indian Agents Latta and Reed had stored, under his annuity contract, in the American Fur Company warehouse at Fort Union in 1863. The Indian Office had refused to pay La Barge for the delivery of those annuities until he had actually carried them to the proper distribution points above Fort Union, and had recontracted with him in 1864, extending the delivery date. On April 16, the *Effie Deans* left for the upper river, and late in June, La Barge went ashore at Fort Union and requested, in the presence of army Captain W. B. Greer as witness, the annuities from the American Fur Company agent in charge of the post. Roulette, the Company agent, demanded a $2,000 storage charge for the goods, and when La Barge agreed to pay the sum, Roulette refused to deliver them until La Barge gave him the receipts the Company had given La Barge in 1863. La Barge suspected that a large portion, if not all, of the annuities were missing—Captain Greer told him that the Company had traded "nearly all [of them] for robes"—and Roulette finally admitted that, under instructions from the Indian Office (instructions he refused to show La Barge), he had delivered most of the annuities to the Indians during the winter. "Captain La Barge became thoroughly convinced

[20] *DMR*, July 22, 1864; Father Pierre Jean De Smet to W. P. Dole, July 15, 1864, 38 Cong., 2 sess., *HED No. 1*, p. 424.

that [the annuities] had been used in trade . . . wisely declined to surrender his receipts . . . [and] went on his way without them."[21]

Above Fort Union, on the way upriver, La Barge met Charles Chouteau and Indian Agent Reed aboard the *Yellowstone* coming downriver from Cow Island. The three men discussed the annuity problem. Although Chouteau "professed to disapprove of Roulette's course," he refused to order his agent to turn over the goods. La Barge, incensed by Chouteau's highhandedness, broke off the meeting and took the *Effie Deans* up to Cow Island, where he loaded the freight and passengers left by the American Fur Company boat and deposited them safely, together with the freight and passengers of the *Effie Deans*, at the mouth of the Marias within a few miles of Fort Benton. Then he headed downstream, carrying a small cargo of buffalo robes and a number of passengers from the mines, and landed the *Effie Deans* on August 5 at the port of St. Louis.[22]

La Barge visited Washington, during the winter of 1864–65 to "secure payment," refused by the Treasury, on his government annuity contracts. Although he failed to convince Secretary of the Treasury Salmon Chase (Chase thought all Missourians were rebels) of the validity of his claim, when he talked with President Lincoln about the problem, the President "smiled at Chase's remark" and arranged for at least part of the money to be paid La Barge immediately. The remainder of the sum, however, particularly La Barge's charge for transporting the Blackfoot and Crow annuities, was disallowed by the Indian Office, since it had received receipts for the annuities, witnessed by American Fur Company agents, from the Blackfeet and Crows. La Barge, certain that the American Fur Company had falsified the receipts, filed a claim with the Secretary of the Interior for $19,914.03 to

[21] Chittenden, *Early Steamboat Navigation*, II, 319–22; Henry H. Reed to W. P. Dole, 1864, 38 Cong., 2 sess., *HED No. 1*, pp. 413–14; *DMR*, March 24, April 13, 1864.

[22] Gad E. Upson to W. P. Dole, September 1, 1864, 38 Cong., 2 sess., *HED No. 1*, pp. 439–40; *DMR*, August 6, 1864.

cover the cost of transportation of the Blackfoot and Crow annuities to the Upper Missouri and for detention of his steamboat, the *Robert Campbell*, in St. Louis between April 10 and May 13, 1863, awaiting the annuities coming from the East. The Interior Department repeatedly turned down the claim, and, in desperation, La Barge finally petitioned the Congress, in 1887, to pass a private bill in his behalf. Between January, 1888, and March, 1909, several representatives introduced private bills in his favor, but none passed the House.[23]

It seems likely that the American Fur Company *was* guilty of using the Blackfoot and Crow annuities of 1863 for Company trading purposes, just as it had used other annuities on other occasions. It also appears that the Company shipped hundreds of gallons of illicit alcohol upriver during the war years to supply the mines, the thirsty passengers aboard river steamers, the riverside settlers, the grog shops near army installations, and, of course, the Indian camps. In the summer of 1864, Indian Agent Reed reported to the Commissioner of Indian Affairs that the Upper Missouri trading posts stocked whiskey and that every boat bound upriver carried a large cargo of alcohol. Indian Agent Mahlon Wilkinson agreed with Reed and wrote the Commissioner, in mid-July, that he had seen American Fur Company boats unload liquor along the upper river and had watched American Fur Company traders sell it to halfbloods and Indians. The Chouteaus, however, as Wilkinson added, always had some of the "best witnesses in the world" to swear that the American Fur Company was innocent of trading illegal alcohol. Nevertheless, Wilkinson was determined to bring the Company to justice, and by early fall, 1864, he had taken several affidavits from Upper Missouri traders willing to testify to the American Fur Company's rumrunning and had written the governor of Dakota Territory charging that Charles Chouteau and Father De Smet ("a good simple minded old man but com-

---

[23] Chittenden, *Early Steamboat Navigation*, II, 323, 342–344; Special File No. 243, OIA, RG 75, NA. See the *Congressional Record*, 1888–1910, for the disposition of the various La Barge relief bills.

pletely under" the Company's control) had held Indian councils along the river during the summer without notifying proper authorities. The Company, in other words, was still using its old tactics. But had it, in final desperation to save itself, added to its bag of trading tricks, or was the Upper Missouri audience of 1864 too large and sophisticated to be fooled for long by the old magician?[24]

By the end of 1864, Charles Chouteau was ready to abandon the upper-river robe and fur business. Trade had declined during the year, and the national and international fur markets were still upset by the Civil War. President Lincoln was re-elected in November, and his victory carried with it at least four more years of trouble for the American Fur Company in the Indian Office. Montana had received territorial status in 1864, and territorial officeholders were likely to meddle in Company business at Fort Benton; and the Congress had chartered a railroad, the Northern Pacific, to run through the heart of the Upper Missouri fur country. In fact, the American Fur Company remained solvent in 1864 only by carrying freight and passengers from lower-river ports to Fort Benton and the mines and by fulfilling special government contracts. American Fur Company steamers no longer dominated the Missouri River above Old Fort Pierre; rather, the river was becoming a major waterway. A variety of shippers used the Missouri, and when the war ended, they profited from an increase in river traffic. One St. Louis merchant and riverboatman, John G. Copelin, organized "The St. Louis and Fort Benton Transportation Line" in 1864, possibly with the assistance of some American Fur Company capital, and sent vessels upriver with freight and passengers to Montana. One of his boats, the little stern-wheeler *Benton*, left St. Louis on March 26,

[24] "Condition of the Indian Tribes" (Testimony of James Havens, September 8, 1865), 39 Cong., 2 sess., *SR Doc. No. 156*, pp. 412–13; Henry H. Reed to W. P. Dole, 1864, 38 Cong., 2 sess., *HED No. 1*, pp. 416–17; Mahlon Wilkinson to James Harlow, July 14, 1864, Letters Received, OIA, RG 75, NA; M. Wilkinson to N. Edmunds, August 31, 1864, and Depositions Taken by M. Wilkinson, July 5, 1864, Dakota Superintendency Field Papers, OIA, RG 76, NA.

1864, despite General Pope's request that no commercial vessel ascend the Missouri in advance of General Sully's expedition. The *Benton* remained on the upper river throughout the summer and carried freight and passengers to Fort Benton from Fort Galpin, where two other Copelin vessels, the *Welcome* and the *Fanny Ogden*, landed. Several of the boats picked up small robe and fur cargoes for the American Fur Company and Robert Campbell on their return trips to St. Louis from the upper river. Copelin earned a substantial profit in 1864 from his river line and the following year, extended service to take advantage of the postwar boom in water transportation.[25]

By the late winter of 1864–65, most upriver American Fur Company trading posts were falling to pieces and Charles Chouteau had decided to dissolve the Company. Fort Pierre II, abandoned in 1863 when Company employees, for protection, moved down to Old Fort Sully to trade with the soldiers, was visited only intermittently by Indians, travelers, traders, and military units. Fort Berthold needed repairs badly, but was still open and doing business. The Assiniboin trade at Fort Union, however, had fallen considerably: the Sioux had killed the livestock at the post and had destroyed the kitchen garden, and only a handful of Company traders remained at the fort. Fort Benton, or "Benton City," as the local citizens preferred to call it, in contrast to Forts Pierre II and Union, prospered from the gold rush. The town, "about as picturesque as a hole in the ground," embraced the old adobe American Fur Company post plus "a dozen uncouth houses"—dwellings, stores, warehouses, and saloons—strung along a single main street facing the river. Miners, drovers, fur traders, and Indian women crowded the community; disregarded what little law existed; drank and brawled, and sometimes killed, with equal facility; and overcharged new arrivals for

[25] *DMR*, February 15, April 6, June 30, July 8, August 21, 1864; Larpenteur, *Forty Years*, II, 355–60; Lass, *Steamboating*, 36–37; M. Wilkinson to N. Edmunds, August 31, 1864, 38 Cong., 2 sess., *HED No. 1*, pp. 406–407.

everything from horses to "lemonade made with syrup, at thirty-eight cents a glass."[26]

When Andrew Dawson, the feeble American Fur Company bourgeois at Fort Benton, retired to Scotland in 1864, Charles Chouteau appointed Isaac G. Baker, who had traded in the Osage River Agency during the 1840's, to supervise the post. Baker, an honest, conscientious businessman, served as chief trader at Fort Benton until the following spring; then, shortly after the American Fur Company withdrew from the upriver trade, he opened a mercantile store in partnership with his brother.[27] Meanwhile, on May 28, 1865, the first steamboat of the season, the "completely refitted and furnished" American Fur Company boat *Yellowstone*, reached Fort Benton, carrying Charles Chouteau and freight and passengers for the mines, and received a warm welcome from a "multitude" gathered at the landing. The citizens presented Captain James Mahood, master of the boat, a prize for early arrival: "a splendid pair of double-pronged Elk horns gaily trimmed." The steamer, leaving St. Louis on March 20, ascended the Missouri on a favorable channel and, in spite of hostile Indians who fired on the boat, a broken rudder, and a mutiny in the deck crew near Old Fort Sully, reached Fort Benton in good time. After a three-day layover (time enough for Chouteau to inform Baker that the American Fur Company was leaving the fur trade and for Captain Mahood to load more than 2,900 bales of robes for the American Fur Company, seventy passengers from the mines, $258,000 in gold dust, and a collection of wild animals and Indian curiosities),

[26] Quotations from E. W. Carpenter, "A Glimpse of Montana," *The Overland Monthly*, Vol. II (April, 1869), 380; Boller, *Among the Indians*, 376–79; Smith, "Fort Pierre II," *Bureau of American Ethnology River Basin Survey Papers*, XVIII, 129; H. D. Upham to Jennie, August 1, 1865, in Paul C. Phillips (ed.), "Upham Letters from the Upper Missouri, 1865," *The Frontier*, Vol. 13 (May, 1933), 316.

[27] D. A. Constable to A. Dawson, February 7, 1864, Dawson (Andrew) Papers, MtHi; I. G. Baker's Invoice of October 1, 1864, Chouteau Family Papers, MoSHi; Bradley, "Affairs," *CHSM*, III, 345–46; Mercier, "Reminiscences," MtHi.

the *Yellowstone* steamed downriver. At Fort Union, she took aboard the garrison left there ten months earlier by General Sully and on June 19 tied up on the St. Louis levee[28]

Three and one-half months before the *Yellowstone* started for the upper river, the Chouteaus had sold "all the interest of the American Fur Company on the upper Missouri" to merchant-banker James Boyd Hubbell of Mankato, Minnesota. Hubbell, "a chameleon-like entrepreneur . . . [who] followed the natural lines of economic development," had taken out a license with the Indian Office in February, 1865, to trade with the Sioux at Forts Sully, Rice, Berthold, and Union and with the Crows at undesignated upriver locations.[29] While in Washington negotiating for his license, he met Charles Chouteau, who was in the capital either to bid on the annuity contract for 1865 or to lobby before the Indian Office for renewal of the American Fur Company trading license—and possibly to do both. The Company, with government approval, had not formally taken out a license in 1863 or 1864. According to Charles Larpenteur, when Chouteau petitioned for a license in 1865, he was denied one because of his "having been reported as a rebel."[30] Whether or not Larpenteur's tale was correct, Chouteau offered to sell the American Fur Company's Upper Missouri posts, equipment, and supplies to Hubbell. The Minnesotan "was well acquainted with the business and knew that there were many articles suitable for the Indian trade at the different [American Fur Company] posts which were difficult to obtain in the market." He quickly accepted the proposal and bought the

28 *DMR*, June 20, 1865; *Kansas City Daily Western Journal of Commerce*, June 18, 1865; *Daily Missouri Democrat*, June 20, 1865. A month later, the American Fur Company sold the *Yellowstone*, for $40,000, to a company engaged in the "St. Louis and White river trade" (see the *Daily Missouri Democrat* of July 29, 1865).

29 James Boyd Hubbell, "The Last of the Old American Fur Company," Hubbell (James Boyd) Papers, MnHi; Lucile M. Kane, "New Light on the Northwestern Fur Company," *Minnesota History*, Vol. 34 (Winter, 1955), 329.

30 Larpenteur, *Forty Years*, II, 366; W. P. Dole to Pierre Chouteau, Jr., and Company, August 25, October 1, 1864, Letters Sent, OIA, RG 75, NA.

Company's Upper Missouri Outfit—neither he nor the Chouteaus ever revealed the exact price—for a cash down payment of 50 per cent, then turned over a half-interest in the business to Alpheus F. Hawley, his partner in the Indian trade.[31]

A few days after the sale, Chouteau's agent in New York City told James A. Smith, an "elderly, well-known and wealthy" Chicago fur dealer, about it, and Smith, together with C. Francis Bates, an important New York City furrier, asked Hubbell to include them in the deal. Hubbell and Hawley agreed to take in Smith and Bates, and in New York City on March 23, 1865, the four men incorporated the Northwestern Fur Company. The managing partners, Hubbell and Hawley, put up $10,000 in cash and their goods stored on the Upper Missouri, and Smith and Bates contributed $50,000 in goods and cash and promised to pay certain rebates guaranteed the American Fur Company. The agreement was to run for four years, with profits to be divided one-fourth to Smith, one-fourth to Bates, and one-half to Hubbell and Hawley.[32]

Both Hubbell and Hawley accompanied Charles Chouteau up the Missouri aboard the *Yellowstone* in March, 1865. The agreement made in New York City on March 23, three days after the *Yellowstone* sailed from St. Louis, either was completed in Hubbell's and Hawley's absence, which seems unlikely, or they dashed from the eastern conference room to the railroad station and boarded a westbound train to meet the steamboat at St. Joseph. At Old Fort Sully, Hubbell, Hawley, and the passengers aboard the *Yellowstone* first heard the news of Lincoln's assassination, and when the boat reached Fort Rice, the military commander of the post arrested everyone aboard "on the charge of jubilating over" the President's death and threatened to shoot Chouteau,

---

[31] Hubbell, "Last of the American Fur Company," Hubbell (James Boyd) Papers, MnHi.

[32] *Ibid.*; Kane, "New Light," *Minnesota History*, Vol. 34, pp. 325–27; Agreement of March 23, 1865, Hubbell (James Boyd) Papers, MnHi: *New-York Tribune* (New York City), September 16, 1865.

"whose Southern proclivities were well understood." Joseph La Barge said in his memoirs that Hubbell and Hawley, anxious to free the steamboat from military arrest, returned on a yawl to Sioux City from Fort Rice, gave General Sully a letter from Chouteau detailing the arbitrary conduct of the commander at Fort Rice, and received from the General an order to release the *Yellowstone*. If La Barge's account is accurate, Hubbell and Hawley set an amazing record for a round trip between Fort Rice and Sioux City, since the memorandum of the *Yellowstone*'s clerk states that the boat arrived at Fort Rice on May 9 and left two days later![33]

By late June, 1865, Lee had surrendered to Grant at Appomattox Courthouse, the American Fur Company had sold its Upper Missouri Outfit to Hubbell and Hawley, and the era of St. Louis control of the Upper Missouri fur and robe trade had ended. Old Pierre Chouteau, Jr., one of the last links between the founders of St. Louis and the Civil War generation, died early in September, 1865, and left his heirs, in addition to other property, a quarter-million-dollar share in the American Fur Company. His son Charles held an equal share in the business, earned by at least fifteen years' hard work perfecting the Company as a family enterprise. Three years after Pierre's death, the *St. Louis Journal of Commerce* editorialized that "the time when large fortunes were made in [the fur trade] has long since passed."[34] The *Journal* was correct, but at the end of the century, the St. Louis fur market revived, and the entire American fur industry was reborn. By then, however, the Upper Missouri trading post, robe-laden steamboat, and buffalo herd had disappeared, replaced, in the twentieth century, by the fur farmer and the hunter, who shipped pelts to market by train and truck. Nevertheless, the fur trade, particularly between 1840 and 1865, indelibly marked the life

[33] Chittenden, *Early Steamboat Navigation*, II, 260–64.

[34] *DMR*, September 7, 1865; Files of Estates of Pierre Chouteau, Jr., No. 7159, and Pierre Chouteau, Jr., and Company, No. 7159-A, Records of the St. Louis Probate Court, St. Louis.

(economic, political, religious, literary, artistic, and scientific) of the Upper Missouri Valley and reached out from the hunting ground of the Sioux, Assiniboin, and Blackfoot to touch the nation —and the world.

Bibliography

I. MANUSCRIPTS

Adams (David) Family Papers, MoSHi.

American Fur Company Ledgers JJ and LL, MoSHi.

American Fur Company Papers, NHi.

Articles of Agreement Between Frost, Todd, and Atkinson, November 4, 1859, Typescript, SdHi.

Baird, Spencer F. Letters Received, 1859; Letters Written, 1, 2, and 18; Private Correspondence, Letters Written; and Private Letters, DSI.

Benton Family Papers, MoSHi.

Boller Papers, NdHi.

Chouteau Family Papers and Chouteau Family Papers (Uncatalogued), MoSHi.

Clark (William) Papers, KHi.

Dawson (Andrew) Papers, MtHi.

Diary of Edwin A. C. Hatch, June 7–October 13, 1856, Typescript, MnHi.

Diary of James Henry Morley, 1862, Typescript, MtHi.

Diary of Peter Garrioche, 1843–1847, Typescript, NdHi.

Dougherty (John) Papers, MoSHi.

Drips (Andrew) Papers, MoSHi.

Drips Family Papers, CU-B.

Engelmann (George) Papers, MOSB.

Ft. Pierre Letter Books, 1845–1846, 1847–1848, and 1849–1850, MoSHi.

"From St. Louis to Ft. Benton in 1862" (The Diary of Jirah Isham Allen), Typescript, MtHi.

Hall (James) Papers, NLA.

"History of the Western Academy of Natural Science," Typescript, MOSA.

Hubbell (James Boyd) Papers, MnHi.

Insurance Record Book of Robert Campbell, 1862–1864, Campbell Family Papers, MoSHi.

"Journal of Daniel G. Taylor" by Steamer *Clermont*, 1846, Steamboats Envelope, 1800–1859, MoSHi.

Journal of George Suckley, 1853, DSI-M.

"Journal of J. Hudson Snowden," 1860, CtY-WA.

La Barge Collection, St. Charles County Historical Society, St. Charles, Missouri.

Letters of A. H. Redfield to John D. Caton, May 12, June 14, 1858, Photostats, SdHi.; Father Augustin Ravoux to Bishop Loras of Dubuque, July 2, September 21, 1847, Dubuque Diocesan Archives, Catholic Chancery Office, Dubuque, Iowa; Lt. George T. Balch to a "Beloved Friend," October 21, 1855, CU-B; Father J. F. Trecy to Bishop James M. O'Gorman, August 4, 1859, and Father Joseph Giorda to Bishop James M. O'Gorman, March 31, 1862, O'Gorman Papers, Archdiocesan Archives of the Catholic Church, Omaha, Nebraska; Malcolm Clark's Daughter to N. P. Langford, n.d., Typescript, MnHi; Samuel T. Hauser to his Sister, May 24–June 17, 1862, CtY-WA; Stephen R. Riggs to David Green, November 9, 1840, ABCFM, MS 141: No. 64, Ayer Collection, ICN; Lt. Thomas W. Sweeny to his Brother (?), December 10, 1855, Sweeny Papers, CSmH; and William Cary to Charles N. Kessler, September 2, 1919, Typescript, Cary Collection, Thomas Gilcrease Institute of American History and Art, Tulsa, Oklahoma.

Manuscript File on the Reverend Thomas Scanlon, Pius XII Library, St. Louis University, St. Louis, Missouri.

Marmaduke (Meredith M.) Papers, State Historical Society of Missouri, Columbia, Missouri.

Meek (Fielding B.) Papers, DSI-M.

Memorandum of W. R. Massie, Typescript, Eugene Stephens Collection–IV, MoSHi.

Mercier, Charles. "Reminiscences," MtHi.

"Minutes of the Academy of Science of St. Louis," Typescript, MOSA.

Montana Manuscripts Collection, CLUC.

Pierre Chouteau, Jr., and Company Letter Book, 1856–1860, MoSHi.

Price Report by Ramsay Crooks' Son and Company, 1859, McKenzie Papers, MoSHi.

"Reminiscences of Antoine A. Juneau," Typescript, MtHi.

Reminiscences of Eli W. McNeal, Typescript, MtHi.

Sire, Joseph A. Log Books, 1841–1846, Typescript, MoSHi.

Two Articles of Agreement made at Ft. George, August 22, 1842, Fur Trade Papers Envelope, MoSHi.

"Up the Missouri River to Montana in the Spring of 1862" (by A. H. Wilcox), Typescript, MtHi.

Walker, Joel P. "Narrative of Adventures," CU-B.

Wimar Papers, MoSHi.

II. PUBLIC RECORDS

Central Superintendency Field Papers, OIA, RG 76, NA.

Complete and Final Record, United States Circuit Court, District of Missouri, Vol. 3, 1841–1850, FRC, KC.

Dakota Superintendency Field Papers, OIA, RG 76, NA.

Files of Estates of Joseph A. Sire, No. 4292; Alexander M. Harvey, No. 4888; John B. Sarpy, No. 4974; Pierre Chouteau, Jr., No. 7159; and Pierre Chouteau, Jr., and Company, No. 7159-A, Records of the St. Louis Probate Court, St. Louis, Missouri.

Files of *U.S.* v. *Charles Kelsey*, Case No. 392; *U.S.* v. *James Lee, Jacob Berger, and Malcolm Clark*, Case No. 393; and *U.S.* v. *Victor Baraser*, Criminal Case No. 410, Records of the United States Circuit Court, District of Missouri, FRC, KC.

Law Record, United States Circuit Court, District of Missouri, Vol. A, 1838–1848, FRC, KC.

Letters Received, 1839–1865, OIA, RG 75, NA.

Letters Received, 1855–1856, 1862, Topographical Bureau, RG 77, NA.

Letters Sent, 1846–1864, OIA, RG 75, NA.

License Books (Steamboats), Port of St. Louis Custom House Records, FRC, KC.

Records of the Solicitor of the Treasury, SOT, RG 206, NA.

Special File No. 70, OIA, RG 76, NA.

Special File No. 243, OIA, RG 75, NA.

Volume Entitled "Licenses for Indian Trade," OIA, RG 76, NA.

III. GOVERNMENT PUBLICATIONS

Bennett, Samuel A. (reporter). *Reports of Cases Argued and Determined in the Supreme Court of the State of Missouri*, XVI. St. Louis, 1853.

"Condition of the Indian Tribes" (Testimony of James Havens, September 8, 1865), 39 Cong., 2 sess., *SR No. 156.*

Culbertson, Thaddeus A. *Journal of an Expedition to the Mauvaises Terres and the Upper Missouri in 1850.* Ed. by John F. McDermott. (*Smithsonian Institution, Bureau of American Ethnology, Bulletin 147*). Washington D.C., 1952.

Denig, Edwin T. *Indian Tribes of the Upper Missouri.* Ed. by J. N. B. Hewitt. (*Forty-sixth Annual Report of the Bureau of American Ethnology, 1928–29*). Washington, D.C., 1930.

Douglas, Edward M. *Boundaries, Areas, Geographic Centers and Altitudes of the United States and the Several States.* (*United States Department of the Interior, Geological Survey, Bulletin 817*). Washington, D.C., 1932.

"Expedition from Fort Abercrombie to Fort Benton," 37 Cong., 3 sess., *HED No. 80.*

"Explorations in the Dacota Country, in the Year 1855," 34 Cong., 1 sess., *SED No. 76.*

"Fifth Annual Report of the Board of Regents of the Smithsonian Institution," 32 Cong., 1 sess., *SMD No. 1.*

Journal of the House of Representatives of the State of Missouri, at the First Session of the Eleventh General Assembly . . . One Thousand Eight Hundred and Forty. Jackson, Missouri, 1841.

Kurz, Rudolph F. *Journal of Rudolph Friedrich Kurz.* Trans. by Myrtis Jarrell; ed. by J. N. B. Hewitt. (*Smithsonian Institu-*

tion, Bureau of American Ethnology, Bulletin 115). Washington, D.C., 1937.

Laws of the General Assembly of the Commonwealth of Pennsylvania, Passed at the Session of 1844. Harrisburg, 1844.

"Memorial of a Number of Citizens of St. Louis, Missouri, Praying an Appropriation for the Removal of Obstructions in the Western Rivers, and for the Improvement of the Harbor of That City," 28 Cong., 1 sess., *SD No. 185.*

Murray, Alexander H. *Journal of the Yukon, 1847–48.* Ed. by L. J. Burpee. (*Publications of the Canadian Archives, No. 4*). Ottawa, 1910.

"Report Intended to Illustrate a Map of the Hydrographical Basin of the Upper Mississippi River Made by I. [*sic*] N. Nicollet, While in Employ Under the Bureau of the Corps of Topographical Engineers," 28 Cong., 2 sess., *HED No. 52.*

"Report of Brevet Colonel W. F. Raynolds, U.S.A., Corps of Engineers, on the Exploration of the Yellowstone and Missouri Rivers, in 1859–'60," 40 Cong., 2 sess., *SED No. 77.*

"Report on the Construction of a Military Road from Fort Walla Walla to Fort Benton," 37 Cong., 3 sess., *SED No. 43.*

"Report on Steamboat Wrecks on Missouri River by Capt. H. M. Chittenden, Corps of Engineers," 55 Cong., 2 sess., *HR Doc. No. 2.*

"Reports of Explorations and Surveys . . . 1853–5," 36 Cong., 1 sess., *HED No. 56.*

Scott, R. N., *et al.* (eds.). *The War of the Rebellion: A Compilation of the Official Records of the Union and Confederate Armies,* Series I, Vol. XXXIV, Parts II–III, and Vol. L, Part II. Washington, D.C., 1891 and 1897.

"Seventh Annual Report of the Board of Regents of the Smithsonian Institution," 32 Cong., 2 sess., *SMD No. 53.*

"[Sixth] Annual Report of the Board of Regents of the Smithsonian Institution," 32 Cong., 1 sess., *SMD No. 108.*

Smith, G. Hubert. "Fort Pierre II (39ST217), a Historic Trading Post in the Oahe Dam Area, South Dakota," *Bureau of American Ethnology River Basin Survey Papers,* XVIII. Washington, D.C., 1960.

Bibliography

Smithsonian Institution River Basin Surveys, "Archeological Progress Report No. 7." Lincoln, Nebraska, October, 1962.

Tenth Annual Report of the Board of Regents of the Smithsonian Institution. Washington, D.C., 1856.

Territorial Council of Dakota. *Report of the Select Committee on Indian Affairs, December 29, 1862.* Yankton, Dakota Territory, 1862.

United States Congress, House of Representatives. 29 Cong., 2 sess., *HED No. 4;* 30 Cong., 2 sess., *HED No. 1;* 33 Cong., 2 sess., *HED No. 1;* 37 Cong., 3 sess., *HED No. 1;* 38 Cong., 1 sess., *HED No. 1;* 38 Cong., 2 sess., *HED No. 1.*

———, Senate. 28 Cong., 1 sess., *SD No. 1;* 28 Cong., 2 sess., *SD No. 1;* 30 Cong., 1 sess., *SED No. 1;* 31 Cong., 1 sess., *SED No. 1;* 31 Cong., 2 sess., *SED No. 1;* 32 Cong., 2 sess., *SED No. 1;* 34 Cong., 1 sess., *SED No. 1;* 34 Cong., 3 sess., *SED No. 5;* 35 Cong., 1 sess., *SED No. 11;* 35 Cong., 2 sess., *SED No. 1;* 36 Cong., 1 sess., *SED No. 2;* 36 Cong., 2 sess., *SED No. 1.*

United States War Department, Surgeon General's Office. *A Report of Barracks and Hospitals.* Washington, D.C., 1870.

IV. NEWSPAPERS

Arkansas Intelligencer (Van Buren), May 17, 1845.

Cherokee Advocate (Tahlequah, Indian Territory), February 5, 1846.

Daily Evening Gazette (St. Louis), July 3, 1839; June 12, September 10, 1840.

Daily Missouri Democrat (St. Louis), 1853–62, 1865.

Daily Missouri Republican (St. Louis), 1837–65, October 17, 1879.

Daily Morning Missourian (St. Louis), July 4, 1846.

Daily People's Organ (St. Louis), August 23, 1842.

Daily St. Louis Times, July 6, 8, 1850.

Dakotian (Yankton, South Dakota), 1861–63.

Freedom's Champion (Atchison, Kansas), March 12, 1859.

Frontier Guardian (Kanesville, Iowa), April 18, October 31, 1851.

Gazette (St. Joseph, Missouri), 1845, 1847–51, 1853–54.

Glasgow (Missouri) *Weekly Times,* June 10, 1852.

Hawkeye and Iowa Patriot (Burlington), April 15, 1841.

Iowa Territorial Gazette and Burlington Advertiser, July 6, 1839.

Jefferson Inquirer (Jefferson City, Missouri), June 7, 1851.

Kansas City Daily Western Journal of Commerce, 1859, 1861, 1865.

Missouri Argus (St. Louis), 1839–40.

Missouri Reporter (St. Louis), May 28, June 6, 7, 1845, Transcripts in Dale Morgan Collection, CSmH.

Native American Bulletin (St. Louis), August 17, 1842, Transcript in Dale Morgan Collection, CSmH.

New York Evening Post (New York City), December 11, 1849.

New-York Tribune (New York City), September 16, 1865.

Niles' National Register (Baltimore), 1843–45, 1847.

St. Joseph Commercial Cycle, May 11, 1855.

Saint Louis American, 1845–46.

Saint Louis Daily Bulletin, May 4, July 30, 1860.

Saint Louis Daily Evening News, 1852–53.

Saint Louis Daily Union (also *Daily Morning Union*), 1846–51.

St. Louis Democrat, May 2, 23, 1844, Transcripts in Dale Morgan Collection, CSmH.

St. Louis Intelligencer, 1850–52.

St. Louis New Era (also *Daily New Era*), 1840–50.

Sioux City (Iowa) *Register*, 1859–60, 1862.

Weekly Reveille (St. Louis), 1844–50.

Weekly Saint Louis Pilot, May 19, 1855.

Weekly Tribune (Liberty, Missouri), September 19, 1846; April 22, 1853; May 11, 1855; October 9, 1857; September 10, 1858.

V. BOOKS, PAMPHLETS, AND THESES

Abel, Annie H. (ed.). *Chardon's Journal at Fort Clark, 1834–1839.* Pierre, South Dakota, 1932.

Albion, Robert G. *Square-Riggers on Schedule.* Princeton, New Jersey, 1938.

———. *The Rise of New York Port.* New York and London, 1939.

Annual Statement of the Trade & Commerce of St. Louis for the Year 1858. St. Louis, 1859.

Athearn, Robert G. *High Country Empire.* New York, 1960.

Audubon, Marie R., and Elliott Coues (eds.). *Audubon and His Journals.* 2 vols. New York, 1900.

Back-Trailing on the Old Frontiers. Great Falls, Montana, 1922.

Beach, Moses Y. *The Wealth and Biography of the Wealthy Citizens of the City of New York.* New York, 1855.

Beckwith, Paul. *Creoles of St. Louis.* St. Louis, 1893.

Bidwell, John. *A Journey to California . . . by John Bidwell.* Ed. by Herbert I. Priestley. San Francisco, 1937.

Boller, Henry A. *Among the Indians.* Ed. by Milo M. Quaife. Chicago, 1959.

Bolton, Henry C. and Reginald P. *The Family of Bolton in England and America, 1100–1894: A Study in Genealogy.* New York, 1895.

Branch, E. Douglas. *The Hunting of the Buffalo.* Lincoln, Nebraska, 1962.

Briggs, Harold E. *Frontiers of the Northwest: A History of the Upper Missouri Valley.* New York, 1940.

Burlingame, Merrill G. *The Military-Indian Frontier in Montana, 1860–1890.* Iowa City, 1938.

Casper, Henry W. *History of the Catholic Church in Nebraska.* Milwaukee, 1960.

Chittenden, Hiram M. *Early Steamboat Navigation on the Missouri River: Life and Adventures of Joseph La Barge.* 2 vols. New York, 1903.

———. *A History of the American Fur Trade of the Far West.* 2 vols. Palo Alto, 1954.

———, and A. T. Richardson (eds.). *Life, Letters and Travels of Father Pierre-Jean de Smet, S.J.* 4 vols. New York, 1905.

Clarke, John M. *James Hall of Albany.* N.p., 1921.

The Commerce and Navigation of the Valley of the Mississippi. St. Louis, 1847.

Denig, Edwin T. *Five Indian Tribes of the Upper Missouri: Sioux, Arickaras, Assiniboines, Crees, Crows.* Ed. by John C. Ewers. Norman, Oklahoma, 1961.

De Smet, Pierre Jean. *Oregon Missions and Travels over the Rocky Mountains in 1845–46.* Ed. by Reuben G. Thwaites as Vol. XXIX of *Early Western Travels, 1748–1846.* Cleveland, 1906.

De Voto, Bernard. *Across the Wide Missouri.* Boston, 1947.

Duratschek, M. Claudia. *The Beginnings of Catholicism in South Dakota.* Washington, D.C., 1943.

Ewers, John C. *The Blackfeet: Raiders on the Northwestern Plains.* Norman, Oklahoma, 1958.

Folwell, William Watts. *A History of Minnesota.* 4 vols. St. Paul, 1921.

Frémont, John Charles. *Memoirs of My Life.* Chicago and New York, 1887.

Fritschel, Erwin G. "A History of the Indian Mission of The Lutheran Iowa Synod, 1856 to 1866." Typescript, Bachelor of Theology Thesis, Wartburg Theological Seminary, Dubuque, 1940.

Gould, E. W. *Fifty Years on the Mississippi.* St. Louis, 1889.

Hafen, LeRoy R., and Francis M. Young. *Fort Laramie and the Pageant of the West 1834–1890.* Glendale, California, 1938.

Harper, Frank B. *Fort Union and Its Neighbors.* N.p., n.d.

Harris, Edward. *Up the Missouri with Audubon: The Journal of Edward Harris.* Ed. by John F. McDermott. Norman, Oklahoma, 1951.

Hoopes, Alban W. *Indian Affairs and Their Administration, with Special Reference to the Far West, 1849–1860.* Philadelphia, 1932.

Hunter, Louis C. *Steamboats on the Western Rivers.* Cambridge, Massachusetts, 1949.

Jones, Robert H. *The Civil War in the Northwest.* Norman, Oklahoma, 1960.

Keiser, Albert. *Lutheran Mission Work Among the American Indians.* Minneapolis, 1922.

Kingsbury, George M. *History of Dakota Territory.* 5 vols. Chicago, 1915.

Lamar, Howard R. *Dakota Territory, 1861–1889.* New Haven, 1956.

Larpenteur, Charles. *Forty Years a Fur Trader on the Upper Missouri.* Ed. by Milo M. Quaife. 2 vols. in 1. Chicago, 1933.

———. *Forty Years a Fur Trader on the Upper Missouri.* Ed. by Elliott Coues. 2 vols. in 1. Minneapolis, 1962.

Lass, William E. *A History of Steamboating on the Upper Missouri River.* Lincoln, Nebraska, 1962.

Laveille, E. *The Life of Father De Smet, S.J. (1801–1873).* New York, 1915.

Leeson, Michael A. *History of Montana, 1739–1885.* Chicago, 1885.

Merrill, George P. *The First One Hundred Years of American Geology*. New Haven, 1924.

Napton, W. B. *Over the Santa Fe Trail in 1857*. Kansas City, Missouri, 1905.

Norton, Mary Aquinas. *Catholic Missionary Activities in the Northwest, 1818–1864*. Washington, D.C., 1930.

Owen, David D. *Report of a Geological Survey of Wisconsin, Iowa, and Minnesota*. Philadelphia, 1852.

Paden, Irene. *The Wake of the Prairie Schooner*. New York, 1943.

Palladino, Lawrence B. *Indian and White in the Northwest*. Baltimore, 1894.

Palliser, John. *The Solitary Hunter; or, Sporting Adventures in the Prairies*. London, 1856.

Parkman, Francis. *The Oregon Trail*. New York, 1946.

Pfaller, Louis. *The Catholic Church in Western North Dakota, 1738–1960*. Mandan, North Dakota, 1960.

Phillips, Paul C. *The Fur Trade*. 2 vols. Norman, Oklahoma, 1961.

Preuss, Charles. *Exploring with Frémont: The Private Diaries of Charles Preuss, Cartographer for John C. Frémont on His First, Second, and Fourth Expeditions to the Far West*. Trans. and ed. by Erwin G. and Elisabeth K. Gudde. Norman, Oklahoma, 1958.

Pritchett, John P. *The Red River Valley, 1811–1849*. New Haven, 1942.

Proceedings of the St. Louis Chamber of Commerce, in Relation to the Improvement of the Navigation of the Mississippi. St. Louis, 1842.

Rathbone, Perry T. *Charles Wimar, 1828–1862*. St. Louis, 1946.

Ravoux, Augustin. *Reminiscences, Memoirs and Lectures*. St. Paul, 1890.

Rickard, Thomas A. *A History of American Mining*. New York, 1932.

Riggs, Stephen R. *Mary and I*. Chicago, 1880.

Schell, Herbert S. *History of South Dakota*. Lincoln, Nebraska, 1961.

Scoville, J. A. *The Old Merchants of New York City*. 4 vols. New York, 1864.

Stevens, Hazard. *The Life of Isaac Ingalls Stevens*. 2 vols. New York and Boston, 1900.

Stevens, Walter B. *St. Louis, the Fourth City, 1764–1909.* 3 vols. St. Louis, 1909.

Stuart, James and Granville. *Forty Years on the Frontier.* Ed. by Paul C. Phillips. 2 vols. Cleveland, 1925.

Taft, Robert. *Artists and Illustrators of the Old West, 1850–1900.* New York and London, 1953.

Taylor, Emerson G. *Gouverneur Kemble Warren.* Boston and New York, 1932.

The Twentieth Annual Report of the Board of Foreign Missions of the Presbyterian Church of the United States of America. New York, 1857.

Van Cleve, Charlotte O. *Three Score Years and Ten.* Minneapolis, 1888.

Vaughan, Robert. *Then and Now.* Minneapolis, 1900.

Weisel, George F. (ed.). *Men and Trade on the Northwest Frontier as Shown by the Fort Owen Ledger.* Missoula, Montana, 1955.

Wheat, Carl I. *Mapping the Transmississippi West, 1540–1861.* Vol. IV. San Francisco, 1960.

White, Leslie A. (ed.). *Lewis Henry Morgan: The Indian Journals, 1859–62.* Ann Arbor, Michigan, 1959.

Wislizenus, F. A. *A Journey to the Rocky Mountains in the Year 1839.* St. Louis, 1912.

Wissler, Clark. *Indians of the United States.* New York, 1940.

VI. ARTICLES

Annales de la Propagation de la Foi, Vol. XXIV (1852), 236–42.

Atkins, C. J. (ed.). "Log of Steamer Robert Campbell, Jr., from St. Louis to Fort Benton, Montana Territory," *Collections of the State Historical Society of North Dakota,* Vol. II (1908), 267–84.

Babcock, Willoughby M. "The Fur Trade As an Aid to Settlement," *North Dakota Historical Quarterly,* Vol. VII (January and April, 1933), 82–93.

Barbier, Charles P. "Recollections of Ft. La Framboise in 1862 and the Rescue of Lake Chetak Captives," *South Dakota Historical Collections,* Vol. XI (1922), 232–42.

Bradley, James H. "Affairs at Fort Benton from 1831 to 1869. From

Lieut. Bradley's Journal," *Contributions to the Historical Society of Montana*, Vol. III (1900), 201–87.

Brayer, Herbert O. "The Western Journal of Edward Shelley," *The Westerners Brand Book* (Chicago), Vol. XIII (January, 1957), 81–83, 85–88.

Brown, John Mason (ed.). "A Trip to the Northwest in 1861, Part I," *The Filson Club History Quarterly*, Vol. 24 (April, 1950), 103–36.

Carpenter, E. W. "A Glimpse of Montana," *The Overland Monthly*, Vol. II (April, 1869), 378–86.

Chittenden, Hiram M. "The Ancient Town of Fort Benton in Montana," *Magazine of American History*, Vol. XXIV (December, 1890), 409–25.

Collection de Précis Historiques, Vol. 7 (1856), 572–76.

The Commercial Review of the South and West, Vol. II (December, 1846), 383.

Cowan, Ian M. "The Fur Trade and the Fur Cycle: 1825–1857," *The British Columbia Historical Quarterly*, Vol. II (January, 1938), 19–30.

The Crayon, Vol. VII (July, 1860), 206.

De Bow's Review and Industrial Resources, Vol. XXVIII (March, 1860), 330.

De Girardin, M. E. "A Trip to the Bad Lands in 1849," *South Dakota Historical Review*, Vol. I (January, 1936), 51–78.

DeLand, Charles E. "Basil Clement (Claymore)," *South Dakota Historical Collections*, Vol. XI (1922), 245–389.

"Diary of Asahel Munger and Wife," *The Quarterly of the Oregon Historical Society*, Vol. VIII (December, 1907), 387–405.

"Diary of James Harkness, of the Firm of La Barge, Harkness and Company," *Contributions to the Historical Society of Montana*, Vol. II (1896), 343–61.

"Diary of Virgil K. Pringle, 1846," *Transactions of the Forty-eighth Annual Reunion of the Oregon Pioneer Association* (1920), 281–300.

Dodd, E. Merrick, Jr. "American Business Association Law a Hundred Years Ago and Today," in *Law: A Century of Progress, 1835–1935*, III. New York, 1937.

Drumm, Stella M. "Pierre Chouteau," in Dumas Malone (ed.), *Dictionary of American Biography*, IV, 93–94.

Ellis, Elmer (ed.). "The Journal of H. E. Maynadier," *North Dakota Historical Quarterly*, Vol. I (January, 1927), 41–51.

The Farmers' Cabinet and American Herd-Book, Vol. XI (August 15, 1846), 25.

"Floating on the Missouri—IV," *Forest and Stream*, Vol. LVIII (March 8, 1902), 183–84.

Garraghan, Gilbert J. "Nicholas Point, Jesuit Missionary in Montana in the Forties," in J. F. Willard and C. B. Goodykoontz (eds.), *The Trans-Mississippi West.* Boulder, Colorado, 1930.

Garver, F. H. "Reminiscences of John H. Charles," *Proceedings of the Academy of Science and Letters of Sioux City, Iowa, 1905–06*, Vol. II (1906), 29–62.

Ghent, William J. "Jean Pierre Chouteau," in Dumas Malone (ed.), *Dictionary of American Biography*, IV, 93.

Graebner, Norman A. "Nebraska's Missouri River Frontier, 1854–1860," *Nebraska History*, Vol. 42 (December, 1961), 213–35.

Grinnell, George B. "Recollections of the Old West," *The American Museum Journal*, Vol. XVII (May, 1917), 333–40.

Guthrie, Chester L., and Leo L. Gerald. "Upper Missouri Agency: An Account of the Indian Administration on the Frontier," *Pacific Historical Review*, Vol. X (March, 1941), 47–56.

Hafen, LeRoy R. "Thomas Fitzpatrick and the First Indian Agency of the Upper Platte and Arkansas," *Mississippi Valley Historical Review*, Vol. XV (December, 1928), 374–84.

Hanson, Charles E., Jr. "Marking the Grave of Alexander Culbertson," *Nebraska History*, Vol. XXXII (June, 1951), 120–29.

Hardin, Martin D. "Up the Missouri and over the Mullan Road" (ed. by John E. Parsons), *The Westerners New York Posse Brand Book*, Vol. V (1958), 1–18.

The Home and Foreign Record of the Presbyterian Church in the United States of America, Vol. VIII (January, 1857), 13.

Howard, Helen A. (ed.). "Diary of Charles Rumley from St. Louis to Portland, 1862," *Frontier and Midland*, Vol. XIX (Spring, 1939), 190–200.

Hunt's Merchants' Magazine, Vol. XI (September, 1844), 291; Vol.

XLII (May, 1860), 617; Vol. XLIV (January, 1861), 103–104.

"In Memoriam Charles Pierre Chouteau," *Transactions of the Academy of Science of St. Louis*, Vol. XI (1901), xxi–xxii.

"In Memoriam—Fielding Bradford Meek," *The American Journal of Science and Arts* (March, 1877), 169–71.

"Journal of Dr. Elias J. Marsh," *South Dakota Historical Review*, Vol. I (January, 1936), 79–123.

Kane, Lucile M. "New Light on the Northwestern Fur Company," *Minnesota History*, Vol. 34 (Winter, 1955), 325–29.

Leidy, Joseph. "Description of the Remains of Extinct Mammalia and Chelonia, from Nebraska Territory," in David D. Owen, *Report of a Geological Survey of Wisconsin, Iowa, and Minnesota*. Philadelphia, 1852.

Lippincott, Isaac. "A Century and a Half of Fur Trade at St. Louis," *Washington University Studies* (Humanistic Series), Vol. III, Pt. 2 (April, 1916), 205–42.

Lowrie, Walter, "North-Western Indian Missions," *The Home and Foreign Record of the Presbyterian Church in the United States of America*, Vol. VII (August, 1856), 240.

McDonnell, Anne (ed.). "The Fort Benton Journal, 1854–56, and the Fort Sarpy Journal, 1855–56," *Contributions to the Historical Society of Montana*, Vol. X (1940).

Mackey, E. D. "Blackfeet Indian Mission," *The Home and Foreign Record of the Presbyterian Church in the United States of America*, Vol. VII (September, 1856), 271–72.

Marks, Constant R. (ed.). "Autobiography of Louis Dace Letellier," *South Dakota Historical Collections*, Vol. IV (1908), 215–53.

Mattison, Ray H. "Report on Historic Sites in the Garrison Reservoir Area, Missouri River," *North Dakota History*, Vol. 22 (January, 1955), 5–73.

———. "The Military Frontier on the Upper Missouri," *Nebraska History*, Vol. 37 (September, 1956), 159–82.

———. "The Upper Missouri Fur Trade: Its Methods of Operation," *Nebraska History*, Vol. 42 (March, 1961), 1–28.

Meyers, Augustus. "Dakota in the Fifties," *South Dakota Historical Collections*, Vol. X (1920), 130–94.

"Missionary Excursion in Iowa." *The United States Catholic Magazine and Monthly Review*, Vol. VII (1848), 19–25 (Part I), 84–87 (Part II).

The Missionary Herald, Vol. XXXVII (April, 1841), 179–86.

Nute, Grace Lee. "The Papers of the American Fur Company: A Brief Estimate of Their Significance," *The American Historical Review*, Vol. XXXII (April, 1927), 519–38.

Partoll, Albert J. "Frank L. Worden, Pioneer Merchant, 1830–1887," *Pacific Northwest Quarterly*, Vol. 40 (July, 1949), 189–202.

Peabody, E. "The Backwoodsman," *The Western Messenger; Devoted to Religion and Literature*, Vols. II–III (1836–37), 661.

Phillips, Paul C. (ed.), "Upham Letters from the Upper Missouri, 1865," *The Frontier*, Vol. 13 (May, 1933), 311–17.

Point, Nicholas. "A Journey in a Barge on the Missouri from the Fort of the Blackfeet [Lewis] to That of the Assiniboines [Union]," *Mid-America*, Vol. XIII (January, 1931), 238–54.

Prout, Hiram A. "Description of a Fossil Maxillary Bone of a Paleotherium, from near White River," *The American Journal of Science and Arts*, Vol. III, Second Series (1847), 248–50.

Rapport sur les Missions, Vol. 7 (July, 1847), 70–76.

Rasmussen, Louise. "Artists of the Explorations Overland, 1840–1860," *Oregon Historical Quarterly*, Vol. XLIII (March, 1942), 56–62.

Reardon, James M. "Father Lacombe, the Black-Robe Voyageur," *Acta et Dicta*, Vol. V (July, 1917), 93–98.

"The Reminiscences of General Bernard Pratte, Jr.," *Bulletin of the Missouri Historical Society*, Vol. VI (October, 1949), 59–71.

"Report of Chas. P. Chouteau to the Secretary of War of a Steamboat Expedition from St. Louis to Fort Benton, 1859," *Contributions to the Historical Society of Montana*, Vol. VII (1910), 253–56.

Ruckman, J. Ward. "Ramsay Crooks and the Fur Trade of the Northwest," *Minnesota History*, Vol. VII (March, 1926), 18–31.

Schieffelin, W. H. "Crossing the Plains in '61," *Recreation*, Vols. II–III (1895), 15–21, 53–56, 115–18, 395–99.

Sibley, Henry H. "Memoir of Jean N. Nicollet," *Collections of the Minnesota Historical Society*, Vol. I (1872), 183–95.

Slaughter, Linda W. "Fort Randall," *Collections of the State Historical Society of North Dakota,* Vol. I (1906), 423–29.

Smith, G. Hubert. "Archeological Work at 32ML2 (Like-A-Fishook Village and Fort Berthold), Garrison Reservoir Area, North Dakota, 1950–1954," *The Plains Anthropologist,* No. 2 (December, 1954), 27–32.

Spence, Clark C. "A Celtic Nimrod in the Old West," *Montana: The Magazine of Western History,* Vol. IX (April, 1959), 56–66.

Sunder, John E. "Up the Missouri to the Montana Mines: John O'Fallon Delany's 'Pocket Diary for 1862,' " Part I, *Bulletin of the Missouri Historical Society,* Vol. XIX (October, 1962), 3–22.

Thomas, Norman. "John Blair Smith Todd, First Dakota Delegate to Congress," *South Dakota Historical Collections,* Vol. XXIV (1949), 178–219.

Thompson, Francis M. "Reminiscences of Four Score Years," *Massachusetts Magazine,* Vol. V, Supplement (1912), 123–67.

Transactions of the Academy of Science of St. Louis, Vol. I (1856–60).

The United States Catholic Magazine and Monthly Review, Vol. VIII (1849), 313–16.

Welty, Raymond L. "The Frontier Army on the Missouri River, 1860–1870," *North Dakota Historical Quarterly,* Vol. II (January, 1928), 81–99.

Westbrook, Harriette J. "The Chouteaus and Their Commercial Enterprises—Part II," *Chronicles of Oklahoma,* Vol. XI (September, 1933), 942–66.

The Western Boatman, Vol. I (June, 1849), 395.

White, Charles A. "Biographical Memoir of Ferdinand Vandeveer Hayden, 1839–1887," *National Academy of Sciences Biographical Memoirs,* Vol. III (1895) 395–413.

Wilson, Frederick T. "Old Fort Pierre and Its Neighbors" (ed. by Charles E. DeLand), *South Dakota Historical Collections,* Vol. I (1902), 263–79.

Index

Academy of Science of St. Louis: 175f., 178, 185f., 189, 203, 209; museum of, 176f., 186

Adobe ("doughboys"): 127

Agassiz, Jean Louis: 153

Albin, William M.: 222

Allen, Jirah Isham: 231

Alone (steamboat): 248ff., 251, 254

Alton (steamboat): 137

Alvord, General Benjamin: 253n.

Amaranth (steamboat): 97

Amelia (steamboat): 109, 117ff., 120

American Fur Company (J. J. Astor): 4, 15f.; Western Department, 4; Upper Missouri Outfit, 4; Northern Department, 14ff.

American Fur Company (Pierre Chouteau, Jr., and Company): 4f., 7, 10, 14, 16f., 19ff., 22f., 27ff., 30, 41, 44, 47, 50, 54f., 58f., 62, 64f., 67, 70, 72, 79ff., 83ff., 86ff., 89–90, 91f., 94f., 97, 104f., 108ff., 112, 114f., 117, 119, 122, 125, 128f., 131ff., 134, 138, 140, 143ff., 146ff., 149–50, 151ff., 156f., 159, 161ff., 166ff., 169, 172f., 175ff., 178f., 182ff., 185, 187ff., 197, 199ff., 202, 204ff., 207f., 210f., 213, 216f., 221f., 224, 227, 229f., 237f., 244f., 248f., 251ff., 254ff., 259ff., 262; in St. Louis, 3, 6, 41, 59, 64, 80, 84, 98, 119, 131f., 179, 209, 216, 220, 229–30, 253; Rocky Mountain trade of, 7, 10ff.; Platte River trade of, 7–8, 18; Upper Missouri River trade of, 8, 14, 18–19, 26, 31, 55, 60ff., 115f.; opposition to, 8ff., 15, 18, 24, 31–32, 33, 37f., 40, 45, 47, 49f., 52, 54f., 59, 63, 68ff., 71f., 77, 79, 82f., 87, 92, 94ff., 100, 105f., 111f., 120ff., 124, 137, 144f., 150, 159, 161ff., 164f., 178, 182f., 185, 188, 191, 197, 199f., 202, 207ff., 214ff., 217, 219, 230, 234ff., 238ff., 251; liquor policy of, 9, 12, 48f., 51, 71, 74–75, 89ff., 113, 115, 139, 228, 258; business practices of, 11, 34, 52, 79; agents of, 20, 24, 28, 33, 56, 58f., 61f., 69, 72, 76, 90f., 99, 105, 112, 119, 129, 132, 134, 148, 161f., 178, 188, 213, 218, 220, 251, 256f.; public relations of, 23–25; political activity of, 26–27, 28–29, 30, 59, 78–79, 82, 111, 114, 149, 157, 221, 223, 243–44; robe and fur returns, 34, 47, 79f., 97, 109, 118ff., 125f., 137, 146ff., 150f., 155, 162f., 167, 175, 185, 188, 191, 201f., 207, 213, 220, 226, 234, 241, 250, 252, 255–56, 260f.; liquor suits against, 90–92, 104, 106, 108–109, 113–14, 115–16, 117; policy toward missionaries, 99f., 198, 214; Upper Missouri Outfit, 106, 112, 132f., 161, 263f.; policy toward scientists, 118, 152, 154, 202ff.; Civil War difficulties, 219–20, 221f.; sold to James Boyd Hubbell, 262–63

Annuities, Indian: 28, 97, 107f., 112, 117f., 142ff., 148, 151, 155, 163f., 166, 173ff., 179, 181, 184f., 191, 193ff., 196f., 200ff., 205, 210, 212f., 216, 221ff., 224, 227ff., 230ff., 244, 246ff., 255ff., 258, 262

Antelope (steamboat): 20, 24, 41
Antelope Island: 94
Arabia (steamboat)· 169
Arapaho Indians: 44, 141, 143
Archembeau (American Fur Company trader): 89
Arikara Indians: 86, 141, 143, 155, 167, 179, 190, 225, 231 f., 236, 245; women, 139–40, 197, 232; government annuities, 164, 194–95
Arkansas River: 143
Arrott, James, Jr.: 72n., 90
Artists: 25, 63f., 110, 119, 140, 156, 192f., 212, 225
Assiniboine (steamboat): 20
Assiniboine River: 110
Assiniboin Indians: 44, 46, 54f., 103, 104f., 123, 140f., 143, 148, 179, 190, 197, 250, 265; trade with, 72, 94, 113, 206, 260; government annuities, 166, 174, 196, 212, 229, 248, 256; burn Roulette's Post, 249–50
Astor, John Jacob: 4, 11, 14f., 19f., 31
Atchison, Senator David R.: 142
Atkinson, Edward G.: 183, 185, 197n., 201
Audubon, John James: 64ff., 67–68, 130
Audubon, Victor: 66

Bad Lands: 118, 127ff., 151, 153f., 176, 254
Bad River: 32, 41, 65, 87
Baily (or Bailey), Captain Robert E.: 230, 233f.
Baird, Professor Spencer F.: 128ff., 156, 176, 203
Baker, Isaac G.: 261
Balch, George T.: 170
Balloon (steamboat): 85f.
Banner State (steamboat): 146f.
Baraser, Victor: 85f.
Bartlett, Reverend John Francis: 237, 239
Bates, C. Francis: 263
Beard, Elias L.: 255n.
Bear's Rib (Sioux chief): 232, 240

Beauchamp, C. A.: 31
Beaver and beaver pelts: 12, 16ff., 19, 44, 50, 58, 78f., 96, 104, 146, 158, 166, 210
Beaver River: 71, 96
Beeman, Frank: 56
Beeson, Henry W.: 197
Belcourt, Father George A.: 101f.
Bell, John G.: 64
Bellevue, Nebraska: 138, 161, 179
Bent, St. Vrain and Company: 8, 13f.
Benton, Senator Thomas Hart: 26, 29f., 71n., 91, 114, 150
Benton (steamboat): 259
"Benton City" (Fort Benton), Montana: 260–61
Bent's Fort, Colorado: 14
Berger, Jacob: 88f.
Bernabé (American Fur Company trader): 89
Berthold, Bartholomew: 4
Berthold, Frederick: 83, 117, 138
Berthold, Pierre: 83
Bertrand (steamboat): 104, 106ff., 109f.
Bidwell, John: 12
Big Head (Sioux chief): 194
Big Horn River: 59f., 162
Big Muddy River: 196, 206, 208
Big Sioux River: 19, 37f., 122, 150, 161, 200
Birch, James H.: 29n.
Black Feet Star (mackinaw): 191
Blackfoot Indians: 44, 60ff., 86, 94, 99, 105, 133, 136, 143, 148, 150, 156f., 165, 168, 179, 181, 185, 187, 190f., 209, 216, 231, 265; trade with, 22, 31, 46, 61ff., 64, 72, 87, 89, 113, 147, 150, 175; attacked at Fort McKenzie, 61, 88; Treaty of 1855, 168, 187; government annuities, 173, 175, 181, 196f., 200, 227ff., 248, 257f.
Black Hawk (Negro slave): 105
Black Hills: 37, 40, 135, 175
Black's Fork (Green River): 13
Blass, John: 137
Bluff City (steamboat): 150

Boller, Colonel F.: 194n.
Boller, Henry A.: 217, 218–19, 220, 222
Bolton, Curtis: 53
Bolton, Fox and Livingston (company): 54ff.
Bouis, Anthony R.: 58, 59n., 82n., 87, 92, 94, 124, 165, 182f.
Boyle, Jack: 57
Braeuninger, Moritz: 198f.
Branch, Harrison B.: 222, 228, 229n.
Brant, Joshua B.: 91f.
Bridger, Jim: 13, 203
Brown, Benjamin Gratz: 142, 225
Brown, John Mason: 225, 231
Bruguier, Théophile: 69
Bruguier and Booge (company): 236
Buchanan, President James: 178, 182
Buffalo meat: 17, 35
Buffalo-robe trade: *see* Fur and buffalo-robe trade
Buffalo-tongue trade: 17, 20, 34, 47, 58, 75, 86, 98, 109
Burleigh, Walter A.: 222

Cabanné, John C.: 9f., 20, 31, 51, 76
Campbell, Colin: 48f., 50n., 107f., 117, 150, 175
Campbell, Hugh: 219
Campbell, Robert: 31, 92–93, 95, 106f., 111, 123, 143, 145f., 150, 163ff., 166, 173, 179, 183ff., 191, 196, 199, 213, 217, 219, 235, 239, 260; R. and W. Campbell (company), 119, 124, 136, 144
Campbell, William: 107; R. and W. Campbell (company); 119, 124, 136, 144
Cannonball River: 141, 254
Carrier (steamboat): 205
Carriveau, Jean (John Bull): 57
Cary, William de la Montaigne: 225, 227, 228n.
Cassilly, Charles P.: 93
Caton, John D.: 193n.
Cerré, Pascal: 65
Chantier Creek: 51, 170, 172

Chardon, Francis A.: 61ff., 83, 85n., 86, 88f., 91, 105, 115, 133n.; attack on Blackfeet at Fort McKenzie, 61, 88
Charles, John H.: 222
Chase, Salmon: 257
Cheyenne Indians: 141, 143
Cheyenne River: 32f., 41, 58f., 71, 73, 102
Chippewa (steamboat): 202, 204ff., 207, 210f., 213, 224f., 229; burns, 226–27, 228
Chippewa Falls (steamboat): 254
Chippewa Indians: 122
Cholera: 117, 120, 122, 124f., 134f., 137ff.
Chouteau, Charles Pierre: 4, 131–32, 161, 166, 173ff., 176f., 185f., 188ff., 191, 201ff., 205ff., 208ff., 211ff., 216, 221f., 224, 226ff., 229f., 232ff., 235, 249ff., 253, 255, 257ff., 260ff., 263f.; patron of science, 152, 175
Chouteau, Émilie (Mrs. John F. A. Sanford): 7
Chouteau, Jean Pierre: 4f., 7, 64
Chouteau, Pierre, Jr.: 3ff., 6ff., 9, 14ff., 17ff., 20f., 24f., 27, 31ff., 38f., 41, 44ff., 48ff., 51f., 59, 62f., 68, 72, 75ff., 79ff., 82, 84, 87, 89, 91f., 95, 99, 105, 111ff., 115ff., 131, 140, 143, 145, 161, 167, 175, 209, 221, 229; description of, 3–4; business career of, 4; wealth of, 4–5; interest in arts and sciences, 24f., 129; political activities of, 26, 29f., 47–48, 90; business practices of, 34; associates and sureties of, 91; dies, 264
Chouteau, Pierre M.: 188
Chouteau, Merle and Sanford (company): 6
Christy, James: 136
Churchill, Samuel: 29n.
Clapp, Benjamin: 40n., 51n., 52n., 59, 79, 81, 91f.
Clara (steamboat): 178f.
Clark, Malcolm: 88f., 118n., 121, 132–

33, 147, 185, 196f., 207, 213, 215, 218, 238, 250–51

Clark, William: 46

Clark, Primeau and Company: 185, 208f., 213–14, 217; robe and fur returns, 185, 188, 197, 199, 208, 213

Clark's Fork (Yellowstone River): 253

Clermont No. 2 (steamboat): 93f.

Collier, George: 68

Collins, John: 69

Constable, D. A.: 261n.

Copelin, John G.: 259f.

Cordelling: 38, 43, 125, 147f., 175, 197, 206, 233

Council Bluffs: 19f., 32, 49, 58, 74, 82, 85, 93, 98, 103f., 109, 118, 124–25, 137, 146, 149f., 154, 160

Cow Island: 22, 255, 257

Crapster, Captain M. H.: 202, 205

Crawford, T. Hartley: 28, 45n., 48n., 49n., 50n., 72n., 81n., 90n.

Crazy Bear (Assiniboin chief): 55

Cree Indians: 140, 148, 190

Crenier (American Fur Company trader): 89

Croke, Father James: 181n.

Crooks, Ramsay: 3n., 9n., 14–15, 16f., 31n., 34, 47n., 75n.

Crow, Wayman: 37, 40

Crow Creek: 107, 248

Crow Indians: 44, 60, 123, 126, 136, 141, 143, 164f., 179, 197ff., 214; trade with, 22, 31, 46, 60, 64, 94, 262; government annuities, 166, 185, 196f., 205, 212, 229, 248, 256ff.; language of, 198

Culbertson, Alexander: 55, 62–63, 67, 86, 88, 89n., 91, 106f., 118n., 121n., 126ff., 129f., 132, 141, 143, 146, 148, 150ff., 156f., 161f., 165f., 173, 175f., 179f., 182, 185, 187f., 190, 197, 202, 209, 221, 230f., 246f.; *Locust Grove*, 187

Culbertson, Mrs. Alexander (Na-ta-wis-ta-cha): 62, 180, 187, 190, 207, 231, 246f.

Culbertson, Ferdinand: 128f.

Culbertson, Joseph: 127, 251n.

Culbertson, Thaddeus: 127ff., 130

Cumming, Alfred: 149, 164n., 166ff., 170n., 173n., 174n., 178, 179n., 185n.

Cummins, Richard W.: 90n.

Curtis, General Samuel R.: 253n.

Cutting, Fulton: 40, 52f., 54–55, 59, 66, 68f., 72f., 75f., 81f., 92; charges against Andrew Drips, 80f., 83

Cutting, Robert: 66

Dakotas, The: 6, 19, 21, 25, 32, 80, 84f., 100, 122, 128, 150, 153, 158, 203; *see also* Dakota Territory

Dakota Territory: 208, 222, 241, 243f., 252f.; Sioux outbreak in, 241f.

Dauphin, Louis: 188

Dawson, Andrew: 132f., 167, 176, 180, 188, 207, 216, 225, 227, 230f., 251, 261

DeBow, J. D. B.: 96

Deer Creek: 199

Deer hides: 17f.

De Girardin, M. E.: 119

Delaney, John O'Fallon: 231

Denig, Edwin T.: 43n., 48n., 121n., 129f., 132, 140–41, 152, 156, 176

Denver, James W.: 178, 201n.

Depau, Francis: 53

Desautel, Joseph: 121n.

Désiré, Jacques: 66

De Smet, Father Pierre Jean (Black Robe): 17, 98–99, 100n., 113, 138ff., 141ff., 153n., 214n., 230f., 236, 255, 256n., 258

Dinkler, Leo: 185

Dole, William P.: 221n., 222f., 228n., 229n., 231n., 244, 246n., 247n., 255n., 257n., 259n.

Donelson, Lieutenant A. J.: 153ff.

Dougherty, John: 29f.

Drips, Andrew: 9, 49f., 52, 56f., 59n., 66, 69ff., 72, 76n., 79f., 84n., 89, 104, 106n., 112n., 144, 145n.; charges against, 80f., 83

Durack, John: 66, 74, 125

Duroc (steamboat): 137

Ebbetts, John A. N.: 37f., 39-40, 51, 52-53, 55ff., 58f., 62, 69, 72, 81f., 92; liquor policy of, 40, 48f., 52, 56

Ebbetts, Cutting and Kelsey (company): 40, 46f., 50, 52, 54, 58; robe and fur returns, 39, 52

Edgerton, Sidney S.: 222

Edmunds, Newton: 222, 259n., 260n.

Effie Deans (steamboat): 256f.

Elk Prairie (Little Dry) Creek: 236

El Paso (steamboat): 125f., 129, 137, 146, 175, 212

Emily (steamboat): 232ff., 236-37, 238f.

Engelmann, George: 153, 154n., 177n.

Evans, Dr. John: 118f., 128f., 138, 151, 153f.

Ewers, John C.: 141

Fanny Ogden (steamboat): 260

Farm Island: 243

Filley, Giles F.: 235, 238

Finch, Captain D.: 117

Fishhook Bend: 83

Fitch, George: 6n.

Fitzpatrick, Thomas: 141f.

Flathead Indians: 255

Florence (steamboat): 207f.

Forsythe, Robert: 87

Fort Alexander, Montana: 60

Fort Andrew, Montana: 240, 253

Fort Atkinson, North Dakota: 195, 217, 240; *see also* Fort Berthold II, North Dakota

Fort Benton, Montana: 22, 43, 55, 63, 94, 99, 121, 125ff., 133, 135, 147f., 155ff., 162, 165ff., 173, 175, 180, 181n., 190, 200ff., 203f., 206f., 209, 211ff., 214, 216, 224ff., 227ff., 230, 233f., 236, 238, 240ff., 249, 251f., 255ff., 259ff., 260-61

Fort Bernard, Wyoming: 9f.

Fort Berthold, North Dakota: 83, 101f., 105, 120, 135, 137, 140f., 164, 174, 178, 182, 190f., 195, 215, 218, 225, 232, 240, 245

Fort Berthold II, North Dakota: 240, 246, 253ff., 260, 262

Fort Bouis, South Dakota: 94, 100ff., 103, 122f., 135

Fort Campbell, Montana: 94f., 99, 103, 106, 114, 120f., 127, 136, 145f., 150, 164, 182, 185, 196, 214, 238

Fort Cass, Montana: 59

Fort Chardon, Montana: 62f., 88

Fort Charles, Montana: 236, 249f., 253

Fort Clark, North Dakota: 46f., 50, 61, 70, 76, 83, 125, 133, 135, 139, 164, 166, 173, 180, 190f., 194, 214, 225, 245; Indian women at, 67

Fort Clay, Montana: *see* Fort Benton, Montana

Fort Cotton, Montana: 55, 63

Fort Galpin, Montana: 219, 240, 245, 253, 260

Fort Garry, Manitoba, Canada: 110

Fort George, South Dakota: 40f., 54, 56ff., 59, 66, 68ff., 72f., 81-82, 96, 110

Fort Hall, Idaho: 14

Fort Henry, Montana: *see* Fort Lewis, Montana

Fort Honoré Picotte, Montana: *see* Fort Lewis, Montana

Fort James, North Dakota: *see* Fort Berthold, North Dakota

Fort John, Wyoming: *see* Fort Laramie, Wyoming

Fort Kipp, Montana: 206, 214, 218, 240, 249

Fort La Barge, Montana: 238, 239-40, 245, 251; sawmill at, 239, 252; robe and fur returns, 252

Fort La Framboise, South Dakota: 240, 245

Fort Laramie, Wyoming: 6, 8, 10, 14, 70, 85, 141, 144, 165, 168, 199

Fort Leavenworth, Kansas: 85

Fort Lewis, Montana: 63, 99, 113

Fort Lookout, South Dakota: 38

Fort McKenzie, Montana: 61ff., 87f., 91, 206, 213; robe and fur returns, 61, 62n.; attack on Blackfeet, 88

Fort Meriwether Lewis, Montana: *see* Fort Lewis, Montana

Fort Mortimer, North Dakota: 54, 68f., 72f., 81f., 94, 110; *see also* Fort William, North Dakota

Fort of the Blackfeet, Montana: *see* Fort Lewis, Montana

Fort Piegan, Montana: 60f.

Fort Pierre, South Dakota: 8, 24, 32f., 38, 40, 46f., 54, 56, 58, 66f., 69f., 76, 78f., 85ff., 91ff., 101f., 105, 110f., 117f., 121, 124ff., 128f., 135, 137, 139, 144, 148, 154f., 162, 164f., 168, 171ff., 174, 177, 179ff., 183f., 186, 189, 193f., 243, 259; description of, 41; robe and fur returns, 79, 85, 97, 104, 118; party for Dr. Evans, 119; sold to U.S. Army, 169–70; winter at, 170–71

Fort Pierre II, South Dakota: 172, 189ff., 203ff., 216, 225, 231, 234, 236f., 240, 246ff., 249f., 260

Fort Platte, Wyoming: 8f., 70

Fort Randall, South Dakota: 65, 160, 171f., 180, 183f., 191, 193, 197, 200, 203, 205, 208f., 211, 222, 237, 242, 245, 250, 252

Fort Rice, North Dakota: 254, 262ff.

Fort Sarpy, Montana: 6, 126, 162, 164f.

Fort Sarpy II, Montana: 162, 197f., 204

Fort Stewart, Montana: 197, 206, 208, 214, 218f., 236, 240, 249

Fort Sully, South Dakota: 243, 253, 260ff., 263

Fort Tecumseh, South Dakota: 20

Fort Uintah, Utah: 13

Fort Uncompahgre, Colorado: 13

Fort Union, North Dakota: 20ff., 31, 33, 41, 44, 50, 54f., 59f., 62, 67ff., 73, 79, 82, 84, 86, 88, 91, 94, 98f., 109f., 112f., 118, 125ff., 129f., 134f., 140f., 144, 146ff., 151, 153, 155ff., 164ff., 167, 173ff., 178, 180ff., 190f., 196ff., 201, 204ff., 207, 210, 212, 216, 218, 221, 225ff., 228f., 231, 233f., 237, 245f., 248ff., 251, 253ff., 256f., 260, 262; description of, 43–44; robe and fur returns, 46, 79, 84f., 97; attacked by Sioux, 215

Fort Van Buren, Montana: 59f.

Fort William, North Dakota: 54, 94, 120f., 123, 156, 164, 185, 196f.; *see also* Fort Mortimer, North Dakota

Fort William, Wyoming: *see* Fort Laramie, Wyoming

Fossils: 127ff., 130, 151, 153f., 170, 176f., 189; *see also* Scientific specimens

Four Bears (Hidatsa chief): 184

Fox, Samuel M.: 53

Fox and Livingston (company): *see* Bolton, Fox and Livingston (company)

Frémont, John Charles: 24, 229; in St. Louis (1845), 80

Frolic (steamboat): 73, 81

Frost, Daniel Marsh: 183, 191f., 196, 199, 208f.

Frost, Todd and Company: 183f., 191, 193, 195, 200f., 207ff., 217

Fur and buffalo-robe trade: 3ff., 7, 15ff., 18, 20, 22f., 32f., 44, 55, 59, 63, 66, 69, 76, 78, 83, 95f., 104, 109ff., 121, 131, 144, 148, 157f., 160, 166f., 172, 187, 210, 217, 223, 232, 237, 256f., 264–65; on Platte River, 8–9; in Rocky Mountains, 11–12, 13; on Arkansas River, 14; in Minnesota, 14f.; on Upper Missouri River, 14, 18f., 25, 29, 38, 72, 86–87, 100, 104, 165, 182, 188, 215, 241, 252; market, 16–17, 52, 79, 104, 159, 201–202, 216, 220; robe preparation, 35; bartering, 35–36; business practices, 36; on Yellowstone River, 60, 86–87, 97; public image of, 100

F. X. Aubrey (steamboat): 150

Galpin, Charles E.: 129, 132f., 162n., 170f., 172, 176f., 205, 209, 230, 234, 237

Galpin's Post, South Dakota: 172

Gantt, Thomas: 89ff., 106, 114–15

Garrioche, Peter: 67

General Brooke (steamboat): 79, 81f., 84, 86f., 95
Genoa (steamboat): 163f., 172, 174
Gerard, Frederic F.: 176, 209
Giorda, Father Joseph: 214
Glasgow, Missouri: 85
Gold and gold mines: 209, 220, 230, 237, 239, 241f., 245, 249, 252, 256, 258ff., 261
Gore, Sir St. George: 181–82
Grand River: 71
Great Cedar Island: 66
Great Council: 141–42, 144; see also Treaty of Fort Laramie
Green, David: 181n.
Greenough, Byron: 34n.
Green River: 11f.
Greenwood, Alfred B.: 198n., 213n., 222
Greer, Captain W. B.: 256
Grosvenor, Lord Richard–De Aquila: 203
Gros Ventre Indians: 44
Gunsollis, Captain John: 146, 151

Hall, James: 151f., 154n., 155
Halleck, General Henry W.: 253, 255n.
Halsey, Jacob: 33n., 106
Hamell, Augustin: 188
Hamilton, Joseph Varnum: 9, 56, 57n., 69, 71n., 170
Handy's Point, South Dakota: 65
Hannum, Captain P. E.: 150
Harkness, James: 234, 238, 251
Harkness, Margaret: 239
Harlow, James: 259n.
Harney, General William S.: 168f., 171, 174
Harris, Edward: 64
Harris, Moses (Black): 12
Harrison, President William Henry: 26ff., 29
Harvey, Alexander: 61, 87, 92ff., 95, 103f., 106, 109, 111, 114f., 121, 124, 136, 145f., 150, 165n., 182; early career of, 87–89; charges against Fran-

cis Chardon, 89; descent from Fort Campbell, 122–23; death of, 164, 166
Harvey, Thomas H.: 70n., 71, 72n., 81, 84n., 89n., 90f., 97n., 98n., 104, 106n., 107n., 109n., 112, 115f.
Harvey and Primeau (company): 87, 93f., 97, 99f., 106, 109, 111, 119, 143, 144–45, 156, 163, 164–65, 166; robe and fur returns, 93, 95, 97, 106–107, 109, 119ff., 123ff., 136f., 145f., 150; Yankton Sioux trading license revoked, 108; post inventories of, 110; liquor policy of, 113
Harvey, Primeau and Company: see Harvey and Primeau (company)
Hatch, Edwin A. C.: 168n., 175, 178, 180f.
Hatton, William S.: 112, 113, 117f., 120, 148
Haverty, John: 167n., 170n., 178, 184n.
Hawley, Alpheus F.: 263f.
Haydee (steamboat): 97, 122
Hayden, Ferdinand Vandeveer: 151ff., 154f., 176ff., 202f.
Hays, William Jacob: 212
Heart River: 20, 37f., 246
Helfenstein, John P.: 163
Henry, Joseph: 129n.
Hidatsa Indians: 83, 101f., 120f., 141, 143, 148, 179, 190, 217f., 225, 231f., 245; government annuities, 164, 195
Highland Mary No. 1 (steamboat): 146, 150
Hitchcock, E. A.: 28n.
Hodgkiss, William D.: 111, 112n., 118n., 121, 124n., 126n., 132, 133n., 176, 183n., 190, 214n., 216n.
Hoecken, Father Christian: 100n., 138–39
Honduras (steamboat): 146
Horse Creek: 141
Hoyt, Joseph Gibson: 237
Hoyt, Mrs. Joseph Gibson: 237
Hubbell, James Boyd: 262, 264
Hudson's Bay Company: 14, 18, 45, 67, 110; business tactics of, 11

Huggins, Alexander G.: 180
Humphreys, Captain William H.: 211, 213, 224, 226, 230, 249
Huntsville (steamboat): 46

Illingsworth, James: 56, 57n.
Indian agents: 6, 9, 27f., 48f., 74, 80, 89f., 93, 95, 97f., 148f., 175, 177, 192, 197, 203, 205, 212, 221ff., 231, 242, 246, 256f.
Indian annuities: *see* Annuities, Indian
Iowa Indians: 149
Isabel (steamboat): 146
Island City (steamboat): 254

Jaccard, Eugene: 234, 238
James River: 37, 40, 200, 208, 243
Jayne, William: 222, 231n.
John J. Roe and Nicholas Wall (company): 252
J. Picotte and Company: 165, 217; robe and fur returns, 172, 179; dissolution of, 182, 185
Judith River: 44, 62, 148, 167, 181, 245

Kansas City, Missouri: 211, 220; robe and fur trade in, 159, 210
Kansas River: 47
Keemle, Charles: 30
Kelsey, Charles: 40, 52ff., 92; at Fort George, 55–57; indicted for murder, 57–58
Kennard, Dr. Thomas: 189
Kennerly, Lewis H.: 183
Kessler, Charles N.: 54n., 126n., 206n., 228n., 251n.
Key West No. 2 (steamboat): 210ff., 213, 230, 233ff.
Killdeer Mountain: 254
Kipp, James: 46, 60, 67, 83, 85, 91, 106, 110, 112n., 113, 118n., 132, 158, 176, 178f., 188, 206
Knife River: 37, 46
Kurz, Rudolph F.: 139f., 144

Labadie, Sylvestre: 91f.

La Barge, Captain John: 95, 185, 188ff., 191, 202, 206, 211ff., 219, 224, 230, 234f., 238f., 244ff., 247f.
La Barge, Captain Joseph: 32f., 64f., 74f., 95, 97, 99, 106, 107n., 119, 124, 138f., 141, 146n., 162, 166f., 169n., 173ff., 219, 230, 232ff., 236ff., 244, 246ff., 251f., 256, 258, 264; Blackfoot-Crow annuities controversy, 256ff.
La Barge, Mrs. Joseph: 138
La Barge, Harkness and Company: 235, 240, 244, 252; robe and fur returns, 239, 241, 245, 248; dissolution of, 251, 256
Lacombe, Father Albert: 102
Lac qui Parle: 37, 101, 180
La Framboise, Françoise: 216, 240
Laidlaw, William: 41n., 61n., 66, 70n., 71n.
Lake of the Woods (steamboat): 100f., 102–103
Lambdin, Robert B.: 149
Lame Bull (Blackfoot chief): 181
Lampson, Curtis M.: 16, 78n., 104
Langford, N. P.: 133n.
Laramie Creek: 6, 8f.
Larpenteur, Charles: 33, 54f., 60, 83, 217ff., 220, 234, 262
Larpenteur, Lemon and Company: 219
Larpenteur, Smith and Company: 216, 218
Latta, Samuel N.: 221n., 222, 228n., 230, 231n., 232, 246ff., 256; charges against American Fur Company, 223, 229
Lawrence, E. N.: 225
Lea, Luke: 142n., 143n., 149
Leavenworth, Kansas: 203, 248
Lee, James: 88f.
Leidy, Professor Joseph: 129, 155
Lemon, Robert H.: 217ff., 220, 251, 252n.
Letellier, Louis: 147f.
Liberty, Missouri: 104, 124, 136
Like-a-Fishhook Village, North Dakota: 83, 195f.

Lincoln, President Abraham: 220ff., 257, 259, 263
Liquor trade: 9, 36, 47–48, 49f., 52, 54, 61, 65, 69, 74, 84, 93, 98, 232; on Platte River, 8ff., 70; in Rocky Mountains, 12f.; John Ebbetts' policy, 38, 40; on Upper Missouri River, 48f., 56, 72, 76, 80–81, 112f., 115, 148; at Fort George, 56f.; Sioux favor end to, 69; in Cheyenne River Valley, 70; American Fur Company policy, 9, 12, 48f., 51, 71, 74–75, 89ff., 113, 115, 139, 228, 258; Pratte and Cabanné policy, 71f.; on Yellowstone River, 80; Union Fur Company policy, 82; on Vermillion River, 139
Lisa, Manuel: 27
Little Big Horn River: 55
Little Missouri River: 37, 135, 254
Little Sioux River: 138f.
Livingston, Mortimer: 53f.
Loras, Bishop of Dubuque: 101, 102n., 103n.
Loup Fork (Platte River): 37
Lupton, Lancaster P.: 8

McBrayer, John H.: 178
McCulloh, T. H.: 221n.
McElderry, Samuel E.: 178n.
McGuffin, Napoleon: 85
Mackay, Colonel Aeneas: 118
McKellops, Dr. J. H.: 238
McKenzie, Kenneth: 20, 31, 59, 83, 84n., 91f.
McKenzie, Owen: 245, 250–51
McKenzie's Butte: 43
McKenzie's Post, Montana: 240, 245
Mackey, Reverend Elkanah D.: 179ff.
Mackey, Mrs. Elkanah D. (Sarah): 179ff.
Mackinaws: 8, 13, 23, 38, 47, 60, 65f., 68f., 72f., 79, 81, 84f., 94, 97, 99, 104, 109f., 119, 123f., 136, 145f., 150, 166, 172, 174f., 190, 197f., 204ff., 215, 218, 227, 230, 242, 245; description of,

22–23; cargoes of, 23, 47, 97, 110, 119, 125, 137, 146, 150, 163, 188
McNeal, Eli W.: 249
Maffitt, Dr. William: 161, 183n., 185n.
Mahood, Captain James: 261
Malcolm Clark's Fort, Montana: 218
Mandan (steamboat): 109
Mandan Indians: 6, 37, 46, 83, 101f., 104, 121, 141, 143, 179, 190, 225, 232, 245; government annuities, 195
Manypenny, George W.: 149, 164n., 167n., 170n., 178
Marias River: 19, 44, 60f., 63, 87, 94, 188, 206, 257
Marley, Michoux: 57
Marmaduke, Meredith M.: 27
Marsh, Dr. Elias J.: 203, 207
Marten, Jacques: 96
Martha (steamboat): 95, 97ff., 100, 106, 108ff., 117; Yankton Sioux attack on, 107ff.
Mary Blane (steamboat): 119, 128
Massie, Captain William R.: 255
Matlock, Gideon C.: 97, 98n., 101, 106ff., 109, 111
May, William P.: 45, 58f.
Maynadier, Lieutenant Henry E.: 203f.
Measles: 101
Medicine Creek: 94, 97
Medill, William: 84n., 91n., 106n., 111n., 112n., 115f.
Meek, Fielding Bradford: 151ff., 154f., 176f.
Meldrum, Robert (Round Iron): 126, 204f., 215, 249
Mendota, Minnesota: 15, 85, 101, 113
Messenger service (express): 41, 66, 79, 112, 123, 177, 199
Meyers, Augustus: 170
Milk River: 44, 125, 129, 136, 175, 188, 190, 200, 206, 212f., 219, 233, 236, 238f., 245, 249f.
Minnesota: 72, 76, 101, 113, 122, 180, 208, 217; Sioux outbreak in, 240–41, 242
Minnesota River: 242

Missionaries: 25, 63, 98, 138ff., 179ff., 191f., 197f., 214, 237; policy of fur companies toward, 99–100

Missouri River: 5f., 8f., 11, 18, 20ff., 23ff., 27f., 37f., 41, 43f., 46ff., 49f., 53ff., 56, 61, 63ff., 68, 70, 72, 76, 78, 81, 83f., 88, 92ff., 95, 100ff., 106, 120, 122, 125ff., 128, 130, 136f., 143, 145f., 148, 153, 155, 160, 162, 165ff., 171ff., 174, 176f., 180ff., 189f., 194, 196f., 200, 203, 206, 208, 211, 213f., 217, 219, 226, 231f., 234, 237, 240, 243, 247, 249, 253ff., 258ff., 263; description of, 6; robe and fur trade on, 18f., 23, 25, 29, 31, 33, 45, 49, 59f., 62, 73, 77ff., 80, 82, 87, 89, 96f., 100, 109, 116, 132f., 136, 159, 161, 188, 199f., 209, 220, 236, 239, 252, 259; navigation on, 21–22, 42–43, 131, 136, 138, 171, 178f., 199, 201f., 206f., 210f., 230f., 233, 246; Great Bend of, 38, 93, 100, 103, 107, 110, 117, 120, 172–73, 180, 189, 191, 193, 207; Little Bend of, 58; channel of, 78f., 86, 125, 136, 141, 143, 211f., 230, 233, 245f., 248f., 261; murder on, 86; Falls of, 104, 133, 188, 207, 209, 239, 242; epidemics on, 135–36, 137ff., 178 (*see also* Cholera *and* Smallpox); Indian unrest on, 165–66, 168, 215, 242; rapids on, 206, 233, 236, 238, 245, 251, 255; military operations on (Civil War), 220–21, 230, 245f.; Disaster Bend of, 226, 228

Mitchell, David Dawson: 30, 44, 48ff., 58f., 61, 69ff., 76n., 87, 90, 112, 113n., 117, 120n., 135n., 141ff., 144, 148n., 149, 184

Mix, C. E.: 187n., 192n., 197n., 201n., 223n.

Montana: 19, 21f., 25, 80, 100, 132, 158, 181, 203, 239, 241, 251ff.

Montana Territory: 222, 259

Moore, Thomas P.: 83–84, 86, 93, 97

Moreau River: 71

Morgan, Lewis Henry: 231, 233f.

Morgan, Robert: 230n.

Morley, James Henry: 231

Morrison, William: 68

Mountain boats: *see* Steamboats

Mullan, John: 204, 209, 211, 216

Munger, Asahel: 12

Murray, Alexander H.: 110

Muskrat skins: 17f.

Musselshell River: 44, 240

Mustang (steamboat): 119

Nellie Rogers (steamboat): 248ff., 251f.

New Haven (steamboat): 68, 70, 72, 75, 100; attacked by Sioux, 68

Nez Percé Indians: 138

Nicholas of Nassau: *see* William Nicholas of Nassau, Prince

Nicollet, Joseph (Jean) Nicolas: 24f., 127

Nimrod (steamboat): 73ff., 91

Niobrara (L'Eau qui Court) River: 139, 171

Noble, Lieutenant Patrick: 65

North Platte River: 7f., 37, 44, 143

North West Company of Canada: 11

Northwestern Fur Company: 263

Norwood, James H.: 135n., 148–49

Oglala Sioux Indians: 168

O'Gorman, Bishop James M.: 181n., 214

Omaha, Nebraska: 65, 160f., 188, 204, 209, 242

Omaha (steamboat): 198f.

Omega (steamboat): 64f., 67

Oregon Fur Company: 77

Osage Indians: 149

Otrante, Comte d' (son of Joseph Fouché): 74

Ottawa Indians: 122

Otter skins: 18

Overland trails: 10, 19, 142, 146, 168, 253f.

Owen, David Dale: 118

Pack trains: 110f.

Papin, Mr.: 138
Parkman, Francis: 84
Patrick Henry (steamboat): 150
Pawnee Indians: 75
Pearsall, John: 202f.
Pease, Luther: 222
Peindry, Comte de: 74
Pembina, North Dakota: 15, 217f.
Pembina River: 37
Peoria, Illinois: 187, 221
Picotte, Honoré: 33, 38, 39n., 47n., 57n., 69, 71, 72n., 73n., 82n., 83n., 85n., 86, 89n., 91f., 105f., 113, 144, 145n.
Picotte, Joseph: 87, 92, 95, 97, 109, 124, 140, 144, 165f., 167n., 182ff., 251
Piegan (Blackfoot) Indians: 44, 61, 95
Pierce, President Franklin: 149, 152
Pierre, South Dakota: 20
Pierre Chouteau, Jr., and Company: *see* American Fur Company (Pierre Chouteau, Jr., and Company)
Pilcher, Joshua: 27, 29f., 49, 61n.
Platte River: 8, 10, 14, 20f., 28, 48, 50, 65, 70, 73, 83f., 96, 110, 136f., 142f., 168, 174, 204
Pocahontas (steamboat): 125
Point, Father Nicholas: 98f.
Polk, President James Knox: 78f.
Ponca Indians: 135, 139
Pope, General John: 243, 244n., 253, 260
Poplar River: 141, 155f., 188, 218, 226f.
Poplar River Post, Montana: 218f.
Porter, James M.: 90n.
Postlewaite, Jon: 231
Potawatomi Indians: 122
Powder River: 37, 44, 143, 174, 197, 199
Powers, Lyman: 226n., 227n.
Pratte, Bernard, Jr.: 5, 7, 9f., 20, 31, 51, 76
Pratte, Bernard, Sr.: 4f., 15
Pratte and Cabanné (company): 70ff., 77, 83, 89; liquor policy of, 70, 72; failure of, 80, 82, 87
Pratte, Chouteau and Company: 4f.

Primeau, Charles: 87, 92ff., 124, 165, 183, 185, 213, 216, 217n., 220n.
Prout, Dr. Hiram A.: 128
Purgatoire River: 14

Raccoon pelts: 16
R. and W. Campbell (company): 119, 124, 136, 144
Ranken, David: 194n.
Ravoux, Father Augustin: 100–101, 102f.
Ray, Captain Thomas: 249f.
Raynald, A.: 50n.
Raynolds, Captain William F.: 177, 198, 203ff., 209
Rea, Isaac (Old Sam Johnson): 231, 234
Redfield, Alexander H.: 178, 184f., 192ff., 195ff., 198f., 203, 205, 222, 223n.
Red River: 15, 37, 45, 102, 110, 113, 195, 208
Ree Indians: *see* Arikara Indians
Ree Post, North Dakota: 140
Reed, Henry H.: 222, 231, 246, 248, 255n., 256ff., 259n.
Rendezvous: 7, 10ff., 14, 18
Richard, John: 10, 49
Riggs, Reverend Stephen R.: 180
Riggs, Thomas: 181
Riter, Frederick G.: 141n., 215
Robert (or Robar; American Fur Company trader): 89
Robert Campbell (steamboat): 125, 136ff., 150f., 153ff., 244ff., 247ff., 258
Robert Fulton (steamboat): 125
Robertson, John: 118
Robidoux brothers: 13
Robinson, Alexander M.: 178, 192n., 197n., 198n., 200–201, 206n., 215n., 216n., 222n.
Rocky Mountain Fur Company: 10f.
Rosebud River: 59, 126
Roulette's Post, Montana: 240, 249
Roy, J. B.: 33
Russell, James: 123f.

Sac and Fox Indians: 14, 135, 149
Sacramento (steamboat): 136
St. Ange (steamboat): 119, 124, 126, 138f., 141, 146, 150, 156
St. Charles, Missouri: 192, 211
St. Croix (steamboat): 119
St. Joseph, Missouri: 23, 97, 109f., 119, 124, 128, 136f., 150, 160, 165, 191, 201, 203, 222, 228, 230, 237, 263
St. Louis, Missouri: 5f., 13, 21, 23, 33, 40, 46, 49f., 53, 66ff., 69, 73, 76, 78, 84, 86f., 89, 92ff., 95f., 99f., 103, 106, 108, 112, 114, 117, 120ff., 123, 126, 128f., 131, 138f., 143, 145, 151ff., 157, 160, 165, 170f., 174, 176, 178, 183f., 187, 191f., 196ff., 199f., 202, 204f., 212, 217, 219f., 224, 226, 229f., 236, 238, 244, 246, 248f., 257f., 261, 263; robe and fur trade in, 15, 17ff., 34ff., 264; robe and fur returns to, 17, 20, 23, 34, 47, 62n., 65, 66n., 68, 72, 75, 79, 81, 85f., 95, 97f., 104, 107, 109, 111, 118f., 124ff., 136f., 141, 144, 146f., 150, 159, 162ff., 167, 175, 179, 182, 185, 207f., 210, 213, 218, 234f., 239, 250, 255–56, 260; commerce in, 18, 159; Missouri River trade (boats), 19f., 38, 47, 67, 75; fire in (1849), 117
St. Louis Fur Company: *see* Harvey and Primeau (company)
St. Mary (steamboat): 166f., 173ff., 176, 179
St. Paul, Minnesota: 152f., 155, 217ff.
St. Peter's (steamboat): 20, 104
Saluda (steamboat): 125
Sandoval, Isadore: 88
Sanford, John F. A.: 5, 6–7, 21n., 24, 28, 49, 59, 104n., 115, 132
Santee Sioux Indians: 65, 68, 112
Saranac (steamboat): 125, 137
Sarpy, John B.: 5–6, 7, 47n., 59, 83, 84n., 89n., 91f., 106f., 117, 132, 151, 154f., 161, 169, 187
Scanlon, Father Thomas: 191
Schieffelin, W. H.: 225

Schlegel (trader at Vermillion Post): 129, 139
Schlieffarth, Charles W.: 206n.
Schmidt, Jacob J.: 198f.
Scholfield, W. F.: 224–25
Schoonover, Bernard S.: 203, 205, 215, 222, 225, 229
Scientific specimens: 127ff., 130, 156, 174ff., 177, 186, 189, 203; *see also* Fossils
Scientists: 25, 64, 118, 127f., 130, 151, 153f., 176f., 202, 231
Sergeant's Bluff: 149
Shaw, Henry: 33
Shaw, John: 96
Shaw, Captain John: 173, 178f., 184f., 191f., 194, 196ff., 201
Shoshoni Indians: 142
Shoup, W. A.: 54n.
Shreveport (steamboat): 234ff., 238f., 244f., 248f., 251; attacked by Sioux, 246–48
Shumard, Benjamin F.: 153f., 176
Sibille, Adams and Company: 8ff.
Sibley, George C.: 30
Sibley, Henry Hastings: 15, 85, 113, 243
Simoneau's Island: 57f., 69
Sioux City, Iowa: 149, 161, 174, 183, 188, 193, 199f., 205, 207, 212, 224, 230, 239, 242, 245, 248, 253f., 264
Sioux Indians: 44, 46, 56, 60, 82, 87, 90, 93f., 101ff., 104, 117ff., 120f., 123, 133, 135f., 141f., 155, 164ff., 168ff., 171, 188f., 196, 199, 216, 231, 236f., 239f., 245f., 249, 252ff., 260, 265; Dakota Sioux, 37–38, 78, 217; favor end to liquor trade, 69; trade with, 70, 262; government annuities, 195, 231, 246f.; attack on Fort Union, 215; uprising of, 242f.; defeated at White Stone Hill, 243; attack *Shreveport*, 246–48
Sire, Joseph A.: 5ff., 41, 43, 46, 52, 59, 64, 67, 74f., 79, 86, 91, 113n., 132, 145, 161

Smallpox: 44, 46, 83, 114, 134ff., 137, 178f.

Smith, Caleb B.: 221n., 244

Smith, James A.: 263

Smith, Jefferson: 217ff., 220

Smutty Bear (Yankton Sioux chief): 107–108

Sonora (steamboat): 146n., 162, 164

Souris River: 44, 218

South Antler Creek: 218

South Platte River: 8, 14

Sprague, Isaac: 64

Spread Eagle (steamboat): 185, 188ff., 191, 202ff., 205, 207, 210ff., 213, 224ff., 230ff., 233ff., 238, 240

Square Buttes: 67

Squires, Lewis M.: 64, 66

Stanley, John Mix: 156

Steamboats: 6, 8, 15, 19f., 22f., 28, 38, 41, 46f., 59, 64, 72f., 79, 84ff., 93ff., 97, 100, 103f., 106, 109f., 117ff., 120f., 124f., 128, 136ff., 139ff., 143f., 146, 150f., 154ff., 162f., 166, 169, 171, 173ff., 179, 184f., 188ff., 191, 193ff., 198, 200ff., 205ff., 208, 210ff., 217, 222, 224, 230, 232ff., 235, 237f., 244f., 247ff., 251, 253ff., 259, 261, 264; wood for, 21, 75, 82, 86, 118, 126, 190, 196, 206, 246, 249; design and construction for Missouri River trade, 21; "warping," 42; "grasshoppering," 42; lightening, 42; landing, 42–43; "sparring," 94; Civil War protection of, 220; race on the Missouri River, 232–33, 237–38; carrying trade, 201, 241, 259; *see also* Cordelling

Steuart, Lieutenant Colonel Adam D.: 197n.

Stevens, Dr. Charles W.: 176

Stevens, Isaac I.: 152–53, 155ff., 167f.

Stinger, William: 247

Sublette, William L.: 31, 54, 93

Sublette and Campbell (company): 54, 163

Suckley, Dr. George: 156

Sully, General Alfred: 262, 264; Sioux campaign, 243, 250, 253f., 260

Sweeny, Lieutenant Thomas W.: 170

Sweetwater River: 44

Talbot, Miss V.: 225

Tamerlane (steamboat): 119f.

Tappan, William Henry: 109–10

Taylor, Captain Daniel G.: 93f.

Taylor, Robert W.: 37, 40; flees Fort George, 58

Taylor, Sinclair: 71n.

Taylor, President Zachary: 110

Teal, Jessie T.: 126n.

Terry, W. Eliphalet: 212

Teton Sioux Indians: 37, 105, 122, 180, 194, 205, 240; government annuities, 193

Tevis, John C.: 151, 165

Thompson, Jacob: 201n.

Throckmorton, Captain Joseph: 163, 200f., 207f.

Tobacco Creek: 246

Tobacco Garden Landing, North Dakota: 246

Tobacco Plant (steamboat): 85

Todd, John Blair: 183, 200, 208f.

Trade medals: 76

Traders and trading posts: 9ff., 14f., 19f., 23, 27ff., 31, 33, 34–35, 37f., 41, 43f., 46ff., 50f., 55ff., 58ff., 61f., 65ff., 68–69, 70ff., 73, 76, 78f., 82ff., 85ff., 88ff., 92ff., 95f., 98ff., 102, 105ff., 108ff., 111ff., 114, 116f., 119ff., 122ff., 126ff., 132, 134ff., 137, 139ff., 143ff., 146, 148ff., 152, 154ff., 157, 160, 162ff., 165ff., 168ff., 171, 174ff., 177ff., 180, 182f., 188, 190, 192, 194ff., 198ff., 204, 206, 208ff., 212f., 215, 217ff., 221, 223, 229, 238ff., 242f., 245, 248, 251, 254, 256, 258, 260ff., 264; morale, 33–34; bartering for robes and furs, 35–36; inventories, 75–76, 110, 132; business problems, 76; post industries, 76; relations with Indians, 121–22; wages,

133–34; daily life, 133–35; livestock, 135

Trapper (steamboat): 41ff., 46, 66, 74

Traverse des Sioux, Minnesota: 101

Treaty of 1855: 168, 187

Treaty of Fort Laramie: 142–43, 148, 195

"Treaty with the Blackfoot Nation": *see* Treaty of 1855

Trecy, Father Jeremiah F.: 180, 181n.

Tributary (steamboat): 85ff.

Turtle Mountains: 37

Twilight (steamboat): 184f., 191ff., 194ff., 197f., 205

Tyler, President John: 26, 29, 90n.

Union Fur Company: 54f., 59, 62, 66, 68, 71ff., 77, 80f., 89; robe and fur returns, 69, 73, 82; liquor policy of, 80–81, 82; failure of, 80ff., 83, 87

United States Army: posts in Upper Missouri country, 169, 243, 252f.

Upson, Gad E.: 222, 257n.

Ute Indians: 13

Vaughan, Alfred J.: 149, 151, 154f., 163ff., 166, 167n., 170, 173, 174n., 176ff., 179n., 182, 184f., 192, 196, 197n., 203, 205, 206n., 213n., 222

Vermillion Post, South Dakota: 65ff.

Vermillion River: 38, 46, 65, 86, 93, 96, 101, 103, 117, 120, 123f., 133, 139, 150, 154, 189, 242

Waddington, William: 117

Walla Walla, Washington: 204, 211, 228

Walsh, Edward: 150

Warren, Lieutenant Gouverneur K.: 174f., 177, 203

Welcome (steamboat): 260

Wessells, Major H. W.: 193f.

Western Academy of Natural Science: 175

Western Engineer (steamboat): 20

Weston, Missouri: 72f., 109

Whigs: 26ff., 29f., 111f., 149

White, Elijah: 95f.

White, William: 57

White Earth River: 122

White River: 32, 37f., 41, 135, 180, 207

White Shield (Arikara chief): 139

Wilcox, A. H.: 231

Wilkinson, Mahlon: 222, 259n., 260n.; charges against Charles Chouteau, 258–59

William Nicholas of Nassau, Prince: 151, 154

Wimar, Carl: 193ff., 197ff., 203

Worden, Francis (Frank) L.: 226n., 227

Wright, Captain Robert: 211f.

Yankton, South Dakota: 200, 208, 225, 230, 235, 255

Yanktonai Sioux Indians: 37

Yankton Sioux Indians: 28, 32, 37, 107ff., 112, 154, 165, 188f., 203, 222; government annuities, 193, 205, 224; cession of land, 200, 205

Yeatman, James E.: 106

Yellowstone (steamboat): 20, 255, 257, 261ff., 264

Yellowstone River: 6, 20, 22, 43f., 54f., 60f., 66f., 72f., 79f., 82, 86, 94, 97f., 103, 108, 118, 120, 124, 126, 136ff., 141, 143, 150, 152, 155f., 162ff., 166ff., 175, 177, 179, 185, 188, 198, 200, 202, 204ff., 207, 224, 226, 236, 238, 245, 248f., 253f.; trade on, 59, 73, 86; cordelling on, 60; navigation on, 60, 201, 254f.

The paper on which the text of *The Fur Trade on the Upper Missouri, 1840–1865* has been printed bears the watermark of the University of Oklahoma Press and is expected to last for at least three hundred years. The type is Janson, a Dutch face of the seventeenth century widely admired today for its legibility and character.

University of Oklahoma Press

Norman